"THAT'S RAVEN TALK"
Holophrastic Readings of Contemporary Indigenous Literatures

"THAT'S RAVEN TALK"

Holophrastic Readings of Contemporary Indigenous Literatures

Mareike Neuhaus

© 2011 Canadian Plains Research Center.

All rights reserved. No part of this work covered by the copyrights hereon may be reproduced or used in any form or by any means—graphic, electronic, or mechanical— without the prior written permission of the publisher. Any request for photocopying, recording, taping or placement in information storage and retrieval systems of any sort shall be directed in writing to Access Copyright.

Printed and bound in Canada at Friesens.
The text of this book is printed on 100% post-consumer recycled paper with earth-friendly vegetable-based inks.

Cover and text design: Duncan Campbell, CPRC.   Copy editor: Dallas Harrison, Dysart, Saskatchewan.
Editor for the Press: Donna Grant, CPRC.   Index by Patricia Furdek, Ottawa, Ontario.

COVER PHOTO: by Carolyn Pihach Photography.
Cree syllabic typewriter is based on a photo from the Sam Waller Museum's website (www.samwallermuseum.ca/feature/?id=12)

Library and Archives Canada Cataloguing in Publication

Neuhaus, Mareike, 1978–
  That's raven talk : holophrastic readings of contemporary indigenous literatures / Mareike Neuhaus.

Includes bibliographical references and index.
ISBN 978-0-88977-233-5

1. Canadian literature (English)—Indian authors—History and criticism.
2. Canadian literature (English)—Inuit authors—History and criticism.
3. Canadian literature (English)—20th century—History and criticism.
4. Native peoples—Canada—Languages—Influence on English.
5. Native peoples—Canada—Languages—Compound words. I. Title.

PS8089.5.I6N48 2011   C810.9'897   C2010-908079-3

10 9 8 7 6 5 4 3 2 1

Excerpts in Chapter 1 from *Call Me Ishmael: Memories of Ishmael Alunik, Inuvialuk Elder*, by Ishmael Alunik, published 1998 by Kolausok Ublaaq Enterprises. Reprinted with permission of the publisher.

Excerpts in Chapter 2 from *Arctic Dream and Nightmares*, by Alootook Ipellie, published c. 1993 by Theytus Books. Reprinted with permission from the publisher.

Excerpts in Chapter 3 from *The Lesser Blessed*, by Richard Van Camp, published 1996 by Douglas & McIntyre: an imprint of D&M Publishers Inc. Reprinted with permission from the publisher.

Excerpts in Chapter 4 from *Green Grass, Running Water* © 1993 by Thomas King, published by HarperCollins Publishers Ltd. All rights reserved. Reprinted with permission from the publisher.

Excerpts in Chapter 5 from *Blue Marrow*, by Louise Halfe, published by Coteau Books, Regina, Canada. Reprinted with permission from the publisher.

Canadian Plains Research Center
University of Regina
Regina, Saskatchewan, Canada, S4S 0A2
tel: (306) 585-4758 fax: (306) 585-4699
e-mail: canadian.plains@uregina.ca web: www.cprcpress.ca

We acknowledge the financial support of the Government of Canada through the Canada Book Fund for our publishing activities.

 Canadian Heritage   Patrimoine canadien

Mixed Sources
Cert no. SW-COC-001271
© 1996 FSC

CONTENTS

ACKNOWLEDGEMENTS—*vii*

INTRODUCTION—*1*
Theorizing Textualized Orality in Indigenous Literatures

CHAPTER 1—*34*
Writing the Oral Tradition: Ishmael Alunik's *Call Me Ishmael*

CHAPTER 2—*69*
Exorcising Guti: Alootook Ipellie's *Arctic Dreams and Nightmares*

CHAPTER 3—*108*
"Busy Looking for Juliet Hope": Richard Van Camp's *The Lesser Blessed*

CHAPTER 4—*142*
"All This Water Imagery Must Mean Something":
Thomas King's *Green Grass, Running Water*

CHAPTER 5—*179*
"Cree-ing Loud into My Night": Louise Bernice Halfe's *Blue Marrow*

CONCLUSION—*216*
Contemporary Indigenous Literatures, Textualized Orality,
and Rhetorical Sovereignty

APPENDIX—*225*
The Narrative Function of Holophrases in Indigenous Languages

GLOSSARY—*229*

NOTES—*233*

WORKS CITED—*275*

INDEX—*295*

ACKNOWLEDGEMENTS

This study began as a dissertation in 2005 with the generous support of Foreign Affairs and International Trade Canada, which funded a research stay at the University of Alberta that sparked my interest in the holophrase. The study continued to grow with the kind assistance of the Andrew W. Mellon Foundation, which sponsored a postdoctoral fellowship at the Jackman Humanities Institute, University of Toronto, during which I turned what was once a dissertation into the book that you are about to read.

No scholarly or creative work ever comes into being without human interaction. I would therefore like to thank all those individuals without whose support I would not have been able to write this book. First of all, I owe an enormous debt of gratitude to Martin Kuester, for being in the best sense of the word my *Doktorvater*, for accompanying me on my journey, for enduring my sometimes stubborn temper, and for continuing to offer support and encouragement. To Ted Dyck I am especially grateful for introducing me to Indigenous literatures and the holophrase, for the numerous discussions that we have had over the years, and for his friendship. I would also like to thank Rüdiger Zimmermann, for his thoughtful suggestions and for agreeing to write a *Zweitgutachten*, as well as Hans-Jürgen Sasse, for providing an additional *Gutachten*.

Special thanks go to the following individuals at the University of Alberta for the help they offered during my stay in 2005: to Cheryl Suzack, for supervising my work; to Dorothy Thunder and Marjorie Memnook-White, for teaching me Cree; to Naomi McIlwraith, for sharing her experiences while

ACKNOWLEDGEMENTS

studying Cree; to Ellen Bielawski and Heather Zwicker, for giving me such a warm welcome; to Ted Bishop, Albert Braz, John Newman, Don Perkins, and Sally A. Rice, for listening to my ideas about Indigenous literatures and the holophrase; to Rania El Saadi and Barry Tonge at Education Abroad, for enabling me to take Intermediate Cree; to Stephen R. Reimer, for letting me use his LitStats program; to Terry Butler, for providing me with access to the TAPoR Workshop facilities; and to Ted Dyck and Penny Snelgrove, Carol and Kevin Kennedy, Myrna Kostash, and Bobbi-Jo Roasting, for reminding me that there is a life besides research.

Deep thanks go to Richard Van Camp, for sending me a then unpublished interview; to Peter Irniq, for sharing his Inuit language and culture; to Mathias Häberle, Johanna Hocke-Szparaga, Jürgen Warmbrunn, and Andrea Wolff-Wölk, as well as Friedrich von Petersdorff and Anca Raluca Radu, for providing me with literature; to Astrid Lohöfer, Alma Mikulinsky, Magda Szych, and Jürgen Warmbrunn, for their translations; to Wolfram Keller, for his helpful suggestions; to Dorothy Thunder, for editing my Cree; to Friedrich von Petersdorff, for his meticulous readings; to the Marburg Centre for Canadian Studies and the Gesellschaft für Kanada-Studien, for much-needed travel grants; to the Jackman Humanities Institute at the University of Toronto, for hosting my fellowship and for creating an environment that stimulates interdisciplinary research; to Ted Dyck, Daniel Heath Justice, Neil ten Kortenaar, Martin Kuester, and Rüdiger Zimmermann, for providing valuable feedback during the completion of this book; to the good people at the Canadian Plains Research Center, particularly Donna Grant, without whom this book would not have seen print; and to everyone else whom I might have missed.

Big thanks go to my parents, Annegret and Alfred, for believing in me from the beginning, and to Jagdwiga Jagiełło, for her prayers and all the good food. *Dziękuję bardzo.*

Finally, I could never give enough thanks to Tereska Jagiełło, who knows that I couldn't have written this book without her. *Dziękuję bardzo* for your Jagiellonian scholarship.

ay ay miikwec dziękuję danke thank you

Toronto, May 2010

INTRODUCTION

Theorizing Textualized Orality in Indigenous Literatures

"It is my conviction that Okanagan, my original language, the language of my people, constitutes the most significant influence on my writing in English."[1] Thus Jeannette Armstrong (Okanagan) begins her essay "Land Speaking" in *Speaking for the Generations*, a collection that brings together the reflections of nine contemporary Indigenous authors on their writing. Each author points to a deep connection to the land and the importance of telling stories, but some, including Armstrong, also raise the issue of writing in English in relation to an ancestral language. *"That's Raven Talk"* explores textualized orality in contemporary Indigenous literatures composed in English, but it is as much a study of Indigenous language influences in contemporary Indigenous writing as it is of oral strategies in writing. In fact, the main premise of this book is that a discussion of textualized orality in contemporary Indigenous literatures ultimately amounts to a discussion of Indigenous language influences in the English written by Indigenous authors and particularly of a linguistic structure called the *holophrase*.

The main idea that I would like to discuss in what follows is that *holophrastic reading*—a reading for (para)holophrases—constitutes a significant reading strategy for textualized orality in Indigenous literatures composed in English—or French, Spanish, or Portuguese, for that matter. I will limit myself, however, to Indigenous literatures written in just one of the "colonizers' languages," though I am positive that my findings are also applicable to Indigenous literatures in languages other than English.

But I am getting ahead of myself. So let me begin by explaining in this introduction the thesis that I have so bluntly stated here, including its key elements—holophrase, holophrastic reading, (para)holophrase, and textualized orality. This discussion is followed by five chapters in which I apply my thesis to readings of *Call Me Ishmael* by Ishmael Alunik (Inuvialuit), *Arctic Dreams and Nightmares* by Alootook Ipellie (Inuit), *The Lesser Blessed* by Richard Van Camp (Dogrib), *Green Grass, Running Water* by Thomas King (Cherokee), and *Blue Marrow* by Louise Bernice Halfe (Cree). I selected these five texts because they are by writers whose ancestral language traditions are all holophrastic[2] and because together they cover a wide enough range of generic, tribal, generational, and linguistic differences to allow for differentiated findings.[3]

WHAT IS THE HOLOPHRASE?

Jeannette Armstrong describes the main difference between her ancestral Okanagan (Southern Interior Salish) and the English language as follows:

> Okanagan is a language guided by active components of reality. Syllables form base units that carry meaning in the language. Root syllables are where meanings reside rather than only in whole or complete words. Words are a combination of syllables, each of which carries meaning and contains function. Each word, when examined, can be broken down into root syllables, each of which has an active meaning and when combined activates a larger animated image.

She further notes that, "In Okanagan, then, language is a constant replay of tiny selected pieces of movement and action that solicit a larger active movement somehow connected to you by the context you arrange for it."[4]

What Armstrong describes here is a structure that linguists refer to as the holophrase. Holophrases are polysyllabic units of utterance that result from *polysynthesis*: that is, they come into being the moment that one joins both lexical and grammatical morphemes into a single word so that, if one translates this word into an Indo-European language such as English, it corresponds to a complete sentence or clause.[5] The example that Armstrong uses to illustrate the language structures of her mother tongue is *kekwep*, the Okanagan word for "dog." It consists of two syllables—*kek* is translated by Armstrong as "happening upon a small (thing)," and *wep* is given as "sprouting profusely (as in fur)." Once put together, Armstrong further explains, these two syllables become "fur growing on a little living thing," which is not only a complete clause but also a very apt description of a dog, one that highlights action and movement as well as connection. As Armstrong explains, "When you say the Okanagan word for dog, you don't 'see' a dog image, you summon an *experience* of a little furred life, the exactness of which is known only by its interaction with you or something."[6] Armstrong's attempt to re-create in her writing in English the action, movement, and connectedness implicated in her mother tongue underlines the significant influence of Okanagan on her work.[7] This attempt would be far less complex if English did not differ considerably from Okanagan in terms of both its morphology and its discourse practices.

There appears to be a general agreement among linguists today that, even though polysynthesis is not found exclusively in North America,[8] it is "especially well developed" there compared with other regions in the world.[9] Moreover, as Marianne Mithun notes, Indigenous North America does not know any "truly analytic languages, in which all words would consist of a single morpheme."[10] Given the relatively high density of polysynthesis on this continent, the holophrase may hence be considered as one of the central features that distinguishes most Indigenous languages from English and from many other Indo-European languages. To explain why I believe that a linguistic structure that does not exist in English grammar is significant in the English written by Indigenous peoples, I need to explore further this linguistic structure and particularly its discourse consequences.

For literary purposes, I define the holophrase as *a productive and ordered concatenation of signs in polysynthetic languages that forms the core of a substantive polysynthetic idea unit and functions as a significant narrative unit in a given polysynthetic discourse.* Each of these notions, of course, requires further explanation and exemplification. Unlike polysynthetic languages such as Okanagan, which "concentrate the expression of information into the verbal word,"[11] English relies on using independent noun phrases and pronouns to express subject and object relationships. Thus, *ra-wir-a-nuhwe's*, a single Mohawk word meaning "he likes the baby,"[12] becomes a four-word sentence in English. The holophrase, then, is a *concatenation of signs* whose central component is always the verb, which, because of its ability to express both an event and its main participant(s), has been described by Wallace Chafe as "holistic."[13] The holistic nature of polysynthetic verbs does not concern morphology alone but "is a difference with discourse consequence,"[14] as we shall see next.

Since they allow speakers to produce fully grammatical sentences with a minimalism of text, polysynthetic grammars contain built-in silences. Whether or not the information provided in a given holophrase is further elaborated on ultimately depends on the situation.¹⁵ The speaker, deciding that (s)he does not need to provide more specific information, such as—to pick up the example of *ra-wir-a-nuhwe's*—*who* likes *whose* baby, may go on with the story. Or, deciding that further information is needed or on being asked by a listener, (s)he may elaborate on the previous utterance. Silences built into polysynthetic grammars—and the resulting minimalism of text—hence create speaker involvement and listener participation, resulting in dialogue.

Textual silences and minimalism of text are an indication of the significance of holophrases in polysynthetic discourse. Holophrases express the key components of grammar needed in telling a story—that is, the event and its participant(s)—and thus they have significant narrative functions in polysynthetic languages. Speech is produced in a series of spurts that Chafe calls *idea units*.¹⁶ Substantive idea units "convey substantive ideas of events, states, or referents."¹⁷ If a substantive idea unit includes a holophrase, the latter will, due to its morphological structure, form the *core of the substantive idea unit* in question—regardless of whether it stands alone or is accompanied by other words. As my interlinear translation of a Cree story in the appendix illustrates more fully, the holophrase represents that part of a polysynthetic idea unit *where signification takes its start*. Everything else needed in telling a story may be loosely grouped around the holophrase; however, for such modifiers to signify, they need to be related to a given holophrase. If one were to drop all the modifiers in a polysynthetic discourse, one would still be left with at least the *grid of a story*; if one were to drop all of its holophrases, however, one would lose the story's grid. Holophrases, then, function as *significant narrative units* by forming the grid, or skeleton, of any given narrative composed in a polysynthetic language.

To further illustrate the significance of holophrases in Indigenous discourse, let me briefly discuss how the holophrase relates to Roland Barthes' notion of narrative functions. Barthes distinguishes narrative units based on "two broad classes of functions" that these units can serve: *cardinal functions* (or *nuclei*) and *catalyses*, which he subsumes under the class "functions," and *indices proper* and *informants*, which he subsumes under the class "indices."¹⁸ Catalyses, indices proper, and informants, according to Barthes, are mere "*expansions* in their relation to the nuclei," whereas nuclei "define the very framework of the narrative," since they point to a complementary and consequential act and thus ensure the continuation of the story.¹⁹ As Barthes puts it,

> it is possible to reduce a sequence [i.e., a small group of functions] to its nuclei, and again a whole hierarchy of sequences to its

principal terms, without altering the meaning of the story. A narrative can be identified even if one reduces its total syntagm to its actants and major functions. In other words, narrative lends itself to *summary* (what used to be called *argument*).[20]

One cannot equate the holophrase with the Barthesian cardinal function because not every holophrase ultimately has a cardinal function; some of them, albeit few, might be only catalyses, indices proper, or informants. For example, the Mohawk holophrase *ra-wir-a-nuhwe's* quoted above may be used in a story only to give additional information about a character, such as the fact that he likes children and would be a good father; not relevant for the continuation of the story, this utterance functions merely as an index proper. If, however, the story is about the kidnapping of a baby, then "he likes the baby" qualifies as a cardinal function because the kidnapper's affection for the baby causes the action to unfold.

Of course, every narrative unit has meaning and is hence functional in one way or another. In both cases, "he likes the baby" is used in the story for a particular purpose, but, as this example shows, narrative units differ in the degree that they function in a given narrative: some units are more important than others.[21] Holophrases in Indigenous discourse form its very hinges (i.e., those parts of the narrative on which everything else depends), whereas the non-holophrastic units fill the narrative with texture. Or, to stay within the metaphor of holophrases as hinges, they are needed for the door to swing, allowing or blocking entrance into the room, but other narrative units are needed for the door to be a full-sized door in the first place. Even more so, one hinge will not do for the door to hold; only the sum of hinges can fulfill the task. Likewise, holophrases do not function in isolation; their potential significance in a narrative becomes possible only because they are interrelated. The holophrase, then, does not fit smoothly into Barthes' typology of narrative functions, yet holophrases and narrative units with cardinal functions have one thing in common: they function as particularly *significant* narrative units.

As we have seen above, much more information can be incorporated into polysynthetic verbs than into English verbs. In fact, speakers of polysynthetic languages constantly invent new holophrases, and their listeners will readily understand them[22]—provided, of course, that the various morphemes within the newly invented holophrases are combined according to the order outlined in the grammar of the respective language. Word formation in the Siglit dialect of Inuvialuktun, for example, always follows a defined pattern: wordbase/lexical suffixes/grammatical suffixes/

enclitic suffixes, with "wordbases and grammatical suffixes form[ing] the minimum requirement to get a grammatical word."[23] The concatenation of signs in holophrases is thus both *productive*[24] and *ordered*. I can summarize the discussion of the holophrase thus: it is a single word, it is built around a verb according to well-defined rules, it forms the core of a substantive polysynthetic idea unit, and it functions as a significant narrative unit in storytelling. Evidently, polysynthesis is more than a morphological phenomenon; its implications go well beyond the range of morphology and reach the realm of larger discourse, such as storytelling. Thus, holophrasis—a phenomenon usually studied by linguists only—might also be of interest for literary critics.[25]

WHY HOLOPHRASTIC READING?

Holophrastic reading constitutes a culturally specific reading strategy for textualized orality in Indigenous literatures in English and describes the search for what I call *(para)holophrases*: that is, the various manifestations of the holophrase in Indigenous discourse composed in English. There are two main reasons that a linguistic structure non-existent in English grammar might be of interest to literary critics working with English-language texts by Indigenous writers. One reason is that ancestral languages and discourse conventions, both directly and indirectly, influence Indigenous uses of English. The other is that, once one accepts that textualized orality marks a universal phenomenon encountered across literatures and cultures, the question arises whether there exist culturally specific strategies in textualizing orality. The holophrase points to one such culturally specific strategy in Indigenous literatures composed in English.

The use of English by the majority of Indigenous peoples in many parts of Canada and the United States today, Craig S. Womack (Muskogee Creek/Cherokee) suggests, has made "English an Indian language."[26] The question, then, is not one of *langue* but one of *parole*, that language is used by real people in real-life situations for specific purposes. Discussing the issue of translations from Indigenous languages into English, Womack also reminds us that what is different must not by definition be bad. Translation always implies a loss; however, as he asks, "what if there are other aspects [...] that are rendered 'better' in English?"[27] or simply rendered *differently*, one could add. After all, English is an Indigenous language for two reasons: first, as Womack notes, because it is *used* by Indigenous people (though, in this sense, it is also an East Indian and Caribbean language), and second—and this will be my focus—because some of its Indigenous uses are inflected by Indigenous mother tongues.

As Guillermo Bartelt has pointed out, "the shift from tribal tongues to English has not at all implied the discontinuity of ethnically marked discourse."[28] Instead of blindly adopting the English language or being helpless victims of English-language policies in Canada and the United States, many Indigenous people have indigenized English, thus creating what is referred to as "Red English"—"a pan-Indian phenomenon, roughly analogous to Black English,"[29] that coexists with standard uses of English all across Indigenous North America. William L. Leap claims that, though other linguistic influences can also exist,[30] the speakers' particular "ancestral language tradition provides the basis for [their] knowledge of Indian English grammar and for their use of that knowledge in specific discourse settings."[31] It follows, then, that there are as many different versions of Indigenous English as there are Indigenous languages in North America.[32]

Indigenous English codes differ from standard English in their sound patterns, word and sentence structures, semantics, and pragmatics.[33] As Leap's research on Ute students' writing suggests, moreover, Indigenous language influences in written English go beyond the sentence level. Leap finds that written Ute students' compositions are organized according to a "nonexhaustive presentation of meaning; [an] active engagement of the reader; and [the] communicative value of the text-form." Not only do these principles point to oral strategies of language use (namely, involvement and participation; see below), but they also do not correspond with "expectations of standard English literacy."[34] What is even more important, Leap argues that written Ute English "parallels in many ways the patterns of oral discourse found within the students' ancestral language tradition."[35] If his findings about Ute students' writing are generalizable—which, I would argue, is plausible—the expectations that speakers of Indigenous English codes have regarding writing are based on principles of composition in the respective spoken Indigenous English code and, by extension, the respective Indigenous language. Many Indigenous writers' use of English, then, cannot simply be equated with orality or the colloquial use of language. As Allison Adelle Hedge Coke (Huron/Cherokee) further explains, "*Colloquialism* refers to regional usage of certain words or informal oral speech rather than the written form of dialogue. This description does not quite explain Indianizing, but I have to resort to the word *colloquial* to convey what I mean about this use. I find this frustrating but necessary."[36] Hedge Coke here points to the limits of describing Indigenous language practices using Euro-Western languages—linguistics, on the one hand, and English, on the other hand. What her observation also suggests, however, is that Indigenous writers' use of English is not simply a form of textualized orality; rather, it is a *specific* form of textualized orality given that Indigenous writers both oralize and indigenize English when composing in it.

The Indigenous mother tongues of North America have suffered immensely through colonization. Many of these languages have become extinct in the past 500 years; others are in danger of becoming extinct in the near future.[37] Thus, English, French, Portuguese, and Spanish have become the first languages for most Indigenous people living in North America today, including many contemporary Indigenous writers. Richard Van Camp and Thomas King, for example, two of the five authors included in this study, write in English because they do not speak their ancestral languages (Dogrib in the case of Van Camp; Cherokee in the case of King). Hence, these two writers have not been influenced by Indigenous languages in any immediate way. Yet I think that we should not readily assume the absence of all ancestral linguistic contexts in the works of writers such as Van Camp and King. Indigenous language influences sometimes figure in more indirect ways. Writers speaking only English will know other writers and storytellers, and have family members and friends, who still speak their ancestral languages. King's writing, for example, has been much influenced by his experiences living and working with Blackfoot people during his time in Lethbridge, Alberta. The storytelling of Harry Robinson (Okanagan) has also had a notable impact on King's work. As King noted in an interview with Peter Gzowski, Robinson's stories had been "inspirational" in showing him a way to "recreate the sense of an oral storytelling voice in a written form."[38] Finally, Indigenous language influences are not restricted to purely grammatical notions that end with the sentence level. After all, the holophrase not only concerns morphology but also affects Indigenous discourse practices at large.

Indigenous oratures[39] constitute the immediate contexts of contemporary Indigenous literatures not just in *poetic* and *cultural* terms but also, as the discussion above illustrates, in *linguistic* terms. Given that they continue traditions of Indigenous oratures using not only a different medium but also a different language, contemporary Indigenous literatures are always, then, "some version of [a] translation project," as Arnold Krupat argues:

> Even though contemporary Native writers write in English and configure their texts in apparent consonance with Western or Euramerican literary forms—that is, they give us texts that look like novels, short stories, poems, and autobiographies—they do so in ways that present an "English" nonetheless "powerfully affected by the foreign tongue," not by Hindi, Greek, or German, of course,

and not actually by a "foreign" language, inasmuch as the "tongue" and "tongues" in question are indigenous to America.[40]

The logical consequence of Krupat's observation is, to use Margery Fee's words, that "we, as literary critics, cannot rely on our knowledge of our own discourse conventions to see us through an interpretation" of works by Indigenous writers.[41] That is, we need to study the influences of Indigenous language structures and the resulting principles of verbal composition on the writing by Indigenous authors if we want to gain a better understanding of Indigenous literatures, including their strategies in textualizing orality.

The holophrase has been known as a distinguishing feature of many North American Indigenous languages since the first half of the nineteenth century (the first use of the word *holophrastic* goes back to Francis Lieber in 1837[42]). Yet this category has not yet entered the critical discussion of Indigenous literatures, which so far has limited its consideration of questions of language either to notions of code switching[43] or, more recently, to Creenglish, a Cree English code, in Cree and Métis poetry.[44] I intend to correct this historical oversight by developing a reading strategy for textualized orality that is derived from the holophrase. I call this reading strategy "holophrastic reading": that is, a search for (para)holophrases, the various manifestations of the holophrase in Indigenous discourse composed in English. Holophrastic reading paves the way for a less ethnocentric approach to Indigenous literatures by developing a notion of orality in these literatures from inside, rather than outside, Indigenous languages. Equally important is that this method of reading not only offers an approach to textualized orality in Indigenous literatures that can account for these literatures' *culturally specific* strategies in textualizing orality (i.e., strategies commonly found in Indigenous as opposed to Euro-Western literatures); it also lays the ground for future studies on ancestral language influences in Indigenous literatures that focus on the *tribal specificity* of these literatures and might thus contribute to the growing corpus of scholarship in the field of Indigenous literatures "that takes seriously the intellectual and political sovereignty of the People."[45]

The notion of culturally specific strategies in textualizing orality in Indigenous literatures reflects more than just the history and development of Indigenous verbal traditions; it is also significant in light of the abundance of material that literary critics, but also linguists, have gathered together in support of the notion of literature as not just writing but also writing of a hybrid nature that always displays, at least to some degree, strategies of orality.[46] Reading literature as hybrid writing seems to counter the Derridean notion of all sign systems as *writing* caught up in the process of the infinite deferral of meaning.⁴⁷ My interest here lies not so much in the principles of signification. Nor am I interested in poststructuralist readings of Indigenous literatures, as proposed by Arnold Krupat in "Post-Structuralism and Oral Literature"⁴⁸—such readings would only undermine Indigenous notions of "[l]anguage and the sacred [as] indivisible."⁴⁹ What I am interested in, rather, are the nuances that exist between different types of discourse, between, for example, expository prose and what literary critics call literature.

As Boris M. Éjchenbaum noted in an essay originally published in 1918,

> elements of oral narration and of live, oral improvisation can still be discerned in written literature. A writer often imagines himself to be an oral narrator and by various devices tries to give his written language the illusion of *skaz*. There are, of course, literary forms that are specifically written forms, but they do not comprise all of literature (or, more precisely, all of belles lettres [...]), and traces of colloquial spoken language can be found even in these forms.⁵⁰

Thus, Éjchenbaum observes, "written language is not always beneficial to the literary artist. The real artist carries within him the primitive but organic forces of living oral narration."⁵¹ Similarly, John Willinsky argues, "the level of sophistication of the highly literate text is dependent on sustaining an oral sensibility."⁵² Consequently, as Robert Kellogg suggests, "to answer the question about what kinds of books many of our greatest works of narrative art are, it can be useful to ask what kind of oral narratives some of them are pretending to be."⁵³ In an essay on what he calls *fingierte Mündlichkeit* ("simulated orality"), Paul Goetsch has noted that written narrative "intends to induce the reader to reading, to capture his attention, to inspire his imagination, and to offer him points of identification. Above all, however, it asks him to invent the narrated world in the act of reading." Thus, as Goetsch further notes, "textualized orality is part of the potential effectiveness of written narrative, an aspect of the general rhetoric of fictional texts (Wayne C. Booth) as well as their unique appellative structure (Wolfgang Iser)."⁵⁴

Susan Berry Brill de Ramírez correctly observes that "the problematic emphasis in Native studies on past oral traditions has perpetuated colonial romanticizations and, thereby, the continuing marginalization of American Indian literatures."⁵⁵ At the same time, she does not want to leave the oral aesthetic of contemporary Indigenous literatures completely undiscussed— and why should she? After all, the oral aesthetic of Euro-Western literatures has not remained unanalyzed, either, even if the recent emphasis in North

America on textualized orality in Indigenous literatures appears to suggest otherwise.⁵⁶ The issue, then, is not so much *that* orality, in whatever form, is discussed in relation to Indigenous nations and their literatures but *how* it is discussed. The oral-literate theories proposed by Marshall McLuhan, Jack Goody, Ian Watt, Walter Ong, Eric Havelock, and David Olson have prompted strong criticism—and rightly so—for claiming, "roughly, that writing is necessary for the forms of consciousness found in modern Western thought," as Carol Fleisher Feldman summarizes the ideological disposition of these theories.⁵⁷ J. Edward Chamberlin has aptly described the choice between the oral and the written as "[o]ne of the most debilitating choices that colonialism seems to have imposed on us." No culture, he argues, is ever purely oral or purely written; rather, every culture engages in some forms of listening and speaking as well as reading and writing. Chamberlin thus reminds us to "be deeply uncertain about where to draw the line between oral and written traditions and indeed about whether there should be any lines at all."⁵⁸ That Euro-Western oral traditions have vanished almost completely from Euro-Western consciousness, whereas Indigenous oral traditions are still very much alive despite colonization, does not make Euro-Western literatures any less concerned with the oral than Indigenous literatures. When the oral and the written in contemporary Indigenous literatures are described as forming an interwoven relationship, this description, then, applies just as well to Euro-Western literatures,⁵⁹ albeit not necessarily in the same fashion and/or degree—but even Indigenous writing varies in the degree to and way in which it displays oral strategies.⁶⁰ As Margery Fee has pointed out, "Different cultures have different oral conventions as well as different written ones."⁶¹ Any discussion of textualized orality in Indigenous literatures remains superficial as long as it does not address this question in terms of the cultural specificity of the strategies used. A culturally specific approach to textualized orality in Indigenous literatures has, then, as much to do with avoiding ethnocentrism as with avoiding the romantic notion that contemporary Indigenous literatures are the only literatures engaging with the oral.

This brings me back to the holophrase, which, as noted earlier, has been largely ignored in the study of Indigenous literatures. It has figured in the work of a few scholars (Mary Austin and Lester Standiford), but even there it has been given very limited attention. The one aspect emphasized in previous approaches to the oral aesthetic in Indigenous literatures has not been the holophrase but the dialogic quality of Indigenous writing. Kimberly M. Blaeser (Anishinaabe) explains the critical interest in the oral dimension of contemporary Indigenous literatures as follows:

INTRODUCTION

There is a movement in Native written literature connected to its roots in orality. Attention to this connection has resulted in a certain style of writing. Tribally based aesthetic patterns may appear inadvertently in the work of some writers, quite self-consciously in the work of others. Regardless, Native authors show similarities in the way they attempt to encourage *a response-able way of reading—an imaginative, interactive, participatory creation of story*. More than that, I believe that Native literatures have supra-literary intentions. [...] Native stories have goals beyond entertainment just as their predecessors in the oral literatures did. They work to make us into communities, form our identity, ensure our survival. Native authors, like authors of many postcolonial cultures, write revolution; their "tongue is fire."[62]

The notion of "participatory creation of story" is also present in Blanca Schorcht's discussion of the relationship between Indigenous oral storytelling and contemporary Indigenous literatures. Employing the Bakhtinian notion of dialogue, Schorcht discusses how Harry Robinson, Thomas King, James Welch (Blackfoot/Gros Ventre), and Leslie Marmon Silko (Laguna Pueblo) write novels that allow "readers [to] become a part of the stories that are being told in these novels, just as the audience is a part of any storytelling performance." The "dialogic fluidity" thus created, Schorcht further argues, "resonates with the power of the oral tradition and its ability to continually transform itself."[63]

In contrast to Schorcht, Susan Berry Brill de Ramírez finds Bakhtinian readings of Indigenous literatures flawed because they "reclaim the oral within the textual [...] from a discursively textual and decidedly Western framework that privileges the textual at the expense of the oral." Arguing for a reading of "literatures closer to their oral roots" that is "based within the very traditions from which those literatures are based,"[64] Brill de Ramírez hence proposes what she calls a *conversive* approach to Indigenous literatures that borrows from "the conjunctive reality of traditional storytelling through both its transformational and regenerative power (conversion) and the intersubjective relationality between the storyteller and listener (conversation)."[65] Unlike reader-response criticism, which, Brill de Ramírez argues, "privilege[s] the role of the reader at the expense of the writer-teller," conversive criticism attempts to read Indigenous literary texts as growing out of a co-creation of both reader and story writer.[66] Reader-response criticism emphasizes a component of verbal communication—the creative role of the receptor of the message—that appears to get lost in the process of putting words into writing or print but never actually disappears in literature. Reader-response criticism, then, has undoubtedly contributed to the acknowledgement of the oral aesthetics of all literatures. Its terminology might have emphasized the role of the reader, yet reader participation ultimately implies author involvement; the two are always correlated. Schorcht's and Brill de Ramírez's readings of textualized orality in Indigenous literatures thus differ more in terminology than in conception: both approach Indigenous literary texts as having a dialogic quality.

What strategies are employed to achieve this dialogic quality in Indigenous literatures? Discussing the work of Gerald Vizenor (Anishinaabe), Blaeser devotes some time to a discussion of "stylistic characteristics of orality."[67] Along with other characteristics, she refers to minimalism of text as a key component of Indigenous oratures. Pointing out how minimalism of text relates to audience (and reader) participation and how it is employed in Vizenor's own writing to open up the text (e.g., by way of implication, absence, contradiction, and ambiguity or by use of allegory, metaphor, satire, shock, and humour),[68] Blaeser also briefly mentions the holophrastic character of North American Indigenous languages and, in this context, quotes Lester Standiford, who has observed a correlation in Indigenous verbal traditions between holophrasis and minimalism of text:[69] "Lester Standiford draws a parallel between the 'dense *holophrastic* nature' of tribal language, the 'compactness of the literature,' and the 'embedding technique' and 'cryptic nature' that characterize contemporary Native American literature. He claims that this 'nondirective approach [...] allows a reader the feeling and the meaning of the experience in his or her own turn.'"[70] As Blaeser notes elsewhere, the "tensions between oral and written, and between English and Native languages, still have currency even though many Native American writers grew up with English and with the written mode," so that Indigenous literatures include "many tangible manifestations of a commitment to as well as descent from *orality* and *Native speech patterns*."[71] Blaeser's observation points to the interconnectedness of discourse mode and language that calls for a culturally specific approach to textualized orality in Indigenous literatures composed in English—an approach that may be provided by the holophrase. After all, the reader participation that Blaeser sees invited by Vizenor's style is due to a minimalism of text, which lies at the core of Indigenous oratures and is encouraged by the holophrastic nature of many North American Indigenous languages and their holistic verbs.

WHAT ARE (PARA)HOLOPHRASES?

The holophrase, then, is a key element for developing a culturally specific reading strategy for textualized orality in Indigenous literatures composed in English. But how does the holophrase carry over into English discourse? Code switching, a conversational strategy involving "the use of more than one language in the course of a single communicative episode,"[72] marks a strategy in textualizing orality that is found across cultures. When Indigenous authors composing in English weave words from Indigenous languages into their writing—and there are more and more contemporary Indigenous authors who do so (e.g., Louise Bernice Halfe, Neal McLeod [Cree], Tomson Highway [Cree], Gregory Scofield [Métis], LeAnne Howe [Choctaw], and Richard Wagamese [Anishinaabe])—they show involvement with their readers by marking readers' relationships to their compositions as either cultural insiders or outsiders, thus defining the terms by which readers may participate with the texts. The moment that code switching in Indigenous literatures in English includes the use of Indigenous holophrases, this strategy in textualizing orality becomes culturally specific since the holophrase is one of the defining features that distinguishes many Indigenous languages from English and most other Indo-European languages. The significant question, however, is whether the culturally specific strategies in textualizing orality found in Indigenous literatures composed in English go beyond the mere use of code switching in the form of holophrases. To put the question more bluntly, do contemporary Indigenous authors writing in English weave into their works equivalents to the linguistic structure referred to as the holophrase? And, if this is the case, how do Indigenous authors reinvent this particular cultural code in their writing in English? In other words, we need to explore what other forms, besides code switching, holophrastic manifestations in English-language discourse can take.

The movement from holophrases in Indigenous languages to equivalents in English implies a process of translation. In *The Theory and Practice of Translation* (1969), Eugene Nida and Charles Taber introduced a concept of translation that shifts the focus "from the form of the message to the response of the receptor" and proposes the priority of what they call *dynamic equivalence* over *formal correspondence*.[73] Formal correspondence is concerned with "the message itself, in both form and content," whereas dynamic equivalence is always based upon "the principle of equivalent effect."[74] The effects of a given text on its readers can only be assumed. However, what can more or less objectively be observed in a text are its functions. Hence, if one modifies Nida and Taber's notion of dynamic equivalence to encompass primarily function—which, of course, has certain, if non-specifiable, effects—the focus can again be shifted to the object of translation, the text. As we will see in the discussion that follows, Nida and Taber's theory of translation, in this modified form, proves to be helpful in illuminating the relationship between the holophrase and its possible formal and functional equivalents in English discourse.

Formal Equivalents to the Holophrase
English certainly does not qualify as a polysynthetic language; in fact, historically, it has moved further and further away from polysynthesis.[75] Given its morphology, the holophrase in *English grammar* simply does not exist. A translation of the holophrase into English that aims for an equivalence of *form* (i.e., grammar), then, is a failed translation.[76] Despite their differences in morphology, however, Indigenous languages and English are far from being incompatible.[77] Thus, the remnants of this failed translation are worth analyzing. Although English is a largely analytic language, its morphology and syntax leave its speakers some room, however limited, for the production of words or phrases that *suggest* the holophrase in terms of grammar and may thus be regarded as *holophrastic traces*: that is, as traces of the holophrase on the level of form (i.e., grammar). As we have seen above, polysynthesis does not concern morphology alone but has larger discourse consequences. Traces of the holophrase may hence involve not only the imitation of this particular morphological structure within the limits defined by English grammar but also the imitation of discourse features that result from polysynthesis or that may be associated with polysynthesis. It makes sense, then, to distinguish between *direct holophrastic traces* (traces of the morphological structure of the holophrase) and *indirect holophrastic traces* (traces of discourse features invited by polysynthesis). Depending on their form, however, there may be considerable differences in the degree to which these holophrastic traces evoke holophrases. Obviously, direct holophrastic traces come closer to actual holophrases in Indigenous languages than do indirect holophrastic traces, which evoke the *use* of the holophrase in discourse rather than its morphological structure. Further differences naturally exist within each of the two groups of holophrastic traces.

Direct holophrastic traces are reminiscent of the morphological structure of holophrases to varying degrees, depending on the specific type of linguistic structure involved. For instance, linguists distinguish between root or *primary compounds*, simply concatenations of words (e.g., "houseboat"), and *synthetic compounds*, concatenations of words in which the head (i.e., the main component that determines the semantic category of the compound) is derived from a verb (e.g., "taxi driver").[78] *Complex root compounds*, that is, root compounds that concatenate more than two words (e.g., "university teaching award committee"), suggest the possibility found in polysynthetic languages of combining various morphemes into a new word. However, *complex noun-noun compounds* (*N N compounds*), such as "willow frame sod huts" in Alunik's *Call Me Ishmael*,[79] are unable to evoke the holistic nature of polysynthetic verbs unless they contain a deverbal noun: that is, a noun derived by affixation of a verb. *Deverbal N N compounds*, such as "breathing holes" and "societal cut-throat rat races" in Ipellie's *Arctic Dreams and Nightmares*,[80] on the other hand, are less reminiscent of the significance of verbs in polysynthetic languages than *compound nouns with a verbal modifier* (*V N compounds*; e.g., "drawbridge" and "pickpocket"), which in turn are less evocative of the holistic nature of the holophrase than *synthetic compounds*, such as "Will Horse Capture" in King's *Green Grass, Running Water*,[81] because English assigns more importance to heads than to modifiers. *Quotation compounds* (e.g., "'dontwasteit' grip" in Van Camp's *The Lesser Blessed*),[82] and *idiom-like lexical phrases* (e.g., "Young Man Walking On Water" in *Green Grass, Running Water*),[83] both of which can involve the attempt to create (the illusion of) *loan translations into English*,[84] come even closer to the morphological structure of holophrases in Indigenous languages than synthetic compounds: not only are quotation compounds and idiom-like lexical phrases very descriptive, but also, unlike synthetic compounds, they are essentially phrasal.

Like their direct counterparts, indirect holophrastic traces can be more or less suggestive of holophrases, depending on how common these discourse features are in other writings in English discourse as well as on how directly these features can be associated with the use of holophrases in Indigenous discourse. Indirect holophrastic traces include *subject dropping*, *highly descriptive* or *figurative language*, *textual silences*, as well as *evidentials* and *pronoun copying*. All of these indirect holophrastic traces may be read as echoing—each one in its own unique way—discourse consequences that relate to the complexity of verbs in Indigenous languages or, in the case of descriptive and figurative uses of language, of Indigenous words more generally. However, because evidentials and pronoun copying are more clearly related to the discourse consequences of polysynthesis than the others, they warrant a more detailed discussion.

Evidentiality has been strongly connected with Indigenous languages in North America[85]—a circumstance that can correlate with the fact that these languages still represent oral languages. As Chafe notes of Seneca speakers, "when they think about an event, [they] immediately and unconsciously associate it with how they know about it and with the extent to which it accords with their perception of reality, whereas English speakers immediately and unconsciously associate it with its temporal relation to the time of speaking."[86]

While evidentials have also been identified for other, including non-polysynthetic, languages,[87] the "entire Western Hemisphere," Wallace L. Chafe and Johanna Nichols note, "shows an *unusual* concern for the linguistic marking of epistemology."⁸⁸ Cree speakers, for example, usually begin and/or end reported speech either with *ê-itêyihtahk*, "[this is] what he thought," or *itêyihtam*, "so he thought."⁸⁹ These holophrases mark the previous utterance as verbal report, one of the two types of indirect evidence identified by linguists besides inference.⁹⁰ Take, for example, the following excerpt from "Chahkabesh and the Giant Women," as told by Xavier Sutherland (Cree) in Swampy Cree and translated by C. Douglas Ellis.

"šââ!" *mamâ itwêw* ana iskwêw. "'kwâni kwayask kâ-kî-pêci-kîwêyin," *manâ itwêw*. "mistâpêskwêwak oš' ân' ê-kêkišêpâ-manihtêcik, anima kâ-pêhtaman," *manâ itwêw*, " ê-matwê-kahikêcik oš' âni animêniw kâ-itihtâkwaninik," *manâ itwêw*. "'kâwina mîna wîskâc antê ohc'-îtohtê, kâ-k'-îsi-pêhtaman anima kêkwân," *itwêw*.⁹¹

"O-oh dear!" *said that woman*. "Then it was right that you came back home," *she said*. "It was the giant women, you realize, gathering wood early in the morning, that is what you heard," *she said*. "As they were noisily cutting it, indeed that is what made the sound," *she said*. "Don't ever go there again where you heard that thing," *she said*.⁹²

The continuous repetition of *manâ itwêw* at the end of each idea unit in this passage is rather striking. The regular use of quotatives creates rhythm and—as M. Dale Kinkade and Anthony Mattina have noted analyzing quotatives in a Tunica example—"may even help to mark folktales or myths as a genre different from ordinary narrative or other discourse inasmuch as it regularly distances the speaker from the time and content of the tale, which is likely to be believed to take place in a special myth time."⁹³ Evidentiality in Indigenous verbal traditions, then, functions as "an important structural marker."⁹⁴

As it turns out, this observation applies not just to Indigenous-language texts but also to English compositions, such as in this excerpt from "Twins: White and Indian," a story in Harry Robinson's *Write It on Your Heart*, where evidentials again take the form of attributive clauses or tags (in this case, "he says"):

But when he come back and they both of 'em there.
And *he says*,
 "Where is that paper?
 I laid 'em right here.
 And what you fellas do with it?"
The older one.

> He ask the older one first.
> "I don't know.
> I seen 'em there but I take a walk and come back.
> I didn't know.
> I don't know where it went."
> And he ask the younger one.
> *Says* the same thing.
> *He says,*
> "I don't know."
> And, *he says,*
> "I put some stone on 'em,
> and it should not slide away."[95]

Repetition of the tag at the end of this scene, or in the story told by Sutherland, might seem to be superfluous to a reader familiar only with Euro-Western literatures, but the repeated use of evidentials is an integral component in many Indigenous literary traditions, regardless of whether they are composed in an Indigenous language or in English.

There is, of course, nothing holophrastic per se about the use of evidentials in Indigenous discourse. At the same time, however, their widespread use in Indigenous discourse seems to be invited by the holistic nature of polysynthetic verbs and, by extension, of polysynthesis itself. Since speakers of polysynthetic languages are not occupied with identifying events and participants using separate signifiers, they can provide more detailed information on the subject addressed, such as the source of their knowledge. Evidentials can hence function as strong indirect holophrastic traces in Indigenous literatures composed in English.

Pronoun copying is another significant indirect holophrastic trace. This is "the practice of adding a pronoun after the subject noun or object noun," which is, according to Bartelt, a "very common syntactic feature in Indian English,"[96] but not very common in Euro-American English, where it is restricted primarily to colloquial discourse.[97] Pronoun copying, then, marks one means by which standard English is inflected with Indigenous tongues, and it can be found in significant texts such as *Stories of the Road Allowance People*, compiled and translated by Maria Campbell (Métis):

> "Oh dats your dog Bob" *Dah woman he* say.
> "He always sleep under dere when your gone."
> *Dah man he* put hees han on dah floor an he say
> "Astum Bob."[98]

Although ancestral language influence may not be the only explanation for the existence of pronoun copying in Indigenous English codes,[99] it still provides one possible explanation. After all, when translated literally into English, sentences in Indigenous languages with independent noun phrases contain dislocated nouns, since subjects and objects in Indigenous languages are usually already expressed by way of an affix that is part of the holistic verb, as in this example from Plains Cree:

> *iskwew kîwâpamew maskwa*
> woman—something animate saw something animate—bear
> * woman he/she saw him/her bear.
> "The woman saw a bear."

Pronoun copying in Indigenous English codes, then, can be read as an echo of the verb complexity found in many Indigenous languages.

In the end, however, the presence in Indigenous discourse composed in English of holophrastic traces—whether direct or indirect—always implies a negation or gap. These traces essentially evoke (the use of) a structure that does not exist in English grammar and can always only be hinted at. Yet, depending on the context of their use, holophrastic traces can serve important discourse functions in Indigenous literatures composed in English—for example, by establishing linguistic, cultural, or other contexts. The significance of holophrastic traces as a kind of *formal* manifestation of the holophrase in English discourse will therefore not be underestimated.

Dynamic Equivalents to the Holophrase

The notion of holophrastic *traces* speaks of the impossibility of successfully translating the holophrase into English grammar. As we have seen in the discussion of Nida and Taber's notion of dynamic equivalence, however, translation concerns not only *form* but also *function*. If two things have the same or similar functions, and hence effects, then they can be described as equivalent even if their formal features differ considerably. Indeed, there is nothing intrinsic to English grammar that points to the non-existence of a structure in this language that is equivalent *in function* to the holophrase in Indigenous languages. That a formal translation of the holophrase into English grammar fails, then, does not imply that the holophrase is by definition untranslatable into English discourse.

With a translation of the holophrase into English discourse that aims at creating a *dynamic equivalence* between source and target object, the significance shifts from linguistics to *rhetoric* or *literary criticism*. Of course, both the source object of such a translation (i.e., the holophrase) and the target object (its dynamic equivalent) belong to the body of linguistics and the body of rhetoric simultaneously: both have their basis in language, and hence grammar, and can be used for rhetorical effect. Yet, while the holophrase is a *significant linguistic object* because it represents a unique morphological structure, the target object will be a *significant rhetorical object*, which lacks the unique morphological structure of its source object. The metaphor "Young Man Walking On Water," for example, as used in *Green Grass, Running Water*, is not a one-word sentence, yet it carries a bundle of meaning with it and, together with all of the other examples of water imagery in the novel, helps to hold its multiple narratives together. Similarly, the synecdoche "dah Prees" (the priest as one of many facets of colonialism) functions as a significant narrative unit in *Stories of the Road Allowance People* by tying seemingly unrelated stories into a coherent narrative of cultural memory.[100] Likewise, in *Porcupines and China Dolls*, a novel by Gwich'in author Robert Arthur Alexie, the simile "like a million porcupines crying in the dark" and its various repetitions throughout the novel contribute to the narrative's dark tone.[101] Performing functions that are similar to those performed by actual holophrases in Indigenous languages and expressing a complex idea, each of these concatenations of signs can be said to be dynamically equivalent to the holophrase. As the dynamic equivalent to the holophrase in Indigenous languages, the target object is analogous to, but separate from, the holophrase; shifting the focus from linguistics to rhetoric, the target object can even be said to go *beyond* the holophrase. In English, the Greek prefix *para*—meaning "analogous or parallel to, but separate from or going beyond, what is denoted by the root word"—can be used to express such a relationship between two objects.[102] *Paraholophrase* thus appears to be an appropriate term to denote the dynamic equivalent in Indigenous literatures in English to the holophrase in Indigenous languages.[103] Not only does this term mark the close relationship between the product of the translation and its source, but it also marks the target object as an independent category existing on a different level (rhetoric) than the category from which it derives (linguistics). As a dynamic equivalent to the holophrase, the paraholophrase exists not in contrast to but beside or parallel to the holophrase; it is a "repetition with difference," to use Linda Hutcheon's notion of parody,[104] the repetition of a linguistic category in a rhetorical/literary realm.

My definition of the holophrase—*a productive and ordered concatenation of signs that forms the core of a substantive polysynthetic idea unit and functions as a significant narrative unit in a given polysynthetic discourse*—focuses on function rather than form (i.e., grammar). The definition of the dynamic equivalent to the holophrase can thus be derived from this particular definition. Since the paraholophrase is a rhetorical/literary category, this process naturally implies dropping and/or replacing all those components in the functional definition of the holophrase that represent purely linguistic notions: that is, "productive," "unit" in "idea unit," and consequently "substantive" as well as "polysynthetic." The metaphor "Young Man Walking On Water," for example, is a concatenation of signs, yet literary critics would not describe this phrase as an indicator of productivity, a term reserved for linguistics, nor would they describe it as the core of a substantive polysynthetic idea unit, again terms used primarily in linguistics. A more rhetorical/literary description of phrases such as "Young Man Walking On Water," "dah Prees," and "like a million porcupines crying in the dark," which I will henceforth use as a definition of the paraholophrase, reads as follows: *a paraholophrase is a creative and ordered concatenation of signs that forms the core of a complex idea and functions as a significant narrative unit in a given discourse.*

This definition, of course, bears further analysis, so let me discuss its various components in more detail to illustrate how paraholophrases actually work in discourse. Cognitive linguists assume that language output—regardless of the language in question—is formed based not so much on the smallest components of language (i.e., words) but on larger *chunks* of language. Chunks in polysynthetic languages can be, but do not have to be, represented by one signifier (i.e., a holophrase), whereas chunks in analytic or synthetic languages are always represented by a series of signifiers. From a semiotic point of view, however, chunks are always *concatenations of signs*: whatever the language in question, chunks are series of interconnected signs that are processed by the listener (or reader) as forming one unit: that is, a complex sign (see Fig. 0.1). Take, for example, the word *storytelling*: it consists of two signs: "story" (sign$_1$) and "telling" (sign$_2$). As with any other sign, these signs are defined by the association between the actual expression, that is, the *signifier* (abbr. "sr"), and the concept that it represents, that is, the *signified* (abbr. "sd"), but these two individual signs are also combined to form a new and ultimately more complex sign that exists in its own right: "storytelling." Chunks can consist of more than two interconnected signs; in fact, the possible number of signs that can be combined to form a chunk is infinite (as suggested by the subscript "n" in Fig. 0.1).

Figure 0.1. Chunks as complex signs.

That is, the paraholophrase can be (depending on the language in which it is composed) polylexical, such as the examples used above, "Young Man Walking On Water," "dah Prees," and "like a million porcupines crying in the dark,"[105] whereas the holophrase is by definition *monolexical*. The concatenation of signs in paraholophrases, by the way, is as productive and ordered as the concatenation of signs in holophrases. In both cases, new signs are produced according to defined rules—with the only difference being that the technical term for the ability to form new words or expressions is "productive" in linguistics and concerns *langue*, whereas in literary analysis this ability is usually referred to as "creative" and concerns *parole*.

However, not all concatenations of signs, or chunks, ultimately qualify as paraholophrases. To distinguish a paraholophrase from other chunks of language, context must be considered. The following two sentences will serve as an illustration:

(a) He saw a young man walking on water.
(b) "Old Woman leaves *Young Man Walking On Water* and his apostles and floats around for a while."[106]

Both sentences include the noun phrase "young man walking on water," which I have used above as an example of the paraholophrase; however, only the phrase in (b) qualifies as a paraholophrase. Each example can be considered a concatenation of signs—a grammatical chunk, to be more precise. The most obvious difference between (a) and (b) is the capitalization used in the latter, which indicates to the reader that it should be treated as a proper name. The capitalization changes the nature of this particular kind of concatenation of signs: these five words mark the *core of a complex idea* that is self-contained, but to which readers of *Green Grass, Running Water* are expected to attach further meaning, which is left unspoken. Of course, readers will, on a first reading of this proper name, stumble over its descriptiveness; in fact, they even witness its very invention:

So Old Woman is floating in the water. And she looks around. And she sees *a man. Young man. A young man walking on water.*
Hello, says Old Woman. Nice day for a walk.
Yes, it is, says *Young Man Walking On Water*.[107]

In the course of the story, the descriptive meaning of "young man walking on water" will become secondary. It will no longer be understood to refer to a man who actually walks on water but to a person who takes this phrase as his personal name, with all of its intertextual implications (Jesus, the Bible, the role of the Church in the colonization of North America, the residential and boarding school systems in Canada and the United States, and their social, mental, physical, spiritual, political, and cultural effects on Indigenous nations). So, whereas the concatenation of signs in (a) is a purely grammatical chunk, the concatenation of signs in (b) also represents a *psychological* chunk. That is, the latter is processed by readers according not only to defined rules of grammar but also to the idea's *context* (in this case, historical, political, and literary). Hence, the concatenation of signs in (b) is a paraholophrase—provided that it is used in the text as a significant narrative unit—whereas the sentence in (a) is not. Reader participation—and, by implication, author involvement—is, then, central to the processing of paraholophrases—as it is to the processing of holophrases.

A phrase that serves as a paraholophrase in one text—for example, "Young Man Walking On Water" in *Green Grass, Running Water*—can, technically speaking, also be found in other texts, for example in a parish newsletter retelling the story of Jesus approaching the apostles' boat by walking on water,[108] using as a proper name "Young Man Walking On Water" instead of "Jesus." Or the same phrase can be found in a description of Paul Cézanne's painting *Bather* (1885) as displaying a "pensive *young man walking on water* in a spare blue and beige landscape."[109] In the last two examples, however, the *context of the phrase* will be completely different from its context in King's novel. In King's case, the context is ultimately Indigenous since the phrase occurs in a variation of a Blackfoot myth involving the figure of Old Woman. The parish newsletter and the description of the Cézanne painting lack this Indigenous context. As Bronisław Malinowski has pointed out, "the sentence is not a self-contained, self-sufficient unit of speech. Exactly as a single word is—save in exceptional circumstances—meaningless, and receives significance only through the context of other words, so a sentence usually appears in the context of other sentences and has meaning only as a part of a larger significant whole."[110] Context, then, is also con*text*: that is, all the other utterances surrounding a particular phrase or, in other words, the very discourse that this phrase is placed in, which gives the phrase its *particular* meaning. "Young Man Walking On Water" in *Green Grass, Running Water* receives its real significance only when seen in conjunction with the remainder of the novel, particularly with its other paraholophrases, for example "Where did all that water come from?"[111] When seen in its immediate con*text*, "Young Man Walking On Water" fulfills a significant narrative function in King's novel—a function that the same phrase in the parish newsletter or in the description of the Cézanne painting will ultimately lack, hence distinguishing the latter two from the former. The holophrase and the paraholophrase, then, differ from each other also in that the holophrase can be identified without its immediate con*text* because it describes a unique morphological structure that can easily be recognized (and thus concerns primarily *langue*), whereas the paraholophrase is a rhetorical device (and thus concerns primarily *parole*) that can never be identified without consideration of its immediate con*text*.

The kind of signification at play in the paraholophrase "Young Man Walking On Water" resembles the use of figurative language in polysynthetic languages. For example, let us return to Jeannette Armstrong's Okanagan word for "dog," *kekwep*: "In English," Armstrong writes, its two syllables put "together would not make specific sense. However, when these two syllables are combined in Okanagan, they immediately join together to become an activator of a larger *image*."[112] That is, the meaning of this holophrase is not readily accessible to an outsider by merely "unchunking" it into its individual signs. When put together, these signs form a complex sign that is more than its individual pieces added together: it is a *figure of speech*. In a similar fashion, Thomas King's "Young Man Walking On Water" is a concatenation of signs whose actual meaning goes beyond simple algebra. It takes more than a simple addition of all its individual signs to derive its meaning, or, to use Gérard Genette's description of figures, it marks "a gap between sign and meaning," whose "value [...] is not given in the words that make it up, since it depends on the gap between these words and those that the reader perceives, mentally, beyond them."[113] A paraholophrase that forms a figure of speech comes into being, then, only after the reader has identified it as such. However, since there is no rule stating that holophrases must be figurative, we can assume that the figure is only one of various forms that paraholophrases can take in Indigenous literatures composed in English. Moreover, not every figure of speech necessarily qualifies as a paraholophrase; a particular figure of speech can be regarded as a paraholophrase only if, besides carrying a bundle of meaning, it also serves a significant narrative function in the text.

The notion of the paraholophrase that I am proposing is, of course, grounded in Euro-Western discourses of theorizing. Yet the concept behind it partly overlaps with thoughts expressed by Indigenous people. To quote from an interview with Maria Campbell,[114]

> Yeah, it's the word bundle. I always tell my students don't just settle for the word, but imagine that the word is carrying this big huge bundle. What's inside? What are the roots of that word? What is

the story? Is there a song in the bundle, a ceremony, a protocol? Where did it come from? The word bundle is full of treasure.[115]

The paraholophrase is similar to the word bundle. I cannot claim that the two are identical or even equivalent, but there seems to be some significant overlap between these two notions, for both the word bundle and the paraholophrase carry with them a significant amount of meaning and function, just like the holophrase but in a different language.[116]

Let me summarize my theoretical musings about the paraholophrase thus far. I have argued that it is a dynamic equivalent to the holophrase: that is, the paraholophrase is neither identical with nor formally (i.e., grammatically) equivalent to the holophrase, but it performs functions of language that are equivalent to those performed by the holophrase in Indigenous languages. The paraholophrase is the product of a translation of the holophrase based on *dynamic equivalence*; as such, it implies leaving the realm of linguistics to enter the realm of rhetoric or literary criticism. Thus, whereas the holophrase is a significant *linguistic* object, the paraholophrase is a significant *rhetorical* object. It has its basis in grammar, but beyond these rules the forces of discourse and its particular context ask the author/reader to bind together certain signs to form a new and more complex sign, thus creating a paraholophrase. Paraholophrases can exist only within the constraints defined by the grammar of the language in which they are composed, which is why they are usually polylexical and cannot be identified without their immediate contexts.

The (Para)Holophrase as a Culturally Specific Signifier of Textualized Orality

Holophrastic traces and paraholophrases can be read as culturally specific strategies in textualizing orality because they are the products of more or less successful translations of the holophrase into English discourse, on the level of either form or function. Reading the various manifestations of the holophrase in Indigenous literatures composed in English as culturally specific strategies in textualizing orality points to the third and connotative level of multi-staggered systems of signification à la Roland Barthes,[117] which unmistakably grounds these literatures' textualization of orality in Indigenous oratures.

My translation of the holophrase into English discourse describes two systems of signification: namely, Indigenous discourse composed in Indigenous languages (SYSTEM A), on the one hand, and Indigenous discourse composed in non-Indigenous languages such as English (SYSTEM B), on the other hand (see Fig. 0.2).

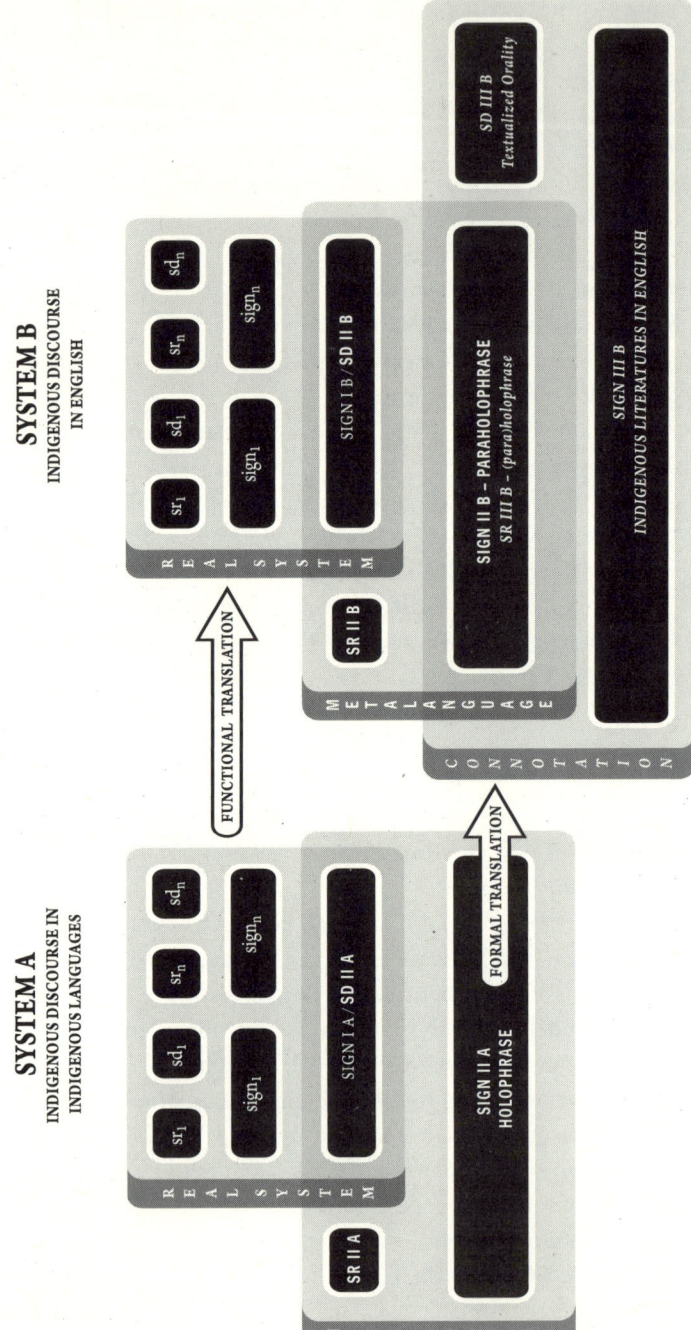

Figure 0.2. The (Para)Holophrase as a Signifier of Textualized Orality in Indigenous Literatures

In SYSTEM A, the real system is formed by the actual signs in a given Indigenous language (SIGN I A) and consists of concatenations of signifiers—for example, *kikînohtenitawikociwîci-nehiyaw'kiskinohamâkosiminâwâw* "you folks wanted to come and try to learn Cree with me"—and their signifieds. The moment that linguists describe these signs as "holophrases," they have entered the realm of a second level of signification, a metalanguage, in this case *linguistics*. In this metalanguage, the real system (i.e., the actual signs in a given Indigenous language) becomes a signified of the second system HOLOPHRASE (SIGN II A). That is, this real system becomes the concept associated with the expression "holophrase," which acts as a signifier of a whole class of expressions with a unique morphological structure that I have defined as *a productive and ordered concatenation of signs in polysynthetic languages that forms the core of a substantive polysynthetic idea unit and functions as a significant narrative unit in a given polysynthetic discourse.*

In SYSTEM B, the real system is formed by the actual signs in Indigenous discourse composed in English (or other non-Indigenous languages). SYSTEM B is the result of translating SYSTEM A onto a different level—namely, Indigenous discourse in non-Indigenous languages—with the attempt to create dynamic equivalence between the two systems. That is, SIGN I B of SYSTEM B is constructed so that it is equivalent to SIGN I A of SYSTEM A in function rather than in form (i.e., grammar): it lacks the unique morphological structure of SIGN I A, but it is equivalent to the latter in function. I have hence defined SIGN I B in analogy to SIGN I A as *a creative and ordered concatenation of signs that forms the core of a complex idea and functions as a significant narrative unit in a given discourse.* The moment that I refer to SIGN I B as a *paraholophrase* I have again entered the level of a metalanguage, in this case *rhetoric* or *literary criticism*. In this metalanguage, the real system (i.e., the signs in Indigenous discourse composed in non-Indigenous languages) becomes a signified of the second system PARAHOLOPHRASE (SIGN II B). That is, the real system becomes the concept associated with the expression "paraholophrase."

In other words, my discussion of the holophrase and its functional equivalent (the paraholophrase) relies on two different metalanguages. As part of the metalanguages of two different systems of signification, the HOLOPHRASE (SIGN II A) and the PARAHOLOPHRASE (SIGN II B) mark two separate and self-contained categories that are nonetheless interrelated because one has evolved from the other. This interrelatedness is of substantial significance in the context of discussing Indigenous language influences in Indigenous literatures composed in English. In fact, the close relationship between the holophrase and the paraholophrase is expressed in the fact that both of these second-level signs turn into what Barthes calls *connotators* in SYSTEM B. That is, they become signifiers of connotation, which consist of "several denoted signs [...] grouped together to form a single connotator—provided the latter has a single signified of connotation";[118] in my case, this "single signified of connotation" is textualized orality in the connoted system, "Indigenous literatures in English," which forms the third level of signification in SYSTEM B. The plane of connotation in SYSTEM B, then, contains my thesis statement: *the (para)holophrase serves as a culturally specific signifier of textualized orality in Indigenous literatures composed in English*. The (para)holophrase encompasses the two kinds of manifestations of the holophrase in English discourse, which include as discussed above:

1. its *functional manifestations* in the form of *paraholophrases* (i.e., the products of translating the holophrase (SIGN II A) based on an equivalence of function); and
2. its *formal manifestations* in the form of *code switching* and *holophrastic traces*, the latter of which are the remnants of an unsuccessful translation of the holophrase into English discourse striving for an equivalence of form (i.e., grammar).

The Cree holophrase *sîpi-kiskisiyân* ("I stretch my memory") in Neal McLeod's poem "Indian Summer,"[119] for example, functions as a signifier of textualized orality in Indigenous literatures in English because it marks a culturally specific way of code switching. Similarly, the phrase "Young Man Walking On Water" can serve as a culturally specific signifier of textualized orality because it forms a *holophrastic trace*—as an idiom-like lexical phrase, it is suggestive of the holistic structure of verbs in polysynthetic languages—or because it qualifies as a *paraholophrase* (provided, of course, that this creative and ordered concatenation of signs forming the core of a complex idea also functions as a significant narrative unit in a given Indigenous text composed in English).

In *Mythologies*, Barthes has shown how myth functions as "*a second-order semiological system*,"[120] that is, as a connoted system. The motivation underlying mythical signification, according to Barthes, "unavoidably contains some analogy" between form (second-level signifier) and concept (second-level signified) that "is never anything but partial," since a signified can have multiple signifiers.[121] Applied to holophrastic reading, this means that, though the (para)holophrase is only one of many signifiers of textualized orality in Indigenous literatures composed in English, it is arguably a significant one. Not only does the notion of the (para)holophrase point to the twofold transition from Indigenous oratures to Indigenous literatures as concerning both the mode of discourse and the choice of language, but it also helps to distinguish Indigenous literatures' strategies in textualizing orality from those found in other cultural settings. But what *is* textualized orality?

WHAT IS TEXTUALIZED ORALITY?

The term "textualized orality" has been suggested by Susan Gingell in an attempt to distinguish oral discourse that has been put into writing—what she calls "textualized orature"—from written discourse that exhibits "a writer's representation of the non-standard speech habits and oral strategies of communication used by speakers of a variety of a language other than that of the dominant socio-cultural group."[122] When I adopt Gingell's terminology here, I do so extending her notion of vernacular or sociolect in writing to oral strategies displayed in writing more generally, because I don't think that oral strategies are restricted to vernaculars and sociolects.

The notion of oral strategies in writing suggests a set of language uses independent of the medium. Distinguishing verbal discourse based on its medium and its conception (i.e., the degree of immediacy or distance between sender and receiver), as suggested by Peter Koch and Wulf Oesterreicher,[123] indeed makes a lot of sense. After all, the *particular contexts* of language production ("the moment and situation of [a] text's creation by speaker or writer") and language use ("the occasion on which [a] text is actually processed by the hearer or reader")[124] determine the "nature" of a given discourse just as much as the medium chosen for its composition. Koch and Oesterreicher propose to classify discourse also according to the degree of deviation from two ideal types at either end of a continuum: namely, the *language of immediacy* and the *language of distance*.[125] Like many other linguists,[126] Koch and Oesterreicher have chosen intimate conversation and expository prose (i.e., an administrative fiat) as ideal types to describe the languages of immediacy and distance, however relative and skewed such comparisons might be.[127] Accordingly, they define the language of immediacy as involving dialogue, free turn-taking between speakers, familiarity of partners, face-to-face interaction, free development of topics, non-public setting, spontaneity, involvement, and high context, which in turn result in low degrees of information density, compactness of language, integration, complexity, elaborateness, planning, and so on.[128] As such, the language describing what could be called *conceptual orality* corresponds with *characteristics of spoken discourse* that linguists have described as resulting from the context of *language production*—prosodic, redundant, fragmented, and fuzzy—or the context of *language use*—contextualized, involved, and participatory.[129] Oral strategies, then, can be found in both oral and written texts because they describe conceptual orality, which is independent of the medium. Used in texts[130] that are composed and transmitted in writing, oral strategies indicate textualized orality, which ultimately is a specific kind of conceptual orality.

All of this is not to say, of course, that textualized orality describes a homogeneous phenomenon. Any two novels, whether Indigenous or not, will differ in terms of the degree to which and the ways in which they employ oral strategies. In other words, textualized orality is a construct that we use to better understand the creation of meaning in literary texts. Thus, to echo a description that Ruth Finnegan once gave of orality, textualized orality "is *not* anything: or at any rate not anything in the apparently unitary sense that the term seems to imply."[131] What textualized orality *does*, however, again echoing Finnegan's words, is direct "us to certain kinds of investigations and insights, labelling and identifying certain aspects of human behaviour, forming a link between scholars interested in a range (even if not a fully agreed one) of party-shared questions and insights."[132] Textualized orality is more a means than a reality, but used with caution it can provide us with more understanding of the dynamics of verbal communication, of which the holophrase is only one of many facets.

READING INDIGENOUS LITERATURES FOR (PARA)HOLOPHRASES

I have used this introduction to explain the key elements of my thesis—that holophrastic reading constitutes a significant reading strategy for textualized orality in Indigenous literatures in English. In doing so, I have pointed out two possible ways of translating the holophrase into English discourse—one that strives for an equivalence of form (i.e., grammar) but ultimately remains unsuccessful, and one that strives for an equivalence of function and proves to be successful. I have further described and defined the objects resulting from these two acts of translation as holophrastic traces, on the one hand, and as paraholophrases, on the other. Finally, I have argued that the (para)-holophrase functions as a culturally specific signifier of textualized orality in Indigenous literatures in English. That these observations are indeed corroborated by Indigenous literary texts will be demonstrated in the holophrastic readings that follow in Chapters 1 to 5. Before ending this introduction, though, let me conclude with a few practical observations relating to both the specific structure of these readings and the results that they bring to light.

A holophrastic reading of Indigenous literatures in English—that is, a reading for (para)holophrases—implies crossing disciplinary boundaries because it combines two analyses into one reading. The holophrase and holophrastic traces are linguistic categories, whereas the paraholophrase belongs to the realm of rhetoric or literary criticism. Thus, the (linguistic) analysis of a text's use of holophrases and holophrastic traces is concerned with particular uses of language (code switching, borrowing, compounding), whereas the (literary) analysis of paraholophrases is concerned with the text's form and content. Paraholophrases, unlike holophrases, then, can only be determined from the con*text* into which they are placed. A reading for paraholophrases hence demands close textual analysis but also reveals a better understanding of the text in question. It is appropriate, therefore, to discuss the use of paraholophrases (literary analysis) in the works selected for this study before analyzing their use of holophrases and holophrastic traces (linguistic analysis).

To facilitate a comparison of the holophrastic readings conducted in the chapters that follow, each reading proceeds along the same lines. Introductory remarks concerning the work in question point out its relevant contexts. A discussion of paraholophrases in relation to textualized orality follows and is succeeded by an analysis of the use of holophrases and holophrastic traces as oral strategies. A short summary closes each holophrastic reading. Because the paraholophrase lacks the unique morphological structure of the holophrase, it might not always be apparent if and why a particular phrase in an Indigenous text serves as a paraholophrase. Phrases that qualify as paraholophrases are thus marked in boldface on first mention, even if the reasons why they serve as such can only be discussed later in the analysis.[133]

Ishmael Alunik's *Call Me Ishmael*, Alootook Ipellie's *Arctic Dreams and Nightmares*, Richard Van Camp's *The Lesser Blessed*, Thomas King's *Green Grass, Running Water*, and Louise Bernice Halfe's *Blue Marrow* represent a wide range of contemporary Indigenous writing, not only in terms of tribal affiliation and genre but also with regard to the authors' linguistic backgrounds and the immediate concerns of the individual texts. As the succeeding chapters will show, however, all five works engage in holophrastic "play." Although the degree to which these texts employ holophrastic traces and code switching involving holophrases proper varies considerably, paraholophrases figure prominently as significant discourse devices in all five texts. These paraholophrases create semantic density by taking the form of figures of speech (primarily tropes), formulae, or intertextual and intratextual references. Even more intriguing is that the paraholophrases created by Alunik, Ipellie, Van Camp, King, and Halfe serve narrative functions that are always tied to Indigenous generic conventions (narrative frames, cyclical narration, open and fluid discourse).

Despite notable differences in their use of holophrases and holophrastic traces, on the one hand, and paraholophrases, on the other, *Call Me Ishmael*,

Arctic Dreams and Nightmares, *The Lesser Blessed*, *Green Grass, Running Water*, and *Blue Marrow* employ as oral strategies both the formal and the functional manifestations of holophrases in English. Holophrases in these texts generally help to create the proper linguistic contexts, whereas holophrastic traces are used as strategies of conceptual orality that result from the context of language production (prosody, redundancy, fragmentation), from the context of language use (involvement, participation, context), or, in some cases, from both. The paraholophrases employed by Alunik, Ipellie, Van Camp, King, and Halfe, however, create only those features of conceptual orality that result from the context in which language is used: that is, involvement, participation, and context. As oral strategies, holophrases, holophrastic traces, and paraholophrases hence cover the whole breadth of conceptual orality.

The three characteristics of conceptual orality resulting from the context of language use deserve more explanation than I have given them thus far. Reader participation and author involvement are interdependent elements of conceptual orality. There is no reader participation without author involvement and vice versa; both are equally important in the creation of a work that welcomes a dialogue between speaker and audience. Just how important this interplay is for literary works will become evident in the holophrastic readings of this study: the selected texts demand readers' full engagement in the creation of meaning, largely because of the works' continuation of Indigenous generic conventions.

Context is always a significant component of a literary work, but it becomes all the more relevant once writers choose different media and languages to continue their respective traditions. Hence, the contexts established by means of paraholophrases in the texts selected for analysis are not only extremely significant but often take on multiple forms (linguistic, religious, cultural, historical, interpretative, etc.). One specific context that proves to be particularly significant in many of the works discussed is their interpretative context: it is often established by means of opening and closing frames, which are generally an integral component of Indigenous oratures; in the texts analyzed here, these opening and closing frames are constructed with the help of paraholophrases.

As noted above, the holophrastic readings of *Call Me Ishmael*, *Arctic Dreams and Nightmares*, *The Lesser Blessed*, *Green Grass, Running Water*, and *Blue Marrow* included here are primarily meant to demonstrate the usefulness of my thesis that holophrastic reading constitutes a culturally specific reading strategy for textualized orality in Indigenous literatures in English. What these exemplary readings ultimately attest to, however, is the practicing of Indigenous rhetorical sovereignties. As culturally specific oral strategies, (para)holophrases function as discourse devices that are fully grounded in Indigenous languages and rhetorics and that hence empower Indigenous writers in their own stories and in their own conventions of discourse—(para)holophrases are, to use Van Camp's words, "Raven talk."[134]

CHAPTER 1

Writing the Oral Tradition: Ishmael Alunik's *Call Me Ishmael*

Call Me Ishmael (1998) is a collection of stories and essays by Ishmael Alunik, a storyteller from Inuvik, Northwest Territories, who passed away in the summer of 2006 at the age of eighty-three. Alunik was born in 1923 at Old Crow Flats, Yukon Territory. He learned the traditional Inuvialuit way of life from his parents and grandparents, who were originally from northern Alaska and are thus properly referred to as Inupiat (35). The Inupiat had moved into the Mackenzie Delta in the late nineteenth century and early twentieth century after the Inuvialuit population had been considerably diminished by new diseases, such as measles, smallpox, and influenza.[1] Alunik's traditional knowledge, then, is also partly Inupiat. Even though Alunik eventually began working for wages, he lived most of his life as a trapper and hunter (97–98). During his lifetime, he thus belonged to an ever-decreasing group of Inuvialuit who, knowing about Inuvialuit life in the old days, served their communities as elders. His role as an elder is significant to *Call Me Ishmael*. Its stories and essays are not fiction but are meant to preserve and to pass on Inuvialuit/Inupiat traditional knowledge. The fact that stories belonging to an oral tradition are told using a written form makes *Call Me Ishmael* exceptionally valuable for anyone studying textualized orality in Indigenous literatures.

THE TEXT: *CALL ME ISHMAEL*

Although published in 1998, *Call Me Ishmael* is very much a traditional Inuit text, particularly with regard to authorship and genre, both of which must be considered in order to place Alunik's narrative in its appropriate context.

The Question of Authorship

When it comes to questions of authorship, *Call Me Ishmael* is a rather unconventional book, to say the least. According to the copyright page, the book was authored by Ishmael Alunik and edited and published by Eddie D. Kolausok (Inuvialuit/Gwich'in). The question of who acts as author and who acts as editor of *Call Me Ishmael* is far from clear, however. The chapters attributed to Alunik in *Across Time and Tundra* (2003), a book on the Inuvialuit co-authored by Ishmael Alunik, Eddie D. Kolausok, and David Morrison, rely at least partly on *Call Me Ishmael*. These chapters include "Legends from Long Ago" (Ch. 2), "Nuyaviak's Story: Life around Tuktoyaktuk Long Ago" (Ch. 6), and "A Trapper's Life in the 20th Century" (Ch. 7). While Chapters 6 and 7 in *Across Time and Tundra*, though evoking *Call Me Ishmael* thematically, tell new stories, Chapter 2—apart from some minor differences that appear to be caused by editorial changes rather than changes based on the same story composed at different occasions—is a direct reproduction of the two Tulugak stories in *Call Me Ishmael* (26–30, 31–34).

All of Alunik's contributions to *Across Time and Tundra*, as listed on the contents page, include a note in parentheses that reads "as told to Eddie D. Kolausok," which can be interpreted in two ways: either Alunik told his stories in *Across Time and Tundra* to Kolausok, who recorded and transcribed them, or Alunik composed these stories in writing, and Kolausok edited them later. I believe the latter scenario to be more likely, partly because, as noted above, one of Alunik's contributions in *Across Time and Tundra* is a reproduction of two chapters from *Call Me Ishmael*.[2] This assumption is further strengthened by the fact that David Morrison, in Chapter 1 of *Across Time and Tundra*, twice cites from passages from *Call Me Ishmael* (60–61, 63) but gives as a reference "Ishmael Alunik, as told to Eddie D. Kolausok," instead of the respective pages from *Call Me Ishmael*.[3] Although it seems unlikely that *Call Me Ishmael* is a work of textualized orature, we must assume that Kolausok had a considerable share in its composition. The extent of his influence, however, is difficult to determine without access to the manuscript itself.

The question of the authorship of *Call Me Ishmael* turns out to be even more complicated, however, since the Tulugak stories in *Across Time and Tundra* and *Call Me Ishmael* were, in fact, authored neither by Alunik nor by Kolausok. *Across Time and Tundra* acknowledges on its copyright page that its first Tulugak story (Ch. 2, 47–50) is "retold from a version first published in a collection of stories by Simon Bennettin in the magazine *Inuvialuit* (Summer 1981: 13–15)."[4] But *Across Time and Tundra* (Ch. 2, 51–53) also includes a second Tulugak story by Simon Bennett[5] (as he is referred to in *Inuvialuit*) from the same publication—in this case, however, there is no acknowledgement whatsoever. Moreover, what *Across Time and Tundra* refers to as a retelling is really a *reproduction*: except for minor changes especially at the beginning and the end, the Tulugak stories in *Across Time and Tundra*, and consequently also those in *Call Me Ishmael*, are Bennett's stories almost verbatim, even though the credit for these stories is given to Alunik (and/or Kolausok).[6]

Amid all of this uncertainty regarding its authorial origins, then, what *is* certain is that *Call Me Ishmael* does not conform to Euro-Western notions of authorship, editorship, and copyright. As noted by Agnes Grant, composers of traditional Indigenous poetry "took no credit, for it was believed that nature's poems were discovered, not composed; the poet merely nourished them and gave them back to the people, thus remaining humble before nature and the tribe."[7] At the same time, Indigenous peoples have always known what Alexander Wolfe (Saulteaux) calls "a copyright system based on trust,"[8] according to which "one storyteller cannot tell another's story without permisson"[9] and without giving the story's source. In Indigenous traditions, the question, then, is not so much who composes a particular piece but who is permitted to pass it on in whatever form. When Morrison—after the book had gone to print—pointed out to Kolausok the similarities between Alunik's first chapter in *Across Time and Tundra* and the Tulugak story by Bennett, Kolausok "insisted that the similarities in text were due to a common oral tradition and that Ishmael as an Inuvialuit elder (80+) had every right to tell these stories in the way he did."[10] Alunik again and again cites the sources of the stories that he tells in *Call Me Ishmael*, ironically one of them being Bennett himself ("A Story of a Caribou Hunt," 45–46). Without access to the manuscript, which might yield some clues, the question is impossible to answer; all one can do, in the end, is treat *Call Me Ishmael* as one would treat oral traditions more generally—that is, owned not by a tribal member individually but by the tribe collectively. Seen from this perspective, Alunik's role in *Call Me Ishmael* is more that of "narrator" and keeper of an oral tradition than its "author."

The question of authorship is but one reason why *Call Me Ishmael* does not easily fit into Euro-Western notions of literature; the fact that the narrative escapes all attempts to classify it according to Euro-Western–defined categories of genre further adds to the text's complexity.

The Question of Genre

Robin McGrath distinguishes between four basic categories of modern Inuit prose: "1) modern stories, 2) memoirs or reminiscences, 3) history of the material culture, and 4) articles and essays on contemporary life."[11] These categories, however, are chosen only for the sake of convenience; as McGrath notes, "The prose is often loosely structured and the forms tend to blend together," so classifications are possible only when one remembers that they are not fixed.[12] Being rather traditional in its purpose and its content, *Call Me Ishmael* does not fit into the first or the fourth category suggested by McGrath. This leaves only memoirs and reminiscences and history of the material culture as possible categories for Alunik's narrative—but even this categorization is not without difficulties.

Memoirs and the Oral Tradition

Robin McGrath, noting that "autobiography is one of the first forms of written literature to emerge in newly literate societies," gives as a probable reason that "the easiest subject for a new writer to attempt is that which he knows best: himself."[13] The subtitle of *Call Me Ishmael—Memories of Ishmael Alunik, Inuvialuk Elder*—seemingly marks Alunik's narrative as a particular form of autobiography. Often, however, Indigenous autobiography is actually oral tradition disguised as autobiography, for the importance of many Inuit autobiographies, such as *I, Nuligak* (1966) or Peter Pitseolak's *People from Our Side* (1975), lies not so much in their depiction of the life or memories of one particular Inuk as in their depiction of traditional Inuit life per se. Such is the case with *Call Me Ishmael*.

As Alunik notes at the end of Chapter 1 (25), his narrative is diverse in (sub)genres, containing stories, both mythical and modern, histories, personal memories, and essays. Some of its content is based on his own experiences, but many of the stories that he tells in *Call Me Ishmael* were given to him by others. In particular, his descriptions of Inuvialuit material culture are based on knowledge that Alunik received from his grandparents. The subtitle of his collection thus correctly marks the narrative not as someone's memoirs but as the memoirs of an Inuvialuk elder: that is, of someone who is entitled to pass on a particular kind of knowledge that is generally referred to as traditional, or Indigenous, knowledge and is meant to ensure a given people's survival.

The first chapter of Alunik's collection, entitled "Our Name Is Inuit," forms an interesting opposition to the narrative's main title: the individual versus the community. This pair is often understood in Euro-Western traditions of thought as an example of *binary contraries*, things that are thus opposed to one another that nothing can possibly lie between them.¹⁴ As the first chapter in Alunik's collection so eloquently illustrates, however, his concern is that of the people, the community for which Alunik serves as a keeper of tradition. As such, he is not *opposed to* but very much *within* the community. Even as *Call Me Ishmael* embraces a definition of self as always related to community, it deconstructs the Euro-Western notion of memoirs, offering instead a concept of balance that is central to Indigenous worldviews. Hence, the collection's subtitle marks the narrative not so much as the memoirs of Ishmael Alunik as part of the whole that is the oral tradition of the Inuvialuit and Inupiat peoples.¹⁵

Essays on Material Culture and Tradition
One half of *Call Me Ishmael* is indeed dedicated to Inuvialuit/Inupiat material culture (Chs. 10–22 and Ch. 24). In this part of the narrative, Alunik passes on the life skills that he learned from his parents and grandparents. These skills include the building of umiaks and kayaks, the making of hunting tools (bows and arrows), the hunting and snaring of animals, the building of shelters, and the making of clothing. Alunik's essays are very matter-of-fact, as is usually the case with cultural histories, but are complemented with illustrations to trigger the reader's participation. For the same reason, Alunik's essays on Inuit material culture are sometimes interwoven with personal details. In "How William Kuptana Hunted Polar Bears," for example, Kuptana is not so much a character as an informant (70–71), yet the essay is rendered more vivid because the reader is invited to participate in the narrative by imagining Kuptana hunting polar bears in the fashion outlined by Alunik. The weaving of personal details into an essay draws readers into the text and hence functions as a strategy in textualizing orality.¹⁶

As McGrath notes, for Inuit people, the value of cultural histories lies in the detailed depictions that they give of traditional Inuit life.¹⁷ She argues further, however, that "for the most part they have only secondary value to the student of Eskimo literature."¹⁸ I would argue differently—and not just in the case of *Call Me Ishmael*. Indigenous texts such as Alunik's collection challenge the narrow definitions of literature often encountered in Euro-Western traditions of thought. All of the stories and essays found in Alunik's collection are worthy of the attention of literary critics because Alunik finds all of them—not just the Tulugak stories and the story of the flood—worth preserving; after all, it is the entirety of texts, broadly defined, that forms Inuvialuit/Inupiat literary traditions.

Call Me Ishmael, then, runs counter to our attempts to classify it according to Euro-Western notions of genre: the collection is neither just a memoir nor just a history of the Inuvialuit/Inupiat material culture; it is both and even more. Instead of compromising his people's stories to make them fit into Euro-Western notions of genre, Alunik attempts to do the opposite: his narrative compromises the fixed form of the written word for the fluidity of oral stories to fulfill the purpose of the oral tradition: that is, to pass on traditional knowledge. The best way to make sense of his narrative in terms of genre, then, is to see it as translating the Inuvialuit/Inupiat oral tradition into the written form. It is against this background of reading *Call Me Ishmael* as *writing the oral tradition* that the holophrastic analysis below is undertaken.

A HOLOPHRASTIC READING OF *CALL ME ISHMAEL*
Paraholophrases
Most paraholophrases in *Call Me Ishmael* are found in the opening and the closing of the narrative and thus frame it. Because an analysis of these paraholophrases will shed more light on the narrative's structure, I will discuss those constituting the narrative frame first and then turn to paraholophrases found elsewhere in the narrative.

Paraholophrases Constituting the Narrative's Frame
Although, grammatically speaking, the collection's title phrase, "**call me Ishmael**," is an imperative, it lacks the authoritativeness of a command. Instead, readers are *invited* to call the narrator by his first name. The direct address to readers is a call for their attention as much as it is an offer: echoing in print a handshake in person, the title draws readers in, thereby establishing a strong tie between narrator and audience, as if to imitate the intimate experience of an oral performance. The title also assures readers of Alunik's presence as the performer of the narrative, for it gives Alunik the opportunity to "narrate [himself] into the text via [his] name," a strategy in textualizing orality often found in Inuit literature.[19] Although Alunik's first name appears only once in the narrative, the importance of a title ensures that its use will have a lasting effect. In the attempt to write back the performative nature of storytelling via its title, Alunik's narrative thus textualizes the oral in more general terms.

"**Call me Ishmael**," of course, is also an intertextual reference to Melville's *Moby-Dick*, which opens, famously, with this very phrase. Whether the choice of the title goes back to the book's editor, Eddie D. Kolausok, or to Alunik himself is impossible to decide. At the same time, there is the chance that, even if Alunik did pick the title himself, he did not consciously make the connection with *Moby-Dick*.[20] Readers can only work with what a text offers them, and most readers familiar with Anglo-American traditions will certainly see the connection between the title of Alunik's collection and Melville's novel. Both the Alunik and the Melville narratives are heterogeneous texts, and both concern whales and whaling, though Melville's text does so more exclusively and from a different perspective.[21]

The function of the collection's title does not become apparent, however, unless one reads the first chapter of *Call Me Ishmael*, entitled "**Our Name Is Inuit**" (24). This chapter defines the purpose of Alunik's narrative—the passing on of tradition to both Inuvialuit and non-Inuvialuit. The statement "our name is Inuit" thus defines the origin of Alunik's narrative—that is, the tradition passed on is Inuvialuit/Inupiat as opposed to Euro-Western—but above all it comments on another intertext: namely, the non-Inuit habit of referring to Inuit people, either in speech or in writing, as "Eskimos." Alunik "do[es] not like to be called that name" because he finds this exonym offensive (24). Instead, he prefers the endonym *Inuit* or its variations—*Inupiaq* for the Inuit in Alaska, *Inuvialuit* for those in the western Arctic, and *Inuinat* for the Kitikmeot[22] Inuit—all of which mean "real people, or human beings," in the respective language variant (25). The insistence with which Alunik emphasizes the appropriate way of referring to his people—the word *Inuit* and the specific designations for the various Inuit people are repeated thirteen times throughout Chapter 1—is an ironic commentary on his initial titular introduction, "**Call me Ishmael**." He subverts two sets of binaries simultaneously here: the self (Ishmael) versus the community (the Inuit), and English versus Inuvialuktun: his memoirs and his way of composing are hence marked as essentially Inuit or, more precisely, Inuvialuit/Inupiat. And so Alunik ends the first chapter in his story collection by abruptly shifting from the issue of naming to the purpose of the book:

> As human beings with a rich culture and long history, we Inuit passed on many stories, tales, legends, life skills and our history in the traditional oral way of our ancestors. The following stories are a collection [of] legends, personal experiences and stories which were given to me by my ancestors and friends. In my elderly years, I wish to preserve these stories for future people to share and experience. (25)

In this simple and straightforward statement, we find, in a nutshell, the core of Indigenous cultures: the oral tradition that elders pass on from generation to generation to ensure their people's survival.

The next stage in Alunik's narrative involves the depiction of Inuit perceptions of the world. In Chapters 2 and 3 of *Call Me Ishmael*, Alunik retells two stories of Tulugak (Inupiaq and Inuvialuktun for "raven").[23] Unlike other Indigenous peoples (e.g., the Crees[24]), the Inuit do not seem to differentiate creation or origin stories from other stories since the supernatural is believed to still play a prominent role in the present world.[25] Most Euro-Western observers, however, will likely read the Tulugak stories in *Call Me Ishmael* as creation or origin stories.

From material that the ethnologist Edward William Nelson collected in northern Alaska between 1877 and 1881, we know that the Tulugak stories that Alunik shares in *Call Me Ishmael* are part of a much larger *cycle of stories* that features Tulugak as creator and cultural hero.[26] The extensive "Raven Creation Myth" that Nelson transcribed from an old Unalit man living at Kigiktauik can be summarized as follows.[27]

Tulugak travels down from the sky and creates earth, man, and all the wildlife. He appears in the form of a raven for most parts of the story but can change into man any time he sees fit. Tulugak teaches Man (the first man on earth, thus capitalized) everything that he needs to know in order to survive and takes him, on what seem to be shamanic journeys,[28] to the sea and to the sky, where the dwarves dwell. Eventually, the people whom Tulugak has created become so abundant that he is afraid they will kill all the animals. So he decides to take away the sun and returns to the sky, much to the distress of the people. The son of Tulugak's brother eventually manages to steal the light from Tulugak, but, before bringing it back to the people, he divides day and night. The Raven boy continues to live among the people on earth, but he loses his power to return to the sky. His children eventually turn into normal ravens as Inuit know them today.

Tulugak, as creator "of the earth and everything upon it,"[29] is a very important figure among northern Alaskan Inuit (i.e., Inupiat). Robert F. Spencer quotes an Inuit who, when confronted with the biblical creation story, said, "Very well, God made the world, but Raven made it first."[30] It seems natural, then, that Alunik begins a collection designed to pass on Inuvialuit/Inupiat tradition with this Inuvialuit/Inupiat creation story featuring the western Arctic creator and cultural hero. The Tulugak cycle is indeed restricted to the western Arctic,[31] including the Mackenzie Delta.[32] Researchers generally point out its resemblance to northwest coast and even Siberian raven cycles.[33] In the tribal traditions of all three cultural groups—northwest coast First Nations, Siberian people, western Arctic Inuit—Raven takes the role of a creator and cultural hero who is "responsible for establishing distinctive features of a culture."[34] The stories told about Raven vary a great deal, however. The Tulugak stories told by Alunik, for example, feature beluga whales and snowbirds—animals that one is not likely to find among the tribes of the northwest coast. In most First Nations traditions, Raven is also generally described as a "trickster."[35] Alunik's narrative, however, connects Tulugak with both the shaman and the trickster[36] and in doing so emphasizes particularly Tulugak's transformative powers. When Tulugak says at one point in the story, "**I am a seed,** [...] so I must find some place to grow" (28), this statement refers to his being stuck in the stomach of a woman, trying to figure out how to get out. At the same time, however, the phrase "**I am a seed**" also serves as a metaphor of Tulugak's role as a creator and cultural hero in Inuvialuit and Inupiat culture.[37]

The issue of naming first raised in *Call Me Ishmael* in Chapter 1 is picked up again in Chapter 4, in which Alunik establishes his authority as an Inuvialuit/Inupiat storyteller. The chapter begins with the following statement: "**My father's fathers passed on stories to me from before the time the first white men came North to the Arctic**" (35). In the account that follows, Alunik mentions his grandparents, where and when they were born, and what they taught him as he was growing up. Interestingly, Alunik gives the place of his birth, Old Crow Flats, but not the year of his birth. He does mention, however, that "In 1927 I was only four years old. From then I start [sic] learning the culture of my people, the Inupiat from Alaska, and the Inuvialuit of Kitty (Kittigazuit) and Herschel Island" (35). Evidently, Alunik wants to emphasize that what he will present in his narrative was passed on to him from a very early age. Pointing out that "**It was through living off the land and listening to my elders that I learned the stories and history of my people**" (37), Alunik ends Chapter 4 by echoing its beginning. This echo is more than a pure repetition, however, as the frame thus established within Chapter 4 stresses what is so vital for the survival of Inu(vialu)it people: to listen to the elders as the carriers of tradition. The ending of Chapter 4 thus takes readers back both to the beginning of Chapter 4 and to the ending of Chapter 1. Here, as pointed out above, Alunik has defined the purpose of his narrative as preserving the stories of his people for future generations (25). An attentive reader will understand that the ending of Chapter 4 entails an obligation to listen to Alunik to ensure that the oral tradition he is passing on will not get lost. Chapter 4, then, establishes a contract between the narrator, Alunik, and his readers that resembles the implicit contract between storyteller and audience.

In Chapter 4, Alunik also includes one of the few more biographical accounts found in his narrative. He writes, a "layman named me Joseph and

after I got baptized I died." Alunik tells us that he "had no heartbeat for over half an hour," and if it had not been for an "old Gwich'in lady"—evidently a shaman—who saved his life he would have remained dead.[38] Later he was baptized a second time, this time as Ishmael, "the father of the Arabs" (36). Thus, we know that the narrative's title also is an explicit intertextual reference to the Old Testament and the story of Abraham, his maid Hagar, and their son Ishmael. Considering this biblical reference, the phrase "**after I got baptized I died**" can also be read as a metaphor of the involvement of the Church in the colonization of the Inuit, which marked the beginning of the end of traditional Inuit culture. Just as a Gwich'in shaman saved Alunik physically, so too he hopes that the writing of the Inuvialuit/Inupiat oral tradition in *Call Me Ishmael* will eventually save his people.

So what does a discussion of the opening chapters in *Call Me Ishmael* have to do with paraholophrases? Using the phrases that I have just discussed—all of which, in fact, qualify as paraholophrases—Alunik is able to construct a narrative opening that, together with the closing at the end of the book, gives his collection its narrative frame. And this narrative frame is significant for our discussion because formulaic openings and closings are considered common elements of Indigenous oratures.[39]

Melville Jacobs has observed formulaic opening and closing frames in Clackamas Chinook myths and tales, though he calls them introductions, epilogues, and endings.[40] The same narrative structures have been noted by Dennis Tedlock in fictional narratives among the Zuni. Tedlock has pointed out particularly the "mirror-image structure" of these frames—the opening stages are repeated backward in the closing stages—and the lack of "transparent referential meaning" of some of the formulae used in the frames, an abstractness that he assumes to be found also in the narrative frames among "Seneca, Wintu, Karok, Klikitat, and probably many other North American tale-telling traditions."[41] In that they include several stages whereby the storyteller carefully takes the audience into the story and carefully leads them out again, opening and closing frames serve primarily narrative functions in Indigenous oratures. Picking up Gregory Bateson's notion of frame as a "defined interpretive context," Richard Bauman has argued that performance—which he conceives as "*constitutive* of the domain of verbal art as spoken communication"—"sets up, or represents, an interpretative frame within which the messages being communicated are to be understood."[42] Opening and closing frames, then, provide the audience with explicit or implicit clues about how to interpret the narratives' messages.[43]

Leaving aside the introduction by Uluksuk,[44] what follows after the titular invitation to "listen" to Ishmael's writing resembles in part the prologues often found in works of Euro-Western literary traditions. Granted, there is no title in *Call Me Ishmael* that reads "Prologue." Neither is there text set apart from the first chapter that might be understood as a prologue. In fact, the very idea of a prologue does not make sense. The word derives from the Greek *prologos*, from *pro-* "before" and *logos* "saying," but Alunik has already spoken, even if in no more than three words. Instead, what I refer to as the prologue of *Call Me Ishmael* is really an opening that readers must identify as such on their own and that includes several stages: Alunik attentively guides his readers into *Call Me Ishmael* by defining the narrative's origin in Inuit cultures (Ch. 1), by explaining Inuit perceptions of the world (Chs. 1 and 2), and by establishing his authority as an Inuvialuit storyteller (Ch. 4).

A reader familiar with Euro-Western cultural and literary traditions will likely wonder about the purpose of such a long opening.[45] Whereas in Euro-Western literatures the question of context does not usually feature prominently, context is of central importance in traditional oratures. Only after having read this opening is Alunik's audience prepared to "hear" his narrative, because it is this opening that lends his narrative its proper cultural context, which, to use Bauman's words, defines its "interpretative frame." As Thomas King has noted,

> For Native storytellers, there is generally a proper place and time to tell a story. [...] So when Native stories began appearing in print, concern arose that the context in which these stories had existed was in danger of being destroyed and the stories themselves were being compromised. The printed word, after all, once set on a page, has no master, no voice, no sense of time or place.[46]

The context of time and place gets lost once an oral story turns into ink. Alunik's narrative, however, saves at least some of this context by emphasizing its origin, hence the significance of the narrative's three-step opening.

As suggested above, however, the existence of the opening in *Call Me Ishmael*—like any opening in orature—depends entirely on readers being aware that they are being guided into the narrative, which in itself depends on their recognition of phrases that feature prominently in the narrative's opening chapters and mark them as the narrative's opening:

 a. "Call me Ishmael" (intertextuality),
 b. "Our Name Is Inuit" (24; intertextuality),

c. "I am a seed" (28; metaphor),
d. "My father's fathers passed on stories to me from before the time the first white men came North to the Arctic" (35; intratextuality),
e. "after I got baptized I died" (36; metaphor), and
f. "It was through living off the land and listening to my elders that I learned the stories and history of my people" (37; intratextuality).

As figures of speech (c, e) or examples of inter- or intratextuality (a, b, d, f), these phrases form the cores of complex ideas: they are self-contained but carry with them a surplus of meaning that is not explicitly stated in the text but that must be discerned by readers: namely, "a gap between sign and meaning" (i.e., a figure of speech),[47] a reference to a different text (intertextuality), or a reference to the narrative itself (intratextuality). Constituting the narrative's opening, so central to the overall narrative structure of the text, these phrases, moreover, function as significant narrative units.[48] Although the opening in *Call Me Ishmael* is not formulaic and is much longer than traditional openings in Indigenous oratures,[49] it nonetheless fulfills the same function as the latter.

Due to their semantic density and narrative significance, the phrases discussed above are equivalent *in function* to holophrases in Indigenous languages; they can thus be referred to as paraholophrases. Their use in the opening marks the narrator's involvement with his audience as much as it invites reader participation, without which the opening would not exist. Since the opening forms part of the narrative's "grid" and provides the cultural and interpretative context of the narrative, these paraholophrases are not only key components of the composition of *Call Me Ishmael*; given that context, involvement, and participation are oral strategies resulting from the context of language use, these paraholophrases also function as a strategy in textualizing orality that is culturally specific.

The effectiveness of the opening of *Call Me Ishmael* is enhanced by the narrative's closing, which intentionally alludes back to its opening or to other preceding parts of the narrative, thereby establishing a frame in which to place the narrative. This closing is not explicitly marked in the text, however, and most readers will not notice it until they have reached the last chapter. In fact, it is difficult to make out the exact beginning of this closing, but the first hints are found in the intratextual references in "Inuvialuit and Indian Confrontations" (Ch. 23, 85–89).

Here we find a variation of a story already told in Chapter 8 (43–44) about a group of Inuit who moved to Greenland to escape the Kittigakyuit because their chief's son had killed a Kittigakyuk man and eaten his liver

(43–44, 87–88). Because of this incident, the Kittigakyuit called this group of Inuit Inuktoyuit, which means "**man eaters**" (44) or "**human body eater[s]**" (88). That Alunik repeats this story, albeit in variation, toward the end of his narrative is interesting, also considering that between these two tellings of the story he stresses in "Fishing and Hunting" (Ch. 14, 60–67) that, despite the hostile climate and environment in the Arctic, his "grandfather and other old Inupiat and Inuvialuit in Canada [...] never spoke of their **people eating humans**" (67). This statement is obviously linked to the story of the Inuktoyuit, but it also seems to point to the paraholophrase "**Our Name Is Inuit**" of Chapter 1. The common, albeit wrong, translation of the word *Eskimo* is "eater of raw meat." Although this does not necessarily mean human meat,[50] the connection between "man eaters" and "Eskimo" is readily made.

The next intratextual reference in the narrative's closing is found in the second-last chapter, "Navigating the Tundra by Stars, Moon, and Snowdrifts" (90–96), which relates how the Inuit managed to get around in the Arctic without getting lost. Halfway through the chapter, Alunik relates a story about the origins of the Inuit of Canada and Greenland, into which he incorporates information about the findings of archaeologists and anthropologists (94). When he concludes that the story of how the Inuit moved east from Alaska is indeed true, however, he does not refer to scientific findings to support this claim. Instead, he claims that this information is true "**[a]ccording to the stories we heard from our grandfathers and our grandfathers heard from their ancestors back to hundreds of years ago, could be thousands of years**" (95). Aside from stressing the Inuit version of migration patterns, Alunik's account of his people's origins in this chapter becomes relevant when seen in direct relation to the Tulugak stories, which happen to form part of the narrative's opening. The reference to Alunik's ancestors provides even further links to the opening: namely, the ending of Chapter 1 (25) and the beginning and ending of Chapter 4 (35, 37), in which Alunik has situated himself as a carrier and transmitter of traditional Inuvialuit/Inupiat knowledge. By reminding his readers once again of his sources, the ancestors, and by taking his readers back to origins of the Inuit, Alunik not only establishes a cyclical narration but also ensures that the cultural context established in the narrative's opening does not get lost toward the narrative's ending. The reference to the ancestors toward the end of *Call Me Ishmael* is, then, a reminder of what readers are reading: that is, an oral tradition translated into writing.

"Navigating the Tundra by Stars, Moon, and Snowdrifts" also tells about the times when Christian missionaries started arriving in the Mackenzie area in the nineteenth century. This particular story contains intratextual references to the Tulugak stories of Chapters 2 and 3 and creates an interesting connection between the culture hero, Tulugak or Raven, and that of the shaman (*angakkuq*[51]):

> There were some Inuit with powerful Shaman powers. My grandmother, named Rebecca by a Presbyterian minister in Alaska around Point Hope, told me of the Shaman showing off his power. He put the light out in a sod house and let people tie him up. In the dark he turn [*sic*] into a Raven. **He was a raven when light was put on**. (95–96)

When Christian missionaries arrived in the Arctic, they set out to "**cast the devils out of the Inuit**" (96), as Alunik puts it. From the account of a shaman turning into a raven, which immediately precedes this observation, a reader might assume that "**cast the devils out of the Inuit**" here reads metaphorically as wiping out the practice of shamanism among the Inuit because it was considered an "act of the devil."[52] Indeed, Alunik ends this episode about the shaman who turned into a raven by noting, "**Yes, the Inuit know about the devil because some Shaman were real evil**" (96).

It is impossible to analyze these two remarks without discussing more extensively the Christian misreading of Inuit shamanism as an act of the devil—a misreading that not only points to Euro-Western ethnocentrism but also proves to be yet another manifestation of translation as a discourse of domination. Before it was eradicated in the 1940s, a process largely fostered through the use of translations of the Bible into Inuktitut using syllabics, shamanism served as "the major frame of reference for Inuit life," taking care of "community life, education of young people and health care."[53] In the replacement of shamanism with Christianity, Inuit were thus robbed of "the foundation of [their] entire system of [...] beliefs and practices before the coming of the Whites."[54] The central role assigned to the shaman in traditional Inuit religion and culture is reflected in the belief that the community's well-being rested upon the shaman, who, using his spirit powers, could cure diseases, bring better weather, ensure good hunting, and help a woman have a child.[55] Contemporary Inuit elders from Nunavut do point out "that there were two sides to shamanism":[56] "There were two types of *angakkuit* ['shamans']," Inuit elder Lucassie Nutaraaluk says. "Those that used their powers to kill people and those that tried to help by healing people."[57] Yet, though there were apparently also evil shamans (*angakkuutsianngittuq*[58]), Inuit shamanism did not by definition imply evil. The fact that shamanism is viewed skeptically or is even fully rejected by many contemporary Inuit[59] is due entirely to Christian propaganda, which started with the arrival of the first missionaries in the Arctic.[60] The arrival of Pentecostal preachers in the Arctic in the 1960s, Bernard Saladin d'Anglure points out, further "strengthened the polarization between the forces of good and the forces of evil—between God and the Devil. Everything before Christianity was depicted as the Devil's work and any relationship with spirits, other than Christian ones, became cases of demonic possession. Specialists were brought in from the South to teach Inuit techniques and rituals of exorcism."[61]

In his story about the Christian missionaries' arrival in the Arctic, Alunik gives the respective Inuit names for "devil," *tupilak* among the Inupiat and *tuungak*, or *toongak*, among the Inuvialuit (96).[62] Ronald Lowe also gives "devil" as a translation of *tupilak* in his *Basic Siglit Inuvialuit Eskimo Dictionary*,[63] but this does not appear to be the original meaning of the word, as Peter Irniq (Inuit) suggests when pointing out that "Tupilak is thought to have been a terrible spirit who placed hardships on people. And it had to take a very powerful shaman to get rid of it."[64] The killing of a *tupilak* (*tupilanniq* in Inuktitut) is described as follows: "There is an enormous amount of blood when the *tupilaq* is killed. The *angakkuq*'s hands become covered in blood while he is killing a *tupilaq* which cannot be seen by ordinary people. This blood can only be washed off by human urine."[65] Aupilaarjuk et al. add that, for some people (e.g., the Caribou Inuit[66]), *tupilak* is an evil *tuurngaq* (i.e., spirit), while for others (e.g., the Iglulik Inuit[67]) "it is the unsatisfied soul of a deceased person."[68] *Tupilait* (pl.), then, were known among Inuit in precontact times and represented evil spirits that could be fought off only by shamans.[69]

Tuungak, or *toongak*, which Alunik gives as Inuvialuktun equivalents to the English "devil," translate simply as "spirit; sprite; ghost; presence of a dream or vision; helping spirit."[70] "A *tuurngaq* [...] does not mean Satan," the Inuit elder Victor Tungilik points out: "Satan works against people and wants people to do bad things. A *tuurngaq* is there to help people."[71] In fact, *tuurngait* (pl.) are often described as a shaman's helping spirits,[72] whose nature depends on the respective *angakkuq*. So "tuurnngaq [sic] is only a bad spirit, when a shaman places a curse on another person, but it takes a shaman to drive away the bad spirit, through his or her spirits."[73] Hence, "there are two kinds of *tuurngait*: the evil ones, and the good ones."[74] While *tuurngaq*, depending on the context, denotes either a good spirit or an evil spirit, the Inuktitut word for "evil spirit" is *tuurngaaluk*,[75] which is formed by the word *tuurngaq*—which really means "spirit" but which Alunik translates as "devil"—plus an affix that turns "spirit" into "evil spirit."[76]

The Netsilik, Iglulik, and Baffin Island Inuit considered many of the spirits to be evil creatures, but for all the other Canadian Inuit groups, as well as the Inuit in Greenland, spirits could be either good or bad depending on whether the spirit was sought out by someone and hence was misused.[77] There is no evidence, then, in either Inuit cultures or Inuit languages of shamanism as personifying *nothing but evil*. True, shamanism had its dire side since shamans could misuse their power to hurt others,[78] but, first and foremost, shamanism served the welfare of the people. As much as competition among shamans was always part of Inuit shamanism, Laugrand, Oosten, and Trudel note, there existed at the same time "a strong moral concern in shamanism not to turn against your fellow men."[79]

I should stress, then, that when Alunik translates *tupilak* and *tuurngaq* as "devil" in *Call Me Ishmael* he does not give the original meanings of these words but their contemporary meaning, which was coined by Christian missionaries in their attempt to Christianize the Inuit. Missionaries' use of *tupilak* and *tuurngaq* as referring to the Christian notion of devil was based on a deliberate mistranslation that served no purpose other than to distort Inuit religion in an attempt to promote Christianity among the Inuit.[80] That early missionaries, as Seidelman and Turner put it, saw "themselves in a contest for influence with the angakoqs"[81] might explain their deliberate deformation of Inuit shamanism, but it does not excuse it.

Given the deliberate mistranslation of *tupilak* and *tuurngaq* by Christian colonizers, Alunik's comments in *Call Me Ishmael* regarding devils and shamanism—"**cast the devils out of the Inuit**" and "**Yes, the Inuit know about the devil because some Shaman were real evil**"— can be read as deeply ironic, even though this irony might not have been intended by Alunik himself. Given the traditional meanings of the words *tupilak* and *tuurngaq*, what the missionaries cast out of the Inuit was not the devil but their "spirit," the foundation of their whole system of beliefs—shamanism. The irony in this part of Alunik's narrative hence serves to subvert the discourse of domination implied in the Christian mistranslation of *tupilak* and *tuurngaq*.

Alunik's account of the Christian missionizing in the western Canadian Arctic also casts an ironic light back on two stories from the narrative's opening. The first story concerns Alunik's near-death after his first baptism (Ch. 4); that Alunik himself was saved by an old Gwich'in shaman underscores the life-affirming nature of shamanism as opposed to the Christian reading of shamanism as the work of the devil. The second story is that of the shaman who "**was a raven when light was put on**," which obviously connects with shamanism the figure of Tulugak, the creator and cultural hero, whom

Alunik's readers have already encountered in Chapters 2 and 3. Readers, of course, will understand the irony at the end of Alunik's narrative only if they have sufficient knowledge of the Inuit language and Inuit shamanism. However, this circumstance serves only to emphasize the importance of context and reader participation in *Call Me Ishmael* and points to the use of figures of speech as a strategy in textualizing orality.

Eventually, Alunik's narrative reaches its last chapter, curiously entitled "**Ishmael: Yesterday and Today.**" For the first time in the narrative, we are given Alunik's year of birth, 1923 (98), as well as a chronological account of his life, which some readers might have expected in Chapter 1. The subtitle might strengthen the impression that one is reading an afterword. Yet this last chapter is not a mere postscript. The title, "**Ishmael: Yesterday and Today,**" refers readers back to the main title of the narrative. Moreover, the biographical information in this chapter provides links to Chapter 4, filling in all those biographical gaps left in the opening. Finally, *Call Me Ishmael* closes with an intratextual reminder of the narrative's initial invitation and original purpose, "**sharing my stories with friends and family**" (99), thereby echoing the ending of Chapter 1: "In my elderly years, I wish to preserve these stories for future people to share and experience" (25). The cyclical narration already established in "Navigating the Tundra by Stars, Moon, and Snowdrifts" is thus perfected in the last chapter.

That the phrases I have pointed out in my discussion of the closing in *Call Me Ishmael*—except for the two figures of speech (metaphor/irony: "cast the devils out of the Inuit"; irony: "Yes, the Inuit know about the devil because some Shaman were real evil"; 96)—all mark intratextual references to the narrative's opening, then, is anything but accidental. Incorporated into new stories, these phrases—

a. "man eaters" (44), "human body eater" (88), and "people eating humans" (67; intratextuality),
b. "According to the stories we heard from our grandfathers and our grandfathers heard from their ancestors back to hundreds of years ago, could be thousands of years" (95; intratextuality),
c. "He was a raven when light was put on" (96; intratextuality),
d. "Ishmael: Yesterday and Today" (97; intratextuality), and
e. "sharing my stories with friends and family" (99; intratextuality)

— deliberately establish direct connections to the narrative's opening, thus perfecting the narrative's frame, whereas the two figures of speech in the story about the Christian missionizing in the western Canadian

Arctic guarantee that the establishment of cultural context does not rest on intratextuality alone.

The narrative's closing does not imply closure, then; instead, the frame (though it is far from being formulaic and rather long compared with narrative frames in Indigenous oratures) ensures that the narrative both is ended and can begin again. Just like the opening, the closing in *Call Me Ishmael*, then, depends on paraholophrases. These intratextual references and the figures of speech form *cores* of complex ideas, whose *full* meanings must be deciphered by readers, and they perform a significant narrative function—in this case, the establishment of a closing to complete a narrative frame. In other words, these phrases might not be holophrases, but, given their semantic density and their narrative significance, they are equivalent *in function* to holophrases in Indigenous languages. The narrative frame in *Call Me Ishmael* not only evokes the generic conventions of traditional Indigenous oratures but also writes back the cultural context of the narrative, all the while defining its interpretative frame. Since Alunik does not explicitly mark the narrative frame, readers depend entirely on deciphering the paraholophrases constituting the frame to make sense of the narrative. The audience's participation thus invited is also an indication of Alunik's involvement with his readers. Displaying strategies of conceptual orality that result from the context of language usage (context, involvement, and participation), the paraholophrases constituting the opening and closing in *Call Me Ishmael* hence function as a strategy in textualizing orality. The textualization of the oral achieved through the use of paraholophrases, however, is not restricted to the opening and closing frame, as will become apparent in the following discussion of further paraholophrases in *Call Me Ishmael*.

Paraholophrases with Other Narrative Functions

Some paraholophrases in Alunik's narrative do not constitute its frame but fulfill slightly different, though equally significant, narrative functions. For example, at the end of the story entitled "Caribou Used for Many Things" (Ch. 21, 80–82), Alunik alludes to "**One story about a little orphan boy with dirty clothes who eventually grows up to become a good hunter**"—a story, he writes, that was often told during wintertime gatherings (82). This story is actually the famous narrative of Kaujjarjuk, a story that is "known from Alaska to Greenland."[82] Alunik does not retell the story of Kaujjarjuk, however; his short—and understated—allusion alone points the knowledgeable reader to this well-known story from Inuit oral traditions. By referring to this story, Alunik not only provides further cultural context for his narrative but also breaks the line of his narration and engages readers in his narrative, regardless of whether they can make the connection. He thus plays with the interconnectedness of stories in Inuit oratures: although the stories in *Call Me Ishmael* are self-contained, they are also part of a much larger body of works and thus are always interrelated. In mimicking this interrelatedness, *Call Me Ishmael* manages to evade some of the fixity inherent in the written word.

An intertextual reference at the end of the second Tulugak story (Ch. 3) also functions in the same way: "But what a tale of his adventures he'd have to tell his children and friends when he got back. **And what other adventures would he** [Tulugak] **have before he got there?** Kow-kow" (34). The ending of this story suggests that more stories about Tulugak exist than the two included in Alunik's narrative. As noted above, Inuvialuit and Inupiat oral traditions feature a larger story cycle telling the adventures of Tulugak as he travels the world, helping to shape its present form. Most Inuvialuit and Inupiat readers will know of the adventures of Tulugak; they have probably heard these stories numerous times. They will thus easily recognize Alunik's allusion at the end of the second Tulugak story. The intimacy created by this mutual knowledge of even more stories represents a trace of the intimacy that Alunik's story would create if performed orally—at least for informed readers. Non-Inuvialuit/Inupiat readers will realize that more Tulugak stories exist but likely will not know them. Yet, even if these stories are not known to non-Inuvialuit/Inupiat readers, the knowledge of their existence—whether or not it leads to research on their part—can still be regarded as reader participation. Participation in the composition of a narrative does not require success. Awareness that one lacks knowledge and is partly left out of the narrative can also count as a form of participation: ignorant readers are motivated to learn and thus to overcome their ignorance. The same kind of participation is also achieved in Chapters 6 ("The Legend of Super Little Man," 40–41) and 7 ("Another Short, True Story Told by Many Inupiat and Inuvialuit," 42), in which Alunik recounts stories about the dwarves, or Little People, one of the legendary races with whom Inuit lived at the beginning of time and about which Inuit oral traditions include many different stories.

Another example of a story found in *Call Me Ishmael* that is part of a much larger story cycle is the story about the flood (Ch. 5, 38–39). Stories of a flood that destroys earlier civilizations can be found in the Old Testament (Genesis 6–8) and in many creation stories around the world, including in the Americas.[83] Chapter 5 in *Call Me Ishmael* is an example of the flood story from Inuit oral traditions. However, what in Alunik's narrative takes the form of only one story is really a story-within-a-story in some Inuit oral traditions, such as the one found in *The Epic of Qayaq* by Lela Kiana Oman (Inupiat),[84] an Inupiat retelling of a famous narrative known in various versions around the circumpolar world.[85] The story of the flood in Oman's version is so old that it can be said to have emerged without biblical influence. As Priscilla Tyler and Maree Brooks point out, "dogs are mentioned in the 'Preamble' [of Oman's version of the epic] but not in the epic itself. Dogs were introduced into Alaska about 1000 C.E., so these stories are very, very old."[86] Similarly, Alunik writes, "he [Alunik's grandfather] said it [the story of the flood] was an Inuit story. The story has been told for more than 5,000 years since the days of Noah, but it was so old that Inuit said it was an Inuk that was told the story by the Creator in Heaven, and some Inuit believe that" (38). Interestingly, both Oman's and Alunik's retelling of the story of the flood feature the character of Tulugak (or Tuluqak, as the name is spelled in Oman's version).[87] In both versions, Tulugak saves the first people from the flood by fixing the earth with his harpoon (in Alunik's story) or his spear (in Oman's story).[88] As Alunik puts it at the end of his version, "So the Raven got a harpoon and when the earth comes up again, he harpoons the earth and he hangs on to it until it was dead, **and ever since it never goes under the water again**" (39). The ending of Alunik's story of the flood echoes the ending of his first Tulugak story, in which Tulugak harpoons the land that would always "disappear under the water [...] before anyone could land on it" (30). His narrative hence refers to itself here; however, with the story of the flood being only one component of much richer oral traditions that include similar stories across the circumpolar world, his narrative also establishes within its main part (i.e., outside its frame) an intertextual reference.

There is another very interesting connection between the Inuit epic of Qayaq and *Call Me Ishmael*. Oman's retelling of the story of Qayaq includes one episode in which Qayaq leaves his wife and her family to wander once again. Before he leaves, his wife tells him to "take a few steps and look back. You will know what we are."[89] As it turns out, Qayaq was among hawks, though they appeared to be human to him while he was living with them. Similarly, Tulugak in Alunik's narrative wanders and unknowingly spends a night among a group of beluga whales and then a night among bowhead whales. His hosts say to him, "**we ask you to look back after you've gone a little way so you will remember us**" (26–27) and "**But look back after you leave so you will remember us**" (27). Only when Tulugak leaves and does as he is asked does he realize with whom he has spent the two nights.

These intertextual references open up Alunik's narrative to the large corpus of Inuit oral traditions, thus making it more fluid. The same effect is also produced by some of the *intra*textual references featured in *Call Me Ishmael*. "Caribou-Horn Bows" (Ch. 15, 68–69) is an elaboration of a preceding chapter entitled "I Learned to Make Bows and Arrows" (Ch. 10, 47–50). In "Caribou-Horn Bows," Alunik retells a story that William Kuptana told him about "**how bows were made from the horns of a bull caribou**" (68). This phrase is almost a literal repetition of "Inuit would use the horns of a bull caribou to make the bow" (48), found at the beginning of a paragraph in the earlier chapter "I Learned to Make Bows and Arrows." In "Caribou-Horn Bows," Alunik paraphrases this paragraph, but more importantly he proceeds to tell how Kuptana employed such bows to hunt caribou. As an intratextual remark, the phrase "**how bows were made from the horns of a bull caribou**" simultaneously breaks the narrative line and keeps the narrative going, for the chapter "Caribou-Horn Bows" explains not so much how to make bows as how to use them for hunting caribou, thus underlining the importance of the material culture discussed by Alunik in his essays—but this connection is not explicitly made by Alunik; readers have to make it for themselves.

In a similar fashion, "**Inuvialuit and Indian Confrontations**" (Ch. 23, 85–89) turns out to be an extensive elaboration on a casual remark made in an earlier chapter that "the Inuit and Indians would fight over hunting areas" (Ch. 14, 66). In the latter chapter, Alunik tells several stories about confrontations between the Inuvialuit and the First Nations living just south of them that developed primarily over hunting areas and that seem to have been common and to have gone back hundreds of years. The stories in Chapter 23 serve primarily to textualize some of the oral history of the western Canadian Arctic, whereas the chapter's title functions to provide a link to the earlier part of Alunik's narrative, thus breaking the line of the narration. In *Call Me Ishmael*, no single story appears in isolation; instead, they are all connected, as are the various parts of the narrative (its opening, its main part, and its closing).

Call Me Ishmael features two other paraholophrases outside the narrative's frame that are neither intertextual nor intratextual references but take the form of figures of speech with significant narrative function. Both figures involve irony, and the fact that irony is one of the dominant figures in *Call Me Ishmael* (besides metaphor) should not be surprising given the importance of irony in Inuit traditional poetry.[90] Yet irony might take Alunik's readers by surprise, interwoven as it is into the otherwise sincere and matter-of-fact tone of his narrative, as we see in this passage from "Rocks, Fire, and Bows" (Ch. 11, 51–54): "I was in school for five years where I learned to write. All the boys and girls needed to learn new schooling as times were changing. **Thanks for schooling. After I finished school I really began to learn and understand the culture of my people—the Inuit**" (51). Considering the purpose of any oral tradition and the purpose of Alunik's story collection in particular, his remark about the importance of schooling for understanding his own culture can be read as ironic. "Schooling" clearly evokes the residential school system, initiated by Christian missionaries in the Arctic, that only accelerated the erosion of Inuit cultures. Often people do not realize the importance of their own cultural traditions or institutions until they begin losing them. Although Euro-Western schooling might have made Alunik more conscious of the importance of his parents' and grandparents' traditional teachings, this schooling, or rather the system behind it, made this observation possible in the first place. Alunik's "speech of thanks" for receiving Euro-Western schooling, then, is not only linked to the paraholophrase "It was through living off the land and listening to my elders that I learned the stories and history of my people" of Chapter 4 (37); moreover, and more importantly, the irony here emphasizes what his narrative *is essentially*: a preservation in writing of what remains of the oral tradition of a culture that has been colonized with the help of the written word. Alunik expresses the same idea, again with irony, a little later in the same chapter: "It is easy to make fire with [trees and willow], so if some one reads this book, **you can make fire with it and remember how the Inupiat and Inuit used their resources and ingenuity to make fires in the past**" (54). This statement, without a doubt, is ambiguous. Alunik might be saying that his book can instruct readers how to make fire using trees and willow, but the statement also allows a more ironic reading: "you can make fire with it" can be understood as referring to the book itself rather than to the knowledge that it passes on to readers. Following this reading, Alunik asks readers to destroy his own writing, but he also requests that they do so by applying Inuvialuit/Inupiat cultural practices. Although setting fire to his book will lead to its destruction, there remains trust that words have power and can exist beyond the letters in ink—that is, in readers' minds and memories. Alunik's address to his readers here, then, is a subtle but nonetheless powerful reminder not only of the narrative's cultural contexts but also of the responsibilities of those reading it.

The phrases discussed above—

    a. "One story about a little orphan boy with dirty clothes who eventually grows up to become a good hunter" (82; intertextuality),

b. "And what other adventures would he have before he got there?" (34; intertextuality),
c. "and ever since it never goes under the water again" (39; intra- and intertextuality),
d. "we ask you to look back after you've gone a little way so you will remember us" (26–27) and "But look back after you leave so you will remember us" (27; both intertextuality),
e. "how bows were made from the horns of a bull caribou" (68; intratextuality),
f. "Inuvialuit and Indian Confrontations" (85; intratextuality),
g. "Thanks for schooling. After I finished school I really began to learn and understand the culture of my people—the Inuit" (51; intratextuality, irony), and
h. "you can make fire with it and remember how the Inupiat and Inuit used their resources and ingenuity to make fires in the past" (54; metafictionality, irony)

— are dynamically equivalent to holophrases in Indigenous languages. First, these phrases are semantically dense—they express only the *cores* of complex ideas and leave the uncovering of the full meanings entirely to the reader; the subtexts alluded to by these phrases concern either another text found outside or within *Call Me Ishmael* (a–g) or the narrative's own composition (h) or a gap between sign and meaning (g, h). Further, all of these phrases function as significant narrative units because they break the line of the narrative, thus opening up the text and inviting the reader's participation. Each phrase must hence be regarded as a paraholophrase. These paraholophrases do not constitute the narrative frame of *Call Me Ishmael*. Their importance lies, on the one hand, in evoking a particular cultural context via stories from Inuit oratures and, on the other, in helping *Call Me Ishmael* to establish a narrative structure that resembles what Leslie Marmon Silko has referred to as "something like a spider's web—with many little threads radiating from a center, criss-crossing each other."[91] A spider's web is an appropriate structure for a written narrative that is intended to pass on oral tradition because it mimics some of the generic conventions of oral storytelling by ensuring that reader participation is invited by the text per se and not just by some of its parts, such as its frame. In other words, the textualization of orality achieved through paraholophrases in *Call Me Ishmael* (context, involvement, and participation) is ever present in the collection and is not just a peripheral phenomenon.

HOLOPHRASES AND HOLOPHRASTIC TRACES

Compared with the prominence of paraholophrases in *Call Me Ishmael*, the narrative's use of holophrases and holophrastic traces is sparse, but these formal manifestations of Indigenous holophrases in English discourse serve a purpose, nonetheless, as they complement the textualization achieved through the use of paraholophrases. Alunik's narrative contains a number of Inuvialuktun and Inupiaq words—some of them holophrases—that cover themes as diverse as

- place names, such as *Tikihaak* for Point Alaska (35), *Utkiakvik* for Point Barrow (35), *Kingak* for King Point (37), *Itkilisaoyak*, the name of a creek near Aklavik, meaning "its [sic] from the Indians" (86), *Kukluktuk*, meaning waterfall (95), or *Uluksaktuk* for Holman Island, meaning "where they get material for ulus" (95);
- Inuit clothing, such as *pualu* (81; fur mitts made out of wolf and wolverine skins), *isiktut* (83; boots made from two caribou legs), *mukluks* (83; "shoes," boots made from caribou legs), *kaakliks* (83; "seal skin waterproof boots"), *kamiks* (35, 46; "boots [made] out of seal and caribou leg skins"), and *atiki* (44; parka);
- Inuit housing, such as *kataak* (78; the drop door of a sod house) and *inne* (79; literally, "a place," an Inuit underground dwelling);
- Inuit vehicles, such as *umiakpak* (38; big Inuit boat), *mukluk* kayaks (31; seal-skin kayaks), *uniat* (35; "Inupiat sleighs"), *umiak* (35, 55, 56; "walrus or bearded seal or beluga skin covered boats," 35);
- Inuit tools, such as *angmaak* (48, 49, 52, 59, 64, 95; flint stone), *ulus* (52, 54, 60, 64, 81; "women's knife"), and *ingnak* (52; fool's gold);
- religious words, such as *tupilak*, *tuungak*, or *toongak* (96);
- Inuit self-designations, such as *Inuit* (24), *Inupiaq* (24, 25), *Inuvialuit* (25), and *Inuinat* (25, 94) or *Inunat* (70), meaning "real people";
- Inuit nomenclature, such as *Itkili* (88; Inupiat and Inuvialuit ways of referring to Indians), *Naluahmiut* (93; meaning "white men," used in Alaska), *Tan'git* (93; Inuvialuktun for "white men"), *Kablunat* (93; "people with long eye brows," eastern Arctic term for "white men"), *Inuktoyuit* (44; "man eaters") or *Inuktoyuk* (88; "human body eater"), *Akukitukmuit* (44; "they are short from the front side of the parka"), *Inukakuulik* (40; Little Man), and *Inugukalik* (42; Little Boy); and
- other words describing nature or the environment, such as *Tulugak* (26; Inupiaq and Inuvialuktun for "raven"), *muktuk* (34; Inuit meal of whale skin and blubber), *Issungnak* (34; jaegers), or *tatkik* (39; month, moon).

Although Alunik generally gives the meaning of Inuvialuktun and Inupiaq words in his narrative, his translations are not always literal. Thus, to determine whether *Call Me Ishmael* includes other holophrases besides *itkilisaoyak* ("it's from the Indians," 86), *uluksaktuk* ("where they get material for ulus," 95), *Akukitukmuit* ("they are short from the front side of the parka," 44), and *Kablunat* ("people with long eye brows," 93), one must conduct further (linguistic) research. Kukluktuk—or Kugluktuk, the "correct" spelling of the official name for what used to be called Coppermine—serves as a good example here. Kugluktuk lies in western Nunavut where the Inuit speak Inuinnaqtun, a local variant of Inuktitut. The Inuit place name Kugluktuk, however, is already an English rendering of the Inuinnaqtun *qurluqtuq*,[92] which, according to Lowe's *Basic Siglit Inuvialuit Eskimo Dictionary*, literally translates as "water is falling down." Kukluktuk/Kugluktuk is thus an Inuktitut holophrase,[93] even though Alunik's translation of the word as "waterfall" (95) fails to mark it clearly as such.

Some of the Inuvialuktun/Inupiaq words in *Call Me Ishmael*—such as *umiak, umiakpak, ulu*, or *inne*—are incorporated into the English text more than once. When such words are used for a second time in the narrative, they are usually no longer put in italics but turn into foreign words that are directly imported into the English lexicon. When used in the plural form, *umiak* and *ulu* are even integrated into the English grammar by the addition of a final *s*—"umiaks" rather than *umiat* (see 35, 55) and "ulus" rather than *uluuk* (two) or *uluit* (many).[94] These words, then, are no longer foreign words but have become loan words. Although his importing of words from the Inuvialuktun/Inupiaq lexicon does not include actual Inuktitut holophrases, through this importation Alunik nonetheless enhances the overall effect of his code switching in *Call Me Ishmael*, as we shall see in the discussion that follows.

Whether or not the Inuvialuktun/Inupiaq words in *Call Me Ishmael* represent actual holophrases, their inclusion serves to weave the Inuit language into an English narrative. More importantly, the use of Inuvialuktun/Inupiaq adds authority to a narrative that intends to write an oral tradition that only some people have the authority to pass on to future generations. The significance of code switching in *Call Me Ishmael*, then, lies not in its constituting the narrative's backbone—that task is fulfilled entirely by its paraholophrases—but in marking Inuvialuktun/Inupiaq as both the narrative's linguistic context and the traditional knowledge that this narrative intends to pass on. In the meantime, Alunik's code switching shows his involvement with his readers by marking their relationship to his composition as either cultural insiders or outsiders, thus defining the terms under which readers can participate in the text. Even if the meanings of these Inuvialuktun/Inupiaq words are—with the exception of *muktuk*—always provided somewhere in the text, cultural outsiders will likely not know how to pronounce these words properly, particularly long ones such as *Akukitukmuit*.[95] By creating linguistic context, showing the narrator's involvement, and defining the terms of reader participation, Alunik's code switching qualifies as a strategy in textualizing orality that, given that some Inuvialuktun/Inupiaq words are holophrases, is at least partially culturally specific.

Code switching from English to an Indigenous language and back to English is the only possible way for holophrases proper to feature in a discourse composed in English. On the level of grammar, holophrasis in English discourse can only be *indicated* or *suggested* in the form of traces either of the structure of actual holophrases (direct holophrastic traces) or of discourse features that result from or can be associated with polysynthesis (indirect holophrastic traces). A discussion of the various kinds of holophrastic traces found in *Call Me Ishmael* and how they function in the text follows.

To pass on Inuvialuit/Inupiaq traditional knowledge, Alunik not only turns to Inuvialuktun or Inupiaq words but also occasionally makes use of compounds. N N compounds cannot suggest the holistic nature of the holophrase because they lack a verbal component. Although *Call Me Ishmael* features only a few N N compounds, they are nevertheless worth mentioning because of the number of words combined in them. "Hard bone arrow heads" (48), "willow frame sod huts" (35), "birch-bark canoes" (87), and "Bowhead-rib sleigh runners" (49) are examples of *complex* N N compounds that are too long to be frequent in the largely analytic English. Although these compounds might not be able to suggest the holistic nature of the holophrase, they do point to the possibility in polysynthetic languages of combining various different morphemes to produce a new and more complex word, sometimes resulting in a holophrase.

Deverbal N N compounds in *Call Me Ishmael* include

- "bow and arrow hunting skills" (50),
- "geese hunting areas" (51),
- "hunting weapons" (51),
- "hunting tools" (57),
- "sitting hole" (57),
- "eating fish" (62), and
- "sleeping part" (of the house) (78).

CHAPTER 1

These deverbal N N compounds evoke the holistic structure of the holophrase because they include as their modifier a deverbal noun, which is derived from a verb through the process of affixation. *Synthetic* compounds are even more suggestive of the holophrase on a formal (i.e., grammatical) level since they use a verbal component as their head rather than as their modifier. The following two examples from *Call Me Ishmael* clearly qualify as synthetic compounds:

- "three horsepower kicker" (59), which should be read as "a three-horsepower kicker," and
- "raw meat eater" (24), which should be read as "raw-meat eater."

We can further assume that the following examples of synthetic compounds also qualify as direct holophrastic traces because they are re-created based on the two examples just mentioned:

- "*People Eaters* or *Man Eaters*" (43; also see "*Inuktoyuit* meaning man eaters," 44),
- "summer feeding" (61),
- "sweep netting" (61),
- "fur bearing" (72),
- "ice fishing" (63), and
- "fire-makers" (35).

In the synthetic compounds used in *Call Me Ishmael*, the heads are usually turned into nouns through the process of affixation (*-ing* or *-er*). The point, however, is that these heads, which can be compared in function with the root of a holophrase, are derived from a verb, the key component of any holophrase in Indigenous languages.

Thus, the synthetic and deverbal N N compounds used in *Call Me Ishmael* provide the narrative with direct holophrastic traces that are comparatively strong imitations of the structure of holophrases. The complex N N compounds, however, can also be read as direct holophrastic traces, even if they are much less evocative of the holophrase on a formal (i.e., grammatical) level than the other types of compounds. Regardless of their respective internal structure, the compounds used in *Call Me Ishmael* evoke both the descriptiveness of words in polysynthetic languages and their word formation capabilities. The cultural importance of the elements from Inuvialuit/Inupiaq material culture denoted by these compounds, then, is reflected in both their content and their grammatical form. By describing objects (or persons) by way of circumlocution rather than by referring to them by a single given or borrowed word, Alunik manages to engage the participation of his readers: they are allowed to "picture" elements from the Inuvialuit/Inupiat material culture and are hence drawn more fully into his narrative. The long, descriptive compounds featured in *Call Me Ishmael*, then, not only evoke the holophrase in Indigenous languages on a formal (i.e., grammatical) level but also serve, given their effect on readers, as an oral strategy that, like the use of paraholophrases, is culturally specific.

A structure in English that mimics the syntactic structures in Indigenous discourse caused by the use of holophrases is called *pronoun copying*. *Call Me Ishmael* does not seem to feature pronoun copying as such, but it does include syntactic structures that are at least related to pronoun copying:

> I told them not to change *it*, though *the name Ishmael, I did not like* because some people joke and tell me "your mother is Hagar" [...]. (36; emphasis added)

> *The place where he* [Alunik's grandfather, Charlie Koruguk] *made his home raising his family, that place* is called Neakulik. (60; emphasis added)

These two sentences could easily be paraphrased in standard written English:

> I told them not to change the name Ishmael although I did not like it because some people joke and tell me "your mother is Hagar."

> The place where he made his home raising his family is called Neakulik.

Although the pronoun in the first sentence taken from *Call Me Ishmael* and the noun phrase with the demonstrative pronoun in the second sentence are not necessary to form grammatical and informative sentences, they nonetheless serve a particular purpose: they textualize orality. Not only do they appear to be repetitive, but they also happen to be structured into idea units that mimic the intonation units in oral speech, and thus they create a fragmentary kind of discourse. Unlike other colloquial uses of English in *Call Me Ishmael*,[96] these two passages seem to borrow from discourse features that result from holophrasis. They can thus be read as indirect holophrastic traces and be seen to function as a strategy in textualizing orality that is, once again, culturally specific.

The same observation can be made of *subject dropping*, as in the following example: "It doesn't take long for the walrus to die as under the front flipper is where the heart is and Inuit poke it there. *Hit* the heart and it dies quickly" (58; emphasis added). The dropping of a grammatical subject is not uncommon in colloquial language, associated as it is with the more rapid composition of language in speech. However, given the linguistic background of Alunik, the ellipsis in "Hit the heart and it dies quickly" can also be seen as an echo of polysynthetic language structures, in which subjects (and objects) are represented via affixes, which are added to a word base, usually a verb, and thus do not need to take the form of independent noun phrases. Subject dropping evokes the independence of holophrases, which can produce full grammatical sentences without the use of independent noun phrases, and thus qualifies as an indirect holophrastic trace. It functions as a culturally specific strategy in textualizing orality because it re-creates the intonation units of oral speech through the use of ellipses and points to increased author involvement and reader participation.

As we have seen, pronoun copying and subject dropping are found only casually in *Call Me Ishmael*. Indirect holophrastic traces that are more pervasive in Alunik's narrative are *repetitions* and *evidentials*.

The use of *repetitions* is characteristic of Indigenous rhetorics and is encouraged in part by Indigenous language structures. The holistic nature of polysynthetic verbs allows speakers of Indigenous languages to produce idea units with a minimalism of text. If more information is required, whether based on the speaker's or listener's judgment, this information will be given in succeeding idea units but not without repeating bits of the previous idea unit. Within paragraphs or even in consecutive sentences in *Call Me Ishmael*, we find repetitions (indicated by boldface type in the following examples) that mark the respective passages as resembling the information flow in Indigenous discourse:

> They called that a **drop door**. In Inupiaq it is called *kataak*. That means **drop door**. (78)

> **The girls were getting wood** for the bonfire from close to the bank of the creek. **The girls were getting wood** for the Indians who were having a bonfire dance. (86)

> **Angmaak is used to make half-inch thick chisel heads**. It's harder to break. **The Inuit use it for chisels**. (64)

> **It is good for the dogs**. It gets strong if it is mixed with fish or little seal meat. The dogs could get fat on it. I use some myself. **It is good for dogs**. (67)

> In Inuvialuktun they [i.e., white men] were called *Tan'git* or by Eastern Arctic Inuit, *Kablunat*, meaning **people with long eye brows**. I asked one Kitikmeot man what Kablunak meant. He said **a people with big eyebrows**. (93–94)

At times, these repetitions in *Call Me Ishmael* become even more elaborate, such as in the following passage:

> Another true story from around Husky Lakes is of an Inuvialuk Shaman. The Shaman was a strong magic man. He could become invisible and protect the Inuit from the Indians. The Inupiat and Inuvialuit call the Indians *Itkili*. This true story was also told to Joe Teddy at Lucas Point just below DEW Line site number three. This is the story of a Shaman who was a strong magic man and this incident occurred around Tuktoyaktuk. The Shaman could become invisible. (88)

Alunik begins with a plot summary and then introduces the source of the story that he is about to tell, only to circle back to the plot summary already given, before eventually telling the whole story. Such a structure is repetitive, but more importantly it indicates Alunik's involvement with his audience. Since the repetitive structures in Alunik's narrative re-create the information flow in Indigenous discourse, which in turn is influenced in part by the use of holophrases, the textualization of orality achieved through repetition can be considered culturally specific.

This passage also marks an indirect holophrastic trace of another kind that concerns the correlation between polysynthesis and *evidentiality* in Indigenous languages. Since *Call Me Ishmael* is composed in English, evidential meanings in the narrative cannot be conveyed by specific grammatical forms since they are non-existent in English grammar. However, Alunik usually gives the theme and the source of his story at the beginning of the chapter and then generally repeats this information toward the end of the chapter, thereby establishing narrative frames on chapter levels that mimic the larger frame into which the narrative is placed. These frames come exceptionally close to traditional opening and closing frames since they are short and, in most cases, consist of formulaic expressions, such as "here is how"

(47, 76, 83), or "here is what" (51), or "here is a little more" (66), or "here is another story" (85) in chapter openings, or "that is how" (73, 75), or "this is how" (74, 83) in chapter closings. Within these formulaic microframes, one often also finds Alunik's insistence that "this is" or "it is" a true story:

> In Canada beside Kittigakyuit, what they call Kitty in our day, the 1900s, an old Inuvialuk named Levi Aknautsiak also told stories. He heard stories from his ancestors. In his time he passed on many true stories that happened before his time. He was born in the late 1800s. Old Levi told stories to people of his generation about people that came from West of Kittigakyuit—somewhere from Alaska. This is one of his true stories. (43; see also 38, 40, 42, 44)

The way in which this information is presented might seem exaggerated to readers raised within Euro-Western literary traditions. But Wendy Rodgers has noted that "Inuit tellers have traditionally been careful to specify the precise degree of their own knowledge."[97] However, *contemporary* authors and storytellers, Robin McGrath writes, "are aware that what they are writing or saying is deliberately fiction."[98] That *Call Me Ishmael*, authored by a "contemporary" Inuit, still contains the insistence that the narrative presented is fact rather than fiction—just as Alunik's grandfathers and their grandfathers would have insisted that their stories were true—speaks to the fact that *Call Me Ishmael* is writing Inuvialuit/Inupiat oral tradition. Some of Alunik's stories might be more easily accepted as fact by Euro-Western readers, particularly his accounts of local history, as in "Another True Story" (Ch. 8, 43–44). Other stories might be regarded by non-Inuit readers as myths, such as the stories of the Little People that immediately precede "Another True Story" (Chs. 6 and 7, 40–42). For Inuit, all these stories are factual and meaningful because they constitute Inuit traditional knowledge. Regardless of the audience, however, Alunik's source citing metafictionalizes the storytelling act, thereby writing the oral process back into the written text. Since it can be read as a trace of the use of evidentials as structural and copyright devices in Indigenous discourse, the elaborate marking of source in *Call Me Ishmael* can be regarded as a strategy of textualizing orality that is culturally specific.

Although illustrations do not qualify as verbal art, there is a strong connection between Inuit verbal and fine art that might be of interest to the discussion of holophrastic traces in Indigenous literatures composed in English. *Call Me Ishmael* contains eleven illustrations, eight of which can be found in the chapters on material culture (48, 49, 52, 53, 60, 69, 71, and 74). The addition of illustrations in these cultural essays seems intentional, for a visualization of Alunik's description facilitates the reader's understanding and engages the reader more fully with a kind of contemporary Inuit writing—a history of Inuit material culture—that, as McGrath puts it, "does not contain any significant reference to present day culture, and does not include stories or myths."[99] Moreover, aside from drawing readers into the text, the illustrations assume the role of body movements and facial expressions in storytelling, showing statically on the two-dimensional page what the storyteller in an oral performance "acts out" in three-dimensional reality.[100]

In fact, illustrations happen to form one of the bridging elements between the oral word and the written word in Inuit verbal art. "Inuit have a long history of illustrating stories," though the creation of what Euro-Western people would consider works of art was only incidental since, in precontact times, Inuit would produce objects primarily to serve well-defined purposes.[101] Illustrative decorations, McGrath writes, would be used as memory tools for old stories or religious truths. A Thule culture bow drill found on Baffin Island, for example, is decorated with scenes of people and animals engaged in summer activities that apparently tell the story of traditional migration. The Inuit also used a variety of pictographic systems that bridge the "gap" between the oral and the written. One such system is the ancient tradition of story-knifing that supposedly predates the invention of Inuit syllabics. Apparently, story-knifing was a play in which girls telling each other stories would draw the respective scenes in the mud or snow using pointed objects called story-knives. "Storyknifing is still obviously well entrenched in the oral tradition," McGrath notes, but it might have been "a first step into the world of print." Another pictographic system used primarily in Alaskan societies was picture writing: the objects drawn represented an object or an idea but not necessarily the one depicted. McGrath notes that Inuit picture writing was invented only around 1900,[102] but this circumstance makes it even more interesting with regard to the development of a written Inuit tradition during the twentieth century. The importance of illustrations in Inuit cultures was not diminished by the development of a written tradition. In fact, illustrations have become an integral part of Inuit literature, which, according to McGrath, might have to do with the "strong narrative quality of Eskimo art, and what Muriel Whitaker calls the inherent pictorial quality of their beliefs and stories."[103] The similarities between Inuit pictorial and verbal art will be dealt with more extensively in the discussion of Alootook Ipellie's *Arctic Dreams and Nightmares* in the next chapter. For now, it should suffice to point out that the illustrations in *Call Me Ishmael* serve to textualize orality, first, in that they mark the narrator's attempt to facilitate reader understanding and are thus indicative of involvement and participation and, second, in that they are reminiscent of the strong visual images evoked in (Inuktitut) holophrases. That much of the text in *Call Me Ishmael* consists of a narrative of events as opposed to a narration of words (i.e., direct speech in writing) further heightens the significance of the oral effects produced by the illustrations in Alunik's collection.

SUMMARY

We have seen that paraholophrases in *Call Me Ishmael* involve the use of intertextuality, intratextuality, or figurative speech and help either to constitute an opening and closing frame with a cyclical structure or to break the line of narration, thus opening up the text. As semantically dense narrative units that form the narrative grid, they prove to be *dynamically equivalent to holophrases* in Indigenous discourse. By establishing a narrative frame, paraholophrases re-create generic conventions of traditional Indigenous oratures and thus help to define the *interpretative context* of the collection, the uncovering of which is a prerequisite for understanding the narrative. That the frame in *Call Me Ishmael* is not explicitly marked in the narrative and can be made out only by recognizing the paraholophrases that constitute it not only indicates Alunik's *involvement* with his audience but also increases the need for *reader participation* in the composition of the narrative. Finally, by undermining the fixity of the printed page, those paraholophrases in *Call Me Ishmael* that do not constitute its narrative frame create a text that, for a written piece of art, is essentially open and fluid and emphatically asks for the participation of its readers.

While the composition of *Call Me Ishmael* relies heavily on the use of paraholophrases, which function not only to construct a coherent narrative but also to mark strategies of conceptual orality that result from the context of language use (context, involvement, and participation), holophrases and holophrastic traces feature less prominently in the narrative and serve primarily as textual markers to complement the textualization of orality achieved through the use of paraholophrases. Inuvialuktun/Inupiaq words and holophrases in Alunik's narrative, whether as examples of code switching or as loan words, function to mark the latter as Inuvialuit/Inupiat, thus defining its *linguistic context*. The use of holophrases, however, also signals Alunik's *involvement* with his readers, who are thus invited to *participate* in the narrative, either as cultural insiders or as cultural outsiders. Holophrastic traces in *Call Me Ishmael* denote strategies of conceptual orality that result from both the context of *language use* (context, involvement, and participation) and the context of *language production* (prosody, redundancy, and fragmentation). Compounding (complex N N compounds, deverbal N N compounds, and synthetic compounds) results in highly descriptive noun phrases that engage reader participation and usually denote elements from Inuvialuit/Inupiat material culture (food, hunting, houses, etc.). Pronoun copying re-creates the prosody of speech, causes redundancy, and makes the discourse increasingly fragmentary. Subject dropping also re-creates the intonation units of oral speech. Repetitions imitate the structures of and information flows in Indigenous languages. The citing of sources for almost every story produces multiple microframes, mimicking the formulaic frames typically found in orature. Finally, illustrations mark Alunik's involvement with his audience and facilitate reader participation.

None of the different types of holophrastic traces in *Call Me Ishmael* occurs pervasively; in fact, some can be considered rare. Pronoun copying and subject dropping, for example, occur very sporadically compared with compounds, repetition, and evidentials, which have a more notable presence in the text. Moreover, holophrastic traces—even direct holophrastic traces—are not formally (i.e., grammatically) equivalent to the holophrase in Indigenous languages. Instead, these holophrastic traces only *suggest* the structure of holophrases (direct holophrastic traces) or discourse features associated with holophrasis (indirect holophrastic traces). They thus create a narrative that, though it can never successfully translate the holophrase into English discourse on the level of grammar, manages at least to weave into the narrative a series of snippets of what actual holophrases look or sound like in Indigenous discourse.

We cannot be absolutely certain that *Call Me Ishmael* was indeed written by Alunik himself. Regardless of its composition, however, his story collection reads more like the *writing of a hitherto oral tradition* (what in the introduction I have referred to as textualized orality) than like the transcription of an oral tradition (what in the introduction I have referred to as textualized orature) and can hence be regarded as a rare form of story-writing: Alunik's narrative comes exceptionally close to the generic conventions of Inuit orature and, unlike much other Indigenous story-writing, continues a particular form of Inuit oratures—namely, Inuvialuit/Inupiat oral tradition. Written by a *storyteller*, whose craft differs notably from that of a *writer*, *Call Me Ishmael* seems to lean further to the oral traditions than examples of story-writing that are produced by professional authors out of the conscious knowledge of a written tradition. Most contemporary Indigenous story-writers deliberately write fiction. They "are usually quite aware of the influence of European literature on their stories"[104] and avoid the degree of repetition found in Alunik's story collection. *Call Me Ishmael* represents a storyteller's deliberate attempt to write an oral tradition, which explains the insistence on the stories being fact, not fiction, and the many instances of source citing in his collection. Considering these differences, the question arises how (para)holophrases feature in "modern stories" by Indigenous story-writers. In other words, can we detect a difference in the use of (para)-holophrases between a traditional Indigenous text, such as *Call Me Ishmael*, and examples of contemporary Indigenous fiction, such as Ipellie's *Arctic Dreams and Nightmares*, discussed in the chapter that follows?

CHAPTER 2

Exorcising Guti: Alootook Ipellie's *Arctic Dreams and Nightmares*

One of the most prominent figures of contemporary Inuit literature is Alootook Ipellie, who passed away unexpectedly in September 2007. He was born in 1951 in a camp near Iqaluit, the capital of what is now Nunavut. His experience of traditional Inuit life was restricted to his early childhood, for his family turned from a semi-nomadic lifestyle to live in permanent settlements when Ipellie was about four years old. He eventually settled in Ottawa, but emotionally and artistically he never left the North. Over the years, he became an artist, journalist, poet, and writer famous for his pen-and-ink drawings and his love of humour, sarcasm, and sexual allusions, all of which are prevalent in *Arctic Dreams and Nightmares* (1993).

THE TEXT: *ARCTIC DREAMS AND NIGHTMARES*
Alootook Ipellie is one of the first two Inuit writers[1] to have written "more than just an occasional short story."[2] Ipellie published numerous poems and short stories in Inuit magazines such as *Inuit Today*, *Inuit Monthly*, and *Inukshuk* before writing *Arctic Dreams and Nightmares*, "a breakthrough volume," according to Michael Kennedy, "because it is the first single author collection of stories published in the South by an Inuk writer."[3] Ipellie's story collection is also significant because of its genre and narrative structure and

because of the insights into shamanism that it provides to contemporary readers, whether they are Inuit or not.

Questions of Genre and Narration

What started out as a series of pen-and-ink drawings, Ipellie writes in his introduction to *Arctic Dreams and Nightmares*, eventually turned into a collection of drawings *and* stories that he wrote based on the drawings (xviii), a series of which he had already exhibited in Sisimiut, Greenland, in 1989.[4] The drawings and stories in *Arctic Dreams and Nightmares*, Ipellie further explains in the introduction, were inspired by his dreams and nightmares, by people and events of his daily life, and by his ancestors' "gift for inventing myths, stories, and legends," turning the book into what he calls "a smorgasbord of stories and events, modern or traditional, true or imagined" (xix).

The twenty stories in *Arctic Dreams and Nightmares* make sense even when they are read piecemeal or out of sequence. However, their real significance becomes apparent only when one reads the stories sequentially and in their entirety. As a story collection with one recurrent narrator, *Arctic Dreams and Nightmares* resembles many other contemporary short-story cycles or "composite novels," to use the term suggested by Maggie Dunn and Ann Morris.[5] Yet, despite being fiction, Ipellie's story collection comes much closer to Inuit story cycles than it does to other composite novels in Euro-Western traditions. *Arctic Dreams and Nightmares* shares many features with the Qayaq story cycle discussed in the holophrastic reading of *Call Me Ishmael* in the previous chapter. Like Qayaq in the Inupiat epic, the narrator in *Arctic Dreams and Nightmares* travels across the Arctic and meets all kinds of interesting, often highly curious, people. However, whereas Qayaq is a restless wanderer in search of his lost brothers, the first-person narrator in *Arctic Dreams and Nightmares* is journeying on the traditional Inuit seasonal rounds in search of food for his family. Not that his family or even his own hunting and gathering feature prominently in his narration; on the contrary, they provide no more than a loose context for the events that inspire his stories. These stories evolve around similar patterns in that they tell of little incidents in the life of the narrator, which he experiences as curious spectator and/or protagonist. As one story leads to another, they build a never-ending chain, a story cycle that is perfected once readers have read the last story. The events narrated in *Arctic Dreams and Nightmares* (with the exception of the first four stories) are not placed in chronological order. From the descriptions of the seasons, which either are given explicitly or can be assumed from the stories' contexts, one can gather only that these events stretch over several years. The stories concern either hunting or sex or, in some cases, both. The question of survival (through sustenance or procreation) hence features prominently in the narrative and provides a thematic focus for the various stories.

Arctic Dreams and Nightmares tells the story of "a powerful shaman" (xix) who has recently passed away. While the first four stories describe his death and the breaking free of his soul from his body, the remainder of the narrative represents a kind of travelogue of the living soul of the narrator as he remembers his past lives. At the beginning of the narrative, his soul travels into the supernatural world, but, as readers learn a little later, it is not going to stay there for eternity. Instead, it will be reborn in another body. It would indeed be impossible for the narrator to have lived more than one life if his soul was granted eternal life (see 21–22). Ipellie thus conflates two different beliefs found among Inuit groups: the belief in the eternal life of the soul in one of the afterworlds, and the belief in reincarnation (for a discussion, see below).

Some of the characters mentioned in *Arctic Dreams and Nightmares* are based on historical people, but their actual life dates contradict the narrator's claim to have been dead for 1,000 years. Besides, no human could have been a contemporary of both William Shakespeare and Brigitte Bardot at the same time, unless that person was reborn again and again. The narrator's crucifixion (21–25) bears strong references to the crucifixion of Jesus: the "I" is nailed to a cross, he wears a crown of thorns, and his hair dress in the pen-and-ink drawing that accompanies the story looks like many depictions of the crucified Jesus. In fact, in traditional Inuit cultures, the rebirth of the shaman after days spent in a death-like trance was part of the Sedna ritual, a festival dedicated to the mother of the sea animals.[6] If, as the narrator in *Arctic Dreams and Nightmares* claims after his crucifixion, "It would be another one thousand years before I was to be born again as a new physical being on this ever unforgiving planet Earth" (25), the events narrated in the remaining sixteen stories seem to belong to the lives that the narrator lived after this crucifixion, which, we can assume given the biblical allusions, could have taken place around 33 C.E. The time frame underlying the narration seems, then, to be as follows: the events in the stories took place sometime between 1000 C.E. and 2000 C.E., but are narrated in contemporary times.

The time lapse between the actual occurrence of the events and their telling, in fact, accounts for the abundant examples of synchronicity in *Arctic Dreams and Nightmares*. Not only does the narrative mingle diverse components of Euro-Western cultures, such as William Shakespeare, Mary Shelley's Frankenstein, Arthur Conan Doyle's Sherlock Holmes, Brigitte Bardot, Greek mythology, the Christian God, the Bible, the Garden of Eden, the

CHAPTER 2

British Royal Family, Euro-Western pop culture, Wimbledon, wrestling, German Eau de Cologne, ballet, and blues music, to mention only a few, but it further blends all of them with elements of traditional Inuit cultures, most prominently shamanism. Inuit perceptions of the life cycle and of the soul and the spirit, as well as elements of Inuit oral traditions, feature prominently in *Arctic Dreams and Nightmares*. In fact, knowledge of Inuit religion and shamanism offers entrance into a subtext in Ipellie's story cycle that would otherwise be unintelligible for cultural outsiders. A discussion of the main elements of Inuit religion and shamanism is thus required to frame properly my holophrastic reading of *Arctic Dreams and Nightmares*.

Inuit Religion and Shamanism

The following survey of Inuit religion and shamanism does not attempt to be complete; nor is it possible to sketch in a short overview all of the regional differences among Inuit peoples across the Arctic, especially given that Ipellie's story cycle does not focus on just one Inuit group but appears to be pan-Inuit. The following survey, then, is but a short introduction to Inuit religion and shamanism, the main purpose of which is to contextualize Ipellie's story collection.

Traditional Inuit religion can be described as a mixture of animist principles and shamanism that was closely linked to Inuit beliefs and customs regarding personal names, the life cycle, and notions of the soul and the spirit. As the Inuit elder Mariano Aupilaarjuk explains, Inuit traditionally believed that all things, whether human or not, were alive and had *anirniq*, meaning "breath," which forms the soul of every human or animal.[7] *Anirniq*, according to Harold Seidelman and James Turner, was considered part of *sila*, "the spirit of the air that controlled the weather" and "lived in the sky and made the sun go down." In fact, the holophrase *silatuujuk*, often given as "he is intelligent," is translated more literally as "he who is endowed with spirit or life-force."[8] Inuit believed their souls to reside in their living bodies, "in the form of an air bubble containing a scaled-down model of the individual. When the individual died, the air bubble burst. The miniature image then grew to human size and, in an ethereal form, went to live in the land of the dead."[9] Most Inuit refer to a soul as *tarniq*, whereas shamans call it a bubble, *pullaq* or *pullakuluujaaqtuq* ("that which looks like a little bubble"). Unlike ordinary people, Aupilaarjuk notes, shamans can see people's *tarniq* and describe it, but use of the term *pullaq* is also proof of the existence of a shamanic language. Inuit people, even if they knew the meaning of *pullaq*, did not usually use the word themselves to refer to the soul, unless they were shamans.[10] The narrator in *Arctic Dreams and Nightmares* uses this shamanic term for the soul (directly translated into

English) in the metaphor "burst open the bubble of our life-blood" (17), the only instance, in fact, of his use of shamanic language in the story cycle. Although a single use of shamanic language from this powerful shaman-narrator might seem surprising at first, it is not: Inuit shamans traditionally used shamanic language only to speak to their helping spirits or *tuurngait*.[11] In fact, many *tuurngait* names "were derived from shamanic words," which could, however, also be used by anyone wishing "to communicate with the spirits."[12]

Inuit traditionally showed a strong belief in the power of words. For example, in fear of offending the animal's soul, the actual words for animals pursued in hunting were avoided, and circumlocutions were used instead. Seals became "sea lice" or "the things that have blubber"; caribou were referred to as "earth lice"; and polar bears were called "the great white ones."[13] *Arctic Dreams and Nightmares* picks up one such circumlocution when it refers to *nanuq*, the polar bear, as "Nanuq, the White Ghost," the "great white Nanuq" (17), or simply the "Great White Ghost" (17, 18, 19). The tendency for this descriptive use of language is also evoked, if only weakly, in the compounds found in *Arctic Dreams and Nightmares*, for example, in "beluga whale harpoon" (139, 140, 141), "white-coated baby harp seal pup" (106), and "societal cut-throat rat races" (120).[14]

Another implicit reference to Inuit spiritual beliefs and practices in *Arctic Dreams and Nightmares* is in the use of personal names. Code switching in Ipellie's story cycle is restricted to personal names, which are either Inuktitut and involve the use of synecdoche (e.g., Aqaqa, Nalikkaaq, and Ossuk, which suggest the love triangle that these characters are involved in) or are Inuktitutized English names that, through the use of mockery, critique the Christian religion and colonialism. (I will discuss this code switching in more detail below.) Inuit traditionally believed personal names to contain a person's outstanding characteristics. When a name was passed on from one generation to the next, it was believed that these characteristics were passed along as well:

> A person's name is always derived from that of someone deceased, and carries with it the namesake's qualities; one becomes, indeed, a member of the great community of all who have borne the same name back to the ultimate distant past. Each living human being is thus attended by a host of namesake-spirits, who aid and protect him as long as he is faithful to rule and rite, but become inimical on any transgression.[15]

Deceased individuals of the community would often appear in a dream to the pregnant mother, or to the father, and would ask to be given something to drink and to eat. Such dreams were generally interpreted as the deceased's wish to give his or her name to the child.[16] The Inuit naming ritual has been interpreted as "social reincarnation";[17] Nunavut elders, however, explain that it is not reincarnation, "for it is not the soul, but rather the spiritual element that is the name—the name-soul—that joins the child, remaining with him and protecting him throughout his life."[18]

A person could have more than one name, including the names of people from the other sex—a circumstance that fostered gender overlapping among Inuit. As noted by Bernard Saladin d'Anglure in "From Foetus to Shaman," the more names of the other gender given to a person, the more likely the inversion of that person's gender identity, which could involve various forms of transvestism. Cross-gender features among Inuit concerned overlapping not only of clothing but also of technology and religion. Gender overlapping, however, could also be caused by the physical change of sex at birth. Cross-dressing usually lasted until puberty, when the transition to the biological sex would be made final.[19]

Pointing to the Yupiit of Alaska and eastern Siberia as well as to the Inuit of Nunavut for evidence, Saladin d'Anglure argues in "The 'Third Gender' of the Inuit" that gender overlapping invited shamanism because it caused "genuine crises of identity, which opened the way for the emergence of a shamanic vocation." The tripartite system of gender in Inuit cultures was kept intact, he further argues, not only because former transvestites always remained marked as symbolically cross-gendered due to their names but also because some of them eventually became shamans.[20] Saladin d'Anglure thus reads Inuit shamanism as a continuation of what he calls the "third gender," but he does so intentionally *without* "any reference to specific sexual orientation."[21] References to sexual orientation, however, are made by the narrator in *Arctic Dreams and Nightmares* in "The Agony and the Ecstasy" (160–68), which features a cross-dressing Prince Char, whose sexual orientation remains unchanged even after killing his first seal.

According to the Iglulik shaman Aua, the greatest danger for Inuit lay in the fact that their diet consisted entirely of souls.[22] Strict rituals and taboos were to be observed in both the killing of animals and their treatment afterward to prevent misfortune.[23] "All game is difficult hunting if the animal refuses to be taken," the Inuvialuit Nuligak explains. "Of course, it becomes easy when the animal exposes himself."[24] Animals allowed themselves to be caught easily when treated with respect.[25] As we have seen, during the hunt, the proper names of the animals pursued were carefully avoided and circumlocutions used instead. "Dressed in animal skins themselves, Inuit hunters were forced to challenge the spirits of their prey in an unending contest.

If they were defeated in this struggle, they could lose their identity and turn into animals or spirits with no hope of return to the human world."[26] Appropriate behaviour at the camp also influenced the outcome of a hunt.[27] The most important rituals and taboos in hunting, however, concerned the proper treatment of the animal after death, Åke Hultkrantz notes. If the soul of a dead animal or human was not appeased, it could take revenge on its killer. Sea animals were given a drink of fresh water for their souls to return in other seals; land animals were given grease.[28]

The three main deities, those of the sea, the air, and the moon, were believed to personify "the cosmic balance," and they quickly responded to any disturbance of the cosmic harmony (i.e., the breaking of a ritual or taboo) by sending bad weather and sickness or by holding back the animals on which the Inuit fed; in such cases, the deities could be calmed down only with shamanic intervention.[29] Asked about his people's religion, the Netsilik elder Ikinilik told Knud Rasmussen, "We do not believe, we only fear."[30] In a long oration often quoted in accounts of Inuit religion, the Iglulik shaman Aua provided Rasmussen with an extensive list of the things feared by Inuit.[31] The Christian religion, with its comparatively small set of rules in the form of the Ten Commandments, might well have appeared attractive to peoples whose religion dictated observing a large set of rituals and taboos.[32] Inge Kleivan and Birgitte Sonne have convincingly argued, however, that Aua's oration cannot be taken at face value, since Aua seems to have already been influenced by Christianity when he made the oration. Kleivan and Sonne also—and correctly, I think—note that hardly any religion does "not contain a considerable element of fear in practice."[33]

Although Inuit feared the misfortunes caused by the transgressions of rituals or taboos, they did not fear death as such.[34] Once people died, Inuit believed that they lost their *inua*. According to Peter Irniq, *inua* "is physically alive"; in fact, "Inuk comes from the word, 'Inuujuq' 'one who is alive.'"[35] Daniel Merkur describes *inua* as "an idea that indwells in and imparts individual character to a physical phenomenon" or, as one informant told him, the "essential existing force." *Inua* is invisible, but, unlike a spirit, it is anthropomorphic: that is, it is connected to a physical body.[36] Spirits were called *tuurngaq* (or a dialectic variant) and aroused different attitudes among Canadian Inuit. They were perceived by some groups as mostly evil (Netsilik, Iglulik, and Baffin Island), but other groups believed spirits to contain only the possibility of evil, since shamans could misuse them for their personal affairs.[37] Spirits could be deliberately sought out; in fact, Inuit shamans drew their helping spirits from *tuurngait*,[38] which could be virtually anything among most Inuit groups; moreover, a shaman could have numerous helping spirits, the first of which was usually acquired during his or her initiation; other helping spirits followed during the course of the shaman's life.[39] The helping spirits of the narrator in *Arctic Dreams and Nightmares* are never specified, but given his reputation as a powerful shaman (22, 37, 177) it is reasonable to assume that he had many powerful helping spirits.

Most Inuit groups in Canada and Greenland shared a belief in the continuous life of the soul in an afterworld; only the Caribou Inuit believed in reincarnation.[40] Although Inuit beliefs in the afterworld, Hultkrantz writes, differ considerably across the Arctic, most Inuit groups believed in two main afterworlds, one celestial and the other underground.[41] According to Iglulik belief, the dead soul travels either to the Land of Day or to the Narrow Land underneath the sea, depending on the circumstances of death. As Aua pointed out to Rasmussen, the souls of those people who drowned in the sea or were murdered proceed immediately to the Land of Day to live with the *Uvdlormiut* "the People of Day." They lead a happy life and spend most of their time playing soccer with a walrus skull; their game is visible to the people on earth in the form of the northern lights.[42] All other souls, Aua explains further, that have not already been purified through a violent death must first travel to the Narrow Land, which is ruled by Sedna. Once they have completed their penance, however, the *Qimiujarmiut* "the People of the Narrow Land" are allowed either to proceed to the Land of Day or to stay in the Narrow Land, where they continue to live just as happily as the souls in the Land of Day.[43]

As noted by Zebedee Nungak (Inuit) and Eugene Arima, however, George Francis Lyon also records the Iglulik belief in an underworld with four different layers through which the souls of those who had not drowned, starved, or been killed had to travel on the first four days after death, with only the lowest layer representing a pleasant place. On Baffin Island, Inuit know *Qudlivun* "the uppermost ones," who live in the sky in a land that seems to correspond to the Iglulik notion of the Land of Day. Baffin Island Inuit further distinguish between the *adli* "the place where Sedna lives," the *Adlivun* "those who live beneath us," *Alipaq* "the land of the *Adliparmiut*," and *Adliparmiut* "the inhabitants of the country farthest below." Finally, the Netsilik Inuit believe in a celestial afterworld (called *Angerlartarfik* "the place one can always return to") and an underworld (called *Agleet* "those who live down there" or *Aglermiut* "those who live below"), but they also make out an afterworld between these two just below the earth's surface that is called *Nuqumminut* "those who always sit huddled up with a hanging head."[44] In *Arctic Dreams and Nightmares*, Ipellie does not employ the highly descriptive language used by Inuit in their references to the various afterworlds, but he does not evoke these religious beliefs, and he gives his story cycle a pan-Inuit outlook by conflating the belief in an eternal afterlife (Iglulik, Baffin Island, and Netsilik Inuit) with the belief in reincarnation (Caribou Inuit).

Shamans occasionally went on spiritual journeys to the upper world or to the underworld, which were called *pavungaaqtuq* and *nakkaanniq* respectively.[45] Such journeys need not serve a particular function, but they were usually made out of curiosity; the stories of what shamans encountered on such journeys, however, served to reinforce Inuit beliefs in the afterworld.[46] *Arctic Dreams and Nightmares*, then, is not as modern as its many intertextual references to Euro-Western societies suggest. In describing the narrator's journeys both to the afterworld and to Sedna, Ipellie's story cycle communicates traditional notions of Inuit religion and shamanism. Although missionaries picked up the Inuktitut word for "evil spirit" to refer to the devil, they refrained from using Inuit designations of underworlds to refer to the Christian notion of hell—probably because the belief in an unpleasant afterworld was not strongly developed among Inuit groups. Instead, missionaries coined the words *kappianakturvik* and *ikumaaluk* for "hell."[47] The narrator in *Arctic Dreams and Nightmares* uses neither coinage, but, given the context of the story, the personal name Kappia in "The Exorcism" (story twenty) can easily be associated with *kappianakturvik*.

Inuit oral traditions include stories about legendary races that, like the animals, fall under the category of humanoid beings.[48] Inuit believed man to have lived in promiscuity with animals at the beginning of time and to have shared the Arctic with other human-like races.[49] These legendary races include giants and (as seen in the discussion of *Call Me Ishmael* in Chapter 1) dwarves. The giants, Seidelman and Turner write, were superior to humans because of their size, but humans used their cunning to outwit them. Dwarves, on the other hand, were said to be more dangerous to humans because of their craftiness and unpredictability.[50] The legendary race of dwarves is evoked in the title story of Ipellie's story cycle, in which the narrator turns into "the incredible shrinking man" (129).

Of the three principal deities in Inuit cosmology, the most prominent is Sedna; she also controls the moon spirit and the air spirit, who act as her agents.[51] Sedna's myth is told all across the circumpolar world, albeit with local variations that concern, among other things, her name.[52] Most versions of the Sedna myth agree that she was a young girl who, after a series of events, is thrown out of her kayak. Here the versions differ considerably: while she tries to hold on to the kayak, she has her fingers chopped off by her father (first variant) or by members in her community (second variant).

The violence against her is tied to her not having any relatives (second variant) or to her unwillingness to marry a human (first variant).⁵³ Her chopped-off fingers turn into sea mammals, whereas Sedna herself metamorphosizes into their guardian living at the bottom of the sea.⁵⁴ Her story, Nungak and Arima note, is often fused with another story, that of "the girl who married a dog"⁵⁵ and from whose dog-children originate—depending on the version—Inuit, First Nations, whites, and several legendary races.⁵⁶ However, Nungak and Arima also point out that Frank Boas and Knud Rasmussen consider the accounts of Sedna and of the girl who married a dog to be separate stories.⁵⁷

As the Goddess of the Sea, Sedna (also known by the name Nuliajuk) is in charge of those animals upon which Inuit communities traditionally depended for food and, hence, survival. When the Netsilik elder Ikinilik told Rasmussen that the Inuit did not believe but only feared, he added that "most of all we fear Nuliajuk."⁵⁸ Only powerful shamans "had the ability to communicate directly with Sedna";⁵⁹ accordingly, the narrator in *Arctic Dreams and Nightmares* is selected to prepare a meeting with Sedna because he happens to be one of the most powerful shamans in the Arctic (37). Seidelman and Turner, referring to an account given by Rasmussen, describe a shaman's visit with Sedna as follows. The shaman would call upon his *tuurngait*, who would accompany him or her on the spirit journey. When the shaman reached Sedna's house at the bottom of the sea, he or she would comb her hair because Sedna was no longer able to take care of it, having lost her fingers. Then the shaman would put her into a trance by magical formulae and songs. Once Sedna was calmed down, she would promise to release the sea animals so that people could hunt and feed on them again.⁶⁰ "Summit with Sedna, the Mother of Sea Beasts" in *Arctic Dreams and Nightmares* includes the main elements of this traditional shamanic journey but adds to it a sexually explicit nuance.

Merkur has identified three functions of shamans in Inuit cultures. The story of Sedna alludes to their *remedial* function in securing the hunt. Inuit shamans were also capable of predicting the future and of *clairvoyance*. Yet their main function, according to Merkur, was *healing*, understood by Inuit to encompass more than just the curing of bodily illnesses. To find out the cause of an illness, Merkur writes, the shaman went on "a 'spirit journey,' i.e., a journey in disembodied form as a free-soul" accompanied by his or her helping spirit.⁶¹ Although shamans represent "a central figure" in Inuit religion,⁶² their exceptional position did not grant them any benefits aside from the *tunijjuuti*, the services that they received as compensation for their work; shamans carried out the same duties as their fellow Inuit.⁶³ If it were not for his occasional spirit journeys, then, the narrator in *Arctic Dreams and Nightmares* could not be differentiated from the other Inuit hunters whom he encounters during his travels.

Defining the shaman as "a social functionary who, with the help of guardian spirits, attains ecstasy in order to create a rapport with the supernatural world on behalf of the group members," Hultkrantz pays attention to two features of Inuit shamanism that are stressed to very different degrees by Euro-Western scholars and by Inuit.[64] Whereas the former tend to emphasize particularly the ecstatic elements in shamanism—Mircea Eliade, for example, has equated shamanism with the "technique of ecstasy"[65]—Inuit understand the possession of helping spirits to be the defining feature of shamanism, as Merkur has observed based on Inuit habits of designation. Although *angakkuq* has become a pan-Inuit term for "shaman," its etymology, according to Merkur, is elusive; as he further notes, synonyms for "shaman" in different dialectal variants are sometimes chosen over the use of *angakkuq* (e.g., the Chugach *kalalik*, the Bering Sea Inuit *tunghak*, the Copper variant *tonngaq*, or the Labrador *torngevok*), all of which refer to someone who possesses a helping spirit.[66]

Other synonyms for *angakkuq* represent circumlocutions in the language of shamans. A shaman in west and east Greenland is called "he who is half hidden" and "he who holds himself hidden" in the respective shamanic language; similarly, the Netsilik word is *tarejumangorsalertoq* "one who starts making shadows."[67] To refer to objects or living beings only indirectly to avoid evoking their spirits, Inuit shamans would use figures of speech.[68] Shamanic language, then, is not a language of its own; it simply uses the productiveness of the Inuit language for its own purposes: "the Eskimo language is capable of a great extent of metaphorical expression—to the extent that the great spiritual intellectuals of the Eskimo society were capable of speaking an entire language using metaphors of every part of speech, for religious, ceremonial, poetic and mediumistic purposes."[69] This description of Inuktitut and its use by shamans not only suggests the importance of words in Inuit cultures and religion but also points to the polysynthetic nature of Inuktitut. Whether Ipellie's *Arctic Dreams and Nightmares* mimics Inuit traditions not just in terms of content but also in terms of its use of language will be discussed in the holophrastic reading that follows.

A HOLOPHRASTIC READING OF *ARCTIC DREAMS AND NIGHTMARES*
Paraholophrases
However different the two texts are in terms of their degree of fiction, *Arctic Dreams and Nightmares* does resemble Ishmael Alunik's *Call Me Ishmael*

(discussed in Chapter 1) in content and structure. Both narratives represent a collection of stories (and essays, in the case of Alunik) with explicit (Alunik) or implicit (Ipellie) references to Inuit traditional knowledge concerning either Inuit material culture (Alunik) or Inuit religion and shamanism (Ipellie). Furthermore, both narratives include an elaborate narrative frame that consists of an opening and a closing and that is meant to re-create the proper context for the respective narrative. As in my reading of *Call Me Ishmael*, I will discuss first those paraholophrases in *Arctic Dreams and Nightmares* that constitute its narrative frame before turning to paraholophrases with other narrative functions in the story cycle.

Paraholophrases Constituting the Narrative's Frame

The first four stories in Ipellie's story cycle introduce its narrative situation, which for some critics seems to be enough to identify them as part of a frame.[70] That the first four stories differ from the remainder of the collection is reflected in the type of narration, which switches from the experiencing self of the first four stories to the narrating and reflecting self of the remaining stories. The first four stories, however, also tell a much deeper story that sets the theme and mood for the remainder of *Arctic Dreams and Nightmares*.

It is not until story four that readers discover that the first-person narrator is "one of the most powerful shamans living in the Arctic" (22), but there are hints in the preceding stories that he is a shaman well before he admits to being one—hints that are visible, however, only to those readers familiar with Inuit religion and shamanism. In story one, "Self-Portrait: Inverse Ten Commandments" (2–9), the narrator wakes up in the middle of the night to find himself face to face with a devil whose hands are outstretched, ugly little faces on each finger. When the narrator eventually realizes that this frightening image is an incarnation of himself, he fights the image, and when it finally disappears he realizes that his soul has just gotten rid of its own devilish being to be freed and to be granted a happy afterlife (8–9). In other words, the narrator seems to have died.

Given its references to Satan, the Ten Commandments, the Garden of Eden, and life in the afterworld, this first story appears to have a very Christian tone to it. This impression is further strengthened in story two, "Ascension of My Soul in Death" (10–15), which describes the journey of the narrator's soul into the supernatural world. But the story takes an unexpected turn when the narrator states, suddenly, that "There is no truth to anyone being able to live for an eternity" (15). According to the narrator, one's soul is indeed granted a life in the afterworld, but only for the period of time that one spent on earth. Once this period is over, so the narrator notes, one's soul is reborn. Here is the first hint that the apparently Christian context of the narrator's account is not very Christian at all but instead is influenced by a mixture of Inuit religious beliefs (i.e., the Caribou Inuit belief in reincarnation and other Inuit groups' beliefs in an afterlife).

In story three, "Nanuq, the White Ghost, Repents" (16–19), the narrator finally explains the circumstances of his death. While he and his father were out on the ice hunting seal, a polar bear came upon them. "With a few powerful swipes of its claws and life-ending bites from its hungry jaws, **the great White Ghost** had cut through our flesh and burst open **the bubble of our life-blood**" (17). The expression "great white one" is a direct translation of *qakurturjuaq*, which, as noted above, is the circumlocution for "polar bear" (*nanuq*) used during hunting or the "name given to the polar bear by shamans & hunters in Inuit song and myth."[71] *Nanuq* often also functioned as an animal helper of shamans, and a very strong one at that, due to "[t]he special status of the polar bear among the animal species."[72] The narrator uses variations of the expression "great white one" throughout story three, including in its title: he is referred to as "Nanuq, the White Ghost," the "great white Nanuq" (17), or the "Great White Ghost" (17, 18, 19). These phrases provide the first indication of the narrator's involvement with shamanism; the second indication follows in the second part of the phrase quoted above, "the bubble of our life-blood." The narrator's use of the word *bubble* to refer to his soul might not prove that he is a shaman, but it is nonetheless a strong indication. His narrative, then, can be read as the subversive narrative of an Inuit shaman who shares with his fellow Inuit (and potential non-Inuit readers) his knowledge of death and the journey of his soul into the afterworld.

This being said, the first two stories must be reconsidered from an entirely different perspective. In spite of their apparent Christian tone, our reading of them, in fact, should not assume a Christian perspective. Some phrases, particularly in story one, can now be seen as rather ambiguous. The narrator initially describes the apparition in front of him as an "**incarnation** of myself" (5; boldface in original). Indeed, when the ugly faces on the fingers of his incarnation start telling him stories about "Hell's **Garden of Nede**" (5; boldface in original)—apparently the devil's version of the Garden of Eden—the narrator realizes that what he is seeing is the "**image of myself as Satan incarnate**"[73] and that the "ten squalid heads represented the **Inverse Ten Commandments in Hell's Garden of Nede**" (6).[74] What puzzles the narrator even more is that all of this is happening even though he has followed the good advice of the "so-called Christian minister" to be good so as to "be assured a place in God's Heaven" (6).

CHAPTER 2

Given the history of Christian propaganda against Inuit religion and particularly Inuit shamanism, it is not the devil per se that the narrator fights in this story but the Christian reading of Inuit shamanism as a deed of the devil: being a shaman, the narrator represents, in the eyes of Christians, the devil who inverts the Christian religion by inverting the Ten Commandments in a place that hence can only be called a "Garden of *Nede*," a place seemingly in *need* of Christian proselytizing—one possible way of interpreting the Nede/Eden anagram in *Arctic Dreams and Nightmares*. In story one, fighting the image of shamanism as devilish is an individual act of the narrator in which he saves himself; as will be seen in the discussion of the narrative's closing below, this fight becomes a matter of a whole Inuit community in the last of the narrator's stories, "The Exorcism." For the moment, however, when in story two the narrator's soul "finally acquires **the distinction of being the 'free spirit' it had longed to be** for the better part of its life on planet Earth" (14), it has escaped the struggles of human life on earth (which will become a focus in the title story, "Arctic Dreams and Nightmares"), and, even more important, it has escaped Christian proselytizing. The narrator's eventual "**ascension of my soul**" (11, 13) might refer to both of these escapes, since "ascension," with its Christian connotation (Christ's ascent to heaven), puts the narrator on an almost equal level with God, thereby reversing the Christian propaganda against Inuit shamanism.

The title of story four, "**I, Crucified**" (20–25), can be read as an intertextual reference to *I, Nuligak*, the first Inuvialuit autobiography ever published. Nuligak (1895–1966) was born in the Mackenzie River Delta and started keeping a journal in 1940,[75] which served as the basis for the manuscript that became *I, Nuligak*. It documents the time of growing Euro-Western influence in the Arctic, which was to change Inuvialuit life forever. In both form and content, *I, Nuligak* repeatedly echoes the well-known, pan-Inuit story of the orphan boy Kaujjarjuk.[76] Thus, by way of his intertextual references to *I, Nuligak* (and, by implication, to the story of Kaujjarjuk), the narrator of *Arctic Dreams and Nightmares* situates his narrative well within the tradition of Inuit verbal art, be it oral or written: this might be the fictional life story of an Inuit shaman, but it documents features of Inuit cultures that would originally have been preserved in Inuit oral traditions.

The phrase "**I, Crucified**" can, of course, also be understood as an intertextual reference to the biblical account of Jesus' crucifixion. In story four, out of fear of his shamanic powers, fellow shamans conspire against the narrator to crucify him. The narrator sees himself "**hanging from a cross, crucified**" (21), his hands, feet, and side punctured and his head crowned with thorns. The story ends with the narrator's "slow death **hanging from**

the whalebone crucifix. Crucified" (25). Given the obvious analogy here between the narrator-shaman and Jesus, then, the narrator's earlier use of the phrase "**incarnation** of myself" (5; boldface in original) is highly ambiguous: it might refer to the narrator's multiple lives on earth, and/or it might refer to himself as the embodiment of a deity in human form.

In the course of the first four stories of *Arctic Dreams and Nightmares*, then, the narrator moves from devil to deity, and he does so while describing features of death and the afterworld that reflect Inuit, not Christian, beliefs: falling back on Inuit shamanic language, he refers to his soul as a bubble and describes how it has to linger near his dead body for four days before it can travel on into "the cosmic land of souls" (15), thus evoking the Iglulik belief (recorded by Lyon) in an underworld with different layers through which a deceased soul has to travel for the first four days after death.

As noted in the holophrastic reading of *Call Me Ishmael* in the previous chapter, openings are usually not explicitly marked as such in Indigenous oratures (or literatures) but depend on a reader being aware that he or she is reading an opening, which itself depends on other signals, such as certain phrases that feature prominently in the first chapters of the narrative. In *Arctic Dreams and Nightmares*, such phrases include

a. "the great White Ghost" (17; metonymy),
b. "the bubble of our life-blood" (17; metaphor),
c. "image of myself as Satan incarnate," "Inverse Ten Commandments in Hell's Garden of Nede," and their variations[77] (6; symbols),
d. "the distinction of being the 'free spirit' it had longed to be" (14; symbol),
e. "ascension of my soul" (11, 13; metaphor),
f. "hanging from a cross, crucified" (21; symbol, intertextuality) and "hanging from the whalebone crucifix. Crucified" (25; symbol, intertextuality), and
g. "I, Crucified" (21; intertextuality).

As figures of speech (a–f) and/or intertextual references (f, g), these phrases refer to complex ideas but explicitly mention only the cores of these ideas: that is, though self-contained, these phrases include a subtext that is entirely left for readers to uncover. "[T]**he great White Ghost**" and "**the bubble of our life-blood**" function as indicators of Inuit religion and shamanism. The phrases "**image of myself as Satan incarnate**" and "**Inverse Ten Commandments in Hell's Garden of Nede**" describe the narrator's apparition, but more importantly they point to the Christian misreading of Inuit shamanism. The phrase "**the distinction of being the free spirit it had longed to be**" describes the narrator's soul attaining its freedom by leaving the often perilous life on earth behind. More significant, though, is the fact that this phrase also points to the narrator's successful fight against the image of himself as the devil, as propagated in the Arctic by Christian missionaries. This fight is also connoted in "**ascension of my soul**" as well as in "**hanging from a cross, crucified**" and "**hanging from the whalebone crucifix. Crucified**," all of which carry strong intertextual significance as references to the Euro-Western master narrative, the Bible. Finally, "**I, Crucified**" draws another important intertextual reference, placing *Arctic Dreams and Nightmares* within the tradition of Inuit verbal art, all the while comparing the narrator to Jesus.

Ironically, the crucifixion means the narrator's death; however, since in some streams of Inuit religion a soul can be reincarnated, this death does not imply the end of his story. In fact, his story is only now ready to be told. The importance of the phrases discussed above is not so much that they introduce the narrative situation but that they define the narrative's cultural, religious, and even historical contexts, all of which provide the grounds for the narrative's interpretative context. The phrases listed above are not only semantically dense; constituting the opening in *Arctic Dreams and Nightmares*, they also function as significant narrative units. They are hence equivalent in function to holophrases in Indigenous languages and can thus be referred to as paraholophrases. As part of the narrative grid, these paraholophrases help in the composition of the story cycle, yet their significance does not rest on this function alone. After all, these phrases also show the author's involvement with his readers, who are invited to participate actively in its composition by tracing the narrative's interpretative and other contexts.

Thus, the deciphering of the opening's paraholophrases is even more demanding on readers of *Arctic Dreams and Nightmares* than on those of *Call Me Ishmael*, in which Alunik states from the outset that he wants to ensure the preservation of the stories passed on to him. In Ipellie's book, the first-person narrator leaves his readers in ignorance of the purpose of his stories, a purpose that can only be gathered by reading between the lines. Creating context, involvement, and participation in writing, the opening's paraholophrases thus clearly serve as strategies in textualizing orality that are culturally specific.

It is from the position of an Inuit shaman—a position that the narrator reaffirms in the course of this opening—that he remembers and tells his life stories, which are meant to reinforce Inuit religious beliefs and to carry on traditional knowledge of shamanism in contemporary times. Since I am discussing paraholophrases in the narrative frame, I will focus on the closing of *Arctic Dreams and Nightmares* before turning to its main part. The circle back to the narrative's opening is established in the title story (story fifteen). "Arctic Dreams and Nightmares" (124–33) marks a break in the narrative in many ways. First, it is the most reflective story in the cycle: story fifteen has the narrator meditating on the harshness of Arctic life rather than narrating an actual story. The tone of the story is rather sombre compared with the tones of previous stories; even the stories narrating the death of the narrator seem to be more cheerful than this one. The title story also marks the first time that the narrator opens up to the reader emotionally: he shares his dreams and nightmares, admits suffering from alcoholism, and, again, dies at the end of the story. By this time, he has died twice (in stories three and four); in story fifteen, however, he dies a figurative death that changes the course of the narrative. The remaining stories go back to the surreal, happy, humorous narration of the stories in the middle part, though they focus more clearly on traditional Inuit life than the previous stories.

"Arctic Dreams and Nightmares" begins with a fictional conversation between the narrator, representative of man, and the animals that he hunts—a conversation that addresses the question of survival and echoes two previous stories, "Nanuq, the White Ghost, Repents" (story three, 16–19) and "Survival of the Most Violent" (story eleven, 88–94). In the first story, the narrator is killed by a polar bear while hunting seal. In the second story, however, the natural food chain is reversed, and the narrator is hunted by a seal. This "was the nature of our precarious lives; both man and beasts," the narrator explains in story three. "In the land of the wild, no individual is ever favoured over another. When the time comes, no individual is ever spared. No law of nature protects or galvanizes the lives of men or beasts alike" (19). The law of nature includes the narrator, who dies yet another death at the end of the title story (see below). In "Survival of the Most Violent," the narrator takes the issue of survival to a more general (and more political) level. Writing from the perspective of the seals, he notes that "They [i.e., humans] have come to understand that the brutal force of the harpoon is used [by seals] so that another creature, in a shared planet, may survive for another moment and another day" (93).

In "Arctic Dreams and Nightmares," the surreal reversal of "The Survival of the Most Violent" is at last undone, and the narrator pleads for the animals' understanding:

> Nature has to have its victims. And it is not out of malice that we go
> out to torture all other living things walking in the vicinity of our

birth places. It is only for the simple requirement that we have to eat you animals out there. Please do not be offended by this dictum. It is the way it is. It is the law of nature. The law of predator and prey. (125–26)

Survival, then, becomes the focus of the title story, echoing all the previous hunting stories—and there are many in *Arctic Dreams and Nightmares*—that culminate in this meditation on survival in the Arctic.

Although the narrator seems to be calm and focused at the outset of the story, the conversation with the animals puts him into a psychological spin. He says that he "dream[s] the undreamable dream" of a paradise "[j]ust around the next mountain" in which "we don't need to go out hunting" because the "Kamikaze animals" readily sacrifice themselves to the hunters. Of course, the narrator knows that he can never reach this paradise, but he is dreaming of it nonetheless "because we live on the edge of hell. Some days it is hell itself when an empty stomach beckons the bounty of paradise" (126). When he goes to sleep at night, he hopes that the next day will bring food for his family, but often enough all that sleep brings are nightmares in whose "midst [...] hell's creatures crawl over [his] soul" (127). Yet, the narrator realizes, man "would not be very different from a wild animal" "had he not been able to dream" (128). So it is that one night he dreams about paradise:

> [...] Paradise, you see, is not at all like the biblical perception of paradise. **It is not quite like the Garden of Eden**. When one lives in the Arctic tundra, one is unlikely ever to see as much as a bush, but only low shrubs and tiny, intricate flowers in all the colors of the rainbow. This was a different sort of paradise.
>
> In my dream, **I became the incredible shrinking man!** (129)

The paradise that the narrator dreams about is "not quite like the Garden of Eden," but it is not quite like the paradise about which he dreamed earlier either. In this particular dream, the narrator turns into a dwarf who lives in the shrubs and becomes a vegetarian, thus avoiding the need to hunt animals. His life "among the shrubs" is such a happy occasion that he is convinced this "must be **how the Christian God lives in His paradise, not in the far off Heaven, but between the shrubs underfoot in the middle of the Great White Arctic**" (130).

The references here to the Garden of Eden and to the Christian God are no coincidence, for they take readers back to story one, "Self-Portrait:

Inverse Ten Commandments," in which the narrator fights the notions of shamanism as devilish and of the Arctic as hell's Garden of Nede. Fourteen stories later the same idea is picked up again, but here the criticism goes one step further by putting Christianity and Inuit shamanism on the same level: in this story, the narrator and God live in the same paradise, not the Bible's Eden, but the "Great White Arctic."[78] That this dream is firmly located in an Inuit rather than a Christian context is also suggested by the narrator's comparison of himself to the **"incredible shrinking man,"** an intertextual reference to one of the legendary races dating back to the days of the first people in Inuit oral traditions.[79] In the Tulugak creation story recorded by Edward William Nelson, the first land that Tulugak makes is found not on the earth but in the sky, where he himself resides. When he takes Man to this land, Man learns that the people living there are dwarves.[80] *Arctic Dreams and Nightmares* appears to be pan-Inuit in outlook,[81] but even if we assume a strong eastern Inuit influence in the story cycle—on the ground that the author's birthplace is Iqaluit—we cannot deny the importance of little people in Inuit mythology throughout the Arctic. The comparison made by the narrator between himself and a dwarf hence links his dream about paradise closely with Inuit oral traditions.

"Arctic Dreams and Nightmares" ends not with this dream about paradise but with a nightmare. The narrator is lying on a platform "with this huge eagle ripping out of [his] chest" (131); only eventually does the eagle break out of his body. Once the narrator figures out the meaning of this nightmare, he realizes that the eagle has been "a mere blood cell" that became "unhappy because [his] body had become unsafe to live in," since nothing but "ravaging alcohol" "passed through [its] vessels" (132). The blood cell persuaded others to join it to form an eagle in order to break out of the narrator's body, leaving the narrator behind as "just another vegetating dead human being." With "the most important cells that [he] needed to continue living" leaving him "to perish," the narrator, apparently suffering from alcoholism, dies a figurative death—figurative because, as he himself explains, "This was an **incarnation of a different eaglekind**" (133). Perhaps he has transformed from man into eagle, or perhaps—considering the reference to the "different eaglekind"—one of his spirit helpers, the eagle, has given him the power to fly and leave his own body. Ipellie's choice of the eagle here seems anything but coincidental given the cultural importance attached to the eagle in Alaskan, Canadian, and Greenland Inuit cultures, regarding both hunting and shamanism.[82] Neither is the transformation here at all unusual given that the narrator is a shaman. In fact, in the preceding story, "Walrus Ballet Stories" (114–23), he also transforms himself—in this case, into a walrus to

CHAPTER 2

lure walruses from Siberia to the Canadian Arctic and provide Inuit communities with food.

To summarize, the phrases from the title story "Arctic Dreams and Nightmares"—

a. "It is not quite like the Garden of Eden" (129; simile),
b. "I became the incredible shrinking man" (129; metaphor),
c. "how the Christian God lives in His paradise, not in the far off Heaven, but between the shrubs underfoot in the middle of the Great White Arctic" (130; symbol), and
d. "incarnation of a different eaglekind" (133; symbol)

— are significant for the narrative not only because they are figures of speech but also because they establish direct or indirect links with the opening in the form of inter- or intratextual references. The phrase "**It is not quite like the Garden of Eden**" evokes the Garden of Nede introduced in story one and, together with "**how the Christian God lives in His paradise, not in the far off Heaven, but between the shrubs underfoot in the middle of the Great White Arctic,**" elaborates on an idea developed in the first four chapters (the problematic relationship between the Christian religion and Inuit shamanism). The phrase "**I became the incredible shrinking man**" draws an intertextual connection to Inuit oral traditions, in this case to stories featuring the legendary race of dwarves, as in the Tulugak story cycle. The intertext alluded to in "**incarnation of a different eaglekind**" is religious rather than literary and evokes the role of shamanic helping spirits and Inuit beliefs concerning the afterlife. At the same time, this phrase also establishes a link to story one, in which the narrator has to face an incarnation of himself as the devil. These phrases form the cores of complex ideas as the surplus of meaning, which is alluded to in them but has yet to be identified by readers, is doubled: these phrases function as both figures of speech and inter- or intratextual references. Because they constitute direct or indirect links to the narrative's opening, particularly to stories one, two, and four, these phrases also function as significant narrative units, for they mark the beginning of the closing in *Arctic Dreams and Nightmares*. As equivalents in function to the holophrase in Indigenous languages, these phrases thus qualify as paraholophrases, but they would, of course, be much less effective if they were not accompanied by other paraholophrases that complete the narrative's closing, thus perfecting its frame. Let us turn, then, to the stories that follow the title story and complete the narrative frame of *Arctic Dreams and Nightmares*.

Despite the sombreness of "Arctic Dreams and Nightmares" and his confession of being an alcoholic, the narrator seems to walk out of the collection's title story in a strengthened position. That he overcomes his alcoholism using his spiritual powers is significant for the remainder of the story cycle given that the narrative seeks to reaffirm Inuit cultures over the cultures of colonizers and against all odds, be it Christianity (one of the facets of colonization) or alcoholism (one of its consequences). Compared with the stories in the middle part of the cycle, the five stories that follow "Arctic Dreams and Nightmares" contain few references to Euro-Western cultures; thus, traditional features of Inuit cultures move into the foreground of the narrative. In "Love Triangle" (story sixteen, 134–53), the "wrestling" match between husband and lover that is suggested by the narrator to solve their conflict resembles traditional "Inuit 'boxing,'" one of the socially recognized solutions employed in traditional Inuit communities.[83] In what might be perceived by most Euro-Western readers as a bizarre and shocking story, "Hunting for Skins and Furs" (story seventeen, 154–59) evokes both the lack of taboos in pre-Christian Inuit society regarding sex and the need for a mixing of blood to prevent degeneration.[84] In "The Agony and the Ecstasy" (story eighteen, 160–68), traditional gender roles are evoked, including the Inuit construction of a third gender. "The Woman Who Married a Goose" (story nineteen, 170–74) is a variation of a traditional Inuit story that tells of an ancient past when humans and animals would marry and have sexual intercourse with each other. Finally, "The Exorcism" (story twenty, 176–81) describes a shamanic ritual, the chasing away of a *tupilak*, an evil spirit.[85]

The narrator admits that the ritual described in "The Exorcism" is unusual, even for a powerful shaman. "One of the most frightening experiences I've ever had as a powerful shaman," he tells his readers at the beginning of the story, "was the longest ten days I've spent in my entire life." It took him ten days to free a family of ten "possessed by the demon of a recently deceased shaman" whose name was Guti, meaning God, as the narrator explains.[86] Guti was an evil shaman who took advantage of his position and abused many women in his camp "in return for his shamanic services, which were usually total failures" (177). One night Guti and Kappia, a man in Guti's camp, got into a fight, and Kappia killed Guti. Before he died, Guti, in an act of revenge, put a curse on Kappia's family (178). Because his family proved to be heavily affected by the curse, Kappia called on the narrator for help to perform what the narrator ironically refers to as an exorcism (179)—the use of this term is ironic because much in his narration points to the ritual being a *tupilanniq*: that is, the killing of an evil spirit by an Inuit shaman.

CHAPTER 2

During this particular ritual, the narrator arouses "**Shaman Guti's demons**" "for the purpose of exorcising them from Kappia and his family" (179). Since the demons, or *tupilait*, have affected all members of the family, a ritual must be performed for each one. When it is Kappia's wife's turn—as the mother of the family's children she is exorcised last—the narrator must strip her naked "so that the demon would have nothing to cling onto when it was being pulled out." The scene conjures up images of childbirth:

> The first thing I saw were the **horns of the demon** as its head began to come out of Kappia's wife's vagina in the manner of an infant being born! As the head came out it was **hissing like a snake** with its mouth wide open. I was surprised to learn that the demon was **wearing a chained cross around its neck**.
>
> Kappia's wife screamed with the kind of pain she had never felt before. The excruciating pain didn't even compare to pains of childbirth. (180–81)

The narrator does not mention how bloody the ritual is, but the comparison with childbirth is enough to suggest that the ritual is very bloody, as is typically the case in *tupilanniq*. The references to the "**horns of the demon**" (180), its "**hissing like a snake**" (180), and its "**wearing a chained cross around its neck**" (181), however, clearly mark the demon as Christian, not Inuit. Considering that the evil shaman's name is an Inuktitutized version of "God," there are grounds for the assumption that it is God himself whom the narrator is exorcising in the final story of *Arctic Dreams and Nightmares*. Then again, the exorcism itself, as well as the horns and the demon's snake-like behaviour, suggest descriptions and depictions of Satan and evoke how he tempted Eve to eat from the Tree of the Knowledge of Good and Evil, thus provoking God into expelling Adam and Eve from the Garden of Eden. Given these allusions to the Christian creation story, it does not appear to be a coincidence that the name Kappia is translated as "scared" in the glossary at the end of the book (184) and forms part of one of the two Inuktitut words coined by missionaries to denote "hell," *kappianakturvik*, which is related to *kappianaktuq* "that which is frightening or causing fear."[87] Given the course of the story, we can assume that Kappia is scared of Shaman Guti, and he has every reason to be. After all, Shaman Guti is an evil shaman resembling the devil even though he appears to be none other than God himself: "**After all, Shaman Guti's name meant 'God'**" (181).

"The Exorcism" is not the first time in *Arctic Dreams and Nightmares* that the Christian God is associated with his adversary, Satan. In "When God Sings the Blues" (story seven, 44–57), the narrator tells readers about one of his "yearly spirit journey[s] to visit God," visits that he cherishes because they give him "the opportunity to try [his] hand at outwitting this particular God" (45). The narrator leaves no doubt that "this particular God" is the Christian God when he states that this God has "exclusive rights to the biggest-selling book of all time, called **The Bible**" (49; boldface in original). Yet readers learn at the beginning of the story that this God goes by the name of Sattaanassee (46), an Inuktitutized version of the word Satan used by Roman Catholic and Anglican missionaries in the Arctic about 100 years ago.[88] That the narrator undertakes his yearly spirit journey to visit the Christian God "on winter solstice" (45) is ironic given that the traditional Inuit winter solstice festivities were replaced with Christmas after the introduction of Christianity in the Arctic.[89] Although "When God Sings the Blues" represents a more lenient treatment of Christian religion than does "The Exorcism," it is nonetheless clearly satiric in its use of irony and mockery and in its representation of the Christian God that borders on the blasphemous.[90] The satire here thus helps to lay the groundwork for the radical reading of Christianity in the last story of Ipellie's cycle.

In "The Exorcism," as we have seen, "**Shaman Guti's demons**" are linked to God and equated with the devil. They are also connected with evil shamanism, however, and thus link the latter with Christianity. It might seem ironic that the narrator ends his life story as one of the most powerful shamans in the Arctic world by saying, "After all, Shaman Guti's name meant God." This last sentence, however, is very subversive. At the beginning of his narration, the narrator fights the Christian notion of shamanism as devilish. Given the ending of his narration, what he is really fighting is Christianity itself. As readers learn in the course of his narration, shamanism is not evil per se. Instead, the Christian religion amounts to a form of evil shamanism, at least in the context of the colonization of the Inuit: the demons that befall Kappia's *family of ten* are the *ten faces* mocking the narrator in story one, "Self-Portrait: Inverse Ten Commandments." The reversal that began with the narrator's "ascension" to a Jesus-like position, as suggested in the description of his crucifixion (story four), is thus completed when the narrator equates the Christian God with both the devil and an evil shaman. In other words, as Christianity is exorcised from contemporary Inuit cultures with the help of *tupilanniq*, an ancient shamanic ritual, Inuit shamanism is restored as the main reference point for traditional Inuit peoples. That the narrator describes the ritual performed to expel God from the Arctic as an exorcism doubles the irony in this last story—especially considering that the techniques and rituals of exorcism taught to Canadian Inuit by Christian missionaries were meant for exorcising their shamanic beliefs (see Ch. 1 in this volume).

The phrases discussed above—

a. "Shaman Guti's demons" (179; oxymoron),
b. "horns of the demon" (180; symbol),
c. "hissing like a snake" (180; simile),
d. "wearing a chained cross around its neck" (181; symbol), and
e. "After all, Shaman Guti's name meant 'God'" (181; metaphor)

— are dynamically equivalent to holophrases in Indigenous languages because they have equivalent functions. First, as figures of speech, each phrase expresses the core of a complex idea whose hidden meaning readers must gather for themselves. Second, within "The Exorcism," these phrases stand as significant narrative units that provide important links to previous stories, links that are anything but accidental. The description of "**Shaman Guti's demons**" associates God with the devil and simultaneously links the last story in Ipellie's story cycle with "When God Sings the Blues" and "Self-Portrait: Inverse Ten Commandments." The description of the demon that befalls Kappia's wife—"**horns of the demon**," "**hissing like a snake**," and "**wearing a chained cross around its neck**"—evokes the story of how Adam and Eve are expelled from the Garden of Eden but also contains an intratextual reference to the Garden of Nede in story one, "Self-Portrait: Inverse Ten Commandments."[91] The description of the demon's necklace as "a chained cross around its neck" also connects "The Exorcism" with "I, Crucified," the last story in the narrative's opening, which tells the story of the narrator's crucifixion and contains intertextual references to the Bible. The phrase "**After all, Shaman Guti's name meant 'God'**" completes the equation of Christianity with the devil and evil shamanism already alluded to in the phrases describing Shaman Guti's demons. As such, this phrase simultaneously provides a link to the first story, which now more clearly than before can be interpreted as an embracing and celebration of Inuit shamanism.

As significant narrative units that are semantically dense, the phrases that I have pointed out as significant in "The Exorcism" can thus also be regarded as paraholophrases. However, unlike those found in "Arctic Dreams and Nightmares," they point to a far more overt criticism of Christianity. Drawing intratextual references particularly to the opening of Ipellie's story cycle, the paraholophrases of "The Exorcism" not only complete the narrative's frame, then, by ending the closing that began in "Arctic Dreams and Nightmares" but also mark the culmination of the narrator's concatenation of stories, which move from a seemingly Christian point of view to a mocking of the Christian God and which eventually end in his figurative exorcism.

The closing of *Arctic Dreams and Nightmares* differs slightly from its opening in that it contains within it stories that do not include any paraholophrases. These stories, nonetheless, are part of the closing and therefore bear a certain narrative importance. As noted above, they are very traditional compared with the other stories in the cycle, which also include traditional features of Inuit cultures but interweave them with elements from Euro-Western cultures. Stories sixteen through nineteen are intriguing as well because they explicitly focus on one thing: sex. "Love Triangle" tells a well-known story of adultery, but the names of the characters provide an added twist. Ossuk is having an affair with Aqaqa, the wife of Nalikkaaq. When the names are translated into English, however, Penis is having an affair with Vagina, the wife of Crotch. These names, therefore, are examples of synecdoche. Phrases such as "Ossuk is a stranger in my life" (137) or "The thought of Ossuk entering the private parts of his wife Aqaqa" (139) thus become highly ambiguous. So "Love Triangle" ends with a wrestling match between the two men in which Ossuk's penis is torn off by Nalikkaaq; the story's subtext seems to promote procreation as much as it suggests Nalikkaaq's homosexuality, a theme that is elaborated on in story eighteen, "The Agony and the Ecstasy." This story also showcases the skilful use of personal names. Prince Char is the homosexual son of Queen Elisapee (a common Inukttitutization of Elisabeth) and Prince Pilipoosee. Since the correct Inuktitutization of Philip would be Pilipi,[92] Prince Char's father's name can be seen as a play on words suggesting the female sexual organ and can be read as an indication of the Inuit third gender that Prince Char's father represents, if unknowingly. The character of Prince Char also strengthens the notion of a third gender: not only does he lament that he should have been born a female (168), but his parents are also immensely relieved when, after years of cross-dressing, Prince Char symbolically turns into a man by capturing his first seal (167). Curiously enough, this life-shaping event occurs at the end of his puberty: that is, at that point in Inuit transvestites' lives when their transvestism would usually be reversed.[93] Story seventeen, "Hunting for Skins and Fur" (154–59), is similarly provocative when it compares prostitution with an ancient hunting ritual involving the abuse of exotic dancers. Story nineteen, "The Woman Who Married a Goose," is far less reproachful in that it is a variation of stories from ancient times that tell of humans having sexual intercourse with animals. With sex as their central theme, these four stories embraced by "Arctic Dreams and Nightmares" and "The Exorcism" literally build up to the final story, which bears strong sexual and reproductive references in the nakedness of Kappia's wife, her vagina, and the images of childbirth evident in the exorcism of Shaman Guti. More importantly, however, these four stories—more clearly than the preceding stories so rich in references to Euro-Western cultures—*write back* Inuit cultural traditions (including the lack of sexual taboos) and thus make possible the move from the implied criticism of Christianity in "Arctic Dreams and Nightmares" to its overt criticism in "The Exorcism," which, in turn, paves the way for a more explicit embracing of Inuit shamanism.

Having finished the telling of "The Exorcism," the narrator ends his life story; however, with Shaman Guti's ten demons pointing to the ten squalid heads in the narrator's self-portrait in story one, his life story begins yet again. The cyclical narration thus achieved emphasizes the importance of the narrator's performance of a *tupilanniq*. Once this frame becomes obvious—and on a first reading it can become obvious only once readers have reached the last sentence—*Arctic Dreams and Nightmares* appears to be even more traditional in outlook than is suggested by the use of elements from traditional Inuit cultures in the various stories, which include references to Sedna (story six), the blanket toss (story nine), husky dogs (story ten), seal hunting (story thirteen), and the role of the shaman in providing communities with sufficient food (stories six and fourteen). *Arctic Dreams and Nightmares* features a shaman as narrator and sometimes as protagonist. As the cycle tells his life story, readers witness his shamanic powers through writing. The interweaving of the stories with Euro-Western cultural elements suggests not a conflation of cultures but the possibility that shamanism—and by equation Inuit cultural traditions—can thrive in a contemporary world, no matter how strong the Euro-Western influences in the Arctic.

The stories in Ipellie's collection make sense when read in isolation; however, by arranging them within a narrative frame that symbolically exorcises the Christian influence in the Arctic, Ipellie has invested them with additional meaning and power. This narrative frame relies on the extensive use of paraholophrases to evoke the generic conventions of traditional Indigenous oratures and define the narrative's interpretative context. As in Alunik's *Call Me Ishmael*, this frame is not marked in the text but must be uncovered by readers, whose participation in the composition of *Arctic Dreams and Nightmares* is therefore doubly invited. The paraholophrases constituting the narrative's frame, then, serve as a strategy in textualizing orality. Not only do they provide the cultural and interpretative context of the story cycle, but they also indicate the author's involvement with his audience, on whose participation the composition of *Arctic Dreams and Nightmares* ultimately depends.

Paraholophrases with Other Narrative Functions

Paraholophrases in the main part of *Arctic Dreams and Nightmares* often establish connections with the narrative's opening or closing. In "**Summit with Sedna**, the Mother of Sea Beasts" (story six, 34–42), the narrator and other shamans calm down a sexually frustrated Sedna by putting her into a dream-trance that leads her to have an orgasm. Once she is sexually satisfied, she releases the sea mammals that the Inuit so desperately depend on for survival (41). The explicit sexual references in this story (35), including the ambiguity of its title, are anticipated by the "**ecstatic journey to the Milky Way**" in "I, Crucified" (story four). In this last story of the opening, the first-person narrator is lured into a community's camp under the pretext that he and other shamans "attempt" this journey. The narrator is fascinated by the idea of "eventually explor[ing] beyond the universe" (23)—most readers will thus associate this planned ecstatic journey with an exploration of outer space, an endeavour that is far from unusual given that Inuit shamans traditionally travelled to the different Inuit afterworlds. The name Milky Way for the galaxy in which our solar system is located goes back to the Greek word for galaxy, *galaxias*, meaning "milky." According to the astronomer Eratosthenes (third century B.C.E.), the Milky Way formed when Heracles, while suckled by Hera, bit into her nipple, thus causing her to shoot milk into the sky.[94] Milky Way has thus also been used poetically to refer to a woman's breasts, particularly in the seventeenth century, which proved to be a "particularly good time for the Milky Way in English literature."[95] Providing a link to the thus equally ambiguous "**ecstatic journey to the Milky Way**," "**Summit with Sedna**" helps to disrupt the linearity of the narrative by way of an intratextual reference.

"When God Sings the Blues" (story seven) also contains two strong references to the narrative's opening. Sattaanassee—the name that the Christian God has assigned to himself, according to the narrator—evokes notions of the devil as found in story one, "Self-Portrait: Inverse Ten Commandments." Moreover, "When God Sings the Blues" twice picks up the Inuit notion of the soul as a bubble, first introduced in "Nanuq, the White Ghost, Repents" (story three):

> [...] Entering the Magical Kingdom was a lot like entering a **soap bubble** without bursting it. No wonder the Magical Kingdom had

a scent similar to an underarm deodorant. One could not take a sniff and feel like a well-washed soul. [...]

Sattaanassee was a bit of an eccentric who dwelled inside a **huge bubble** that hovered right at the edge of the universe. (47–48)

The narrator's description of Sattaanassee's dwelling as a bubble can be read as an equation of Sattaanassee with the soul of Christianity—a very subversive suggestion considering the etymology of the name. The comparison of Sattaanassee's residence to a particular kind of bubble, a soap bubble that smells like deodorant, has another connotation. Not only does this comparison ridicule Christianity, but it also hints at the eventual downfall of Christianity in the last story of *Arctic Dreams and Nightmares*. After all, soap bubbles do not last longer than a few moments before they burst. True, the narrator mentions that this particular soap bubble does not burst when *he* enters it, but the possibility that it will eventually burst remains nonetheless. Both phrases, "**soap bubble**" and "**huge bubble**," thus carry a surplus of meaning that points readers to both the opening and the closing of the narrative.

Finally, "**Trying to Get to Heaven**" (story nine, 68–74) evokes story two of the opening, "Ascension of My Soul in Death." In story nine, the narrator comes upon a group of people gathering for what he believes to be "the annual blanket toss": a man is tossed up into the air in a huge hide blanket, his "palms together as if he was presenting himself to the gods" (70).[96] When the narrator inquires about the scene, he learns that the man's name is Shaman Qilaliaq and that he is "**trying to get to Heaven**" (69, 72). The narrator laughs at the thought but is assured by an onlooker that "This is serious business" (72). Still, the narrator cannot quit laughing and ends up being put onto the blanket and tossed into the sky. Unlike Shaman Qilaliaq, however, the narrator disappears into the clouds (74); in other words, he leaves the earth and "dies," thus ending one of the many lives that he hints at in the narrative's opening. Before he dies, however, he remembers another shaman, Tookeetooq, who, after the introduction of Christianity in the Arctic, thought he was able to get to heaven by his own power. Tookeetooq built a big igloo that lacked a roof and told everyone that he would jump through its opening, ascending to heaven. He undressed until he was completely naked and jumped, "balls and penis thrashing about as he leaped higher and higher" (73–74), making himself an object of ridicule. The story of Tookeetooq is an abridged parody of a story told by Peter Pitseolak in *People from Our Side* about "the first religious time" when people "overdid their religion."[97] The version in *Arctic Dreams and Nightmares* includes important details, such as the shaman's "male organs [...] swinging all over the place."[98] Pitseolak's story is discussed by Robin McGrath as an important example of new Inuit satire in prose.[99] The satiric element remains in the parody in *Arctic Dreams and Nightmares*, but as a story-within-a-story its context is shifted slightly with the effect that its criticism surpasses that of Pitseolak. Not only does the narrator ridicule Tookeetooq and Shaman Qilaliaq, but by making himself the protagonist of the story he is no longer merely an observer, as Pitseolak is in his telling. When the narrator manages to ascend to heaven (physically this time), he deliberately sets himself apart from Shaman Qilaliaq and Tookeetooq, who, "[b]eing mere mortal[s]," are "total failure[s]" (74). Ipellie's parody of "the first religious time," then, takes Pitseolak's satire a step further to achieve his narrative goals in *Arctic Dreams and Nightmares*—to write back shamanism into contemporary Inuit cultures against the presence of Christianity. Besides the intertextual reference to Pitseolak's story, story nine contains intratextual references to story two, "Ascension of My Soul in Death," in which the narrator puts himself on an equal level with Jesus, as well as to story fifteen, "Arctic Dreams and Nightmares," which has the narrator and God living in the same kind of paradise.

To summarize, these phrases (and possible compounds[100])—

a. "ecstatic journey to the Milky Way" (23; metaphor),
b. "Summit with Sedna" (35; metaphor),
c. "soap bubble" (47; symbol),
d. "huge bubble" (48; symbol), and
e. "trying to get to Heaven" (69, 72; metaphor)

— feature prominently in *Arctic Dreams and Nightmares* because, as figures of speech, these phrases refer to complex ideas but explicitly mention only their cores; thus, though these phrases can stand on their own, they also connote a surplus of meaning that readers have to decipher on their own. Moreover, as intra- and/or intertextual references, they function as significant narrative units: first, they establish a narrative line that connects stories that do not immediately follow one another, thus ensuring that the narrative frame does not hang loosely but is attached to a narrative body in which Inuit cultural knowledge is intentionally re-evoked; second, by establishing occasional intertextual references, they keep the narrative exceptionally open and fluid. Given their functions, the phrases (and possible compounds) listed above, then, are dynamically equivalent to holophrases in Indigenous languages and thus qualify as paraholophrases. The narrative structure that they establish—a narrative line that nonetheless remains open and fluid—is visible, however, only to readers who make these connections because they recognize the contexts evoked by these paraholophrases. In other words, like the paraholophrases in the main part of *Call Me Ishmael*, those in the main part of *Arctic Dreams and Nightmares* complement and complete the textualization of orality achieved through the paraholophrases constituting the narrative's frame.

HOLOPHRASES AND HOLOPHRASTIC TRACES

Holophrases in *Arctic Dreams and Nightmares* are found solely in the narrative's personal names. Since the meanings of characters' names usually underscore the meanings of the stories in which these characters are featured, the "Glossary of Inuktitut Words and Their Meanings" at the end of Ipellie's book (183–84) is all the more essential for readers without any knowledge of Inuktitut. The glossary lists all the personal names that the first-person narrator does not translate directly in his narrative. Personal names are (1) taken from animals or nature (Nanuq—"polar bear," Nuna—"land," Ukjuarluk—"big bearded seal," Aivialuk—"big walrus"); (2) describe a character's appearance or an emotion (Tusujuarluk—"envious," Piu—"pretty," Too(t)keetooq[101]—"stupid," Kappia—"scared"); (3) concern sex or marital status (Ossuk—"penis," Nalikkaaq—"crotch," Aqaqa—"vagina," **Oiqangi**—"without a husband," **Nuliaqangi**—"without a wife"); or (4) have a religious background (Shaman **Qilaliaq**—Shaman "Going to Heaven").[102] Whether the personal names used in Ipellie's story cycle qualify as Inuktitut holophrases is difficult to decide when one does not speak Inuktitut. Even a dictionary might not always help, given the polysynthetic nature of Inuktitut. However, regardless of whether these names represent actual Inuktitut holophrases or not, they clearly mark the narrative as Inuit and serve to engage particularly non-Inuit readers, who are forced to overcome their ignorance if they want to participate fully in the narrative.

This participation is required also because of the particular way in which Ipellie uses Inuktitut words in his narrative: they are not foreign words incorporated into a sentence composed in English but are meant to function as personal names, hence their capitalization. The following examples will illustrate the difference. "[...] [M]y fellow shaman, *Ukjuarlak*, was discovered to be a hermaphrodite" (27; emphasis added). This statement can be translated in different ways. Paying attention only to the Inuktitut word's literal meaning, it translates thus: "[...] my fellow shaman, *big bearded seal*, was discovered to be a hermaphrodite." However, taking into account the capitalization of the Inuktitut word in the English text, this phrase should be translated as in the glossary (183). After all, the first-person narrator's fellow shaman, Ukjuarlak, is not a big bearded seal but either *looks* or *acts* like one: "[...] my fellow shaman, *Big Bearded Seal*, was discovered to be a hermaphrodite." This translation, however, is already a paraphrase of the following translation: "[...] my fellow shaman, *he who is like (or resembles) a big bearded seal*, was discovered to be a hermaphrodite."

Similarly, in another example, the Inuktitut word can be translated in different ways: "Then, *Tusujuarluk*, who happened to have the closest shamanic powers as mine, stabbed me in the right ribs" (25; emphasis added). It can be translated literally without consideration of its context: "Then, *envious*, who happened to have the closest shamanic powers as mine, stabbed me in the right ribs." Or it can be translated in accordance with the translation given in the glossary (183): "Then, *Envious*, who happened to have the closest shamanic powers as mine, stabbed me in the right ribs." However, as in the case of Ukjuarlak, the translation above is actually already a paraphrase of the following: "Then, *he who is envious*, who happened to have the closest shamanic powers as mine, stabbed me in the right ribs." Because of the way in which the name Tusujuarluk is incorporated into the narrative, it does not mean "envious" but "he who is envious."

As already noted in the discussion of the personal names of Aqaqa, Nalikkaaq, and Ossuk, Inuktitut words in *Arctic Dreams and Nightmares* involve synecdoche: they use for a person's name that person's defining characteristic.[103] As such, these words can be read as examples of traditional Indigenous name giving. Indigenous personal names tend to be very descriptive, and, as pointed out by David and Kathrine French, personal names "not only designated persons but also 'meant,' or alluded to, something else," such as place of birth, astronomical or climatic phenomena, the environment, the person's characteristics, or life events. Because Indigenous personal names translated literally into English make up a whole phrase (at times even a holophrase), they usually cannot be "directly matched with a name lexeme in English."[104] That Inuktitut words in *Arctic Dreams and Nightmares* are used as personal names reminiscent of traditional Indigenous name giving, however, is not the only reason why they are suggestive of holophrasis in Indigenous discourse. Ipellie's use of Inuktitut words as examples of synecdoche is based on a grammatical feature of many Indigenous languages, including Inuktitut: the lack of a copula (the verb *to be* and its various forms).[105] Inuktitut words in Ipellie's story cycle, then, might not always qualify as holophrases, but their function within the narrative, their very context of use, makes them holophrase-like: every time readers stumble across an Inuktitut word in the text, they must add "(s)he who is like/resembles" to the word's translation into English. Because they suggest complex ideas, Inuktitut words in *Arctic Dreams and Nightmares* function as figures of speech: that is, they invite reader participation and thus further strengthen the culturally specific nature of the strategies in textualizing orality employed by Ipellie in his story cycle.

Not included in the glossary of *Arctic Dreams and Nightmares* are a number of personal names that could be described as Inuktitutized English names: Sattaanassee (46) for Satan;[106] Joanassee (12) for John; Elisapee (161) for Elisabeth; Pilipoosee (161), a wordplay on Pilipi, for Philip; and Guti (177) for God. These Inuktitutized personal names must sound fake to native speakers of Inuktitut and, as such, can be assumed to indicate a tone of mockery. Since all characters bearing such fake Inuktitut personal names have a clearly Euro-Western frame of reference—the biblical John, God, Satan, and the British Royal Family—this mocking tone should not surprise us: it is consistent with Ipellie's criticism of colonialism and of the Christian religion and its influence in the Arctic.

In *Arctic Dreams and Nightmares*, then, Inuktitut words and holophrases have several functions. First, they function as textual markers that "write back" Inuktitut into a text composed in the colonizer's tongue, thus situating the text within its appropriate linguistic context. Second, the use of Inuktitut words indicates the author's involvement with his audience by defining readers' relationship to the text and hence the terms and conditions of their participation; since they function as personal names and involve synecdoche, these Inuktitut words are even more demanding of readers than if they were used in a more literal sense. Third and above all, however, Ipellie's careful choice of personal names—either in Inuktitut or in Inuktitutized form—underscores the political stance implied in the narrative. It makes sense that a narrative that involves a reinvention of Inuit (religious) traditions also applies the traditional naming habits practised by Inuit in the precontact era, particularly given the importance of personal names in Inuit religion. Ipellie's code switching in the form of Indigenous name giving, then, functions as a strategy in textualizing orality that is doubly culturally specific: it points to the narrative's linguistic origin, indicates the author's involvement, and invites readers' participation, all the while enforcing the narrative's message, which rests on a considered use of paraholophrases.

While *Arctic Dreams and Nightmares* thus effectively employs holophrase-like code switching in its Inuktitut and Inuktitutized names, *holophrastic traces*, on the other hand, play only a marginal role in this text. *Arctic Dreams and Nightmares* features *complex N N compounds*, such as "caribou skin-blanket" (3), "life-long sexual history" (39), "beluga whale harpoon" (139, 140, 141), "championship tennis match" (97), "Dog People Society" (87), "European Economic Community Parliament" (109), and "male gender exclusive club" (157). These examples are partially reminiscent of the possibility in Indigenous languages of combining an infinite number of morphemes to form a new and more complex word. As noted in the previous chapter, however, these complex N N compounds are not as suggestive of holophrastic structures in Indigenous languages as, for example, *synthetic compounds* or *deverbal N N compounds*. Most compounds in Ipellie's story cycle that contain a verbal component use the latter as (part of) a modifier, such as in "breathing holes" (42), "shrinking man" (129), "white-coated baby harp seal pup" (106), and "societal cut-throat rat races" (120). One of the few *synthetic compounds* in his story cycle is "blues shouter" (53). What is interesting about the compounds in *Arctic Dreams and Nightmares*, aside from their specific makeup, is the fact that, unlike those in *Call Me Ishmael* (see the previous chapter), they no longer concern only traditional elements from Inuit cultures but also denote Euro-Western or contemporary objects or ideas.

As noted in the discussion of Alunik's collection of stories and essays in the previous chapter, compounding marks an inventive use of language that produces semantically dense words; it therefore indicates the author's involvement with reality as much as it demands the participation of readers, who must decode the compounds and are thus invited to picture certain parts of the story more vividly.[107] The closer that compounds in *Arctic Dreams and Nightmares* come to re-creating the structure of holophrases (i.e., synthetic compounds such as "blues shouter" rather than complex root compounds such as "caribou skin-blanket"), the more culturally specific this strategy in textualizing orality becomes. Nominal compounds with a verbal constituent, particularly as heads, however, are relatively rare in *Arctic Dreams and Nightmares*. Thus, the use of direct holophrastic traces is a relatively minor strategy in the textualizing of orality in Ipellie's story cycle.

Indirect holophrastic traces in *Arctic Dreams and Nightmares* are also fairly sparse: features of discourse that can be associated with holophrasis are restricted entirely to *pronoun copying* and *subject dropping*. Several examples of pronoun copying include "Kamikaze animals, them" (126), "There they were. Two, fully grown, sagging breasts!" (31), and "Yes. Just around the next mountain. Paradise can be found there" (126). Such sentences produce an oral effect: they create fragmentary discourse and mimic intonation units in oral speech. Reminiscent of the seemingly (i.e., from the perspective of Indo-European languages) redundant structure in Indigenous discourse caused by the holistic nature of polysynthetic verbs, these examples of pronoun copying or, more generally, of dislocation textualize orality by recourse to a culturally specific strategy. Examples occur only randomly in *Arctic Dreams and Nightmares*.

Most instances of subject dropping in *Arctic Dreams and Nightmares* do not concern conjugated verb forms (as in "Fine. Suits me" [139]) but involve infinitives or present participles:

> This is how we humans evolve. *To attain* nourishment from the flesh of animals. *To drink* from nature. *To pluck* out the plants of the tundra. (125; emphasis added)

> And there, in the midst, hell's creatures crawl over my soul. *Drawing* blood. *Amputating* my limbs. *Sucking* out my lifeblood. (127; emphasis added)

> It is this dizziness that we take into our waking hours. Never *knowing* whether or not we are really awake or still asleep. *Thinking* that we are actually awake when we are not. (128; emphasis added)

Regardless of the particular grammatical verb form, subject dropping always imitates the intonation units in oral speech and is indicative of both author involvement and reader participation. These instances of subject dropping in *Arctic Dreams and Nightmares* concerning verbs in infinitives or present participles, moreover, involve the use of parallelism, a "rhetorical device found widely in North American folktales."[108] By attempting to express grammatical subjects through context, subject dropping in English discourse mimics the independence of holophrases, which produce meaningful sentences without the use of independent noun phrases. Subject dropping in *Arctic Dreams and Nightmares* can thus be regarded as a holophrastic trace that functions as a strategy in textualizing orality that is culturally specific. Its oral effect notwithstanding, subject dropping, like pronoun copying, is found only rarely in Ipellie's story cycle.

There remains yet another interesting connection to holophrastic language structures in *Arctic Dreams and Nightmares*: the pen-and-ink drawings that accompany the various stories. Each story begins with a full-page pen-and-ink drawing. Since the drawing is also found, albeit in a smaller size, on every left-hand margin of the respective story, it can hardly be ignored by a reader. The story titles seem to apply as much to the corresponding pen-and-ink drawings as to the stories themselves.

As noted in the previous chapter, illustration has been part of Inuit storytelling traditions. In "Image Making in Arctic Art," Edmund Carpenter describes the connection between Inuit stories and Inuit ivory carvings as follows: "Eskimo tales share this quality [of being independent, self-contained]. Generally the narrator speaks only of things you can touch and see. He constantly chooses the concrete word, in phrase after phrase, forcing you to touch and see. No speaker so insistently teaches the general through the particular. *He has mastery over the definite, detailed, particular, visualized image.*"[109] The connecting piece between story and carving, for Carpenter, is the polysynthetic nature of the Inuit language: "What we call action," he explains, "Eskimos see and describe as a pattern of succeeding *impressions*."[110]

By including both writing and drawings, *Arctic Dreams and Nightmares* ignores the boundaries between distinct kinds of arts. The provocative drawings do not leave observers with much room for avoidance. A reader not wishing to engage with a story can readily escape it; confronted with a drawing, however, a reader cannot escape it so easily: it captures the attention, instantly and fully, causing either interest or disgust.[111] At the same time, however, the visual is not enough to carry the full message. It needs the story to complete the narrative line, to draw the connections, to add tone and "voice"—that is, to form the narrative cycle. Verbal art and fine art thus complement each other in Ipellie's story cycle.

Illustrations are found in much contemporary Inuit writing, including Markoosie's *Harpoon of the Hunter*, Peter Pitseolak's *People from Our Side* and *Pictures out of My Life*, and Ishmael Alunik's *Call Me Ishmael*, discussed in the previous chapter. Their presence in *Arctic Dreams and Nightmares*, though, is stark and pervasive. In fact, as visual depictions of the cores of the respective stories, Ipellie's pen-and-ink drawings can be said to function as "visualized holophrases": they express both the main event of the story and the main participant(s) involved. The ink drawing opening the story "The Dogteam Family" (76), for example, shows a "man [...] using a woman, probably his wife, for a sledge! A team of infant children were pulling their mother with their umbilical cords still attached to their belly buttons from their mother's vagina" (83). And, just as the man in the story is travelling away from the narrator, so too the man in the drawing is rushing away from the observer's (thus reader's) eye. Narrator and audience thus become equals.

Even though *Arctic Dreams and Nightmares* is a publication rather than an exhibition, the blurring of generic boundaries that results from the inclusion of the pen-and-ink drawings increases its potential for engaging its audience, over and above what might be possible if this were simply a collection of stories. The "visualized holophrases" therefore lend the textualization of orality in *Arctic Dreams and Nightmares* a further culturally specific dimension and share the same function as the code switching in the story cycle: namely, to emphasize the political message hidden in the narrative.

SUMMARY

Paraholophrases in *Arctic Dreams and Nightmares* primarily serve two narrative purposes: (1) they help to construct a cyclical narrative frame that evokes one of the generic conventions of traditional Indigenous oratures, all the while defining its *interpretative context*; and (2) they constitute a narrative line that is nonetheless open and fluid in order to construct a narrative body without which the narrative frame would have little force. These paraholophrases are *dynamic equivalents* to holophrases in that they serve functions in English discourse similar to the functions of holophrases in Indigenous languages: not only do paraholophrases in Ipellie's story cycle function as significant narrative units, but they are also semantically dense and, as holophrases proper in Indigenous languages (see the introduction), denote a minimalism of text that invites readers' participation in the creation of meaning. Whether the text's message comes across to readers depends, however, on whether they become engaged with the narrative and can identify both the frame and the narrative line—and the connection between the two; this, in turn, depends heavily on whether readers are able to recognize the narrative's paraholophrases. Paraholophrases in *Arctic Dreams and Nightmares* thus not only show the *author's involvement* with his readers but also mark the author's invitation to his readers to *participate* in the text's composition, which involves, in particular, the uncovering of its religious, and ultimately historical, *context*. "Uncovering," in this case, begins with reading the stories sequentially and entirely, because otherwise the narrative's structure, on which the text's message rests, falls apart completely. In other words, Ipellie's story *cycle* points to the importance of the interconnectedness of stories in Indigenous oratures and hence places *Arctic Dreams and Nightmares* well within Inuit verbal art traditions despite its rather contemporary outlook.

Although holophrases and holophrastic traces are not prominent in *Arctic Dreams and Nightmares*, we can identify some of them. Code switching in *Arctic Dreams and Nightmares* is holophrase-like because it involves the use of Inuktitut words as examples of synecdoche. The narrative assigns Inuktitut names to some of its characters by using for a person's name that person's defining characteristic. These monolexical Inuktitut words translate into whole phrases in English; they are therefore semantically dense. Code switching in *Arctic Dreams and Nightmares*, then, not only provides the narrative with its *linguistic context*. Functioning as figures of speech, Inuktitut words in Ipellie's story cycle further increase the *reader participation* already achieved through the code switching. Ipellie's code switching, then, points to strategies of conceptual orality that result from the context of language use (context, involvement, and participation) and qualifies as a culturally specific strategy at least insofar as it applies Inuktitut to an English text in a way that is holophrase-like. That Ipellie continues Indigenous traditions of name giving in a narrative featuring an Inuit shaman as protagonist and narrator strengthens the narrative's message and therefore complements the effect of the narrative's paraholophrases.

Holophrastic traces in *Arctic Dreams and Nightmares* include *compounds* (complex N N and deverbal compounds as well as, to a lesser degree, synthetic compounds) as well as *pronoun copying* and *subject dropping*. With the inclusion of these particular types of holophrastic traces, Ipellie's story cycle ensures that its use of culturally specific strategies in textualizing orality concerns elements of conceptual orality that result from both the context of language *production*—pronoun copying and subject dropping create prosody, redundancy, and fragmentation—and the context of language *use*—the compounds used by Ipellie are indicative of author involvement and create reader participation.

Finally, the pen-and-ink drawings in Ipellie's story cycle assume the role of "visualized holophrases": they express the cores of the respective stories and, as such, invite reader participation and thereby textualize orality. Conflating verbal and fine art in one whole, Ipellie points to the correlation between the verbal and the visual—both are semiotic systems—and the role that this correlation plays particularly in Inuktitut. As visualized holophrases, the pen-and-ink drawings thus compensate for the relative paucity of holophrases and holophrastic traces in *Arctic Dreams and Nightmares*.

That Ipellie's book employs comparatively few holophrases and holophrastic traces might be surprising given his knowledge of Inuktitut as an ancestral language; however, Ipellie already belongs to a generation of contemporary Inuit *authors* who write fiction and are well aware of the diversity of their audience, whereas Alunik, as I argued in the previous chapter, remains a *storyteller* in his writing. *Arctic Dreams and Nightmares* is a story cycle but a fictional one. Although Ipellie admits in the introduction to the book that "Some of the stories and drawings inspired are true in a sense they happened in [his] dreams and nightmares," and though the first drawing in the collection has been described as his "self portrait,"[112] Ipellie also points out that "Still other stories and drawings came to [him] inspired by [his] ancestors' gift for inventing myths, stories, and legends" (xix). *Arctic Dreams and Nightmares*, then, was inspired by his personal life, his people's history, and their cultural, religious, and literary traditions—just as any other work referred to as fiction is inspired by this complex web of personal, communal, and other stories.

Although there is a strong insistence in *Call Me Ishmael* on the stories being "fact," we do not encounter this insistence in Ipellie's story cycle. Accordingly, *Arctic Dreams and Nightmares* does not feature the frequent source citing found in Alunik's collection. The lack of source citing has another reason, of course. In *Call Me Ishmael*, Alunik tells his memoirs rather than his autobiography; hence, his stories are not completely his own; some of them have been given to him by others. The first-person narrator in Ipellie's story cycle, however, tells *nothing but* his own stories, which accordingly feature only events that he immediately experienced in his past lives. Moreover, whereas the I in *Call Me Ishmael* can be, and in fact should be, equated with Ishmael Alunik, the I in *Arctic Dreams and Nightmares* must not be confused with Alootook Ipellie. Although Ipellie's story cycle thus lacks the authority usually assigned to a storyteller (even if s/he appears in print), the position of the narrator in *Arctic Dreams and Nightmares* as one of the most powerful Inuit shamans in the Arctic grants him authority at least in the realm of fiction. Given his spiritual abilities, the shaman is the one who can best fulfill the role of maintaining the (religious) tradition of Inuit peoples. "You [i.e., an ordinary person] can't see spirits," the Inuinnait Hellen Kongitok says. "Only the shamans can see them or talk to them."[113] Some Inuit groups even traditionally associated the *angakkuq* with a storyteller.[114] The narrator in *Arctic Dreams and Nightmares* has therefore been read by Hanne Birk as both *angakkuq* and storyteller, who serves as "the nexus of the culturally specific construction of collective memory" on the levels of both story and discourse. By sharing his life stories and his knowledge of the spiritual world, the shaman-narrator of *Arctic Dreams and Nightmares* reinforces traditional Inuit religious beliefs and customs. This traditional knowledge is imparted to readers in the fitting form of a story cycle, with the first-person narrator, a powerful shaman, as its focal point. That is, traditional knowledge is passed on by way of constructing a narrative "voice" representing an *angakkuq*.[115] When, during the first exhibition of his *Arctic Dreams and Nightmares* drawings in 1989, Ipellie was asked about the rather awkward beginning of this series of drawings, he commented "that the images are not of death as an ending, but of death as a new beginning, a rebirth—the artist's new life as a soul."[116] Although Ipellie refers here to the artist-narrator's rebirth, on a much broader level *Arctic Dreams and Nightmares* is about the rebirth of a whole culture. Transforming the role of the *angakkuq* into that of a story-writer, Ipellie sketches a way to preserve Inuit traditional cultures in writing and against the odds of modern Canadian society: his story cycle writes back Inuit shamanism—and thus the essence of the traditional Inuit belief system—into the contemporary Inuit world.[117]

As we move from Alunik to Ipellie, we see that the stories have changed from fact to fiction; the former *writes a hitherto oral tradition* (Inuvialuit/Inupiat), whereas the latter *reinvents Inuit cultural traditions* using fiction. Despite their differences, however, these story-writers both turn to the paraholophrase as a discourse device to help them construct their texts in attempts to pass on their ancestors' heritage. That Ipellie's story cycle has moved further away from some traditional Indigenous storytelling practices (such as source citing) has much to do with its engagement with Euro-Western literary forms. Yet *Arctic Dreams and Nightmares* does not refrain completely from the use of Inuktitut holophrases and holophrastic traces. They might be less diverse and less frequent than those in *Call Me Ishmael*, but as catalysts of the message passed on in Ipellie's story cycle, which in turn rests heavily on the use of paraholophrases, they are nevertheless employed to a maximum effect.

Our focus thus far has been on holophrastic readings of story (and essay) collections, which, though they can and should be read as containing one narrative, nonetheless come closer to traditional Indigenous oratures and their story cycles than do contemporary Indigenous novels in English, which engage more freely with Euro-Western literary traditions. How (para)holophrases feature in contemporary Indigenous novels in English is discussed in the holophrastic readings of Richard Van Camp's *The Lesser Blessed* and Thomas King's *Green Grass, Running Water* in the chapters that follow.

CHAPTER 3

"Busy Looking for Juliet Hope":
Richard Van Camp's *The Lesser Blessed*

Richard Van Camp was born in 1971 and belongs to a generation of young Indigenous authors in Canada that marks a new period in Indigenous writing. Members of this new generation often do not speak their ancestral languages, have sometimes taken extensive training in creative writing, and either address Indigenous matters without reservation or, in some cases, turn to non-Indigenous themes altogether, as does Eden Robinson (Haisla/Heiltsuk) in her second novel, *Blood Sports* (2006). Van Camp grew up in Fort Smith, Northwest Territories, or, as he refers to the town, "the homeland of my traditional enemy, the Chipewyan and Cree."[1] His parents, who are both Dogrib, had moved there to ensure that their children received the best available schooling. Although his mother speaks Dogrib despite having attended residential school, Van Camp does not speak his ancestral language because his parents decided that he should learn French instead so that he could go to college or university. He has thus always had to use translators to communicate with his grandparents, who speak only Dogrib, but what Van Camp calls his "horrible French" did not prevent him from receiving a university education.[2] He attended the En'owkin International School of Writing in Penticton, British Columbia, graduated from the University of Victoria with a bachelor's degree in writing, and obtained a master's degree in creative writing from the University of British Columbia. His first novel, *The Lesser Blessed*, was published in 1996 and earned him the 1997 Canadian Authors Association Air Canada Award.

THE TEXT: *THE LESSER BLESSED*

The title of *The Lesser Blessed* is taken from "Celebrate," a song by the British gothic rock band Fields of the Nephilim (see Van Camp's acknowledgements). A quotation from the song and the funeral scriptural reading "He accepted them as a holocaust" (Book of Wisdom 3: 1–9) serve as the novel's epigraph. Fallen angels, fire, death, God, and hope—*The Lesser Blessed* wavers between extremes. As one reviewer put it, *The Lesser Blessed*

> is not just painfully honest, it is hysterically funny. Van Camp mixes pleasure and pain so well in this first novel that as the reader wipes away the tears, they can't help but uproariously laugh out loud. Van Camp also reminds us that although we all may be the lesser blessed, our lives are blessed with love and laughter.[3]

Another reviewer, Geary Hobson (Cherokee-Quapaw/Chickasaw), has called *The Lesser Blessed* "a well-wrought tragi-comedy"[4] that, I might add, feels anything but constructed. On the contrary, the fusing of prose with poetry, of catastrophe with romance, of tears with laughter comes across naturally in Van Camp's debut novel. So does the weaving together of various different narrative strands as well as the incorporation of traditional Dogrib stories into a novel set in contemporary times.

Plot and Narrative Structure

Van Camp himself has described *The Lesser Blessed* as "a brutal account of growing up in the Northwest Territories," a story that "is so sexual, so brutal, so gorgeous in its darkness and faith"[5] that, despite qualifying as juvenile literature, it reaches an audience that goes well beyond adolescents. The novel's first-person narrator, Larry Sole, is a sixteen-year-old Dogrib who lives in the fictional town of Fort Simmer, Northwest Territories. His mother's partner, Jed, is a Slavey who works as "a firefighter, a bush cook, a Ranger, a tour guide and a whole lot of other things as well" (3). He lives with Larry and his mother on and off only, but Larry identifies him as a father figure nonetheless. Larry comes across as a typical teenager: he loves hanging out with his best friend, Johnny Beck, listens to heavy metal, gets into occasional fistfights, smokes, hot-knives; most of all, he secretly fantasizes about Juliet Hope, who is, however, sexually involved with Johnny. When Juliet gets pregnant, Johnny abandons her, and she plans to go live with her aunt in Edmonton. Before she leaves town, however, Larry has a surprising and brief sexual encounter with her that helps him to face his future and brings the novel to a close.

The Lesser Blessed bears some resemblance to Richard Wagamese's novel *Keeper'n Me* (1994), which has a young Anishinaabe male (Garnet Raven) as one of its main characters and a homing plot (to use the term from William Bevis[6]) that tells the story of Garnet's return to his family's reserve in northern Ontario after having spent most of his life completely estranged from his cultural roots. However, there are marked differences as well between the two novels: Larry's return in *The Lesser Blessed* is not a physical one, his voice is much rawer than Garnet's, and much of Larry's story is never overtly told in the novel. Moreover, the narrative structure of *The Lesser Blessed*, despite involving only one instead of two first-person narrators, is far more complex than that of *Keeper 'n Me*. Van Camp's novel consists of three narrative strands composed primarily of prose but occasionally interwoven with poetic prose and free verse poems.

In the "main" narrative strand, Larry befriends Johnny Beck, a Métis and newcomer to Fort Simmer, and tells—so it seems—the story of losing his virginity. In the "psychological" narrative strand, which frequently interrupts the main narrative "through a number of finely crafted, fragmented flashbacks,"[7] Larry unwillingly revisits what, in the main narrative strand, he cryptically refers to as "my accident" (3) or "the accident" (58). Larry witnessed his dad raping both his mom (58) and his aunt (87–88). When one day his dad rapes him, too, by demanding oral sex from him (78), Larry finds a hammer, his "secret tusk," and slams it down onto his passed-out father (40, 56, 77, 78; quotation at 78). It is not clear how seriously Larry has injured him, but, when a fire breaks out in their house that Larry seems to have lit after having sniffed gas with his cousins (78–80), his father dies in the fire (1–2), while Larry and his cousins are able to flee the inferno, albeit with serious burns. Larry is transferred to the burn victim wing of the children's hospital in Edmonton (79–80, 86) and undergoes psychological treatment (1). Although the main narrative strand tells the real story of Larry's coming to grips with his accident and its consequences, the novel's core, in fact, is formed by the psychological narrative strand, even if it reveals the story of the accident only in short sketches that readers have to piece together for themselves. The key to Larry's future, however, is finally provided in the "mythological" narrative strand, which consists of a series of traditional Dogrib stories told either by Jed or by Larry, who receives most of his stories from Jed. These three narrative strands—main, psychological, and mythological—are intertwined with each other to form a closely knit narrative—or "a jigsaw puzzle," as Juliet calls Larry's burnt back (111)—that readers must untangle, or put together, for the novel to make sense.

The Lesser Blessed would read much like any other coming-of-age story if it did not include the psychological and mythological narrative strands. That the novel's first-person narrator is Native is not of great significance to the *main narrative*. Of course, Jazz the Jackal's racist jokes (45–46), the Raven talk (14, 22, 29, 31), the instances of code switching to Dogrib or Slavey (15, 16, 66, 83, 84), the references to bannock (6–7, 14–19), rat root (83–84), and going out hunting moose and caribou (24), as well as Larry's remark that "I'm Indian and I gotta watch it" (2),[8] all mark the main narrative as that of a Native person. Yet Larry's identity as a Native rather than a white teenager does not advance the plot in the main narrative, which is about what most teenagers love doing: listening to music, dancing, smoking, hotknifing, getting into occasional fist fights, and being in love. The mythological and psychological narrative strands, however, add cultural and historical contexts to *The Lesser Blessed* that turn this coming-of-age story into both a revival of Dogrib oral traditions in writing and a powerful social commentary on the legacy of the residential school system. *The Lesser Blessed* clearly discusses Indigenous issues, then, but it does so less overtly—if no less powerfully—than many other examples of contemporary Indigenous literatures in English, such as *Porcupines and China Dolls* by Robert Alexie.

"Half Dogrib and Half Pop Culture"

Richard Van Camp's writing has a strong contemporary edge to it. In fact, the inclusion of elements from popular culture in his work is one of the main differences that Van Camp, who describes himself as "half Dogrib and half pop culture," sees between his work and that of more established Indigenous writers:

> Well, I think a lot of our senior authors can speak their language. They certainly know more. They are a lot wiser. But, at the same time, I feel that I bring pop culture, a young wisdom, sensuality, and sexuality to my writing that maybe some of the older authors shy away from. Sometimes I find our trailbreakers shy away from erotica and from talking about medicine, but I don't. I write with respect, but I'm not afraid.[9]

With its sexual explicitness and use of pop culture, *The Lesser Blessed* makes a strong case for this kind of argument.

CHAPTER 3

Pop culture in *The Lesser Blessed* features mainly as references to popular music, particularly heavy metal music (Iron Maiden, AC/DC, Ozzy Osbourne, Van Halen, etc.), but there are also references to Patsy Cline, Creedence Clearwater Revival, and John Fogerty, the kind of music that Larry's mother and Jed like listening to. The references to particular songs or bands give Larry's narrative a contemporary touch, but at times they also function as intertextual references. Larry mentions, for example, the song "High School Confidential" by the Canadian new wave band Rough Trade, which he believes to have been "written for Juliet Hope" (27).

Yet, despite the strong influences of popular culture in *The Lesser Blessed*, Van Camp, who happens to be the first Dogrib author ever published, also includes ties to Dogrib culture and tradition in his work. The Dogribs are a northern Athabascan-speaking group of Dene who traditionally occupied the territory east of the Mackenzie River between Great Bear and Great Slave Lakes in the Northwest Territories.[10] Thus, their immediate neighbours were the Bearlakes (or Sahtú Denes), the Slaveys, the Chipewyans, and the Inuvialuit.[11] According to Kerry Abel, it is believed that the Dene, which today include the Gwich'ins, Bearlakes, Hares, Dogribs, Slaveys, Chipewyans, and Mountains, originally occupied the mountains along the Alaska-Yukon border and, probably after some catastrophe, dispersed into smaller groups that migrated in different directions to find new hunting grounds in the drainage system of the Mackenzie River, the Deh-cho. Thus, despite their shared ancestry, Abel further notes, the various Dene groups form heterogeneous peoples showing notable linguistic, cultural, and social differences.[12]

"Dogrib identity," according to June Helm, "remains elusive until after 1850." French and English sources between 1680 and 1770 make occasional references to the Dogribs, though none of the European explorers or traders at the time actually made contact with the people assigned this name. Moreover, Helm notes, early fur traders often subsumed the Dogribs under the Slaveys, who were eventually identified as an independent group in the 1860s.[13] The Dogribs generally refer to themselves as *doné*, meaning "the people,"[14] but to distinguish themselves from other Dene groups they call themselves "dog's rib," or *tłįchǫ*, though this does not seem to have been a term of self-designation prior to contact.[15] Europeans first heard of the Dogribs through the Crees, whom Helm believes to have referred to Athabascans in general as *atimospikay*,[16] meaning "dog's rib" (from *atim* "dog" and *ospikay* "rib"),[17] supposedly through "knowledge of the widely shared Athabascan legend of tribal creation by the mating of a woman with a dog."[18]

According to Helm, Dogrib oral traditions are a conflation of stories distinctive to the Dogribs with those that the Dogribs share with neighbouring

Dene (Slaveys, Chipewyans, and Yellowknives), including a story called "The Two Brothers" and the aforementioned story of "tribal creation by the mating of a woman with a dog."[19] Other historians and ethnologists, however, regard this creation story as distinctive to the Dogribs. Abel, for example, makes a distinction between the "Dogrib[, who] believed themselves to have descended from a dog, and other northern groups[, who] demonstrated considerable respect for canines, calling them brothers and relatives."[20] In fact, in an earlier article that Helm co-authored with the Dogrib elder Vital Thomas, she included his retellings of both the Two Brothers story and the Dogrib creation story but marked only the former as shared with other Dene groups.[21]

Besides the fieldnotes that Helm collected between 1959 and 1971, she refers to Alexander Mackenzie and Émile Petitot to support her observation regarding a shared creation story among Dogribs, Slaveys, Chipewyans, and Yellowknives.[22] Mackenzie (1822–92) notes in his *Journals and Letters* that the Chipewyans "were produced from a dog," but he does not mention any more details regarding this ancestry.[23] Similarly, Petitot (1838–1917) remarks in his *Autour du Grand Lac des Esclaves* that the "*Dènè Étcha-Ottinè* or Slaves, the *Dounié Espa-tpa-Ottinè* or Men of Goats, and the *Éta-Gottinè* or Men of the Mountains [...] claim the same origin" as the Dogribs, whose creation story Petitot retells in the same volume.[24] Petitot also refers to his *Traditions indiennes du Canada nord-ouest* for "all the variants of the fable on the Men-Dogs, among the Dene."[25] These other versions, however, are quite different from the Dogrib creation story that he presents in both volumes; though all these stories concern *hommes-chiens* (Men-Dogs), only the two Dogrib stories—"Légende nationale des Flancs-de-Chien" and "Origine des indiens flancs-de-chiens d'après eux-mêmes"—tell the story of a woman who marries a dog and whose offspring eventually become the first Dogrib people.[26]

Curiously enough, textualizations of non-Dogrib oral traditions designed as histories from within—at least those of which I am aware (Sahtú Dene and Slavey)—do not contain references to a story of a woman mating with a dog. Finally, one of the traditional Dogrib stories that Van Camp retells in *The Lesser Blessed* is explicitly identified in the narrative as a Dogrib, not a Dene, creation story (51–52).[27] Although there are notable similarities, then, among the Dene oral traditions, and though other Dene groups also claim to originate from dogs, we can thus assume that *the story of tribal creation* by a woman's mating with a dog, as told by Petitot and Van Camp, appears to be *distinctive to the Dogribs*. The distinctiveness of the Dogrib creation story might seem to be of interest only to anthropologists and critics of Indigenous oratures. However, since this creation story is woven into *The Lesser Blessed* with other Dogrib stories to form the mythological strand and, in many ways, provides the key to the novel, the question of its distinctiveness ultimately concerns literary critics studying Van Camp's debut novel.

A number of contemporary publications compile traditional stories of the Dene and Dogrib peoples. George Blondin (Sahtú Dene) has published three books of traditional Sahtú Dene stories,[28] and Slavey traditions from northern Alberta can be accessed in *Wolverine Myths and Visions*, a bilingual collection of Slavey stories compiled by the Dene Wodih Society.[29] Dogrib oral traditions have been textualized and published as well, though mainly by non-Dogribs. *The Book of Dene*, an English translation of Dene traditions that Petitot collected in the North, contains traditional Dogrib stories.[30] *Tale Spinners in a Spruce Tipi* is a collection of traditional Dogrib stories that the Nova Scotian Evalyn Gautreau recorded while living in the Great Slave Lake area in the 1970s.[31] In *Prophecy and Power among the Dogrib Indians*, June Helm relates Dogrib stories concerning Dogrib medicine power.[32] Armin Wiebe has combined various traditional Dogrib stories into one narrative in his novel *Tatsea*.[33] Of the Dogrib stories contained in *The Lesser Blessed*, I have been able to trace only one in the works just listed: namely, the Dogrib creation story.[34] Given that Van Camp's sources for his novel largely consisted of Dogrib material collected in the NWT Archives in Yellowknife and through interviews conducted with family members and relatives,[35] this is not surprising.

The first Dogrib story related in *The Lesser Blessed* is more a cultural teaching than an actual story. It describes how a Dogrib woman has to burn her hair when she gets it cut to avoid having to pick up every hair she dropped in her lifetime before going to heaven (6). The second Dogrib story in the novel is the Dogrib creation story. Larry's retelling of this widely told story—which is rather brief compared with other versions—relates how a Dogrib woman living alone in the bush gives birth to six puppies (51) (there are only three in Gautreau's version).[36] Larry does not mention why she gives birth to puppies instead of children, but, according to the versions told by Petitot, Gautreau, and Wiebe, this woman, before being thrown out of her brother's camp, was married to a magical dog who was human by day but dog at night.[37] According to Larry's story in *The Lesser Blessed*, one day the woman hears strange human noises when leaving her camp to check her snares and, upon further inquiries, finds out that her puppies have turned into children. The woman chases after them, and the puppies try to get back to the bag in which the woman kept them. Only three of them make it, and they turn back into puppies. The woman catches the other three, a girl and two boys, and they remain human and become the first Dogrib people (52). While Wiebe's version of this creation story remains silent about the fate of the three children who turn back into puppies, in

The Lesser Blessed Larry eventually learns from Jed that the Dogrib woman killed them (105).[38] Larry's telling is hence a rather dark version of this important Dogrib story and, as such, bears some resemblance to the third Dogrib story included in *The Lesser Blessed*.

In this third story, a Dogrib woman drowns her six starving children after having been deserted by her husband, who went out hunting but got killed by a muskox that he had been pursuing (69–70). Finally, in what appears to be the last Dogrib story in Van Camp's novel (99–100), a woman takes offence at her son for accusing her husband of something that she believes to be untrue. She throws her son out of her house in the midst of winter, thus causing his death: he falls through the ice and dies. Ever since his death, the woman sees his ghost every time there is a fire or someone lights a match. Only after she consults a medicine woman and burns his clothes in a fire one night, telling her son "to sleep, to rest, to die" (100), does his ghost finally leave her alone. These four Dogrib stories form the mythological narrative strand in the novel; all concern death in one way or another, and all feature a female protagonist. Three of the four stories are narrated by Larry himself, but the first two stories are also *retellings* of stories that have been given to Larry by Jed.

The Lesser Blessed contains yet another story-within-a-story, which is not Dogrib and which is contained in the psychological rather than the mythological narrative strand. It resembles the traditional Dogrib stories insofar as it conflates realist and fantastic elements: the story features cruelly disfigured monkeys in India that steal people's dope. The story about the Blue Monkeys is told by Larry, but it was given to him by Jed, the main character in this story. The four traditional Dogrib stories and the story about the Blue Monkeys all function as allegories in the novel, though on different levels. Whereas the Blue Monkeys story is part of the psychological narrative strand and points to Larry's guilty conscience, the four traditional stories make up the mythological narrative strand and provide Larry with lessons that sketch out the path of healing that he will eventually begin to walk on in the main narrative strand.

A HOLOPHRASTIC READING OF *THE LESSER BLESSED*

The previous chapters showed how (para)holophrases contribute to the narrative purposes in Ishmael Alunik's *Call Me Ishmael* and Alootook Ipellie's *Arctic Dreams and Nightmares*. On the surface, Richard Van Camp's *The Lesser Blessed* differs significantly from Alunik's and Ipellie's rather traditional story collections given that this is a novel written by a fairly young Indigenous author who has lost his tribal language. As we will see in the discussion that follows, however, Van Camp's novel is as reliant on (para)holophrases as the Inuit texts discussed earlier and, despite its paucity of code switching, features a very effective and skilful use of language.

Paraholophrases

Although more contemporary in tone and language than the texts analyzed thus far, *The Lesser Blessed* nonetheless contains an opening and a closing similar to those that traditionally frame most Indigenous oratures and that have been identified in *Call Me Ishmael* and *Arctic Dreams and Nightmares*. Similar to these two texts, *The Lesser Blessed* also features paraholophrases whose narrative function lies in weaving together a coherent narrative.

Paraholophrases Constituting the Narrative's Frame

Van Camp's novel begins with Larry's death, so it seems. "It is the summer of my crucifixion," Larry writes in "Me," the half-page chapter opening the novel. Only underwater can he hear his heartbeat; the skin on his back dries, cracks, and "make[s] the noise of splitting wood when [he] walks." Larry denies everything around him: the mirrors in his house, his mother, his father, and the world at large. Standing "daringly close" to the road leading to Edzo and Yellowknife, he appears to negate even himself:

> I see a therapist who asks me to draw how I see myself. I hand in a picture of a forest.
> He looks closely, says there is no one. I say, "Look there, I am already buried."
> There is NO a hundred million times on every rock, tree and leaf… (1)

The title of the opening chapter, "Me," thus forms an ironic juxtaposition to the chapter's main idea. Larry might be physically alive, but spiritually he is dead: "**I am already buried**." But what makes him feel this way? The next chapter, "Them," consists of the transcription of a newspaper clipping reporting the death of a Dogrib man in a fire that broke out in the man's house in Fort Rae (1–2). Obviously, this man cannot be Larry himself, but when he refers to his accident two chapters later (3), the suspicion arises that this accident and the skin drying on his back from the first chapter might be related to the fire reported in the newspaper clipping. Even more so, given that, between the newspaper clipping and the reference to his accident, Larry introduces his mother and her boyfriend, Jed, readers can assume that the man who died in the fire was Larry's father.

In Chapter 3, Larry introduces Johnny Beck, who will become his best friend over the course of the main narrative. When Johnny arrives in Fort Simmer, he arouses a lot of interest among the high school students—not from Larry, however: "I didn't do a thing. I was too **busy looking for Juliet Hope**" (2). Juliet, he will later tell his readers, is Fort Simmer's high school tramp, and, as he puts it, "[his] love for Juliet has claimed [him]" (28), so he is "too busy" watching the one person with whom he would like to do it "doggy-style" (see 22, 25, 27, 101) to lose his virginity (43).[39] When his new friend Johnny starts "dating" Juliet, Larry's amorous intentions appear to have become futile. Yet, in the course of the novel, "looking for Juliet Hope" will become more than what its literal meaning suggests. What Larry, a "*North of 60* Romeo,"[40] is looking for is twofold: his own *Juliet*, symbolizing love and a sense of belonging, and *hope*, something to keep him going in life, and he does indeed find all this in the end in Juliet Hope. The phrase "busy looking for Juliet Hope" can thus be read as a metaphor of Larry's quest.

The novel continues in Chapter 4, entitled "Mom," by introducing Larry's mother and her boyfriend, Jed, and alluding to Larry's accident; the brief introduction in Chapters 3 and 4 to the novel's main characters (Johnny, Juliet, Darcy,[41] Larry's mother, and Jed) does not, however, mark the end of the novel's opening. That opening continues, in fact, for several more chapters.

In Chapter 5, Larry tells readers Jed's story about running into the "**Blue Monkeys of Corruption**" (4–6). Jed was smoking up with friends in his apartment in India when "eight wonderful monkeys" (5)—"five of them were missing an arm or a hand, and they had these mean eyes" (4)—showed up on his balcony. The monkeys appeared to be harmless until they "turned into the Blue Monkeys" and started hammering the door. Jed and his friends ended up fleeing their apartment; when they returned, their pipe was gone (5). The capitalization of Blue Monkeys suggests that they are more a symbol of someone's guilty conscience—in this case Jed's—than just monkeys with blue fur. Larry does not comment on why he tells Jed's story at this point in the narrative or how the story relates to his personal situation. The Blue Monkeys, however, appear repeatedly throughout the narrative, primarily in the psychological narrative strand; the telling of this story hence functions as a first indication of this strand, which will eventually form one of the keys for readers to understand what happens to Larry in the novel.

After the story about the Blue Monkeys, Larry tells readers more about his mother (6–7) and seemingly by chance mentions the Dogrib belief that "**if a Dogrib woman cuts her hair she has to burn it. If not, when she dies, she has to go back all through her life and pick up every single hair she**

CHAPTER 3

ever dropped before going up to heaven" (6). The story about a Dogrib woman's hair is the first of four Dogrib stories that Larry weaves into his narrative. It represents the first instance of the mythological narrative strand, which—as will become apparent in the discussion of those paraholophrases not constituting the narrative frame—provides Larry with guidance in his quest. Why he weaves the story about the Dogrib woman's hair into his narrative might not be immediately apparent to readers, but given that this story, as part of a larger tradition, differs extensively from the remainder of the narrative there are grounds for the assumption that it might function as a kind of allegory.

We can begin to detect the end of the novel's opening in Chapter 7, where Larry's narration turns to his life at school (8). As Larry looks around the classroom, making a mental list of its desolate state, it becomes evident that his thoughts are drifting, signalled by the compound word "**weakdizzydemented**" and his repetition of the phrase "The crunch under my runners." Finally, when he mentions his father's teeth—a detail fully out of context considering that Larry is sitting in a classroom—it becomes clear that he has temporarily lost touch with reality and that his feeling "weakdizzydemented" probably has nothing to do with being in class. The word suggests a more serious mental chaos than the state of simply feeling weak, dizzy, and demented—a mental chaos that we might speculate is related to his feeling buried alive in Chapter 1 and to his accident. Indeed, Larry eventually ends this chapter by saying to himself that "**it is every parent's dream to watch his child burn**" (10).

Chapter 8, curiously entitled "Six Stages of Rigor Mortis" (10–12), finally marks the end of the novel's opening. Larry's description of the conjugation of the verb *être* as the "**six stages of rigor mortis**," the stiffening of a body after death, is ironic, and so is his comparison of the students with "worker bees singing this death chant mantra" (11). This oxymoronic association of life and death makes sense, however, given his "crucifixion" at the outset of the novel: Larry appears to be a living dead. That his father, ever since his time at residential school, "always talked French when he drank" (58) also helps to explain Larry's negative associations with the French language. Yet his French class offers hope as well: his French teacher's name is Mademoiselle Sauvé, and though Larry's reference to her is stereotypically adolescent—"For crisis management, I only went [to French class] because of **Mademoiselle Sauvé's French titties**" (11)—his interest in the breasts of a woman whose name means "saved" is significant and can be considered proleptic, for it points to the closing of the novel, when Larry is "saved" by none other than Juliet Hope's breasts (110). So Chapter 8 serves two functions:

it draws a circle to his "crucifixion" and burial in the opening chapter of the novel as Larry and his classmates repetitively conjugate the verb *to be* through "six stages of rigor mortis," thus completing the novel's opening and it also provides a narrative thread concerning his salvation that will be spun in the main part of the novel, which can now begin.

As in any Indigenous orature (or literature), the opening in *The Lesser Blessed* rests on the awareness of readers that they are, in fact, being guided into the narrative. This awareness, in turn, depends on their recognition of those chunks of language that feature prominently in the novel's opening chapters, that is, the chunks just discussed:

a. "I am already buried" (1; metaphor),
b. "busy looking for Juliet Hope" (2; metaphor),
c. "Blue Monkeys of Corruption" (4; metaphor),
d. "if a Dogrib woman cuts her hair she has to burn it. If not, when she dies, she has to go back all through her life and pick up every single hair she ever dropped before going up to heaven" (6; allegory and intertextuality),
e. "weakdizzydemented" (8; symbol),
f. "it is every parent's dream to watch his child burn" (10; irony),
g. "six stages of rigor mortis" (11; metaphor), and
h. "Mademoiselle Sauvé's French titties" (11; prolepsis).[42]

These chunks of language feature prominently in the opening pages of *The Lesser Blessed* for two reasons. First, as figures of speech (and, in one case, as an example of intertextuality), they form the cores of complex ideas: they are self-contained but carry a surplus of meaning that readers must uncover for themselves. Second, these chunks function as significant narrative units by constituting the novel's opening and thus marking part of the novel's interpretative context. That is, as semantically dense narrative units that perform a significant narrative function, these chunks are equivalent in function to holophrases in Indigenous languages and thus qualify as paraholophrases. Moreover, by establishing part of the interpretative context of the novel, they indicate the author's involvement with his readers, who are invited to participate in the composition of the novel. The paraholophrases constituting the opening in *The Lesser Blessed* thus clearly mark a strategy in textualizing orality that is culturally specific.

Of all the paraholophrases in the novel's opening, "busy looking for Juliet Hope" and "Blue Monkeys" appear to be particularly significant because they not only reappear in the main part of the novel, either explicitly ("Blue

Monkeys") or implicitly ("busy looking for Juliet Hope"), but also are featured in the novel's closing, which picks up the main ideas of the opening, thus perfecting the narrative frame of the novel. This closing begins with the lovemaking scene between Larry and Juliet, which happens to mark the end of his quest—he has finally "found" Juliet Hope, if for "[o]ne night" only (109)—and which is composed of a combination of prose, poetic prose, and free verse (109–11).

Curiously enough, this lovemaking scene contains numerous allusions to Larry's accident. Juliet becomes a fire that consumes Larry, but he lets it be and rides the waves of pleasure that she is giving him. His **tusk** is no longer the hammer with which he ends his father's life (78) but a tusk that gives "sweet violation." The metaphors ("**It burned my eyes and mind**," "**I was on fire**," "We went for spice"), the oxymoron ("sweet violation"), the simile ("**like flames like blades of a wicked fire**"), the run-on lines, and the lack of proper punctuation turn this passage into a prose poem that reflects the emotional intensity of the scene. Moreover, the fire imagery skilfully connects this scene to the newspaper clipping reporting Larry's father's death in a blaze. Unlike then, however, the fire can no longer do Larry any harm.

Under Larry, Juliet does not turn into a caribou that he hunts and spares out of respect and awe (29); instead, she becomes a fox, then a snowbird, and finally a raven. The sleeping **monkeys**, of course, are the "Blue Monkeys of Corruption," whose story readers have already read in the novel's opening and who visit Larry each time he experiences a flashback in the psychological narrative strand (39, 41–42, 77–81). The Blue Monkeys function as a metaphor of his guilty conscience—he is responsible for his father's death—and only disappear when he "finds Juliet Hope" and is reborn. Now the Blue Monkeys are sleeping and silent, and Larry is healed.

A free verse poem at the end of Larry and Juliet's lovemaking scene expresses this healing:

"Look at me," I said. "Look at me, just look at me."
She did
and I wasn't alone
I wasn't forgotten
I wasn't dead
There was no small town
There was no killing
I wasn't bad I was clean (110)

Here Larry repeats two lines from a poetic prose section immediately preceding this poem, "I was not alone; I was not forgotten" (110). These two lines and the additional "I wasn't dead" connect the novel's closing to two paraholophrases found in its opening: "I am already buried" and the "six stages of rigor mortis." The significance of these lines—**"and I wasn't alone / I wasn't forgotten / I wasn't dead"**—is further heightened when they are repeated yet again, albeit in variation, in the free verse poem that ends the novel. But in this second occurrence, the negatives of the litotes-like "and I wasn't alone / I wasn't forgotten / I wasn't dead" are expressed in the positive: "[...] I knew **I had someone / someone to remember my name / ... / I would in time / find one to call my own / mine to disappear in / to be ...** " (119).

Larry's closing words here express again his having found Juliet Hope, but they also erase the understatement found in the earlier lovemaking poem and are thus more life-affirming. Even more important, though, is the fact that these closing words are actually a formulaic cluster that echoes an earlier passage from the psychological narrative strand when Larry, after having been beaten up by Jazz the Jackal, remembers how he and his cousins escaped the blaze in his father's house: "And we wept because we knew we had no one. No one to remember our names, no one to cry them out, no one to greet us naked in snow, to mourn us in death, to feel us there, in our sacred place. We wept because we did not belong to anyone" (79). Ignoring the change from plural to singular as well as from poetic prose to free verse, Larry's closing poem is a perfect inversion of the passage above. This transition from a self-destroying to a life-affirming attitude is possible for Larry only after his encounter with Juliet Hope. He has lost his guilty conscience—the Blue Monkeys are asleep—and he has found both his own Juliet and hope: he has become alive again.

The significance of Larry finding Juliet is further indicated by another intratextual reference: "[...] I picked up the brush and pulled out the longest hair I could find. I wrapped it around my finger. I kissed it. I put it between the mattress and the box spring. **This way, when she died, she'd have to come back, find this one hair, remember me, remember us, remember what happened before flying back to heaven**" (114–15). Here the reference to the Dogrib teaching points again to the opening of the novel; rather than telling it, however, Larry *performs it* and thus finds a way to make Juliet (and himself) remember the one night that they shared together.

Eventually, Larry has to say goodbye to Juliet. He leaves her house, goes back onto the street, and buries the dead ptarmigan that he hit on his way to see her. The burial place that he chooses is where earlier in the narrative he drew a heart into the snow with the inscription "LARRY + JULIET T.I.D." (29).

CHAPTER 3

His longing for her has been fulfilled, but it is a short-lived fulfillment, as was that of Shakespeare's Romeo. Larry weeps over the fact that he has to remain without a mate since Juliet is leaving town because she is expecting Johnny's child. Unlike Romeo, however, Larry walks out of his story with a future, for by burying the ptarmigan he unburies himself:

> I placed the ptarmigan in the snow and covered her.
> **I said, "Rest."**
> **I said, "Sleep."**
> **I said, "Die."** (118–19)

His words as he buries the ptarmigan echo words from a story that Larry told to Juliet just a few evenings before. The story is about a mother who, having caused her son's death, is haunted by his spirit and gains peace only after seeking advice from a medicine woman and then burning all her son's clothes in a big fire (99–100). Unlike the other three Dogrib stories contained in the mythological narrative strand of *The Lesser Blessed*, this story is not explicitly marked as Dogrib; the references here to medicine power and spirituality, however, suggest that it could well be a traditional Dogrib story. However, when sharing stories or teachings with other characters (and/or his audience, readers), Larry usually mentions the source of the story; here he does not. And, in fact, the text makes it clear that this particular story in the mythological narrative strand is his own invention: "I knew that this was my chance to completely give Juliet something that was mine so much that I would be nothing else. I closed my eyes and decided to let the story lead. I was just the voice, and I knew the story would tell itself" (99). Apparently, Larry invents this Dogrib story for Juliet. That he is capable of invention, of creating something seemingly out of nothing, marks the beginning of his healing process. That he begins walking on the path of healing by telling a story is not without cultural significance: stories in Indigenous cultures also take on survival functions. Even more important, though, is the fact that Larry dresses his story as a traditional Dogrib story, an indication that he feels comfortable in his own cultural tradition. This is clearly Jed's doing who, throughout much of the narrative, has taken on the role of Larry's dead father by introducing Larry to Dogrib culture.

While Juliet is impressed by Larry's story and finds it beautiful, Larry disagrees, replying, "'No, […] that's the truth'" (100–01). By hiding his personal story about the accident in an allegory that resembles a traditional Dogrib story and anticipates the burning imagery in his lovemaking scene with Juliet, Larry lays down a way to unbury himself. Like the woman in his story, he can escape his "fire nightmares" (71) and his guilty conscience, expressed in the form of the Blue Monkeys, only by symbolically setting himself on fire, thereby putting the past to rest. When he buries the ptarmigan in the snow (which happens to be where the woman's son died in his story), Larry repeats the woman's ritualistic formula, saying, "rest, sleep, die." In doing so, he symbolically "buries" his nightmares, the Blue Monkeys, and his traumatic past, as the ptarmigan now takes his place under the earth.

Like the opening and closing frames in *Call Me Ishmael* and *Arctic Dreams and Nightmares* (discussed in the previous chapters), the narrative frame in *The Lesser Blessed* is not explicitly marked in the text but can only be gathered from a series of phrases that feature prominently in the narrative, either in its opening or in its closing pages. These phrases and phrasal clusters—

a. "It burned my eyes and mind" (109; metaphor),
b. "I was on fire" (109; metaphor),
c. "like flames like blades of a wicked fire" (110; simile),
d. "the monkeys" (110; metaphor),
e. "and I wasn't alone / I wasn't forgotten / I wasn't dead" (110; symbol),
f. "I had someone / someone to remember my name / [...] / I would in time / find one to call my own / mine to disappear in / to be ..." (119; symbol),
g. "This way, when she died, she'd have to come back [...] " (114–15; allegory), and
h. "I said, 'Rest.' / I said, 'Sleep.' / I said, 'Die'" (118–19; allegory and intra- and intertextuality)

—perfect the novel's frame by constituting its closing: Larry's story is closed—but not ended—because, in moving from the buried me at the beginning of his narrative to a me whose "life was still / unwrapped" (119), Larry is now reborn and ready to live his life. As figures of speech and intratextual references (either to the opening or to the main part of the novel), these phrases and phrasal clusters form the cores of complex ideas: that is, they are self-contained but carry a surplus of meaning, which readers have to gather for themselves. Serving functions that are equivalent to those of holophrases in Indigenous languages, the phrases and phrasal clusters listed above must hence be considered paraholophrases.

The closing of *The Lesser Blessed* not only provides links to the novel's opening, thus completing its narrative frame, but also picks up the narrative threads of the mythological and psychological narrative strands, thus fusing these different narrative strands into one. Larry builds his own "tradition" by hiding one of Juliet's hairs under her bed (114–15, see 6); as he buries the ptarmigan, he asks for forgiveness for his wrongdoing (i.e., killing his father) using the Dogrib woman's ritualistic formula (118–19, see 100); he realizes that the fact he is still without a mate might have legitimate reasons (119, see 69–70); and, most of all, he lives his own people's creation story: Larry is reborn through his lovemaking with Juliet (119, see 51–52), thus embracing his heritage and underlining how creation stories are as much for the present and the future as they are about the past. Following the teachings revealed in his people's tradition, and assuming the guise of a storyteller in the meantime, Larry is healed: finding strength in Dogrib tradition, he buries his guilty conscience by putting the Blue Monkeys to sleep (110, see 4–6) and is finally allowed to move on with his life—and to end his narrative.

The cyclical frame established in the novel by way of paraholophrases not only brings *The Lesser Blessed* closer to generic conventions of Indigenous oratures but also defines the novel's interpretative context. Van Camp's narrative embraces the Euro-Western tradition of the realist novel openly but with added cultural context through the incorporation of, in particular, the mythological narrative strand and its stories from Dogrib oral tradition. And though *The Lesser Blessed* does not overtly mark non-Indigenous readers as outsiders, it nonetheless demands the readers' *participation*. Whether readers can make sense of the novel or not depends heavily on whether they can untangle its narrative structure, which implies noting the connections between its opening and its closing, on the one hand, and between the closing and the psychological and mythological narrative strands, on the other— that is, connections that are drawn by the author in the form of paraholophrases. By establishing the narrative's interpretative context and by inviting readers' participation in the creation of meaning, these paraholophrases, modelled on the holophrase in Indigenous languages, thus also function as strategies of conceptual orality that are culturally specific.

Paraholophrases with Other Narrative Functions
While the majority of paraholophrases in *The Lesser Blessed* constitute the novel's frame, other paraholophrases link either the psychological or the mythological strand with the main narrative strand, whose story would never be able to develop without its connections to the other two narrative strands.

The Blue Monkeys are encountered in both the novel's opening and its closing: initially a metaphor of Jed's guilty conscience, the Blue Monkeys eventually turn into a metaphor of Larry's own guilty conscience in the course of the main part of his narrative. The function of this particular paraholophrase is thus not restricted to the novel's frame alone. Larry sees the Blue Monkeys for the first time when hot-knifing at Juliet's aunt's house (39). The Blue Monkeys disappear as quickly as they have shown up—but Larry is left hallucinating, thus bringing to light, in the form of flashbacks, his tormented past. His narration becomes increasingly mixed up the more the main and the psychological narrative strands flow into each other. Describing the party at Juliet's aunt's house—"I was in the bathtub stoned and hard. My mind was going a million miles an hour"—Larry suddenly remembers his accident: "I was a rabbit, choking in a snare. I was falling through ice. I was slamming the hammer down on my father. I was—" (40). Back in the main narrative strand, Juliet's mother catches the teenagers hot-knifing in the house. At this moment, the Blue Monkeys appear again, and Larry experiences another flashback, revealing more details about his accident:

Slaughter.
  I was the beast.
  I was close to the beast.
  He was running beside me.
  I could hear the hoofs scrape against the pavement before the deliverance kick to a swelling face.
  And there were scorch marks on the road where we danced.
  Someone was screaming at me to kick
  to scrape a face raw
  the skin and slaughter
  to sniff again
  to scrape again through the window
  to hear my cousin pop and burn
  shards of glass in my back
  screaming glass
  to see my father fuck—(41–42; emphasis added)

Johnny and Larry manage to get away from Juliet's aunt before she can call the police and before the Blue Monkeys can get Larry. However, the Blue Monkeys appear again later in the narrative, after Larry is beaten up by Jazz the Jackal. Larry is forced to relive his accident yet again, and the pieces of this story finally come together for readers: "[…] I could see the Blue Monkeys standing with steam coming out of their eyes and I went black and *heard the hoofs scraping the pavement before he kicked again*. I was close to the beast, and he was laughing" (77–78; emphasis added). Jazz the Jackal is pushed away by the crowd, and Larry runs home, his head pounding.

CHAPTER 3

As he looks at himself in the mirror, more images of the accident flicker through his mind:

> [...] I got a flash of Rae and our house; me standing over him; fire roaring from room to room; me standing in the crowd with a box of matches and the hammer; oh God in Heaven forgive me, my hammer, my secret tusk; me standing over Dad and bringing it down, slamming it down, knowing Dad's passed out, knowing he's dreaming. (78)

Eventually, it becomes clear that "the hoofs scraping the pavement before he kicked again" are a metaphor of Larry's dad raping his own son:

> [...] I wanted to take it away, the sin and dirt and cum and blood in my mouth. I couldn't breathe. My eyes were crying. My lips were split. I wanted to sew stitches through my lips. I thought he wanted me to pray when he said kneel down. I couldn't breathe. I wanted stitches. I thought, Oh God, why is he feeding me mushroom juice? I couldn't breathe. He jammed it so far in I couldn't. I couldn't. I couldn't. I couldn't breathe. I wanted to sew stitches through my lips so he could never fuck me there again. Mother. The flame light. The flame rush. You stand there frozen. Why am I? Why am I—the snow. My face. My skin. It's not supposed to be black. (78–79)

Larry comes to after passing out on the bathroom floor, and he manages to get into bed. The psychological narrative strand continues as his flashbacks move to images of the fire: "I lit a match. I pushed the air with it and the air pushed back. And me, the Destroying Angel, screaming, 'Let's die! Let's die! Let's die!!' and my cousin Franky, eyes wide and mouth quivering, 'Larry, don't Larry please Larry please—'" (79–80). By the time his stream-of-consciousness narrative has reached his stay in the burn wing of the hospital in Edmonton, where Larry was moved after his accident, he has "slept for way too long" after Jazz the Jackal's beating (79). The flashbacks continue and one of the Blue Monkeys comes to visit him once again:

> I could hear myself screaming. I would have continued screaming but I opened my eyes, and a **Blue Monkey** was sitting on my chest, staring into me.

> "Hello, **Son of Dog**," he said, inches from my face. He punched his stump wrist in my mouth, gagging me. I sat up as Jed rushed into the room and threw on the light. (81)

Although Jed does not embody the apparition of the Blue Monkey visiting Larry, this scene clearly draws a connection between the story of the Blue Monkeys and the story about the Dogrib origin. For the first time in the novel, the psychological and mythological narrative strands not only connect with the main narrative strand but also meet and overlap each other, thus anticipating the final merging of all three narrative strands in the novel's closing.

What helps Larry put his Blue Monkeys to sleep and find his Juliet Hope is Dogrib oral tradition. His retelling of the Dogrib creation story (51–52) not only establishes an intertextual allusion to Dogrib oral tradition but also is an interesting *intra*textual reference to his own asides about doing it "**doggy-style**" (22, 25, 27, 101). These asides can be downplayed as being pubertal—which they are to a certain point—but they can also be read as Larry's own reading of the Dogrib origin myth. When Larry finds Juliet Hope at the end of the novel, the act of making love, the "doing it doggy-style"—not necessarily in its literal meaning, then, but perhaps "Dogrib-style"—turns him into a new person. Larry is reborn by connecting with his tradition, by returning to where he, the "Son of Dog" (81), came from: "[Juliet] looked at me and I felt it. I felt alive, like I had fallen from the sky with the grace of God, with the petals of God, and I had finally spread my wings" (109).[43] Of course, doing it doggy-style (preferably with Juliet) has been on Larry's mind for most of the main narrative; at the same time, however, having sexual intercourse also implies that Larry must face his dark past and the source of his fire nightmares. After all, it has been a series of forced acts of sexual intercourse, either witnessed or experienced, that makes him kill his father: "What he [Shamus, a janitor at the hospital] doesn't tell me is that *murder* is a song. A smooth and silent hymn. One I keep inside. For I was raised by butchers" (80; emphasis added).

The realization that he has murdered his father, however, is preceded by a long period of denial. Larry never tells the story of his accident coherently, not even to Johnny. When Johnny asks him about the scars on his back, Larry tells him the story of his aunt's rape instead (87–88); Larry simply cannot force himself to tell the truth until late in the novel, and even when he does tell Juliet the story of his accident he does so in the form of an allegory. Despite his denial, his past does not leave him alone, so readers are able to puzzle together the various pieces of his accident that are revealed in the psychological narrative strand every time Larry experiences a flashback.

In fact, Larry himself seems to be aware that he is in denial. He reads his puppy allergies as an indication that he is suppressing his "whole fuckin' life" (34). When Juliet suggests that Larry should buy a puppy for himself to overcome his "allergies," this advice can be read as a suggestion to face his past by connecting with his (Dogrib) tradition (95–96). At the same time, however, considering the ambiguity of the term "doing it doggy-style," Juliet's suggestion can also be read as a particular proposition. Indeed, Juliet tells Larry that she finds him sweet and thus sends him running out onto the potato field shouting, "So I was sweet! Sweet! Sweet! Didja hear that, you *fuckin' plague monkeys*! Me! Larry! Sweet in the eyes of Juliet." For the first time since his accident, Larry is able to face directly the monkeys haunting him because he has "the answer to [his] allergies." Most of all, however, he has received this answer in the "words of Juliet Hope bathing [him], straight from her pink, hot mouth" (96; emphasis added).

The noun phrase "**Son of Dog**" and the adjective "**doggy-style**," pointing to the Dogrib creation story and to a particular position in sexual intercourse, are ambiguous in meaning and provide important intratextual references to the Dogrib creation story told by Larry in the mythological narrative strand. However, as suggested by the scene in the burn wing of the hospital and the scene in the potato field, "Son of Dog" and "doggy-style" are also linked to a paraholophrase first introduced in the opening of *The Lesser Blessed*, the "**Blue Monkeys**." After all, it is through doing it "doggy-style" that Larry's guilty conscience (symbolized by the Blue Monkeys) is eventually put to sleep. By referring to the core of a more complex idea and thus carrying a surplus of meaning, and by providing a narrative hinge for the novel, both "Son of Dog" and "doggy-style" are equivalent in function to holophrases in Indigenous languages and thus qualify as paraholophrases. They do not constitute the narrative frame of *The Lesser Blessed*, but by forming the "mythological" answer to Larry's "psychological" problem they direct readers to the moment of convergence of the novel's three narrative strands, thus inviting reader participation. By creating context (cultural and interpretative), by showing the author's involvement, and by engaging the readers' participation, "Son of Dog" and "doggy-style" complement the textualization of orality achieved by the paraholophrases constituting the novel's frame and thus ensure that this culturally specific strategy is not restricted to the novel's opening and closing.

Holophrases and Holophrastic Traces

As noted earlier, Richard Van Camp belongs to a generation of young Indigenous authors who have lost their ancestral languages as a consequence of colonization, of which the residential school system was but one facet. His use of Dogrib in *The Lesser Blessed* is very restricted; his overall use of language, however, is astonishingly inventive and effective and relies at least in part on holophrastic traces.

Code switching in *The Lesser Blessed* is almost entirely absent. Indigenous expressions are restricted to a few examples, such as the Dogrib *Edanat'e* "How are you?" (15, 16), the Dogrib *A-me-nay* "Who's this?" (83), the Dogrib *Ischa*, left untranslated (84), the Dogrib *Mahsi Cho* "thank you" (116), and the Slavey greeting *Negha dogondih*, as well as its answer, *Neghadegondee* (66). The paucity of code switching in the novel can be explained, of course, by Van Camp's ignorance of his ancestral language. However, given the novel's setting in contemporary times and the fact that most of the characters and its narrator in particular are teenagers, an abundant use of Dogrib words and/or holophrases would not make much sense. To have contemporary Indigenous youth using Indigenous language in a *realist* novel about youth would be strange considering the threatened state of Indigenous languages in contemporary Canada and the United States. Instead, *The Lesser Blessed* features a colloquial use of language and creates the illusion of an oral storytelling performance, both of which mark the text as imitating oral discourse. While the linguistic context of the story is reflected in its colloquial (and clearly adolescent) use of language, the use of stream-of-consciousness and poetic language also ensures that the language of the novel is never gratuitously offensive.

Reading *The Lesser Blessed* at times feels like flipping through an album full of "photo-booth snapshots":[44] the novel is short and sketchy—its thirty-six chapters cover fewer than 120 pages—yet its effective use of language renders the narration very colourful. As far as direct speech is concerned, Larry's language, as well as that of most of the other characters, is colloquial and often crosses into slang. The colloquialisms create the illusion of oral speech and add a real-life dimension to the speech of the characters. Most colloquialisms in the novel qualify as what Larry refers to as "Raven talk" (14, 22, 29, 31), obviously a Dene/Dogrib English code. In Dene traditions, as in many northwest coast Indigenous traditions, Raven is a cultural hero and one of the First People.[45] Raven talk in *The Lesser Blessed* lends the novel an oral aesthetic: "Seriously" becomes "Shereshly" (31); "See you later" is shortened to "Sol later" (14, 55, 118); and "Mkbuh" (22) is Raven talk's almost unintelligible equivalent to "Okay bye." At the same time, Van Camp's Raven talk points to the important connection between sacred history and language, which, in their interdependence with place/territory and the ceremonial cycle, form what Tom Holm (Cherokee), J. Diane Pearson, and Ben Chavis (Lumbee) have referred to as the "peoplehood matrix," a common model of peoplehood for Indigenous peoples in North America.[46] Thus, Raven talk becomes a metaphor for the ways in which Indigenous authors have oralized and indigenized the English language, turning English *into an Indigenous language* used by Indigenous peoples for Indigenous purposes. Indeed, the significance of this metaphor for the rhetorical sovereignty exercised by Indigenous authors is precisely what makes "Raven talk" an appropriate title for this book. That in her lovemaking with Larry Juliet turns into a fox, then into a snowbird, and finally into a *raven* provides the novel's pivotal scene with another connection to Dogrib sacred history, thus underscoring the importance of the raven imagery in *The Lesser Blessed*—imagery that, by connecting the use of words (Raven talk) with the creation of peoples (Dogrib creation story), is clearly grounded in Indigenous notions of peoplehood.

When contractions are involved, Raven talk in *The Lesser Blessed* can be read as imitating the monolexical form of holophrases. Such a reading applies particularly well to chunks of language such as "safe sex sonovabitch" (31), which should be read as "safe-sex sonovabitch," and "fuckinbitchcow" (42), both of which seem to be original uses of language. Other examples of monolexical Raven talk in *The Lesser Blessed* include

- "sunova" (94),
- "Ohmigod!" (81),
- "Tsa full moon tonight" (34),
- "Getthellouttahere" (10),
- "Shitshitshitshit" (41),
- "Whoopdeefuckindoo!" (42),
- "Fuckinrights! Fuckinrights! Fuckinrights" (116),
- "Manohman" (43), and
- "Fiiiiidemm" (19).

Ignoring the rules of English orthography, Van Camp fuses multiple words into new, monolexical words that invite readers to read the text aloud. Contractions such as the ones listed above qualify as *quotation compounds* because they contain phrases or whole sentences that can be analyzed as a single word. Readers of *The Lesser Blessed* even experience the invention of one such quotation compound in the scene of Larry's first attempt at hot-knifing:

> "Okay, man," he [Darcy] said as he exhaled, "put your mouth over the end of the roll [of toilet paper]. *Don't waste any*... this is from Colombia, man... people died to get this to my main man in Hay River."

> [...] Darcy put the knives down and covered my mouth and nose with his hands. I just about fainted; my knees wanted to buckle and my eyes were crying. The only thing that kept me standing was Darcy and his *gorilla grip.*
> "Fuck, man, *dontwasteitdontwasteitdontwasteit...,*" he commanded.
> [...]
> I hot-knifed about three more times. Never had I smelled or tasted anything so harsh. It felt like I was swallowing fire. I think more smoke went into my hair and eyes than anything. Darcy kept me in his famous "*dontwasteit*" grip. (37; emphasis added)

"Don't waste any" becomes "dontwasteitdontwasteitdontwasteit" and finally constitutes a new adjective that, combined with the noun "grip," produces a quotation compound that adds an interesting connotation to Darcy's "gorilla grip" in the context of doing drugs. Particularly, those quotation compounds in *The Lesser Blessed* that involve more than the mere replication of one word (such as "Shitshitshitshit" or "Manohman") are suggestive of the ability of polysynthetic languages to build long, complex words by combining an infinitude of morphemes to form a single word: the only difference between Indigenous languages and Van Camp's Raven talk is that the latter combines words rather than morphemes to form new words. Because they imitate the ability of polysynthetic languages to construct long, complex words, quotation compounds in *The Lesser Blessed* qualify as direct holophrastic traces. Those quotation compounds that constitute an entire sentence come exceptionally close to translating the structure of the holophrase into English discourse by bypassing the analytic morphology of the English language through a disregard of orthography. In either case, because of the quotation compounds in *The Lesser Blessed*, the dialogue in the novel better reflects actual oral speech and points to the author's involvement with his audience, since these compounds invite reader participation. As direct holophrastic traces, quotation compounds, then, mark a strategy in textualizing orality that is culturally specific.

Compounding in Van Camp's novel is not restricted to quotation compounds in direct discourse. The novel also features a few interesting examples of compounding in its narration of events. "Pissing fire" (44) is a *deverbal N N compound* and suggests the oral in the written through its colloquial use of language. Mostly, however, the effectiveness of these other compounds lies in engaging the reader's imagination through vivid description. For example, the *N N compound* "cornmeal snow" (102) works as a metaphor because it contains an implied comparison of a particular kind of snow with a particular kind of food. Interestingly, Larry gives the source for this metaphor: "That's what Jed called this kind of snow, because it was quite thin and it crunched when we walked on it" (102). Like its probably monolexical equivalents in Inuktitut, Dogrib, or Slavey, "cornmeal snow" gives a detailed description of the object that it denotes—a description that can be crucial for survival in societies reliant on hunting.[47] "Cornmeal snow" invites the reader's participation; at the same time, however, this seemingly casual compound carries a lot of significance at this point in Larry's narrative because it is symbolic of the cultural teachings that Larry has received from Jed and now passes on to readers. The word's importance, then, is reflected not only in its content but also in the attempt to have the form of the word re-create the semantic density of words in polysynthetic languages; even if this compound does not include a verbal constituent, it suggests at least the ability in Indigenous languages to combine multiple morphemes into a new word.

A similar case can be made for the phrase "where Mister Ferguson kept his sled dogs" (101). This adverbial phrase obviously provides a location; however, instead of referring to this place as Ferguson's doghouses, Larry calls it "where Mister Ferguson kept his sled dogs." He uses the phrase not just once but twice ("where Old Man Ferguson kept his dogs" [118]), giving the phrase an *idiom-like* character. This phrase is of further significance, however, because it imitates the descriptiveness of Indigenous geographical names.[48] By highlighting what happens at this place, Larry emphasizes its importance: it is not just a location—it has a *story*. Indigenous peoples are connected to the land through such stories, and this connection is an integral part of Indigenous perceptions of the world. As Thomas D. Andrews and John B. Zoe explain about the Dogribs, "Each place has a story, sometimes many of them, associated with it. These narratives provide information pertinent to Dogrib identity, history, and survival, and in this way geographic features become mnemonic devices for remembering a vast oral tradition."[49] As noted above, *place/territory* along with sacred history, the ceremonial cycle, and *language* form that interdependance of elements that defines Indigenous notions of peoplehood. Van Camp's use of "Where Mister Ferguson kept his sled dogs" points to the interrelatedness of place/territory and language—a toponym that takes the form of a holophrastic trace—and sacred history. The phrase occurs only twice in the novel, but it does so at a decisive moment in the story: when Larry goes to Ferguson's doghouses for the first time, he is joined by Jed, who not only tells him that he and Larry's mother decided to have a permanent relationship (104) but also encourages him to spend time on the land (103). Jed has acted through much of the novel as Larry's "elder." Although he is Slavey, he has taught Larry about his history through the Dogrib creation story and several other stories from Dogrib and Dene traditions. Larry's use of a place name that reflects these cultural teachings indicates that Larry has grown comfortable in this tradition, which in turn will indicate to him a path of healing. Evoking the peoplehood matrix and taking the form of an idiom, which itself contains a complete sentence, make "Where Mister Ferguson kept his sled dogs" an even more powerful holophrastic trace than "cornmeal snow." Although these holophrastic traces—the N N compound ("cornmeal snow"), the deverbal N N compound ("pissing fire"), and the idiom-like toponym ("where Mister Ferguson kept his sled dogs")—are less "oral" than the quotation compounds in *The Lesser Blessed* because they are less colloquial, they nonetheless textualize orality because they invite reader participation by pointing to the descriptiveness of Indigenous languages.

The textualization of orality in *The Lesser Blessed* is further strengthened through the use of onomatopoeic-like words imitating particular sounds. The word *good* spoken with a mouth full of bannock comes out as "Goob" (18); waiting for Juliet to pick up the phone, Larry whispers "Juu-leee-et" (105); the "slish slish slish and the stirring of bubbles" describe Juliet and Johnny's movements on her aunt's waterbed as they are making love (40); Darcy's making fun of the stoned Larry comes out as "Goooo cliiiimb the telephoooone poooole outsiiiide" (38); and, finally, "the neppp-neppp-neppp of a three-wheeler pulling up in [Larry's] driveway" is followed by a "clunk-clunk-clunk of boots" on the stairs and "the ding-dong of the doorbell" (106). Larry eventually turns the "neppp-neppp-neppp" of the three-wheeler into a verb, thus coining a new word: "I heard Darcy's three-wheeler nepp-nepping down the road" (115). The verb "nepp-nepp" denotes not only the movement of the three-wheeler but also the sounds that it makes during the ride. Sound language, as such, is not directly related to holophrasis, but the coining of a new word—particularly of verbs, which play such a significant role in polysynthetic grammars—based on sound language points not only to the descriptiveness but also to the inventiveness of polysynthetic languages. Since this particular coinage in *The Lesser Blessed* shows author involvement and invites reader participation, it can be regarded as a holophrastic trace that functions as a strategy in textualizing orality that is at least partially culturally specific: it might not re-create the structure of holophrases in Indigenous languages, but it reflects the inventiveness of polysynthetic languages when it comes to the processes of word formation.

CHAPTER 3

The inventive and effective use of language is also evident in the narrator's playful description of the disease from which Mr. Harris suffers: "He also had that disease where your head *shimmy, shimmy, shimmies*" (8; emphasis added). His disease is visualized for the reader by way of direct repetition of the verb "shimmy," which is correctly conjugated only upon its third use and therefore translates the visual into the verbal. Some of the personal names in *The Lesser Blessed* are similarly playful and inventive at the same time as they resemble Indigenous traditions of name giving, such as "Darcy 'Hose Cock' McMannus" (29)[50] (whom Johnny also refers to as Thumper [88–89]), Jazz the Jackal (2), and Moustache Sammy (30). Other characters receive their indigenized names during the course of the novel. Mr. Harris' "index finger" (8) or "magic wand finger" (9) is reduced to "babyfingers" (10) before "Babyfingers" (13)—in an act of subversion—becomes his nickname. Similarly, the two town drunks whom Larry and Johnny run into one night eventually become "the Boxer," who shadowboxes through the night, and "Rasp Man" with the "raspy voice" (60). The personal names in *The Lesser Blessed* that imitate Indigenous traditions of name giving provide vivid characterizations of the persons in question, alluding either to their outward appearance (moustache, horse cock, finger, voice) or to their behaviour (jackal, boxing). Although these are usually N N compounds that do not contain a verbal constituent, they always create the *illusion* of English loan translations. The semantic density of the holophrase in Indigenous languages is suggested in these highly descriptive and synecdochic indigenized personal names. Although morphologically different, these names, then, function in the same way as their monolexical Inuktitut counterparts in *Arctic Dreams and Nightmares* (see the previous chapter). The semantic density of the indigenized personal names in Van Camp's novel further increases readers' participation and thus marks these names as a strategy in textualizing orality that can be regarded as culturally specific.

While Van Camp's use of direct holophrastic traces in *The Lesser Blessed*, then, is fairly extensive, indirect holophrastic traces, in the form of subject dropping and pronoun copying, are less so. *Subject dropping* occurs only sporadically in the novel and usually does not concern the narration of words but is found mostly in direct discourse:[51]

- "'Naw,' he said. '*Can't, got barred* for being rowdy'" (35; emphasis added),
- "*Don't think* so. I got a lot of homework to do" (65; emphasis added),
- "*Said* he was going to go on the land" (69; emphasis added),

- "I gotta go. *Think* I'm gonna listen to Jed for a bit" (95; emphasis added),
- "Naw, *rolled* it. *Sent* her out to Hay River to get fixed but I can't pay for it" (106; emphasis added),
- "*Heard* about you and Jazz busting each other up" (106; emphasis added), and
- "'Juliet, what are you going to do?'—'*Go* to Edmonton'" (112; emphasis added).

Pronoun copying, too, is found only occasionally in *The Lesser Blessed* and is restricted mostly to direct discourse:

- "That was the only thing that gave this postcard away. Those eyes" (4),
- "But the monkeys, what they did was they attacked us" (4),
- "There was only her, Juliet" (27),
- "Her room, which one is it?" (108).

Both subject dropping and pronoun copying produce a written discourse that more clearly resembles actual oral speech. The dropping of grammatical subjects here mimics the "shorthand" of a real-life conversation, and pronoun copying creates a rather fragmentary discourse that mimics intonation units in oral speech. Both, therefore, indicate textualized orality as well as author involvement and reader participation. And both imitate polysynthetic language structures: subject dropping imitates the ability of polysynthetic languages to express a complete sentence without using an independent noun phrase elaborating on the grammatical subject, thus having readers rely on context rather than verbal signs, whereas pronoun copying is reminiscent of the structure in Indigenous discourse caused by the holistic nature of polysynthetic verbs. Both subject dropping and pronoun copying in *The Lesser Blessed*, therefore, can be regarded as strategies in textualizing orality that are culturally specific.

Two other language strategies in *The Lesser Blessed*, though further removed from the features of actual Indigenous discourse than subject dropping and pronoun copying, can nonetheless be seen as indirect holophrastic traces: the use of poetic language and the use of silence—what Wolfgang Iser has called *Leerstellen*[52] ("textual gaps")—that produce the minimalism of text that, as noted in the introduction, is so typical of both Indigenous languages and rhetorics.

The interweaving of *poetic language*—poetic prose, prose poems, and free verse—throughout *The Lesser Blessed* serves to "balance" the use of colloquial language and slang and adds to the novel's vivid narration through a considerable amount of figurative language. Indigenous languages often feature the figurative use of language in ordinary speech; it is invited by polysynthesis and increases listener participation. Thus, by incorporating figurative language into a narrative text, *The Lesser Blessed* mimics this tendency of Indigenous languages. "I am my father's scream," "Mommy, your monkey's eating Daddy's banana" (38), and "And listen to my black teeth scream" (3)—all of which anticipate Larry's accident story (the sexual connotations, the violence, the fire)—are figures of speech found in the prose sections of Larry's narrative. On his way from the buried "Me" (1) to the reborn "Me" (119), Larry turns to Dogrib tradition for orientation; in the meantime, his language evolves from plain prose to a more elaborate prose that is interrupted by both poetic prose and poems composed in either prose or free verse. Of course, only those figures of speech in *The Lesser Blessed* that perform a significant narrative function qualify as paraholophrases. Yet all the other figures of speech also form important rhetorical devices because figurative uses of language, whether with or without significant narrative function, always invite reader participation: characterized by a minimalism of text, the poetic passages of *The Lesser Blessed* are key for the story evolving around them. Given the correlation between figurative language and polysynthetic languages, the figurative language in *The Lesser Blessed* adds not only to the textualization of orality in the novel but also to the culturally specific strategies employed for this purpose.

An indirect holophrastic trace of a similar kind is formed by the silences in the psychological narrative strand of *The Lesser Blessed*. This strand is kept fairly short, and, even though the story of Larry's accident is eventually revealed in this strand, this story is never narrated coherently. The silences of the psychological narrative strand result in a minimalism of text and hence invite the readers' participation in the composition of the novel: readers are asked to fill in the blanks left by the narrator/author. Mimicking the silences invited by polysynthetic grammars (see the introduction), the silences of the psychological narrative strand in Van Camp's novel can thus be read as indirect holophrastic traces: they cannot qualify as paraholophrases—silence has no substance—but they nonetheless suggest in writing a communicative situation often found in polysynthetic grammars that calls for more active participation of listeners. The silences in *The Lesser Blessed*, then, not only are indirect holophrastic traces, but they also mark a culturally specific way of textualizing orality.

The imitation of oral speech is pervasive in terms of the construction of dialogue in *The Lesser Blessed*, but the textualization of orality in the novel goes much further. With Larry Sole, Richard Van Camp has invented a narrator who creates the illusion of an oral storytelling performance and who draws attention to the illusion in a number of ways. One example of this attention to the "play" between the oral and the written is in this passage:

> [...] If you've ever seen sand dunes in the Sahara, that was [Juliet's] ass. [...] My hands ached and sang for the chance to grab it!
> P.S.
> I heard she liked it doggy-style.
> But, alas, enough of her ass. It's really her face I want to talk about. (27)

A *post scriptum* (ordinarily reserved for letter-writing, not for oral storytelling or, for that matter, the narrating of novels), instead of an oral "by the way," introduces Larry's aside, which turns into a commentary in which Larry ironizes his sexual fantasies about Juliet in a tongue-in-cheek rhyme: "But, alas, enough of her ass." Yet he ends his metafictional comment by noting what he wants to *talk*, rather than write, about.

Thus clearly aware of the textuality of his narrative, Larry nonetheless places himself in the tradition of Dene storytellers (a tradition to which Jed also belongs). Upon hearing Larry's version of the Dogrib creation story, Johnny is impressed by the story itself but also by Larry's skilful storytelling: "You're a storyteller, man. Your voice even changed when you talked" (52). The reader will obviously not *hear* Larry's voice changing in the course of his telling, but he or she will *see* his change of tense from the past tense to the historical present and back to the past tense toward the story's ending—a movement typically found in (Indigenous) storytelling and generally regarded as an indicator of a speaker's involvement with reality.[53]

The narrator-as-storyteller is further indicated by the fact that Larry frequently interweaves his own narrative with other people's stories or teachings, such as Jed's story about the Blue Monkeys (4–6) and the story about Dogrib creation (51–52), which are found in the psychological and mythological narrative strands respectively. Most of Larry's stories-within-stories are fairly short interludes (6, 32, 97–98, 102) and are directed only at his immediate audience, his readers. In each case, however, he always gives the source for the respective story or teaching (i.e., either his mother or Jed). Larry's source citing evokes the use of evidentials as structural and copyright devices in Indigenous discourse. Given the correlation between polysynthesis and evidentiality, this citing of the sources of stories can be regarded as a holophrastic trace that, through its highlighting of the storytelling act, functions as a strategy in textualizing orality that is clearly culturally specific.

In the course of his narration, Larry frequently shows involvement with both his narrative and his audience. The main narrative strand includes metafictional comments such as "It's really her face I want to talk about" (27) or "Speaking of which, when I first came here, Juliet was on crutches" (28). Conversational asides within parentheses occur frequently in the narrative and provide further information for the reader: "Jed taught me that one" (16), "bubble butt (which is protruding) or a bannock butt (which is flat)" (27), or "That's Raven talk for 'drunk'" (29). In conversations with other characters, his asides often express things that Larry would not dare say out loud: "Don't look at me" (3), "And listen to my black teeth scream" (3), "Juliet! Juliet! Juliet!" (11), "You fuckin' foot-licker" (45), "That fuckin' Johnny" (98), or "call her snowbird" and "call her raven" (110). Parenthetical asides also provide ironic commentary: "'That's pretty smart.' (For a fuckin' asshole)" (44).

Larry's involvement with his audience is further achieved by way of an oral strategy also common in Euro-Western texts. Direct reader addresses in *The Lesser Blessed* either take the form of simple conversational asides, such as "I have to tell you about Darcy McMannus" (19) and "I must tell you more" (28), or become more elaborate, such as the following reader address that serves as a frame for one of the novel's stories-within-stories: "I have this lousy memory because of my accident, but if you were to tell me a neat story, I'd be able to tell it back to you years from now, word by word. For example, the last time Jed was here, he told us about a trip to India. I'll tell it to you. It goes like this: [...]" (3). What follows is Larry's retelling of Jed's story about the "Blue Monkeys of Corruption." Larry ends the story with a comment that mirrors its beginning: "That's the story he told me. It's yours now. Tell anyone you want" (6). Larry does not just tell his readers a story, then; he gives it as an offering, thus bestowing responsibility on readers. Whereas in Richard Wagamese's *Keeper'n Me* Keeper invites readers to listen carefully to Garnet's story because it might also concern their own lives,[54] Larry's address in *The Lesser Blessed* is more demanding because it suggests that the *sharing of stories* is as significant as the stories themselves. Thomas King ends each chapter in his *The Truth about Stories* with an observation similar to Larry's in *The Lesser Blessed*:

> Take Charm's story, for instance. It's yours. Do with it what you will. Tell it to friends. Turn it into a television movie. Forget it. But don't

say in the years to come that you would have lived your life differently if only you had heard this story.

You've heard it now.⁵⁵

Larry's reminder of the responsibility of readers overhearing his narration occurs early in his narrative and thus establishes, from the start, an intimate relationship between the narrator and his readers—a relationship that resembles that between storyteller and audience in Indigenous oratures and is crucial to the success of the narrative as the re-creation of an actual storytelling performance. The techniques that Van Camp employs to re-create this performance—with the exception of source citing—might not be very different from techniques found in Euro-Western texts. The point, however, is that, by creating the illusion of an actual storytelling performance and by constructing dialogue that imitates actual oral speech, he has provided an ideal setting for the direct and indirect holophrastic traces discussed above.

SUMMARY

Unlike Ishmael Alunik's *Call Me Ishmael* and Alootook Ipellie's *Arctic Dreams and Nightmares*, discussed in the previous chapters, Richard Van Camp's *The Lesser Blessed* attempts neither the writing of an oral tradition nor the reimagination of Indigenous cultural traditions. Traditional Dogrib culture does not feature extensively in *The Lesser Blessed*, but the novel does contain retellings of Dogrib oral traditions, and these traditional stories take on significant functions as allegories, on the levels of both content and form. At the same time, Van Camp's novel exhibits a rather flat narrative line, with a narrative frame that takes a cyclical form and is comparable to the opening and closing frames in Alunik's and Ipellie's collections. Like these two Inuit texts, Van Camp's novel depends heavily on the use of paraholophrases to construct its complex narrative structure made up of three narrative strands that eventually flow into each other in the novel's closing, perfecting the cyclical frame first suggested in the narrative's opening. In establishing a narrative frame that evokes one of the generic conventions of Indigenous oratures, paraholophrases in *The Lesser Blessed* provide the *interpretative context* of the narrative. As such, they not only show the *author's involvement* but also invite the *reader's participation*. The reader's successful participation ultimately depends on recognizing the eventual convergence of the novel's three narrative strands, signalled by the paraholophrases marking the mythological answer to Larry's psychological problem.

Unlike those found in *Call Me Ishmael* and *Arctic Dreams and Nightmares*, paraholophrases in *The Lesser Blessed* are usually restricted to figures of speech and intratextual references. The figurative nature of most paraholophrases in *The Lesser Blessed* combined with the narrative structure of the novel and, particularly, the use of Dogrib stories as allegories ensure, nonetheless, that a certain amount of openness is retained in the narrative. Although they do not usually involve intertextuality, the paraholophrases employed in *The Lesser Blessed* function essentially the same as in Alunik's and Ipellie's texts: to construct the narrative's structure and, in the meantime, to serve as oral strategies resulting from the context of language use (context, involvement, and participation). That *The Lesser Blessed* comes relatively close to the Euro-Western realist novel and was written by a young Indigenous author who has lost his tribal language, then, in no way minimizes the significance of paraholophrases in the composition of the novel and its textualization of orality.

Geary Hobson has described Van Camp's debut novel as an exceptional piece of fiction:

> In virtually every generation, in the realm of literary activity, there comes along a book that, by the very nature of its subject matter and place and the sheer exuberance of its utterances reverberant of the place and people depicted, introduces not only a little-known terra firma and people, but sometimes becomes the definer of that era in which it is produced. [...]
>
> In my view, Richard Van Camp [...] is accomplishing virtually the same thing in his first novel, *The Lesser Blessed*, as Hemingway, Kerouac, et al. did in their times. [...] Van Camp's novel introduces a new terrain and language that nonetheless has roots in the fiction of Momaday, Leslie Marmon Silko, and James Welch, while simultaneously exploring the same subject matter as the contemporary stories of Sherman Alexie, Adrian Louis, and Lorne Simon.[56]

Hobson's observations appear to apply particularly to Van Camp's skilful use of language in *The Lesser Blessed*. Van Camp does not speak his ancestral language; his fiction therefore lacks any notable use of Dogrib language, not to mention the use of actual holophrases. The novel, however, compensates for its nearly complete lack of code switching through the wide-ranging use of direct holophrastic traces—rhetorical signals for the self-powerment Larry achieves in the course of his narration. The different kinds of compounds (particularly the quotation compounds) and the inventive use of language not only show the author's involvement but also invite reader participation and thus serve as strategies in textualizing orality. Van Camp employs primarily quotation compounds, whose use is noteworthy despite their comparatively limited frequency. These quotation compounds point out a way to bypass the analytic morphology of the English language in an attempt to imitate the structure of the holophrase, all the while retaining a certain level of colloquial speech. After all, it is through the interweaving of prose with poetry and colloquial with figurative language that *The Lesser Blessed* portrays such a realistic and vivid picture of contemporary Indigenous youth in Canada. While Van Camp's use of figurative language and his use of textual silences mark strategies in creating author *involvement* and reader *participation* that are found universally in literature, the instances of pronoun copying, subject dropping, and source citing in *The Lesser Blessed* are more clearly culturally specific strategies in textualizing orality and, moreover, concern features of language use that result from the context of language production (prosody, redundancy, and fragmentation). As in the two Inuit texts discussed in the earlier chapters, holophrastic traces in Van Camp's novel form textual markers that, though they cannot successfully translate the holophrase into Indigenous literatures in English on a formal (i.e., grammatical) level, provide at least some traces of this particular structure in the English text, all the while adding to the textualization of orality created through the use of paraholophrases.

Although both Van Camp's novel and Ipellie's story cycle are fiction, they differ in that Ipellie's book retains considerable ties to its underlying cultural and linguistic traditions, whereas such ties are less evident in *The Lesser Blessed*. Although the Dogrib language does not feature prominently in *The Lesser Blessed* and Dogrib oral tradition and history are not the novel's *main* focus, the significance of paraholophrases in the composition of the novel is not diminished. With its lack of holophrases and its implicit, rather than explicit, political commentary, *The Lesser Blessed* continues a position in Indigenous literatures in English that tends "towards a stylistic merger with mainstream literature while retaining some Native contents,"[57] a position first introduced by novelists such as Thomas King. Although belonging to different generations of Indigenous writers, King and Van Camp have in common that neither speaks his ancestral language. Compared with *The Lesser Blessed* (and all the other texts discussed in this study), however, King's writing is far richer in intertextual references. How effectively (para)-holophrases can be employed to create a text that engages in *extensive* intertextual play is discussed in the following chapter, using King's *Green Grass, Running Water* as its subject.

CHAPTER 4

"All This Water Imagery Must Mean Something": Thomas King's *Green Grass, Running Water*

Over the past two decades, Thomas King has emerged as one of Canada's most prominent writers of Indigenous descent. He was born in Sacramento, California, in 1943 to a mother of Greek and German descent and a Cherokee father, who left his wife when King was still young. It was not until he was in his teenage years that King began spending time with other Native people.[1] He speaks neither Cherokee nor any other Indigenous language, except, as he says, "[b]its and pieces of some, but not enough to get me fed and a bed to sleep in at night."[2] King sees himself as both "a Native writer and a Canadian writer," rather than a "Canadian Native writer,"[3] thus assuming what many critics of his work have described as a border position:[4] "in some ways," King says, "I'm this Native writer who's out in the middle—not of nowhere, but I don't have strong tribal affiliations. I wasn't raised on Cherokee land";[5] nor did he spend "any large amount of time living on a reserve."[6]

Yet, as Daniel Heath Justice (Cherokee) has argued, King's writing, particularly his *Truth and Bright Water* (1999), still reflects a Cherokee experience, even if it is one that is "made particularly difficult as a result of the demographic scattering of so many Cherokees by the policies of removal."[7] Aside from what Justice has called "a profoundly Cherokee sensibility,"[8] King's writing has also been influenced by his experiences living in Lethbridge, Alberta, for ten years, where King worked extensively with

Blackfoots and Crees who "provided [him] with the basis of much of [his] fiction."[9] "If I think of any place as home," King thus says, "it's the Alberta prairies [...]. I'm not Blackfoot, but that feels like the place I want to go back to."[10] King left Lethbridge for good in 1990, but the prairie landscape is ever-present in much of his fiction. He even, if somewhat ironically, refers to *Medicine River* (1990), *Green Grass, Running Water* (1993), and *Truth and Bright Water* as his "prairie novels."[11] At the same time, however, Plains and Cherokee traditions do not serve as the only sources of King's writing, which freely borrows from numerous Indigenous traditions.

THE TEXT: *GREEN GRASS, RUNNING WATER*

Thomas King's most renowned and highly sophisticated work is *Green Grass, Running Water*.[12] The novel was a finalist for the Governor General's Literary Award in 1993 and, as noted by Hartmut Lutz, "has firmly established contemporary Native Literature in Canada as a field open to and even inviting Western academic study and theorizing."[13] According to a survey by *Quill and Quire* published in its November 2001 issue, *Green Grass, Running Water* was the most-taught novel in undergraduate courses in Canadian literature across Canada.[14]

Green Grass, Running Water can be read as a fictionalized version of King's doctoral dissertation, *Inventing the Indian: White Images, Native Oral Literature, and Contemporary Native Writers*, in which King discusses contemporary Indigenous novels in relation to Indigenous creation stories.[15] *Green Grass, Running Water* is replete with creation stories, both Indigenous and non-Indigenous; in fact, the novel fictionalizes its own creation by way of framing its main story with a conversation between the narrator and his student, Coyote, whose actions bring the novel into being. Because of the significance of creation stories and trickster figures in *Green Grass, Running Water*, I will preface my analysis of the use of (para)holophrases in the novel with, first, a brief review of the traditional roles of creation stories and tricksters in Indigenous oratures and, second, some preliminary remarks about the novel's narrative structure and plot.

The Significance of Indigenous Creation Stories and Trickster Figures

In a study of northwest Indigenous traditions published in 1865, George Gibbs wrote, "Of the Creation of mankind there are probably as many stories as there are tribes."[16] Discussions of North American Indigenous creation stories hence always run the risk of generalization. Yet the various existing Indigenous creation stories have at least two characteristics in common that clearly distinguish them from those of other peoples. First, in contrast to the Judeo-Christian tradition of explaining the world's creation from a void, most Indigenous creation stories propose the existence of "something" before creation.[17] Second, Indigenous creation stories point out perceptions of the world that are ultimately very different from those of Euro-Westeners. The following discussion of creation stories is based on King's generalized view of Indigenous creation stories, as outlined in his dissertation and as summarized in Chapter 1 of his Massey Lectures, *The Truth about Stories* (2003). Of course, King's account does not cover the wealth of creation stories in Indigenous North America. However, his own reading of these stories greatly influences his writing, and for this reason it is appropriate to consider his analysis of Indigenous creation stories here.

"If there is a need to understand a culture, and one can only hear a single story that the culture tells about itself," King argues in his dissertation, "that story should probably be a creation story."[18] Comparing the Christian story of creation in Genesis to the three different categories of Indigenous creation stories, which he identifies based on the degree to which these stories feature a monotheistic deity as in Christianity,[19] King finds that Indigenous creation stories differ from the Christian story of creation in terms of four important relationships: creator to humans, humans to animals, humans to the land, and good to evil. While Genesis features "an omnipotent, patriarchal deity" whose "will controls the universe," King writes, creation in most Indigenous creation stories is a corporate undertaking.[20] In Genesis, God is superior to humans, who have absolutely no control over their lives but whose relationship to animals is the reversal of their relationship to God.[21] In Indigenous creation stories, the lines between deities, humans, and animals are blurred, primarily because the stories lack the Christian idea of a "deity-human-animal hierarchy," as King calls it.[22] Whereas in Genesis humans lose their paradise through a fall from grace and, as punishment, are damned to live in a prison-like world without beauty,[23] the world depicted in Indigenous creation stories is "warm and hospitable"; there exists, according to King, no notion in these stories of "a better world somewhere else."[24] The cosmic forces in the Christian world are good and evil, personified by God and the devil; there exists, King further writes, no position between these two extremes.[25] In Indigenous creation stories, however, good and evil are connected with each other, and if one upsets the balance of good and evil the world will end up in chaos.[26]

King's discussion of the differences between Indigenous creation stories and the book of Genesis, however generalized, becomes relevant for his analysis of their narrative structures. King detects in Genesis two main characters (Adam and Eve), a conflict (the fall from grace), and a climax (God's discovery of their disobedience and their subsequent expulsion from the Garden of Eden), whereas he describes the plot in Indigenous creation stories as "considerably flatter" because they lack the idea of a main character, of conflict, or of climax. Instead, King argues, Indigenous creation stories are "structured like a chain, where one creation leads to another, one understanding to the next," with none of these elements being "any more important or dramatic than the last or the next."[27]

With the incorporation into *Green Grass, Running Water* of several different Indigenous creation stories, all of which make use of the earth diver story,[28] King introduces "a more Native sense of the creation of the world."[29] Given his analysis of the structural differences between Indigenous and Euro-Western creation stories, King ultimately also incorporates into his novel a unique, if admittedly generalized, Indigenous narrative structure that makes *Green Grass, Running Water* resemble what he has termed "associational literature," a type of Indigenous writing that is centred on an Indigenous community and Indigenous realities (i.e., whose main focus is neither a non-Indigenous community nor a conflict between Indigenous and non-Indigenous peoples) and that arranges "the elements of plot along a rather flat narrative line that ignores the ubiquitous climaxes and resolutions that are so valued in non-Native literature."[30]

The notion of balance, whether between different beings or between good and evil, forms an important component in Indigenous perceptions of the universe and is probably nowhere better embodied than in the Indigenous cultural heroes and transformers whom Euro-Western scholars generally refer to as "tricksters."[31] Tricksters populate the Indigenous oral traditions of North America,[32] but they do so taking various shapes and names in narratives that are part of traditions specific to the culture in question. Found in the traditions of Indigenous peoples of the Great Basin, the Plains, central California, the Plateau area, and the Southwest, Coyote is probably the most well-known trickster in North American Indigenous oratures.[33] The origins of Coyote are not always mentioned in the respective tribal traditions,[34] but Coyote, like many other tricksters in North America, is generally considered one of the First People who inhabited the earth at the beginning of time.[35] In some traditions, Coyote is involved in creation, either as the creator's companion (e.g., Chinook, Achumawi, and Kato/Sinkyone) or as the creator himself, as in the case of Old Man Coyote (Crow);[36] other tribal traditions hold Coyote responsible for shaping the world as we know it today, for example, by making sexual intercourse pleasurable (Paiute).[37]

North American Indigenous tricksters have fascinated Euro-Western scholars as far back as the late 1800s. However, as Anne Doueihi has convincingly argued in an essay originally published in 1984, Euro-Western readings of the trickster have often resulted in "a discourse of domination" in which "Western culture turns the discourse about the trickster into a discourse *by Western culture about Western culture*, with the trickster serving only in a nominal function so that the discussion may begin."[38] Craig S. Womack goes even further when arguing that "there is no such thing as a trickster in indigenous cultures, that tricksters were invented by anthropologists."[39] Hence, trickster "is a trope rather than a reality within Native cultures." The very term "trickster," which as Womack notes "is not a term indigenous to an Indian language," further underlines this state of affairs.[40] As Neal McLeod has observed,

> The proper term [for the Cree trickster] is *kistêsinaw*, which denotes the notion of the elder brother. This instantly assumes a state of kinship and relationship between humans and the rest of creation. It also moves beyond the intersubjective limitations of human-based discourse which has dominated the West. It moves beyond the conceptual straitjacket that the term "trickster" puts *wîsahkêcâhk* in: the term suggests to some that this sacred being is little more than a buffoon. The concepts centred on the word in English include such words as "trickery," "tricky," and "trick," which indicate something less than the truth.[41]

Instead, McLeod continues, trickster stories ought to be regarded as sacred stories forming part of the respective tribal tradition; thus, stories of *wîsahkêcâhk* should be considered as belonging to the *âtayôhkêwina*, the sacred narratives of the Crees.[42] Womack's and McLeod's critiques of Euro-Western terminology and readings of tricksters in Indigenous traditions suggest three conclusions: first, that the term "trickster" is part of a discourse of colonization; second, that there are as many tribal-specific names for Indigenous "tricksters" as there are Indigenous cultures in North America; and third, that readings of tricksters in Indigenous traditions need to take into account the "cultural and historical specificity" of trickster narratives, which is how Kristina Fagan (Labrador-Métis) has described the underlying idea of "a new approach to trickster studies" put forward by the contributors of *Troubling Tricksters*, a recent collection of essays on North American Indigenous tricksters.[43]

In her introduction to *Troubling Tricksters*, Fagan also suggests that "the emergence of the trickster in contemporary Native writing took place in a very urban, cross-cultural, organized, and strategic manner." As a "conscious recreation of a tradition," contemporary trickster narratives, she further writes, are tied to "specific and current needs."[44] I believe that this observation applies particularly well to King's Coyote in *Green Grass, Running Water*, which does not seem to be based on any particular Coyote found in Indigenous tribal traditions. Ultimately, I think that it is important to consider the specific function that the figure of Coyote fulfills in *Green Grass, Running Water*, which is, to use King's own words, that of a "sacred clown" introduced into the novel "as a part of the chorus, if you will, and in some ways, as a creator."[45] How exactly Coyote and a conflation of various Indigenous creation stories help King to relate a story set in contemporary Canada will become apparent in the discussion of the plot and narrative structure of the novel that follows.

Plot and Narrative Structure: Preliminary Remarks

Green Grass, Running Water is structured into four volumes and contains three narrative strands: the "realistic" narrative, which tells the story of a group of Canadian Blackfoot Natives; the "mythological" narrative, which tells the stories of First Woman, Changing Woman, Thought Woman, and Old Woman; and the interspersed conversations between the first-person narrator and Coyote, which frame the stories told in the other two narrative strands. The different strands can be distinguished based on formal criteria. Patricia Linton has correctly noted the different structures of tense in the novel's realistic narrative strand, narrated in the past, and its mythological narrative strand, narrated in the present.[46] The continuous dialogue between "I" and Coyote in the framing narrative bears much resemblance to the mythological narrative strand in terms of style of narration. Both employ an oral narrative technique instead of a written one. They are in the present tense and contain various marks of the oral. Unlike the conversations in the mythological narrative strand, however, the conversations between "I" and Coyote employ inverted commas and can be distinguished from the other narrative strands because this text is separated from the other text by empty lines.[47]

The frame narrative consists of the discussions between a teacher—the "I"—and his student, Coyote. By listening to the story told by "I" in the other narrative strands, Coyote is supposed to learn the art of storytelling so that he will eventually be able to tell the story himself. That "I" is indeed the "master narrator" narrating all three narrative strands can only be assumed. Although it is beyond doubt that "I" is relating the frame narrative, which, unlike the other narratives, is narrated in the first person, the omniscient narration in the other two narrative strands suggests a narrator who does not get involved in the action. The only character inside the novel

CHAPTER 4

qualifying as such is the "I" of the frame narrative. Judging from the passage quoted below, "I" is conscious of both the realistic and the mythological narrative strands:[48]

> "But maybe they'll give us a ride," says Coyote.
> "No time for that," I says. "We got to get back to the other story." (237)

Further evidence for the role of "I" as master narrator is provided in the opening of the novel, which ends with the formulaic comment "And here's how it happened" (3)—suggesting that, whatever story comes next, "I" will take responsibility for it since he is assuming the role of narrator. The formula "This according to" (9, 103, 104, 231, 327, 328), however, which marks the beginning of each of the novel's creation stories, indicates that the stories of First Woman, Changing Woman, Thought Woman, and Old Woman are related by the "four old Indians" (97), who also feature as characters in the realistic narrative strand. The master narrator's decision to share his authority as storyteller with the four old Indians turns out to be intentional. When at the end of the creation stories each of the four women assumes the identity of the old Indian narrating her story, it becomes clear that the creation stories are not third-person, but first-person, narrations. Obviously, the master narrator is aware that he "can't tell [the story] all by [him]self" (14) since, in oral traditions, it always takes multiple voices to tell a story properly. But does *Green Grass, Running Water* really tell *one* story? The existence of both a realistic narrative strand and a mythological narrative strand seems to suggest that the novel tells multiple stories that do not intersect, but, as it turns out, the realistic and mythological narrative strands are actually different components of the same story.

The story related in *Green Grass, Running Water* unfolds not in a linear fashion but by means of flashbacks that contain further flashbacks and that cross narrative boundaries. The master narrator's story begins with the introduction of a group of Blackfoots from the southern Alberta town of Blossom and the nearby reserve. The central characters are Lionel Red Dog; his cousin, Charlie Looking Bear; their mutual lover, Alberta Frank; Lionel's and Charlie's uncle, Eli Stands Alone; and Lionel's sister, Latisha. Lionel cannot persuade Alberta to marry him and is stuck in a job that he hates. Alberta wants to have a baby; however, having been divorced once already, she wants to marry neither of her two lovers. Charlie never really recovered from "losing" his father, a once-famous Indigenous actor and now an alcoholic. Charlie did manage, however, to finish law school and was hired by Duplessis International Associates to work on a case against his uncle Eli, who, after the death of his wife, has returned to the reserve and is preventing the completion of the Grand Baleen Dam by refusing to leave his dead mother's cabin, situated in the dam's spillway. Latisha successfully runs the Dead Dog Café, a restaurant and major tourist attraction famous for its (fake) dog dishes, and is raising three children on her own after her divorce from George Morningstar, a white American from Michigan.

As each character is on his or her way to the reserve for the annual Sun Dance, where they all eventually meet at the end of the novel, their life stories are untangled in a series of flashbacks that explain the situations in which they find themselves. The Sun Dance marks both the key event in the novel and its ending. Lionel prevents George Morningstar from taking pictures of the Sun Dance ceremony for a New Age magazine by taking away his rolls of film and chasing him off the Sun Dance grounds (382–88). An earthquake on the morning of the second day of the Sun Dance changes the lives of the various characters considerably, however. Eli drowns in the flood that destroys the dam and his mother's cabin. With no case to work on, Charlie loses his job at Duplessis and decides to visit his father in California. Alberta finally conceives the desired baby (through an immaculate conception), and Lionel considers going back to university. At the end of the novel, it is still unclear how Alberta became pregnant and whether she will marry Lionel or Charlie or neither of them. Despite these major changes in their lives, the characters all seem to be quite hopeful about the future and decide to build a cabin where Eli's once stood. Ironically, the earthquake, a decidedly *non-personal* natural disaster, appears to have forced each of them to face his or her personal problems and finally to sort them out.

As Lionel, Charlie, Alberta, Eli, and Latisha travel to the annual Sun Dance, they meet four mysterious old Indians who have escaped from a psychiatric hospital in Florida and are now travelling through Canada, "trying to fix up the world" (123). As the story progresses, the four old Indians fix *The Mysterious Warrior* (188), a supposedly famous but fictional John Wayne western, by having the Indians shoot Wayne and his companions (316–22). Furthermore, the four old Indians try to fix the life of Lionel by helping him to protect his Blackfoot tradition in front of Alberta, the woman whom he loves. The identities of the four old Indians remain unclear throughout most of the novel. According to the hospital records, their names are "Mr. Red, Mr. White, Mr. Black, and Mr. Blue" (52), but they refer to themselves as the Lone Ranger, Ishmael, Robinson Crusoe, and Hawkeye. And the hospital's janitor, Babo Jones, insists that they are "women, not men" (53). Why the four old Indians were locked up in the security wing of the hospital Dr. J. Hovaugh, in charge of them, cannot really explain; likewise, their escape also remains "a mystery" to him (76). In fact, the mystery surrounding the escape of the Lone Ranger, Ishmael, Robinson Crusoe, and Hawkeye and their return to the hospital by the end of the novel is never explained in the realistic narrative strand but is suggested in the novel's mythological narrative strand.

The creation stories of the mythological narrative strand are told as the four old Indians travel through Canada and meet the characters of the realistic narrative strand. These creation stories thus form a subnarrative of their own, contained within the overall story of the novel in the form of a flashback. Each of the four creation stories follows the same pattern and introduces its respective narrator, thus revealing that the four old Indians are really women. Arranged as flashbacks to the story of First Woman (volume one), the stories of Changing Woman (volume two), Thought Woman (volume three), and Old Woman (volume four) serve to introduce the Lone Ranger's (First Woman's) friends with whom First Woman escapes from Fort Marion at the end of her story (100). But what happens after this escape is not revealed until—at the end of Old Woman's story (418) in volume four—the narration at last resumes where First Woman's story ended in volume one. Of course, there is no suggestion here that the escape of the four old Indians from the fort in the mythological narrative strand is identical to their escape from the hospital in the realistic narrative strand, but readers are invited to see "a pattern" (48): ever since they were first arrested, the four women have left their prison every once in a while to go on a mission to "fix up the world," not as a whole, but a little at a time (123). Once their mission is complete, they return to their prison. In fact, their escape from Fort Marion in the mythological narrative strand was only the first of thirty-seven escapes (47) since their arrival in the psychiatric hospital in 1891 (96). The narrative does not explain why the four women were moved into Dr. Hovaugh's hospital in the first place; nor does it explain how the four old Indians travelled from Florida to Alberta without being seen. These gaps are left for readers to fill.[49]

The realistic and mythological narrative strands in *Green Grass, Running Water* thus form a single story, a fact that the master narrator admits, indirectly, at the end of the novel:

"Earthquake! Earthquake!" yells Coyote.
"Calm down," I says.
"But it's another earthquake," says Coyote.
"Yes," I says. "These things happen."
"But we've already had one earthquake in this story," says Coyote.

"And you never know when something like this is going to happen again," I says.

"Wow!" says Coyote. "Wow!" (418; emphasis added)

At first glance, it might seem impossible to identify a unified reading of the very different narrative strands that run through *Green Grass, Running Water*. The realistic narrative strand, however, is not actually realistic but represents a trickster narrative involving multiple trickster figures (Coyote and the four old Indians). Likewise, the mythological narrative strand not only reinvents actual Indigenous creation stories that rewrite English/Anglo-American (master) narratives (primarily the Bible but also Melville's *Moby-Dick*, Defoe's *Robinson Crusoe*, and Cooper's Leatherstocking novels) but also can be read as the retelling of a specific historical event from an Indigenous perspective: namely, the imprisonment of Kiowa, Comanche, Cheyenne, Arapaho, and Plains Apache at Fort Marion, Florida, in 1874.[50] Blurring generic boundaries, the realistic and mythological narrative strands essentially become one narrative. That these two strands indeed tell one story, then, is reflected not just in terms of content but also in terms of form.

Modelled on various Indigenous cultural heroes with supernatural powers, First Woman,[51] Changing Woman,[52] Thought Woman,[53] and Old Woman[54] belong to the First People, who, according to Indigenous beliefs, populated the earth after creation; as such, these figures are sacred. The presence of the four women in the realistic narrative strand hence reflects Indigenous notions of spirituality.[55] When they return to their hospital disguised as the four old Indians, it is still not clear whether or to what extent they have really fixed Lionel's life, but they are nevertheless content with the result (427–28). The story of the four Indigenous women's first escape from their white oppressors forms a bridge between the two narrative strands in *Green Grass, Running Water*, thus connecting the past with the present. In doing so, the novel does more than merely suggest how one generation affects the generations still to come. Indeed, by having two seemingly different narrative strands float into each other, the novel's structure also embodies the interrelatedness of past and present, of reality and myth, and points to what Paula Gunn Allen (Laguna Pueblo-Sioux) has called "an enduring sense of the fluidity and malleability, the fragility and plasticity of the creative universe in which we live and dwell and have our being."[56] To achieve this fluidity and malleability, *Green Grass, Running Water* relies on elements from Indigenous oral traditions: namely, creation stories and trickster figures. With the basic lines of its plot and narrative structure outlined, let us look at developing a holophrastic reading of King's novel.

CHAPTER 4

A HOLOPHRASTIC READING OF *GREEN GRASS, RUNNING WATER*
Paraholophrases

The frame narrative of *Green Grass, Running Water* consists entirely of direct discourse. In fact, there appear to be only four instances in which the frame narrative briefly shifts from direct speech to a narrative of non-verbal events (41, 238, 293, 300).[57] With no scenic presentations, comments, or descriptions given by the narrator, readers do not know where or when the conversations between "I" and Coyote take place; nor do they know anything about the two characters other than that "I" is telling Coyote a story. Creating the illusion of a live storytelling performance, this frame narrative metafictionalizes the narration of the story told in the novel and invites the reader to participate in its creation by reconstructing this story from the various episodes told by the master narrator in the course of the narration. The *frame narrative* thus works as a frame to the novel's story but not to the novel per se. Instead, as was the case with the three Indigenous texts discussed in the previous chapters, the *narrative frame* in *Green Grass, Running Water* is constituted by an opening and a closing, both of which are constructed with the help of paraholophrases. However, the narrative frame in King's novel forms but the outer part of a much more complex cyclical structure. It seems appropriate, then, to discuss the paraholophrases constituting the novel's narrative frame together with those paraholophrases involved in the construction of its cyclical narrative structure.

Paraholophrases Constituting the Novel's Cyclical Structure

The realistic narrative strand in *Green Grass, Running Water* ends with a flood of water—"Below, in the valley, the water rolled on as it had for eternity" (415)—which is what the mythological narrative strand starts with—"So. In the beginning, there was nothing. Just the water" (1). After the earthquake, the breaking of the Grand Baleen Dam, and Eli's death, Lionel, his aunt Norma, Alberta, Latisha, and Charlie gather near the place where Eli's cabin used to stand. As they examine what is left of it, Norma decides to have it rebuilt: "Norma stuck her stick in the earth. '**We'll start here**,' she said. '**So we can see the sun in the morning**'" (424). Her statement is appropriate since, despite its destructive forces, the earthquake marks a new beginning for each character. But her statement can also be seen as a reference to the story itself, for the allusion to the sun rising in the morning recalls and points back to the title of volume one: "East/red." (The significance of the titles of the four volumes will be further discussed below.) The new beginning evoked at the end of the novel, then, marks a new beginning, or a return to the beginning, both for the characters inside the story and for the readers outside the story. Norma's remark qualifies as a paraholophrase because it is equivalent in function to holophrases in Indigenous languages: through its semantic density—it expresses the core of a complex idea and thus carries a surplus of meaning—and in pointing back to volume one, it helps to create the cyclical shape of the story and thus functions as a significant narrative unit. In taking the form of a circle, the story narrated in *Green Grass, Running Water* represents a story cycle or, as Dee Horne has correctly noted, "a more complex version of the 'story cycle.'"[58] Indeed, this story cycle is made up of various layers of cyclical structures (including the realistic and the mythological narrative strands).

The realistic narrative strand begins with the escape of the four old Indians and ends with their return to the hospital in Florida.[59] The episode about their return (425–26) is a more or less exact repetition of the episode reporting their escape from the same institution at the beginning of the novel (16–17): most portions of the text (some 400 words) are completely identical in both episodes, and those that are not identical are at least analogous. The circle thus established is further emphasized by references in both passages to spring, seasonal cycles, and rebirth. When, upon their return to the hospital, the four old Indians meditate about whose life they will fix up the "next time" they go on a journey and propose to help Dr. Hovaugh—starting, of course, "in the garden" (428) "since everything went 'wrong' there"[60]—it becomes obvious that the realistic narrative strand does not end at this point but will begin anew: that is, it has come full circle. The strand is thus framed by a formulaic opening (the first Dr. Hovaugh scene) and a formulaic closing (the last Dr. Hovaugh scene). We can consider these as *large clusters of paraholophrases*, first, because these formulaic clusters are intratextual, and hence form the core of a complex idea, and, second, because they lend the realistic narrative its cyclical shape and thus function as significant narrative units.

The four creation stories of the mythological narrative strand tell about the first escape of the four old Indians from their prison in Florida. When Old Woman arrives at the fort in Florida (in the fourth volume), the last paragraph of the story of First Woman (from the first volume) is repeated nearly verbatim. This repetition connects the four creation stories into one narrative line, which culminates at the end of volume four and turns back on itself as it echoes the ending of the story of First Woman. The cyclical structure of the four creation stories is thus created with the help of a formulaic cluster of paraholophrases (see Table 4.1).

CHAPTER 4

End of First Woman's Story	End of First Woman's Story Repeated in Volume Four
It's the Lone Ranger, the guards shout. It's the Lone Ranger, they shout again, and they open the gate. So the Lone Ranger walks out of the prison, and the Lone Ranger and Ishmael and Robinson Crusoe and Hawkeye **head west.** Have a nice day, the soldiers say. Say hello to Tonto for us. And all the soldiers wave. (100)	It's the Lone Ranger, the guards shout. It's the Lone Ranger, they shout again. And they open the gate. So the Lone Ranger walks out of the prison, and the Lone Ranger and Ishmael and Hawkeye and Robinson Crusoe **head west.** Have a nice day, the soldiers say. Say hello to Tonto for us. And all those soldiers wave. (418)

Table 4.1 The Cyclical Structure of the Four Creation Stories

The circle established in the mythological narrative strand is also mirrored in the names assigned to the four (wo)men, whose stories suggest movement and growth (see Table 4.2).[61]

Mythological Narrative Strand	Realistic Narrative Strand	Dr. Hovaugh's Files	Volume Headings	Implications of the Colours
First Woman	Lone Ranger	Mr. Red	East/ red	New Generation
Changing Woman	Ishmael	Mr. White	South/ white	Growth
Thought Woman	Robinson Crusoe	Mr. Black	West/ black	Ripeness
Old Woman	Hawkeye	Mr. Blue	North/ blue	Old Age

Table 4.2 The Four (Wo)Men and the Narrative Structure of *Green Grass, Running Water*

Symbolizing the *four cardinal directions*, the *four seasons*, the *course of the sun*, as well as the *four stages of life*, the four (wo)men in the mythological and the realistic narrative strands represent the epitome of the sacred circle in Indigenous cultural traditions. The four colours in the volume headings reappear in the official names of the four (wo)men according to Dr. Hovaugh's files (realistic narrative strand),[62] whereas the four cardinal directions in the volume headings and the course of the sun are evoked in the very order (tracing the four stages of life) and form (circular) in which the four (wo)men tell their stories in the mythological narrative strand. Evidently, the four (wo)men are the key to bridging the "gap" between the realistic and the mythological narrative strands: their travelling from one narrative strand of the story to the other is the "place" where the two circles embodied by the realistic and the mythological narrative strands fall into each other. The two circles of the realistic narrative strand and the mythological narrative strand, both found within the story performed by the master narrator, then, become part of an even larger cyclical structure: namely, the story itself. Thus, the Sun Dance is not merely an element in the story told in *Green Grass, Running Water*; as noted by Marlene Goldman, the story's circular structure is also directly linked "with the circular motion of the sun and, by extension, the Sun Dance," thereby engraving into the novel's structure "an aboriginal conception of the world."[63]

Seen as a complex whole, then, the four (wo)men's names—**First Woman**, **Changing Woman**, **Thought Woman**, and **Old Woman**—provide, through their symbolism, a structural framework for the novel that evokes Indigenous oral generic conventions. Because they form the cores of complex ideas, all the while functioning as significant narrative units, the (wo)men's names are equivalent in function to holophrases in Indigenous languages and can thus be regarded as paraholophrases.

The novel's narrative structure is even more complex, however, than what is suggested by the cyclical structure formed by the realistic and mythological narrative strands, for this structure is part of an even larger circle formed by the novel's narrative frame. Goldman has compared the master narrator in *Green Grass, Running Water* with the announcer at the Sun Dance, who oversees the ceremony and ensures that a certain "standard of traditional behaviour" is kept.[64] Ironically, however, the master narrator's authority must be questioned, considering the involvement of different trickster figures in the novel, in particular the actions of Coyote, the master narrator's student. After all, the *circle formed by the novel proper* is due to none other than Coyote. As becomes evident in the course of *Green Grass, Running Water*, Coyote cares not so much about the story itself as about the playground that this story provides for him: he constantly interrupts the master narrator's narration, hardly ever pays attention to the story, and even jumps into it, thereby changing its outcome. In fact, when Coyote finally gets an opportunity to retell the story just given to him, he "screws up" its beginning, and the master narrator has to start over.

The novel's opening involves the use of the novel's central formulaic expressions, which are repeated at different points in the narrative, either verbatim or in variation:

So.
    In the beginning, there was nothing. Just the water. (1)[65]

Where did all that water come from? (3)[66]

But there is water everywhere. (3)[67]

And here's how it happened. (3)[68]

The colloquial "so" marks the performative situation of the narrative as oral and calls for the reader's attention: the novel is about to start. What follows immediately, however, is not the beginning of the story performed by the master narrator but an introductory scene, the purpose of which is to lead the reader closer to the story told in the novel. In this scene, Coyote is dreaming, and one of his dreams gets loose and thinks that it is in charge of the world. The dream wakes Coyote and complains about wanting to be a "big god." Sick of the dream's constant shouting, Coyote finally gives in (2).

    "Now you've done it," I says.
    "Everything's under control," says Coyote. "Don't panic."
* * *
Where did all that water come from? shouts that GOD.
    "Take it easy," says Coyote. "Sit down. Relax. Watch some television."
    But there is water everywhere, says that GOD.
    "Hmmmm," says Coyote. "So there is."

"That's true," I says. "*And here's how it happened.*" (2–3; emphasis added)

The formulaic "And here's how it happened" indicates that the actual story can now begin. The opening of *Green Grass, Running Water*, then, consists of three stages. "I" opens the novel with a formulaic expression, then moves on to relate an introductory scene, followed by the use of another formula that connotes what lies at the core of the novel: a story and its performance. More importantly, the formulaic expressions used in the novel's opening are repeated in its closing:

> "Okay, okay," says Coyote. "I got it!"
> "Well, it's about time," I says.
> "Okay, okay, here goes," says Coyote. "*In the beginning, there was nothing.*"
> "Nothing?"
> "That's right," says Coyote. "Nothing."
> "No," I says. "*In the beginning, there was just the water.*"
> "Water?" says Coyote.
> "Yes," I says. "Water."
> "Hmmmm," says Coyote. "Are you sure?"
> "Yes," I says, "I'm sure."
> "Okay," says Coyote, "if you say so. *But where did all the water come from?*"
> "*Sit down,*" I says to Coyote.
> "*But there is water everywhere,*" says Coyote.
> "That's true," I says. "*And here's how it happened.*" (431; emphasis added)

With the help of the overarching narrative frame consisting of an opening and a closing, readers are gradually guided into, as well as out of, the *novel proper*, which, just like the stories told within it, has a cyclical shape. We can, therefore, see the novel as a highly complex story cycle, one consisting of a series of cycles intertwined with each other. As in the case of the cyclical structures of the realistic and mythological narrative strands, the opening and closing frame in *Green Grass, Running Water* is established by way of paraholophrases: the formulas constituting the opening and the closing function as significant narrative units and form the cores of complex ideas.

When the master narrator ends his narration on the exact note with which he started it, he does not seem to be aware of the involvement that Coyote had in this turn of events. Without Coyote, however, *Green Grass, Running Water* would lack the circle established in the realistic and mythological narrative strands and, more importantly, the circle established in the novel proper. "By dividing himself" into two, Coyote "both *tells* the story and *is 'in'* the story"[69] and thus assumes the role of *creator* by bringing into being a novel whose narrative structure mimics not only the generic conventions of Indigenous oratures but also Indigenous worldviews. After all, as noted in King's discussion of Indigenous creation stories, creation in Indigenous traditions is usually a shared responsibility. Although Coyote might be responsible for giving the novel its particular shape, the novel would not exist without the "I" who tells the story—and "I" might not tell the story in the first place if Coyote is not willing to be his student. Moreover, the novel's very form is a demonstration of Indigenous notions of the world as opposed to Judeo-Christian concepts of the world: that is, this story does not present a "master narrative" with a beginning, a middle, and an end; instead, its narrative is cyclical rather than linear. This complex narrative structure, of course, is an indication of the author's involvement with his audience, because it not only defines the novel's interpretative context but also invites the readers' participation in the construction of the novel. The paraholophrases constituting the complex narrative structure in *Green Grass, Running Water* hence clearly contribute to the textualization of orality in the novel, and they do so as a strategy that is culturally specific.

Paraholophrases with Other Narrative Functions

In addition to those paraholophrases that constitute the novel's complex cyclical structure, *Green Grass, Running Water* features paraholophrases with other narrative functions; these paraholophrases take the form of formulaic clusters, figures of speech, or intertextual references.

Formulaic clusters in the novel either serve as a bridge between seemingly unrelated subnarratives or help to establish another circle in the narration. Because the frame narrative frequently interrupts the narration of the novel's story, the story is split into numerous smaller parts scattered throughout the other two narrative strands (mythological and realistic). Even within the realistic narrative strand, the narration often switches perspectives or includes subnarratives in the form of flashbacks. Formulaic clusters are employed to bridge some of the various episodes in the realistic narrative strand and, less often, as a connection between different narrative strands. As the realistic narrative strand approaches the Sun Dance, the use of these formulaic clusters becomes less frequent; the narrative bridges that these paraholophrases produce are no longer needed because the narratives are converging as the characters approach the same destination: the Sun Dance and the end/beginning of the circle/story.

These formulaic clusters connecting the subnarratives in the realistic narrative strand occur in a variety of forms. Often they involve repeating the last line of a subnarrative at the beginning of the first line in the subnarrative that follows:

> "**What else would you like to know?**" said the Lone Ranger.
>
> "**What else would you like to know?**" said Babo. (49–50)

Here, two independent subnarratives found in the realistic narrative strand (Lionel and Norma driving to Blossom and the interrogation of Babo Jones at the hospital in Florida) are connected by the repetition of a full line. More often, however, formulaic clusters that are used to bridge subnarratives contain only fragments of a line, such as the phrase "stay awake" in this example:[70]

> The Lone Ranger nodded and got down on his knees. He put his ear to the asphalt and listened. "**Stay awake**," he said. "Our adventure is about to begin."
>
> "Lionel! Lionel! **Stay awake**! You think any harder, you'll be snoring. You better let me drive." (78–79)

At other times, these connections between subnarratives are more indirect in that the repeating lines do not follow immediately one after the other but are separated by intervening text, such as is the case of the two lines below, which occur first at the end of a conversation between Lionel and Norma and are repeated in a conversation among the four old Indians six pages later.[71]

> "**Everybody makes mistakes**, auntie."
> "**Best not to make one with carpet**." (8)
>
> "**Everybody makes mistakes**," said the Lone Ranger.
> "**Best not to make them with stories**." (14)

A particularly significant formulaic cluster occurs near the end of volume one and again near the end of volume four (the end of the novel itself): in the first instance, a "chorus" of four characters asks the same question.

> "**Where did the water come from?**" said Alberta.
>
> "**Where did the water come from?**" said Patrolman Delano.
>
> "**Where did the water come from?**" said Sergeant Cereno.
>
> "**Where did the water come from?**" said Lionel. (98)

CHAPTER 4

This question is eventually answered, in the second instance, by a "chorus" of four different characters:

"Earthquake," yelled Clifford Sifton.

"Earthquake," yelled Bill Bursum.

"Earthquake," yelled Dr. Joseph Hovaugh.

"Earthquake, earthquake!" yells Coyote. "Hee-hee-hee-hee-hee-hee-hee-hee." (410–11)

Each chorus is interesting because it joins characters that, until then, have featured in different subnarratives. In the case of the first chorus, the characters' question about where the water came from refers to different situations: Alberta's memory of her dad's pickup truck sitting on a lake where their outhouse used to be (90), Delano's and Cereno's reaction to the beginning of a creation story told by Babo and Dr. Hovaugh (93, 96), and Lionel's stepping into a puddle of water when getting out of his car (97). Occurring as it does at the end of volume one, this first chorus points the reader to a connection between seemingly unrelated characters and seemingly disjointed subnarratives and thus anticipates their future "meeting." The second chorus again joins characters of different subnarratives in the realistic narrative strand, but their reaction concerns the same event: namely, the earthquake caused by Coyote's singing and dancing.

Although these choruses can be seen as a playful variant of the other formulaic clusters found in the novel, they are also clearly much more. First, repeating a line *four times* points to the Indigenous notion of the circle as sacred.[72] Indeed, with the first chorus anticipating the second chorus and the latter referring again to the former, a cyclical movement is established outside the novel's frame. Second, these choruses bundle up numerous subnarratives, which would otherwise appear to be unrelated to each other, to form formulas that point to the central image of the novel (first chorus: water) and to its main event (second chorus: earthquake). Hence, despite its multiplicity of stories, *Green Grass, Running Water* never runs the risk of losing its focus. Along with the other formulaic clusters in the novel, these choruses form the cores of complex ideas and carry a surplus of meaning; since they also fulfill a significant narrative function—that is, they establish yet another circle in the narration—they can be said to qualify as paraholophrases as well.

Figures of speech, another type of paraholophrase used in *Green Grass, Running Water*, function similarly to, but more subtly than, the two choruses. In volume two, one narrative chunk ends with an exchange between Latisha and Jeanette in the Dead Dog Café about an overflowing toilet, and the next narrative chunk shifts to Eli sitting in front of his cabin contemplating the stress fractures in the Grand Baleen Dam and describing the dam as looking like a toilet:

> "**Watch the toilet**," Latisha called after her. "**Sometimes it overflows.**"
> "Don't they all," Jeanette called back, sounding very far away. "Don't they all."

> From where Eli sat on the porch, he imagined he could see the cracks that were developing near the base of the dam. Stress fractures, they called them, common enough in any dam, but troublesome nonetheless, especially given the relatively young age of the concrete. Of more concern was the slumping that had been discovered.
> "It's a beauty, isn't it?" said Sifton [...]. "You know, if your cabin faced west, you'd have a great view of the dam from your front window."
> "View is fine as it is."
> "It's nice in the morning. Sort of white. Like a shell."
> "Reminds me of a toilet," said Eli. (135–136)

The image of the toilet links two separate subnarratives. More importantly, the comparison of the toilet and the dam here is picked up several hundred pages later, when the water breaking the dam contains "cars [that] tumble [...] over the edge of the world" (414), as though the dam were a big toilet overflowing, with the result that "Below, in the valley, the water rolled on as it had for eternity" (415). The Nissan, the Pinto, and the Karmann-Ghia falling "over the edge of the world" belong to Babo, Charlie, and Dr. Hovaugh, and all have gone missing during the course of the novel (93, 253, 315). This scene evokes the medieval belief that the earth is flat, and the names of the cars are skewed echoes of Columbus's three ships (the *Niña*, the *Pinta*, and the *Santa Maria*) on his 1492 voyage trying to reach India but arriving instead in America.⁷³ The image of the cars tumbling over the dam marks a subversive act of decolonization, then, as it depicts the "washing away of Columbus's colonial heritage."⁷⁴ The metaphor becomes even more powerful through equating the dam with a big toilet, especially considering the trickster's love of violating scatological taboos.⁷⁵ Coyote might not "want to land in poop" (145), but it is none other than *his* dancing that causes the dam to break. Latisha's warning—"**Watch the toilet** […]. **Sometimes it overflows**"—followed by a description of the dam's fractures and a comparison of the dam with a toilet provide the grounds for this forceful metaphor, but in addition Latisha's statement *prefigures* the breaking of the dam.⁷⁶ As a proleptic intratextual reference, this phrase forms the core of a complex idea; by weaving together narrative threads, it functions, moreover, as a significant narrative unit. Latisha's warning, then, is equivalent in function to holophrases in Indigenous languages and can thus be regarded as a paraholophrase.

The water of the overflowing toilet/dam, in fact, is but one instance of one of the novel's central themes. Indeed, water imagery is found throughout *Green Grass, Running Water*, as even Coyote notices:

> "Hmmmm," says Coyote. "All this floating imagery must mean something."
> "That's the way it happens in oral stories," I says.
> "Hmmmm," says Coyote. "All this water imagery must mean something." (352)

Throughout *Green Grass, Running Water*, water imagery involves the use of figurative speech and always entails a surplus of meaning inviting reader participation. For example, in the story of Old Woman, Jesus is not referred to as "Jesus" but as "**Young Man Walking On Water**" (349): that is, this character's name is remodelled to fit into an Indigenous story about the creation of the world, which starts with water instead of a void.

The novel's setting also evokes this notion of the world's creation. *Green Grass, Running Water* is set in Blossom, a fictional town in Alberta, whose name evokes "natural beauty and regeneration."⁷⁷ More importantly, the phrase "**Blossom, Alberta**" (58), is highly ambiguous and can be read as either a reference to the town or as an imperative to one of the novel's characters, who does in fact long to "blossom" (become pregnant). And eventually Alberta does "blossom" through Coyote's doings, while the town of Blossom, with the breaking of the Grand Baleen Dam, also eventually blossoms, though perhaps not so much economically as naturally and, particularly, culturally: "Below, in the valley, the water rolled on as it had for eternity" (415).

The fecundity implicit in the phrase "Blossom, Alberta," is also present in the novel's title, an echo of Eli's words as Bill Bursum attempts to persuade Eli to have his cabin moved so that the Grand Baleen Project can get on its way and Bursum can build his own cabin on a lot that he bought at Parliament Lake:

> "Wouldn't be hard to move the cabin," Bursum had told Eli. "Probably get the government to move it to higher ground for free."
> "Cabin's just fine right here."
> "Might even be able to get a lot on the lake in exchange. What do you think of that?"
> "Like the place right where it is."
> "Can't stay there forever."
> **"As long as the grass is green and the waters run."** (267)

As noted by Jane Flick, Eli's last remark parodies phrases found in treaties between the British and Canadian governments and First Nations peoples that were meant to indicate the significance of the treaties and to reflect their supposed eternal durability—phrases that nonetheless did not prevent the colonial authorities from breaking these treaties. Eli's parody suggests that, with the building of the Grand Baleen Dam, the green grass has been destroyed, and the running of the water has stopped.[78] At the same time, however, his remark is proleptic because it anticipates the eventual destruction of his mother's cabin and his own death. Thus, the water imagery in *Green Grass, Running Water* offers a powerful, life-affirming message and "signifies the supremely powerful, creative-destructive energies of a universe in constant motion."[79]

Robin Ridington's essay "Theorizing Coyote's Canon: Sharing Stories with Thomas King" provides further insight into the importance of the water imagery in *Green Grass, Running Water*: "The oral traditions of many First Nations code information in a way that is analogous to the distribution of visual information in a holographic image. Each story, like each piece of a hologram, contains information about the entire structure of which it is a part. Stories function as metonyms, parts that stand for wholes."[80] This description of what Ridington calls "narrative technology" points not only to Indigenous oral traditions as a closely contexted technology but also to their non-fixity or fluidity.[81] This fluidity is expressed in *Green Grass, Running Water* through a complex narrative structure that has various subnarratives literally floating into each other—after all, the four old Indians cross the boundary between the realistic and the mythological narrative strands by crossing a river (418–19). The fluidity of oral stories, however, is also suggested by the persistent water imagery that I have already discussed, which ultimately provides part of the novel's overarching narrative grid holding together its various scattered subnarratives. So, yes, Coyote is right—all this water imagery indeed means something: it serves a narrative function. All the instances of water imagery in *Green Grass, Running Water* discussed above—**Watch the toilet** [...]. **Sometimes it overflows**" (135), "**Young Man Walking On Water**" (349), "**Blossom, Alberta**" (58), "**As long as the grass is green and the waters run**" (267)—can therefore be regarded as paraholophrases, for as a figure of speech each phrase not only serves a narrative function but also forms the core of a complex idea and thus carries a bundle of meaning that readers must uncover for themselves.

The importance of an Indigenous "narrative technology" in *Green Grass, Running Water* is also revealed in King's elaborate use of intertextuality. Ridington has described the novel as "King's reading of North American literature, literary theory, Native American history, and popular culture through the images and genre conventions of American Indian oral tradition."[82] The novel does owe its sophisticated character not only to its complex narrative structure but also to its "intertextual network of stories rich in subtextual messages about the relationship of European peoples to indigenous cultures throughout the world."[83] Its abundant intertextual references and allusions, Catherine Rainwater has argued, have turned *Green Grass, Running Water* into a novel that "probably best illustrates the maximum effects an author may achieve through a cross-culturally allusive work."[84] Intertextuality primarily helps King to emphasize "the ways in which European settlers to the New World were—and their descendants continue to be—dependent upon a subordinated Other to create their identities and realities."[85] King's use of parody in the conflation of various Indigenous creation stories with Euro-Western master narratives (the Bible and examples of English/Anglo-American literature) in the mythological narrative strand, for example, creates an irony that is utterly empowering for Indigenous peoples. However, intertextuality in *Green Grass, Running Water* also serves as an important *narrative* device.

Arnold E. Davidson, Priscilla L. Walton, and Jennifer Andrews have correctly noted that, "in the desire to pinpoint the myriad of King's allusions," scholars have ignored the "intertextual web of references to his *own* work and characters."[86] They point out, for example, the references in his *Truth and Bright Water* to Lionel Red Dog and his sister Latisha[87] as well as the appearance of Will Horse Capture, the first-person narrator of *Medicine River*, whom Latisha hires in *Green Grass, Running Water* "to make up a bunch of photographs" (109).[88] *Green Grass, Running Water* includes further references to Medicine River (281, 362, 367), the townsite that lends King's first prairie novel its name.[89] These "carry-over[s]"[90] in his prairie trilogy provide a sense of fluidity to these stories and "open up" the novels to form what resembles a story cycle in Indigenous oratures, though this particular story cycle is composed by a single story-writer. Yet the re-creation of an Indigenous narrative technology in *Green Grass, Running Water* does not rest on the intertextual references within King's own work alone. Regardless of whether they create carry-overs, parody Euro-Western discourses, or re-create the cultural context of the narrative—as in the case of the Cherokee divining ceremony (15)—the intertextual references in *Green Grass, Running Water* all function as significant narrative units because they disrupt the linearity of the narrative, which is dictated by its written form, and thus open up the novel for reader participation. The novel's many intertextual references hence serve as a complex web of paraholophrases that makes the novel ultimately very deep, all the while providing a strong connection to the generic conventions of Indigenous oratures, according to which each story evokes a whole universe of still other stories.

To summarize, one can say that those paraholophrases in *Green Grass, Running Water* not employed in the construction of the novel's complex cyclical narrative structure instead ensure that the story framed by the novel's opening and closing remains coherent despite the non-linear, open, and fluid form that King has given the novel. Mimicking generic conventions of Indigenous oratures, *Green Grass, Running Water* forces readers to engage actively with the text: the novel, and by implication its author, demand their full attention; readers can only make sense of the novel if they become participants in its creation. What allow them to become part of the novel's creation essentially are its various formulaic clusters, figures of speech, and intertextual references, which turn the open and fluid discourse into a coherent whole. As such, these rhetorical devices mark the author's involvement with his audience and engage the reader's participation: that is, like the paraholophrases constituting the novel's complex cyclical structure, these paraholophrases function as a strategy in textualizing orality that is ultimately culturally specific.

HOLOPHRASES AND HOLOPHRASTIC TRACES

Green Grass, Running Water features relatively few words in an Indigenous language. Yet these few instances point to a highly effective use of code switching and emphasize the significance of the respective passages in the novel. Interestingly, it is not Blackfoot, the ancestral language of the characters in the realistic narrative strand, but Cherokee, the language of his own nation, that King has chosen for the four volume headings in the novel and for the dialogue opening the story of First Woman, a choice that underscores his sensibility regarding Cherokee traditions.

Each volume heading is composed of words written in the Cherokee syllabary[91] and gives a direction and a colour:[92] East/red (5), South/white (101), West/black (227), and North/blue (325). As Albert Tall Bull (Northern Cheyenne) explains about the Medicine Lodge in a Sun Dance, "each direction has [...] a ceremonial meaning. The East represents the new generation, still green, and just beginning to grow. The South represents further growth. The West represents ripeness. [...] Finally, the north represents old age—the complete generation of a man or being."[93] In naming the volumes after the four cardinal directions and the Cherokee sacred colour system, King avoids a linear enumeration (volume one, two, three, etc.).[94] Continuity in the narration is hence established by means of a metaphor: that is, by the course that the sun takes during its daily "journey." This metaphor not only suggests the Indigenous concept of time as cyclical but also evokes Indigenous notions of the circle as sacred, thereby providing the appropriate cultural setting for the story told in the novel. That the volume headings are composed using Cherokee rather than English words further underlines the importance of the story's cultural contexts.

The only other section in *Green Grass, Running Water* that features the use of an Indigenous language is the opening of the story of First Woman. The Lone Ranger, who is telling this story, uses a number of inappropriate—that is, Euro-Western—formulaic expressions (11-14) before finding "a proper start [for the story] with the mention of First Woman in Cherokee, *Higayv:ligé:i*."[95]

"Gha!" said the Lone Ranger. "Higayv:ligé:i."

"That's better," said Hawkeye. "Tsane:hlan ′v:hi."
"Listen," said Robinson Crusoe. "Hade:lohó:sgi."
"It is beginning," said Ishmael. "Dagvyá:dhv:dv:hní."

"It is begun well," said the Lone Ranger. "Tsada:hnó:nedí niga:v duyughodv: o:sdv." (15)

The beginning of the Lone Ranger's story echoes "the ceremonial opening of storytelling in a Cherokee divining ceremony, divining for water and so in a sense for the future."[96] The opening of the story of First Woman thus undercuts the authoritativeness of Euro-Western texts and offers instead "a beginning rooted in oral performance."[97] More importantly, this beginning is deeply rooted in an Indigenous culture and language given that this opening scene uses Cherokee language to evoke "the most prevalent purification ceremony among the Cherokees" called "'Going to the Water' (*amó:hi* ['water place'] *ats´v:sdi* ['to go and return, one'])."[98] This ceremony was meant either to determine a person's long life, to protect someone from being conjured, or to improve a patient's health.[99] Divining was "a salient part of the Cherokee medicomagical tradition." Its purpose, however, was "not to learn what the future is going to be, but to find out how the component parts of the present stand in relationship to each other. [...] The future will be pretty much what man requests the Provider to provide."[100] About his use of the Cherokee Going to the Water ritual in *Green Grass, Running Water*, King says that

> it is just a request to know the future or to be able to see part of what the future has to offer. It's a device for the reader in some ways to understand that something is going to happen, that these guys [the four old Indians] aren't there just for a little comic relief, as it were, that they're actually about to restructure the world or at least make an attempt at it.[101]

Alan Kilpatrick's *The Night Has a Naked Soul* contains three Going to the Water texts,[102] several Cherokee divinatory spells[103] and protective charms,[104] as well as literal and free translations into English. Following Kilpatrick's translations of the Cherokee texts, as well as Durbin Feeling's *Cherokee-English Dictionary*,[105] the beginning of the Lone Ranger's story (15) in *Green Grass, Running Water* can be translated thus:[106]

Lone Ranger's Story	Proposed Translation
"Gha!" said the Lone Ranger. "Higayv:ligé:i."	"Listen!"[107] said the Lone Ranger. "First Woman."[108]
"That's better," said Hawkeye. "Tsane:hlan´v:hi."	"That's better," said Hawkeye. "Provider, you."[109]
"Listen," said Robinson Crusoe. "Hade:lohó:sgi."	"Listen," said Robinson Crusoe. "One who foresees."[110]
"It is beginning," said Ishmael. "Dagvyá:dhv:dv:hní."	"It is beginning," said Ishmael. "I will question you."[111]
"It is begun well," said the Lone Ranger. "Tsada:hnó:nediniga:v duyughodv: o:sdv."	"It is begun well," said the Lone Ranger. "State the whole truth well."[112]

Table 4.3 Proposed Translation of Lone Ranger's Story

Even if this translation is only approximately accurate, it nonetheless demonstrates that the English text woven into the beginning of the Lone Ranger's story provides neither a loose translation nor an interpretation of the Cherokee phrases. Non-Indigenous readers are thus doubly marked as outsiders by this passage in *Green Grass, Running Water*: first, they will not understand the Cherokee phrases; second, since they lack knowledge of the cultural and religious contexts of the phrases, they will not understand *why* "it is begun well."

Green Grass, Running Water, then, employs Indigenous words and holophrases very economically: the few words from Cherokee that are incorporated into the novel occur at decisive moments in the narrative (at the beginning of the first creation story and in the volume headings); these moments define not only the linguistic, cultural, and religious contexts of the narration but also, ultimately, the grounds on which readers are invited to participate in the composition of the novel. King's code switching thus shows the author's involvement with his audience and complements the other strategies employed to invite reader participation.

The textualization of orality achieved through the economical use of Cherokee in *Green Grass, Running Water* is complemented by a more pervasive use of holophrastic traces. Some of the characters' names in the novel reflect Indigenous traditions of name giving and, in their descriptiveness and semantic density, create the *illusion* of English loan translations. Moreover, like those discussed in *Arctic Dreams and Nightmares* and *The Lesser Blessed*, indigenized personal names in King's novel function as examples of synecdoche. As noted by Flick, "*Alberta* suggests the province in western Canada, and usually Alberta herself is *frank*."[113] As the main female character in the realistic narrative strand, who eventually becomes pregnant, Alberta provides a strong connection with the land. At the same time, her surname can be seen as a reference to the Frank Slide—a natural disaster on Turtle River near Frank, Alberta, in 1903[114]—which points to the interconnectedness of good and evil, as suggested in many Indigenous creation stories. Her lover, Lionel Red Dog, might not be into gambling, but, being rather unambitious and lazy, he prefers to wait for his luck to show up on his doorstep rather than to work for it, unlike his hard-working and determined sister, Latisha. Charlie Looking Bear, the Indigenous Casanova-wanna-be and Alberta's other lover, has never recovered from the disappearance of his father and does not realize that he is unconsciously longing for him. Eli Stands Alone, who has just lost his wife, single-handedly opposes the operation of a dam on Indigenous land by refusing to leave his dead mother's cabin situated in the dam's spillway, thus evoking, in both name and action, Elijah Harper, the Manitoba member of Parliament who scuttled the Meech Lake Accord in 1990.[115] Ishmael's real name, Changing Woman, points to the strong associations of this figure with life and creation in Navajo tradition. Finally, the young man whom Old Woman meets one day as she is floating in the water is referred to as Young Man Walking On Water because he is, in fact, walking on the water when the two meet.

Except for the names Alberta Frank and Lionel Red Dog, which combine a proper noun with either an adjective or an adjective-noun compound (A N compound), the indigenized personal names in *Green Grass, Running Water* all include a verbal component, either a present participle or, in the case of the quotation compound Eli Stands Alone, a conjugated verb. Personal names containing a present participle are usually idiom-like lexical phrases (Charlie Looking Bear, Young Man Walking On Water), but there is also one example that takes the form of a deverbal A N compound (Changing Woman). Regardless of its internal structure, each phrase suggests the holistic nature of the holophrase: it denotes a person, not an event, but it does so by recourse to an event that this person attended at one point or is still involved in (standing alone, changing, looking, walking on water). As noted above, *Green Grass, Running Water* also contains a reference to Will Horse Capture, the narrator in King's *Medicine River*. This character occurs only in the form of an intertextual reference; the synecdoche involved in this personal name might thus be less apparent to some readers. However, as a synthetic compound, Will Horse Capture is nonetheless comparable to the other indigenized personal names. Imitating the holistic nature of the holophrase, the names Charlie Looking Bear, Eli Stands Alone, Changing Woman, Young Man Walking On Water, Will Horse Capture, and, to lesser degrees, Alberta Frank and Lionel Red Dog are textual markers that allow the polysynthetic nature of Indigenous grammars to show through in the English discourse.[116] Moreover, as examples of synecdoche, these direct holophrastic traces suggest the cores of complex ideas and thus engage the readers' participation. The textualization of orality thus achieved points to a culturally specific strategy.

Two more examples of compounding occur in Changing Woman's story, near the end of the novel's second section:

> Pay attention, says Ahab. Keep watching the whales.
> Why does he want a whale? says Changing Woman.
> This is a whaling ship, says Ishmael.
> *Whaleswhaleswhaleswhalesbianswhalesbianswhaleswhales*! shouts Ahab, and everybody grabs their spears and knives...
> [...]

> We're looking for the white whale, Ahab tells his men. Keep looking.
> So Ahab's men look at the ocean and they see something and that something is a whale.
> *Blackwhaleblackwhaleblackwhalesbianblackwhalesbianblackwhale*, they all shout.
> Black whale? yells Ahab. You mean white whale, don't you? Moby-Dick, the great male white whale?
> That's not a white whale, says Changing Woman. That's a female whale and she's black.
> Nonsense, says Ahab. It's Moby-Dick, the great white whale.
> You're mistaken, says Changing Woman, I believe that is Moby-Jane, the Great Black Whale. (195–96; emphasis added)

The critique of homophobia and racism implied in this scene is mirrored in King's inventive use of language. Not only is the shouting of Ahab and, later, that of his crew represented by way of one long, complex signifier, but it also involves a "slip of the tongue." After all, though Ahab might still believe his whale to be white while Changing Woman and his crew point out its blackness, they all agree that the whale is a "whalesbian": that is, "a female whale who prefers other females,"[117] including Changing Woman, with whom Moby-Jane has a short sexual encounter later in the story (224). These two quotation compounds invite reader participation because they are spelled as one word; furthermore, with the pun on whalesbian, King has coined a new word, a N N compound that involves elision, the omission of a sound or syllable when speaking. Indeed, to fully appreciate the pun in the quotation compounds on Moby-Jane, readers must read them aloud. The whale compounds might not contain a verbal constituent, but because of their length—seven or ten words fused into one word—and because they involve an inventive use of language, these two quotation compounds are reminiscent of the structure of holophrases in Indigenous languages and can thus be regarded as direct holophrastic traces. The textualization of orality thus produced derives again from a strategy that can be called culturally specific.

Formulaic uses of language in *Green Grass, Running Water* are not restricted to the elaborate formulaic clusters discussed above but also involve less sophisticated forms. The mythological narrative strand, in particular, contains several noun-epithet formulas, which personify animals, plants, or inanimate objects. As is the case in most Indigenous creation stories, nonhumans featured in the four creation stories of King's novel can speak and are in no way inferior to the other characters involved in the action. As a rule, the noun assigned to a non-human in *Green Grass, Running Water* is capitalized the moment that it begins to talk:

> Thought Woman is walking. It is morning and Thought Woman is walking. So Thought Woman walks to the river.
> Hello, says Thought Woman to the river.
> Hello, says that *River*. Nice day for a walk.
> [...]
> So that Thought Woman takes off her nice clothes, and that one gets into the *River*.
> Whoa! says Thought Woman. That is *one cold River*. This must be a *tricky River*.
> Swim to the middle, says that *tricky River*. It is much warmer there. (231; emphasis added)

The river that Thought Woman runs into one day is not merely a river but "one cold River" and "a tricky River." Similarly, Coyote's dream becomes a "silly Dream" and a "noisy Dream," and its eyes turn into "Dream Eyes" (1). Such noun-epithet formulas might not serve significant narrative functions—which is why they do not qualify as paraholophrases—but they do reflect the figurativity of Indigenous languages, which, in turn, is invited by polysynthesis. That these noun-epithet formulas are found mainly in the mythological narrative strand is particularly interesting given that this strand, with its intertextual references to various Indigenous creation stories, is the closest that *Green Grass, Running Water* comes to Indigenous oral traditions, at least in terms of content. The personification of non-humans in the mythological narrative strand serves, then, to reinforce Indigenous worldviews by reflecting the Indigenous notion that humans and non-humans are equal to one another. Further, because they create long, highly descriptive noun phrases, noun-epithet formulas are reminiscent of the structure of holophrases in Indigenous languages; however, since they do not usually include verbal constituents, they are further removed from actual holophrases than the examples of compounding discussed above. Yet, like the latter, they engage the readers' imagination and therefore invite participation. As a strategy in textualizing orality, then, these noun-epithet formulas can be considered culturally specific.

Indirect holophrastic traces found in *Green Grass, Running Water* are restricted to *pronoun copying* and *subject dropping* and are found predominantly in the least oral of the novel's narrative strands, the realistic strand. There are examples of pronoun copying in its narration of events ("That's right, says First Woman. I guess we better make some land. *So they do. First Woman and grandmother Turtle*" [39; emphasis added]). More frequently, however, pronoun copying is found in direct speech, as in the following examples taken from the realistic narrative strand in the first half of volume one (italics indicate pronoun copying):

- "These Indians. Did *any of them* escape?" (20),
- "Smoking does *that*. To lungs, I mean. *Gets them* all grimy and shrivelled up like raisins and prunes" (25),
- "Pills. *That's* what does it" (27),
- "*That's* what I am doing. *Drinking* my coffee and *walking* and *looking*" (27),
- "'Well,' said Dr. Loomis, 'the boy has a *sore throat. Pretty bad one, too*'" (32),
- "Like I said. They were *Indians. Old ones*" (51),
- "Well, *they* were old. *All of them*" (52), and
- "Stuff like that. *We'd* trade stories too, *the Indians and me. That's* what I could do, you know, *tell you one of the stories they told me*" (53).

Pronoun copying in writing produces discourse that tends to be repetitive, is unusually fragmentary for written language, and imitates the intonation units of oral speech. This kind of fragmentary discourse is also achieved by way of ellipsis, including the dropping of grammatical subjects. Like pronoun copying, subject dropping is found less often in the narration of events and free indirect speech[118] and more often in direct speech—as in the following examples, which again are taken from the realistic narrative strand in the first half of volume one (italics indicate subject dropping):

- "*Wouldn't hold* my breath" (7),
- "Well, I'm going to order the blue. It reminds me of the sky. *Going to get* money to paint the house, too" (7),
- "That's right. *Threw* my smokes on the dash" (25),
- "Smoking does that. To lungs, I mean. *Gets* them all grimy and shrivelled up like raisins and prunes" (25),
- "So today was going to be the day. *Would have been*, too. I was feeling strong. Real strong. *Had* four rolls of Life Savers with me. *Got* to have them when you try to stop" (25–26),
- "*Bought* that car off him. *Always trying to help*" (26),
- "*Can't believe* my own sister let them do that to you. *Got* no more sense than a hubcap" (31),

- "'Well,' said Dr. Loomis, 'the boy has a sore throat. Pretty bad one, too. *Can't do* much about it'" (32),
- "*Course*, the tonsils are inflamed and they don't look all that healthy. *Wouldn't hurt* to get them out sometime" (32),
- "When you put the money in and it starts up, make sure a cup drops down straight. Sometimes it drops crooked. *Makes* a big mess" (50), and
- "'Nope,' said Babo. '*Heard* Dr. Eliot and Dr. Hovaugh talking'" (51).

Both subject dropping and pronoun copying imitate the intonation units in oral speech and thus suggest author involvement and reader participation. Both also draw attention to verbs, which play such a significant role in polysynthetic languages: subject dropping emphasizes the verb, since the absence of a subject means that the verb moves to the beginning of the sentence, whereas pronoun copying mimics the repetitive structures that result from the holistic nature of polysynthetic verbs. Of course, pronoun copying and subject dropping are not restricted to the first half of volume one in *Green Grass, Running Water* but occur throughout the novel. Their pervasiveness makes them strong textual markers with a significance comparable to that of the novel's direct holophrastic traces discussed above.

I have already noted that the three different narrative strands in *Green Grass, Running Water* textualize orality to varying degrees. As a rule, the closer a narrative strand moves to an actual performative situation, the more it textualizes orality. The strategies employed in the textualization of orality differ from narrative strand to narrative strand, and these differences in part concern the cultural specificity of the strategies employed. The frame narrative, in its attempt to re-create an actual storytelling performance, comes exceptionally close to Indigenous generic conventions. Again and again, the frame narrative hints at the fact that readers "overhear" conversations between the master narrator and Coyote. In some cases, these hints are indirect: "We can't hear what's happening if you keep talking" (195), or "Can we get on with this? [...] It's getting late. [...] And people want to go home" (329); in other instances, these hints are more direct but still subtle: "'I wasn't talking to you,' I says.—'Who else is here?' says Coyote" (391). Readers thus become witnesses of the conversations between the two and, like Coyote, are expected to listen patiently and attentively to the master narrator's story so that they can retell it later. Readers are thus invited to participate in the performance, however passively.

The master narrator's indirect addresses to the reader form a culturally *un*specific strategy in textualizing orality, but this strategy is complemented by a culturally *specific* strategy in the form of evidentials. Consisting almost entirely of direct discourse, the frame narrative relies heavily on the use of tags to help readers differentiate between the speech acts of the master narrator and those of Coyote. Their utterances are framed by attributive clauses, which are usually parenthetical and involve "say" as *verbum dicendi*. Ironically, the rather regular use of direct speech in the frame narrative creates a rhythmic effect that free direct speech would never be able to achieve. "Says Coyote" follows "I says" follows "says Coyote" follows "I says" et cetera. King always uses the same *verbum dicendi* to construct a tag, but he inverts subject and verb, depending on the person talking. The rhythm created by the consistent use of this tag in two syntactically different types of attributive clause is simple but astonishingly regular. Aside from helping readers to differentiate between the utterances of the master narrator and those of Coyote, the pattern amounts to an oral, almost musical, effect and mimics the elaborate use of evidentials in Indigenous oratures for structural purposes. As noted in the holophrastic readings in the previous chapters, evidentiality is correlated to polysynthesis. The pervasive use of evidentials in the frame narrative of *Green Grass, Running Water* hence creates an indirect holophrastic trace that, in its textualization of orality—it creates a musical effect and is indicative of the author's involvement with himself [119]—functions as a culturally specific strategy. Although its use is restricted to this rather short portion of text—the frame narrative is the shortest of the three narrative strands—it is nonetheless noticeable in the novel because the frame narrative frequently and regularly interrupts the telling of the story in the other two narrative strands; the use of evidentiality here hence provides a textual marker that is very effective.

The mythological narrative strand is slightly less oral than the frame narrative; however, framed as it is by the four old Indians' conversations regarding the telling of the four creation stories, it is closer to the notion of an actual oral performance than the realistic narrative strand. In that it does not meet the requirements of standard written English, the mythological narrative strand exhibits what might be called an oral style. As Jennifer Andrews has noted about the introductory sentences of the novel, the mythological narrative strand "replicate[s] the terse style of oral delivery and plays with the conventions of standard English."[120] The textualization of orality in the mythological narrative strand includes the following features.

1. *A reliance on the present tense*: Given that the stories told in the mythological narrative strand speak of events that happened in the past, this use of present tense qualifies as *historical present*, which functions as an indicator of the author's/narrator's involvement with reality.[121]

2. *The colloquial use of the particle "so"*: "So" functions as a means to arouse the listener's attention and thus connotes the author's/narrator's involvement with his or her audience.
3. *Deictics such as "this one" or "that one"*: Deictics indicate a relatively low degree of referential explicitness and are indicators of fuzziness; used in writing, they textualize orality.
4. *Violation of the subject-verb concord rule in English* (e.g., "Look, look, all the live rangers says, and they point their fingers at First Woman" [71]): As with any violation of standard English grammar, the violation of the subject-verb concord rule marks the narrative as colloquial and hence oral.
5. *Additive rather than subordinate syntax*: Additive syntax creates a fragmentary, as opposed to an integrated, discourse and marks an oral strategy. See, for example, the following passage: "So that Nasty Bumppo hides behind a big tree and that Nasty Bumppo loads that really big rifle and that Nasty Bumppo aims that really big rifle at Old Woman. /Here we go, says Nasty Bumppo. /And there is a really big explosion. And there is a lot of smoke" (394).
6. *Syntactic fragments*: Syntactic fragments are caused by ellipses and create a fragmentary, as opposed to an integrated, discourse. In at least one instance, the mythological narrative strand arranges these syntactic fragments in the form of verse—"And. / When they catch the whales. / They kill them" (195)—which further emphasizes the fragmentation of text and makes it even more prosodic.

These culturally unspecific strategies in textualizing orality in the mythological narrative strand are complemented by the use of compounds (the two whalesbian quotation compounds, the idiom-like Young Man Walking On Water, and the deverbal A N compound Changing Woman) and noun-epithet formulas, all of which imitate the structure of holophrases to varying degrees, thus adding a culturally specific strategy to the textualization of orality in this narrative strand.

The realistic narrative strand, being the strand that most resembles the Euro-Western realist novel, especially in its use of free indirect speech, is the least oral of the narrative strands in *Green Grass, Running Water* and corresponds, for the most part, to the standards of written English. Nonetheless, it suggests a certain sense of orality, for example, in its use of long passages of completely untagged direct discourse.[122] The realistic narrative strand also attempts to compensate for the lack of sound and prosody in writing through the use of onomatopoeic-like words,[123] italics, or capitalization.[124] Finally, its puns on Jehovah (Dr. J. Hovaugh; see 16–17, 425–26) and Louis Riel (Louis, Ray, and Al; see 334)[125] depend on reading aloud and thus further invite reader participation. Most importantly, however, the realistic narrative strand contains numerous examples of pronoun copying and subject dropping, which, together with the two compounds Eli Stands Alone and Charlie Looking Bear, add a culturally specific dimension to the textualization of orality in this narrative strand. The purpose of pronoun copying and subject dropping is not so much the re-creation of the structure of actual holophrases as the re-creation of discourse features that can be associated with polysynthesis; however, these indirect holophrastic traces are more pervasive than the direct holophrastic traces in the realistic narrative strand, even if the two compounds Eli Stands Alone and Charlie Looking Bear are occasionally repeated in the narration. Holophrastic traces in *Green Grass, Running Water*, whether they qualify as direct or indirect holophrastic traces, then, are found in all of its narrative strands and ensure that a culturally specific strategy in the textualization of orality is pervasive throughout the novel.

SUMMARY

Thomas King's *Green Grass, Running Water* is among the most sophisticated novels of contemporary Indigenous literatures—sophisticated in its narrative structure, its intertextual allusions, and, ultimately, in its use of paraholophrases. Paraholophrases in *Green Grass, Running Water* contribute to the construction of a narrative frame for the novel that highlights its performativeness and establishes a cyclical narrative structure, all the while defining the novel's *interpretative context*. Paraholophrases constituting the narrative frame in *Green Grass, Running Water* often take the form of formulaic clusters. The purpose of these clusters is to help the story-writer compose his story and provide a narrative grid for the novel that readers must decipher to make sense of it. Similarly, reader *participation* is invited by those paraholophrases that establish the novel's complex cyclical narrative structure, which is highly reminiscent of narrative structures in traditional Indigenous oratures. Equally important in *Green Grass, Running Water* are those paraholophrases that help to create a narrative that is astonishingly open and that, in effect, continue in writing what Robin Ridington has called Indigenous "narrative technology." The various subnarratives scattered throughout the novel break the linearity of the narration and thus suggest the fluid nature of oral storytelling. However, were it not for the paraholophrases bridging and providing structure for these various subnarratives, this multiplicity of narratives would prevent reader comprehension and stifle, rather than invite, reader participation. The fluid nature of King's novel is further reinforced by its persistent use of water imagery and its highly complex web of intertextual allusions, both of which are indicative of the author's *involvement* with his audience and illustrate how intertextuality and imagery are employed in Indigenous discourse also for structural purposes. Whether as part of the narrative frame or the novel's cyclical structure or as a mechanism used to construct an open discourse, paraholophrases in *Green Grass, Running Water* are dynamically equivalent to holophrases because they have functions equivalent to holophrases in Indigenous languages: they form the text's narrative grid and are semantically dense. Like the paraholophrases in the other Indigenous texts discussed thus far, paraholophrases in *Green Grass, Running Water* help in the composition of the novel and add a culturally specific dimension to the textualization of orality; as noted above, they ultimately mark oral strategies that result from the context of language use: namely, context, involvement, and participation.

Code switching in *Green Grass, Running Water* is infrequent but not unimportant. In fact, King manages to establish the novel's *cultural and religious contexts* in just one short passage written partly in Cherokee holophrases. Occurring, as it does, at the beginning of the novel, this passage defines the readers' relationship to the text and thus the degree of input necessary to allow their participation. Code switching in King's novel, then, is concerned more with the incorporation of cultural and religious contexts and less with that of mere linguistic context. More frequent than King's use of holophrases is his use of holophrastic traces. *Green Grass, Running Water* contains some personal names that re-create Indigenous traditions of name giving, and thus imitate the word formation processes of polysynthetic languages, creating the illusion of English loan translation. Aside from the few indigenized personal names and the two "whalesbian" quotation compounds, *Green Grass, Running Water* makes use of noun-epithet formulas to imitate the structure of holophrases in Indigenous languages. Overall, even though direct holophrastic traces in *Green Grass, Running Water* are employed rather sporadically, they nonetheless complement the textualization achieved through the use of paraholophrases because these direct holophrastic traces indicate the author's involvement with reality and his audience and, thereby, further engage his readers.

Indirect holophrastic traces are astonishingly pervasive in *Green Grass, Running Water*. The novel exhibits an elaborate use of pronoun copying and subject dropping, both of which produce oral strategies resulting from the context of language production (prosody, redundancy, and fragmentation). The evidentials used in the frame narrative are equally frequent and textualize orality both by creating a musical (and hence oral) effect and by inscribing into the narrative the author's involvement with himself. Since these various holophrastic traces are distributed across all three narrative strands (subject dropping and pronoun copying in the realistic narrative strand; compounding and noun-epithet formulas in the mythological narrative strand; evidentiality in the frame narrative), the textualization of orality achieved through the use of these textual markers is relatively consistent in *Green Grass, Running Water*.

The focus of my holophrastic readings thus far has been on prose narratives. These readings, however, give grounds to the assumption that paraholophrases can also feature as significant components in Indigenous long poems. Not only do some of the paraholophrases that I have pointed out in *Call Me Ishmael, Arctic Dreams and Nightmares, The Lesser Blessed,* and *Green Grass, Running Water* take the form of figures of speech, but the holophrastic reading of *The Lesser Blessed* has also demonstrated how effectively figurative and poetic language can be used for structural purposes in prose narratives. To explore further the usefulness of holophrastic reading, let me close with a reading of *Blue Marrow*, a long poem by Louise Bernice Halfe.

CHAPTER 5

"Cree-ing Loud into My Night":
Louise Bernice Halfe's *Blue Marrow*

Louise Bernice Halfe, whose Cree name translates into Sky Dancer, was born in 1953 on Saddle Lake Reserve in Two Hills, Alberta. She attended Blue Quills Indian Residential School in St. Paul, Alberta, but left it at the age of sixteen to complete school at St. Paul's Regional High School. Halfe received a bachelor's degree in social work from the University of Regina and currently lives and works in Saskatoon. Since her first appearance as a poet in Jeanne Perreault and Sylvia Vance's *Writing the Circle* (1990), Halfe has been a prominent voice in contemporary Cree poetry. In 2005 and 2006, she served as Saskatchewan's poet laureate.[1]

THE TEXT: *BLUE MARROW*
Halfe published her first work of poetry, *Bear Bones and Feathers*, in 1994. Her second book of poetry, *Blue Marrow*, followed in 1998 and was a finalist for many Canadian literary awards, including the Governor General's Literary Award for Poetry. Halfe's third collection, *The Crooked Good* (2007), continues her explorations of Indigenous themes, particularly concerning Indigenous women. Although each collection would provide an interesting ground for holophrastic reading—due to its use of Cree and its genre—the unusual textual history of *Blue Marrow* makes Halfe's second book of poetry particularly intriguing.

CHAPTER 5

Questions of Text

All of Halfe's collections of poetry contain abundant uses of Cree in the English text, which have correctly been referred to as examples of code switching.[2] The conflation of Cree and English in Halfe's poetry is so elaborate that the Cree language is incorporated into the English syntax, a circumstance that has caused Susan Gingell to call Halfe's poems "Creenglish poems."[3] Unlike *Bear Bones and Feathers* and *The Crooked Good*, the first edition of *Blue Marrow* does not contain a glossary giving the meanings of the Cree words. Both Méira Cook and Shelley Stigter have noted this lack of a glossary. Cook suggests that it indicates Halfe's "acknowledgement that she is not writing predominantly for a white English-speaking audience"; Stigter sees it as an interplay of dialogic and dialectical modes of code switching that draws readers into a conversation with the text and makes them rely on contextual understanding.[4] In 2004, Coteau Books published "a rewritten, re-edited, and redesigned edition" of *Blue Marrow*;[5] this edition does include an alphabetically ordered glossary prepared by Halfe and "edited and expanded by Jean Okimâsis and Arok Wolvengrey."[6] The glossary gives the meanings of the words as used in the main text: that is, besides individual words, it also lists phrases and sentences, thus facilitating the understanding of readers with no knowledge of Cree or of the grammatical structures of Indigenous languages in general.

The addition of a Cree glossary to the 2004 edition is not the only difference between the two existing editions of *Blue Marrow*. A brief comparison suggests that the text has been considerably revised. Some of the changes made to the original text are comparatively minor and include the addition of one photograph,[7] changes in the Cree orthography concerning capitalization[8] and the use of macrons,[9] changes of tense,[10] as well as in-line translations of Cree words and phrases.[11] With the addition of line breaks, some of the poetic prose of the first edition turns into free verse poems, thus intensifying the lyrical elements of the sequence and demanding more reader participation.[12] The identification of voices in the form of short indented paragraphs, however, makes the revised edition of *Blue Marrow* more reader friendly. More importantly, however, the revised edition includes additions and deletions of words and phrases as well as completely rewritten paragraphs—changes that have altered the original text of *Blue Marrow* notably.

An extensive discussion of the textual evolution of *Blue Marrow* is a matter of textual scholarship and well beyond the purposes of this study of the role of (para)holophrases in the textualization of orality in Indigenous literatures composed in English. Thus, I will consider the changes in the revised edition of *Blue Marrow* only insofar as they concern the role of (para)holophrases. Since the revised edition presents the most recent version of Halfe's text, my reading will be based on this text.

Questions of Genre

Blue Marrow contains a long sequence of poems written in either prose or free verse and with a strong narrative quality. These poems capture the first-person narratives of numerous voices, identifiable by indentation and the use of italics; the result is an "intensely heteroglossic text."[13] Occasional page breaks divide the poem into eleven sections, which are not titled and which become longer as the narrative progresses; however, with one voice floating into another, the poem forms only a loosely structured sequence of voices, "from the undifferentiated chorus of the foremothers, through the testimony of the fur trader and his wife, the narrator's grandparents, and finally, to the alternating dialogue between the narrator and her father, and her final recollections of her mother."[14]

The poems in *Blue Marrow* are woven together by a first-person narrator, a contemporary Cree woman, "The Keeper of the Stories" (21), as she calls herself. She is in the process of taking dictation from her ancestors' voices.[15] As she weaves together a narrative that empowers both herself and her people—past, present, and future—she eventually "assume[s] the guise of storyteller."[16] Taking an intermediary position between the past generations of her grandmothers and her contemporary readers, the keeper of stories is a "privileged outsider who assumes her position at the margins of narration yet whose insight allows her access to secret histories" for which she becomes a channel.[17] The process of composition lurks beneath the main narrative that she is weaving, but, as Cook has pointed out, "the narrator deflates her heroic function" by trivializing these metafictional moments:[18]

> When the Voices roar,
> I write.
> Sometimes they sing,
> are silent.
> In those times,
> I read, answer overdue letters,
> go for a walk or jog,
> stoke my fire, prepare baloney
> mustard sandwich, wild rice salad. (53)

The Crees traditionally distinguish between two genres of narratives, *âtayohkewina* (pl.) and *âcimowina* (pl.). The former are "spiritual narratives," stories that are generally regarded as sacred.[19] Whereas *âtayohkewina* relate, therefore, to "the time when the world was not yet in its present, definite state,"[20] *âcimowina* are concerned with the present world, particularly with precontact times, and include everything that is not regarded as *âtayohkewina*.[21] With the exception of the Cree earth diver myth (98), sacred legends are never explicitly told in *Blue Marrow*, hence keeping in line with Cree generic conventions that allow the telling of these legends only under certain well-defined conditions.[22] Thus, Halfe's poetry, including *Blue Marrow*, has been categorized as part of the "*âcimôwin* Cree literary tradition."[23]

In combining lyric and epic, *Blue Marrow* can also be seen as part of the long poem tradition, which, as Frank M. Tierney and Angela Robbeson have described David Bentley's reading of the genre, is "a site of tension between the lyric and the epic, between personal and communal expression, a discursive place in which Canadian poets from Thomas Cary to Robert Kroetsch have given individual expression to a community, be it a colony, a region, a city, or a nation."[24] While Cook[25] in her analysis of *Blue Marrow* refers to Susan Stanford Friedman's reading of contemporary women's long poems as insisting on story[26] (contrary to poststructuralist feminist readings of narrative as representing the "repressive masculine, paternal, and oedipal"[27]), Gingell points to the work of Dell Hymes and Dennis Tedlock when discussing Maria Campbell's "generic choice of *poetic form* for recording hitherto oral narratives on the page."[28] Leaving aside for now the gender issues raised by Friedman's argument—of course, narrative is always only one of two main ingredients of any long poem—Cook's and Gingell's contributions, seen not in isolation but as complementing one another, shed light on our understanding of *Blue Marrow* in that they point to *Indigenous traditions* as strong influences in contemporary Indigenous poetry.

The conflation in *Blue Marrow* of epic and lyric is particularly interesting when seen from the perspective of Indigenous languages and rhetorics. Indigenous language structures invite a figurative use of language, which is encountered in Euro-Western literatures more often in poetry than in prose, whereas North American Indigenous oral poetry is usually narrative and contains what Hymes has termed "measured," rather than metered, verse.[29] Finally, the storyteller in Indigenous traditions lends the latter his or her own voice, but only to work as an intermediary. Gingell has read Campbell's and Halfe's choice of poetic style as "appropriating to their own purpose the Western hierarchy of genres that places poetry above prose."[30] Considering its Indigenous context, I suggest reading *Blue Marrow* not so much as an appropriation of the Euro-Western generic hierarchy as a *continuation of Indigenous linguistic and rhetorical traditions*, which happens to fit conveniently into a literary tradition that for "a growing number of literary historians and critics [...] is distinctively Canadian in its documentary aspects, often serving a topographical and memorial function," as Tierney and Robbeson have described the long poem.[31] Halfe's "double voicing" in *Blue Marrow*, to use Stephen Scobie's words, concerns the coexistence of epic and lyrical components and thus can be seen as a "dialogue between the lyric impulse of the short poem and more extended forms of discursive strategy and practice."[32] On a much deeper level, however, this double voicing is a matter not just of different language uses within one literary tradition but also of the conflation of two different literary traditions (Euro-Western/Indigenous) in one literary work. How the use of (para)holophrases adds to this reading of *Blue Marrow* will be the central question of the holophrastic reading that follows.

A HOLOPHRASTIC READING OF *BLUE MARROW*

Unlike the works discussed so far, Halfe's *Blue Marrow* contains an elaborate interweaving of an Indigenous language (Cree) into the English text, a circumstance that clearly marks Halfe as an "inveterate" rather than an occasional code switcher.[33] While her writing in *Blue Marrow* involves frequent code switching (including the use of Cree holophrases), like the work of all the other writers discussed in this study, it also relies heavily on the use of paraholophrases, particularly in the text of the revised edition.

Paraholophrases
Paraholophrases Constituting the Narrative's Frame

Blue Marrow is framed by an opening and a closing that are written in rather oral and intimate genres (i.e., prayer and song), clearly marking this long poem as textualizing orality. The frame owes its importance, however, not just to the fact that it textualizes orality by evoking genres that are universally considered oral but also to the fact that it functions as one of the generic conventions of traditional Cree *âcimowina*, whose dramatic structures were traditionally heightened by the inclusion of a narrative frame.[34]

Although *Blue Marrow* does not belong to the Cree *âtayohkewin* tradition, it nevertheless opens with a prayer:

Voice Dancer *pawâkan*, the Guardian of Dreams and Visions, prayer, brings to you this gift.

> *Glory be to* okâwîmâwaskiy
> *To the* nôhkom âtayôhkan
> *To* pawâkan

CHAPTER 5

As it was in the Beginning,
Is now,
And ever shall be,
World without end.
Amen. Amen. (1)

These opening lines contain a subversive rewriting of the *Gloria Patri*, in which the phrase "*to* okâwîmâwaskiy / *To the* nôhkom âtayôhkan / *To* pawâkan" is substituted for "to the Father and to the Son and to the Holy Spirit," denoting the Holy Trinity, a key belief in most Christian denominations. Instead, the three nouns inserted into Halfe's parody of the *Gloria Patri* express key elements of *Cree* religious beliefs.

Okâwîmâwaskiy—from *okâwîmâw*, the generic word for "mother,"[35] and *askîy*, meaning "earth" or "world"[36]—refers to Mother Earth, who is honoured by many Indigenous peoples in North America, including Crees, as the one who gives life because everything the people feed on they receive from her.[37] This reference to the mother, if only in generic form, is particularly significant in *Blue Marrow* when seen in the context of the Cree women given voice in the poem and the role that *nôhkom âtayôhkan* (see below) plays in passing on their stories.[38] At the same time, *okâwîmâwaskiy* also relates to the bone/marrow imagery permeating much of Halfe's poetry, including *Blue Marrow*: the narrator's ancestors sing to the narrator from beneath the earth, turning their marrow into stories (2).

Nôhkom âtayôhkan[39] is translated as "Grandmother Keeper of Sacred Legends" in the glossary of *Blue Marrow*[40] but as "Grandmother of the legends" in the glossary of *Bear Bones and Feathers*,[41] Halfe's first collection of poetry, which includes two poems entitled "Nōhkom ātayohkān 1" and "Nōhkom ātayohkān 2."[42] The phrase is a compound that consists of *nôhkom*, meaning "my grandmother," and *âtayôhkan*, translated as "a legendary figure" in the *Alberta Elders' Cree Dictionary*.[43] According to Marjorie Memnook-White (Cree), a Cree language instructor, "some prefer to use this term [*âtayôhkan*] associated to some sacred figure," but she also points to the need to consult Elders for further explanation "because there could be many variances and implications."[44] Joseph F. Dion (Cree) describes *âtayôhkanak* (pl.) as good spirits;[45] David G. Mandelbaum calls them spirit powers who acted as "intermediaries between the Creator and man" and whose "number was legion, for they possessed every living thing."[46] In Halfe's use of this term as a compound with *nôhkom*, *âtayôhkan* seems most logically to refer to a female legendary figure. The transition from "Grandmother of the legends" in *Bear Bones and Feathers* to "Grandmother Keeper of the Sacred

Legends" in *Blue Marrow* suggests that this *nôhkom* takes the role of keeper of the *âtayohkewina*. The capitalization of the English translation of the revised edition might even indicate that *nôhkom âtayôhkan* is a proper name. However, considering that the possessive use of the term is left untranslated in the glossaries of both *Bear Bones and Feathers* and *Blue Marrow*—*nôhkom âtayôhkan* is given as "Grandmother Keeper of Sacred Legends," not as "*My* Grandmother Keeper of Sacred Legends"—this proper name both does and does not refer to an actual person. Thus, *nôhkom âtayôhkan* becomes a synecdoche of all Cree fore- and grandmothers whose importance lies in connecting contemporary Crees with their culture's legends, spirituality, and religious beliefs. That the Cree word for "mother" is left in its possessive form has a social explanation that further heightens this connection: Crees, like many other Indigenous peoples, often use kinship terms to refer to non-relatives to express their connection with these people.

Finally, the last of the Cree nouns inserted into the *Gloria Patri*, *pawâkan*, is translated in the glossary of *Blue Marrow* as "Dream Spirit" or "Guardian of Dreams and Visions."[47] The *Alberta Elders' Cree Dictionary* further explains that *pawâkan* is a "tribal totem figure encountered in the dream world and which subsequently represents spiritual power."[48] The Crees, like many other Indigenous tribes in North America, often sought visions through what are usually referred to as vision quests. Mandelbaum describes this custom among the Plains Crees as follows: "When a spirit power appeared to an individual in a vision, it became that person's *pawakan*, his supernatural guardian, or better, his spirit helper. The power did not guard and protect a man against all contingencies, but rather aided him in definite, prescribed situations."[49] Regardless of the powers given to a person during a vision quest, Mandelbaum notes, the person was always "taught a song which had to be sung when the vision capabilities and prerogatives were being exercised." Vision quests were usually restricted to boys, but girls could also be given certain powers during menstrual isolation.[50]

It is not clear what powers have been given to the narrator in *Blue Marrow*, but the invocation of *pawâkan* in the first two lines suggests that whatever words follow have been given to the narrator by her *pawâkan*—they are the song that she has been taught and that must be sung. The narrator addresses *pawâkan*—"**Voice Dancer *pawâkan*, the Guardian of Dreams and Visions**"—in both Cree and English, thus doubling *pawâkan*'s presence in the text, and then evokes *pawâkan*'s spiritual power with the appositional "prayer" before finally ending this enumeration of nouns with "brings to you this gift." *Blue Marrow* knows many "yous"—particularly the narrator's fore- and grandmothers, whom the narrator addresses frequently throughout the sequence. This first "you," however, appears to be directed at the readers as they "overhear" the narrator's "voice." Thus, *pawâkan*'s offering to the narrator—the voices of the fore- and grandmothers that she is privileged to hear—becomes a communal yet intimate experience, with the narrator acting only as intermediary between her spirit power and her readers. *Pawâkan*'s gift to her is passed on as a gift to the readers.

With "**Glory be to okâwîmâwaskiy / To the nôhkom âtayôhkan / To pawâkan**," the narrator in *Blue Marrow* invokes *okâwîmâwaskiy*, Mother Earth, the Cree oral tradition as kept intact by *nôhkom âtayôhkan*, Grandmother Keeper of the Sacred Legends, and the spiritual powers bestowed on people by *pawâkan*, Guardian of Dreams and Visions—all of which are important notions of Cree religion and constitute the basic components of the poem, as will become apparent below. Debra Dudek has noted the importance of Halfe's repeated use of bone imagery in "drawing attention to the *embodied nature of the stories*."[51] Still in the opening, the narrator remarks, "**The prairie is full of bones. The bones stand and sing and I feel the weight of them as they guide my fingers on this page. See the blood**" (2–3). These bones are the very bones of her fore- and grandmothers, the bones of her ancestors, the bones of *nôhkom âtayôhkan*, Grandmother Keeper of the Sacred Legends. Hidden beneath *okâwîmâwaskiy*, Mother Earth, lies the collective memory of the narrator's people, which the narrator is granted to feel through the powers bestowed on her by *pawâkan* so that she can turn into stories the blood produced in her ancestors' marrow.[52] The powerful bone/marrow imagery in *Blue Marrow* thus brings to mind the central religious notions from Cree religion introduced in the opening prayer and points to the land as "the spiritual, historical, and physical connection that gives Native people their identity."[53]

The notions of *okâwîmâwaskiy*, *nôhkom âtayôhkan*, and *pawâkan* are implicitly evoked again and again through the voices of the ancestors transcribed by the narrator and through other instances of the bone/marrow imagery, a theme repeated throughout the poem.[54] However, these Cree religious concepts also reappear more explicitly in the elaborate invocation of the narrator's many foremothers, a long list that comprises the last several pages of the poem's opening (3–7). "Halfe employs the ritual, the repetition, the naming, the prayer, the emotion, the detail of the oral narrative"[55] in this passage of *Blue Marrow* and, as in the beginning of the poem's opening, makes extensive use of parody. The long list of the foremothers' names is interspersed with lines from the opening prayer (3–4), the Hail Mary (3), and the Lord's Prayer (4–7), all rendered to invent a new prayer reflecting Cree religious and cultural concepts (see Table 5.1 and Table 5.2).

First Mother Earth Prayer	**Hail Mary**
okâwîmâwaskiy *full of grace;* *the Creator is filled with thee;* *Blessed art thou among* iskwêwak[56] *And blessed is the fruit of thy womb, Holy Mother of all* *Pray for us* kitânisak,[57] *now and at the hour* *of our death. Amen.* (3)	Hail Mary, full of grace, the Lord is with thee. Blessed art thou among women, and blessed is the fruit of thy womb, Jesus. Holy Mary, Mother of God, pray for us sinners, now and at the hour of our death. Amen.

Table 5.1 *Blue Marrow*'s Parody of the Hail Mary

Thus, the Hail Mary celebrating the incarnation of Jesus becomes a Cree prayer celebrating Mother Earth. *Okâwîmâwaskiy* is addressed again, in a second Mother Earth Prayer, itself a rendering of the Lord's Prayer. This second prayer also includes a reference to *nôhkom âtayôhkan* (6) and, unlike the Christian prayer, communicates a life-affirming message—"temptation" becomes "Celebration."

Second Mother Earth Prayer	**Lord's Prayer[58]**
Okâwîmâwaskiy *who art in* tawahikan[59] *Hallowed be thy name* [...] *Thy Creation come* *Thy will be done* [...] asiskiy[60] *as it is in* kîsik[61]	Our Father which art in heaven; Hallowed be thy Name. Thy kingdom come. Thy will be done in earth, As it is in heaven.
Give us this day our daily reminders [...] *of* sâkihitowin,[62] *of* kisêwâtisiwin[63]	Give us this day our daily bread.

Table 5.2 *Blue Marrow*'s Parody of the Lord's Prayer *(continued next page)*

Second Mother Earth Prayer	Lord's Prayer
And forgive us our shortcomings *As we forgive those who trespass* *against us* [...] *Oh mâmaw-ôhtâwîmâw*[64] *Lead us into Celebration* [...] *We give you thanks for the Four Legged.* *The Winged People. The Swimmers.* [...] *We give thanks to the* piyêsiwak[65]— *Whose voice sings from* kîsik. [...] *We give thanks to the* nôtokwêsiwak[66] *We give thanks to the* kisêyiniwak[67] *The Keeper of the* âcimowinis nôhkom âtayôhkan [...] mâmaw-ôhtâwîmâw, *who art in* tawahikan *Hallowed be thy name* [...] *Lead us to Creation and* *Deliver us into* mâmitonêyihtêstamâsowin[68] *into the* matotisân[69] [...] *For thou art the Parent of All,* *the connection,* *And the Centre, the Universe* *the power* [...] *the glory* *Now and for ever* *Amen. Amen.* (4–7)	And forgive us our trespasses, As we forgive them that trespass against us. And lead us not into temptation; But deliver us from evil: For thine is the kingdom, And the power, and the glory, For ever and ever. Amen.

Table 5.2 *Blue Marrow*'s Parody of the Lord's Prayer

These parodies of Christian prayers in the opening pages of *Blue Marrow*, then, inscribe Cree religious beliefs into the narrative, which the narrator herself describes as a journey. "The walk began before I was a seed," she writes after having said her opening prayer (1). By not naming her final destination, the narrator seems to propose that she was born with an obligation that is not yet revealed to readers and that she herself cannot have been aware of at birth. The reference to her mother stringing her umbilical cord in her moccasins (1) evokes a common Cree custom described by Mandelbaum: a child's navel cord and some tobacco were put into a navel cord bag, which the child wore around his or her neck. When an Elder smoked the tobacco in the bag, "he would offer [the navel cord] to his spirit helpers and ask them to grant good fortune to the child."[70] The reference in *Blue Marrow* to the moccasins, however, also emphasizes the narrator's life-long journey, which turns out to include a vision.[71]

The vision in which the narrator meets her *pawâkan* is not overtly described. However, given the cultural significance of *pawâkan* and its description as **"Voice Dancer *pawâkan*, the Guardian of Dreams and Visions,"** it is possible to read the scattered stories between the opening prayer of the collection and the invocation of the fore- and grandmothers at the end of the opening as a retelling of the narrator's "vision quest" or, as the narrator describes it metaphorically, her awakening after her memory had gone to sleep "Long after *nimosôm* ['my grandfather'] died" (1). So the story of her vision becomes the story of how she hears her ancestors' voices, which cause her walk to become a "walk for them" (3); this story unfolds as follows.

One day, the narrator tells her readers, she awakes "in the mountains lying in the crook of [her] white husband's arms, cocooned in the warmth of [their] tepee," after having dreamed of her grandfather guiding her finger through his "big book" (obviously the Bible) and seeing an old man lifting a pipe with her hand on the stem. In the dream, the narrator touches both book and pipe, but when she returns to her cabin she "fill[s] the pockets between the logs with papers, stack[s] the walls with [her] books" (1), instead of smoking a pipe. Smoking the pipe is an important ritual common to all Plains Cree ceremonies because it connects man with supernatural powers.[72] Not surprisingly, in the narrator's dream, a man with long braids hanging down his shoulders (obviously Indigenous) laughs at her attempt to repair her cabin with the big book rather than by connecting with the spirit powers. The big book not only has silenced the narrator's grandfather ("His fingers traced the path of *cahkipêhikana* / ᐊᕐᒐᐤ, mouth moving quietly" [1]) but also seems to have blinded the narrator. Blinded by the Christian religion, she is without vision.

Realizing her blindness, the narrator decides to go into the mountains, and, while connecting with *okâwîmâwaskiy* ("I picked feathers as I climbed [...]. Soon the mountain too had feet. I swam down her clear water and stood naked beneath her falls" [1]), she hears gunshot, thunder, and "the drumming of the Little People" (2). The presence of the Little People here signals her spiritual awakening, for dwarves among the Plains Crees were believed to have the ability to bestow powers and thus to act as spirit helpers, even if they did not appear in visions.[73] Finally, the narrator awakes to "the brilliant ribbon of Northern Lights melt[ing] into a sunrise," marking a new, yet perilous, beginning for her. As Dion explains,

> It has always been the belief of the Crees that the wondrous display in the northern skies on certain nights was caused by the reflection of the spirits of our departed dancing in the realm of the great beyond. Strange to say, they are not regarded as manifestations of joy or gladness of our people who have passed on, but rather sorrowful reminders, hence we have always taken these signs seriously. They are a phenomenon not to be trifled with.[74]

Although bringing with them the possibility of danger, Dion adds that "In the not too distant past the Crees believed that the spirits of the departed [in the form of the northern lights] were trying to send messages to the living on earth."[75]

The northern lights that the narrator awakes to are the spirits of her ancestors dancing in the night sky, telling their stories of colonization. They will become Halfe's very poem, as her narrator receives her ancestors' stories via *nôhkom*:[76]

> *âstam*, she said. She rubbed my eyes with her sweat and I saw her many faces.
>
> Each face sat at the altar with one large eye.
>
> [...]
>
> In her cabin where *nôhkom* waited was a stoneboat stacked full of her belongings. [...] She invited all my relatives to her feast.
>
> She sang, her Voices echoing through the cabin. (2)

The narrator later identifies her four *kôhkom* by name (8–9), but she does not further identify the *nôhkom* of her vision. When *nôhkom* sings, "her Voices" might refer to *nôhkom*'s own voices—which are multiple because *nôhkom* sings many songs. It seems more likely, however, especially given the capitalization of "Voices," that these are the voices of the narrator's ancestors, heard through *nôhkom*, an intermediary with "many faces" whose role is that of a keeper.[77] The *nôhkom* of the narrator's vision is hence really *nôhkom âtayôhkan*, who was invoked in the Cree opening prayer. And *nôhkom*'s song is that of the narrator's ancestors, whose bones under *okâwîmâwaskiy* guide her fingers on the page, helping the narrator to compose (2). That the scene of the narrator's meeting with *nôhkom* is neither a dream nor reality but a vision—"Each face sat at the altar with one large eye"—is not directly stated in the text, but it can be assumed from the elaborate invocation of *pawâkan* in the Cree opening prayer.

As her vision comes to an end, the narrator is "awake now and remove[s]" her white husband's ring, thus regaining what she lost (*ê-kî-âhtaskêyân*[78]) when she married him (2). At the same time, the act of removing her ring points to the fact that she has accepted her vision and wants to act on it. "**I began the walk for them**," she declares, and the moment that she starts this walk for her ancestors the hoofprint on her left breast disappears (3). She is no longer branded but free, and she shouts out the names of numerous women—four pages of female personal names interspersed, as I have discussed, with the subversive, Cree-infused parodies of the Hail Mary, the *Gloria Patri*, and the Lord's Prayer, names belonging to women whose stories the narrator was given by *nôhkom âtayôhkan*'s many voices in a vision, stories that she now "feeds" to her children and to the readers of the poem:

> Grandmothers hold me.
> I must pass all that I possess,
> every morsel to my children.
> These small gifts. (7)

What the narrator offers to her children, and ultimately to readers, has been given to her by **"Voice Dancer *pawâkan*, the Guardian of Dreams and Visions."** Ending on this notion of passing on stories as gifts, the poem's opening has thus come full circle.

As the narrator accepts her intermediate position between the past generations and those still to come, it also becomes clear that the initial description of *pawâkan* was anything but accidental: **"Voice Dancer *pawâkan*, the Guardian of Dreams and Visions,"** circumscribes the meaning and function of *pawâkan*; however, by evoking both the northern lights ("voice dancer") and its role as "guardian" of the narrator's dreams and vision, this phrase also connects two elements in the opening that are crucial for the poem. It is with this link between the messages of the ancestors and the narrator's dreams and vision that the poem is born. "Voice Dancer *pawâkan*, the Guardian of Dreams and Visions," tells in one phrase the story of the narrator's gaining vision, hence explaining the poem's origin. This phrase, then, is key to understanding the story of the narrator's vision that unfolds in the opening pages of the poem and without which there would be no poem. The roles of those who will accompany the narrator on her walk to vision—Mother Earth, the eternal grandmother and keeper of legends, and the Guardian of Dreams and Visions—are anticipated in the lines "**Glory be to okâwîmâwaskiy / To the nôhkom âtayôhkan / To pawâkan**," but the phrase is also a metonymic invocation of the metaphor that the narrator uses after having had her vision: "**The prairie is full of bones. The bones stand and sing and I feel the weight of them as they guide my fingers on this page. See the blood.**" It is with the help of *okâwîmâwaskiy*, *nôhkom âtayôhkan*, and *pawâkan*, who guide the narrator to vision, that she is finally able to hear her ancestors' stories. The phrase "**I began the walk for them**," then, becomes a metaphor of her decision to speak for the ancestors who surround her so fully (their bones in Mother Earth and their spirits in the sky, dancing as the northern lights), to become their intermediary, and thus to translate their stories—the stories of her vision—into the poem that readers are in the process of reading and that the narrator offers to her children as if it were food: "**every morsel to my children. / These small gifts.**" This metaphor, which ends the poem's opening, points to the importance of the stories that she received from her ancestors and that she will now pass on as the key for the next generation's survival.

The effectiveness of the opening in *Blue Marrow* depends, of course, on the readers' awareness of being guided into the poem, which in turn rests on a number of phrases prominent in the opening pages:

a. "Voice Dancer *pawâkan*, the Guardian of Dreams and Visions" (1; metonymy),
b. "*Glory be to* okâwîmâwaskiy / *To the* nôhkom âtayôhkan / *To* pawâkan" (1; metonymy),
c. "The prairie is full of bones. The bones stand and sing and I feel the weight of them as they guide my fingers on this page. See the blood" (2–3; metaphor),
d. "I began the walk for them" (3; metaphor), and
e. "every morsel to my children. / These small gifts" (7; metaphor).

As figures of speech, these phrases form the cores of complex ideas: they are self-contained, but, because they create a gap between sign and meaning, they also carry a surplus of meaning that readers must uncover for themselves. Moreover, these phrases constitute the structural hinges on which the opening of the revised edition of *Blue Marrow* is constructed, and this opening in turn becomes one of the hinges of the long poem itself. The opening established by these phrases, which are equivalent in function to holophrases in Indigenous languages and thus qualify as paraholophrases, is particularly important because, as part of the poem's frame, it provides the poem's spiritual and cultural contexts and hence heightens the significance of the stories told therein.

The revised edition of *Blue Marrow* differs notably from the text as first published in 1998. Interestingly, some of the changes in the revised edition make the poem's opening more dependent on the paraholophrases that I have just identified. The first edition lacks all the Cree renderings of the three Christian prayers in the poem's opening. It does not begin with the invocation—**"Voice Dancer *pawâkan*, the Guardian of Dreams and Visions"**—and the recitation of the Cree opening prayer; instead, it begins with "The walk began before I was a seed."[79] Furthermore, the enumeration of the narrator's foremothers in the first edition does not include the interspersed prayers that, in the revised edition, serve to recall the three important notions of Cree spirituality that function as the main narrative components of the poem: *okâwîmâwaskiy*, *nôhkom âtayôhkan*, and *pawâkan*. And, finally, what I have pointed out as the end of the opening in the revised edition takes the following form in the first edition:

> Cardinal Woman, Mud Hen Woman, Old Woman. Pray to them.
> Fire Thunder Woman, Kicking Horse Woman, Big Swan Woman,
> *Kytwayhat* (She Who Says So Woman). Pray to them.
> To all my *Nechi* <u>Women throughout this country whose spirit and songs haven't been heard. Who will be heard.</u> All my relations. Amen.
>
> Grandmothers hold me. I must pass all that I possess,
> every morsel to my children. These small gifts
> <u>to see them through life. Raise my fist. Tell the story.</u>
> <u>Tear down barbed-wire fences.</u>[80]

The underlined text here identifies phrases and clauses that have been deleted from the revised edition of *Blue Marrow*. It is futile to speculate about the reasons that led to their removal. One thing, however, is certain: the deleted phrases and clauses *explicitly* point readers to the origin and nature of the poem (songs of the fore- and grandmothers have been imparted to a female narrator in a vision, and she is now going to pass on these songs because of their life-crucial role to others)—a task that in the revised edition is fulfilled exclusively by the paraholophrases added to the opening lines, in the Cree opening prayer, and in their evocations in the other prayers recited in the enumeration of the foremothers.

    The absence of the first edition's more explicit comments forces readers of the revised edition to engage more deeply with the text, for they must interpret the poem's paraholophrases to understand that the opening tells the story of the narrator's vision. The lines deleted from the original edition, then, are not *necessary* for readers of the revised edition to make sense of the poem; in fact, if these parts were kept, they would *tell*, rather than *show*, readers the origin and nature of the narrator's narrative, thus undermining the need for readers to participate in deciphering the poem's interpretative context. Moreover, the paraholophrases used in the construction of the revised opening help to build a narrative frame that marks the poem as a prayer, and not "just" a story, thus lending the text of the revised edition an enhanced cultural and spiritual context over that of the text in the first edition. A comparison of the opening in the two editions of *Blue Marrow* hence reveals that the text in the revised edition is dependent on paraholophrases, which function both in constructing the poem and in textualizing orality. As I discussed earlier, in the introduction to this study, context, involvement, and participation are characteristics of conceptual orality that result from the context of language use. By creating the spiritual, cultural, and interpretative contexts of *Blue Marrow* and by showing Halfe's involvement with her audience as readers are forced to engage with the text in order to interpret it, the paraholophrases constituting the poem's opening, therefore, also function as oral strategies in the text.

    Having said her opening prayer, the narrator of *Blue Marrow* is now ready to begin her narrative. What follows is a series of poems in which different people, primarily Cree women, are given the opportunity to tell *their* stories of First Nations and European contact—stories of rape, hunger, loss, and cultural disorientation. Although these poems are interspersed with passages written in the voice of the narrator, these narratorial passages are fairly short. It is only toward the end of the narrative that the narrator's voice itself becomes more dominant as the narrator becomes "an active participant in the 'membering' of her own story through the reluctant, but compliant, voices of her father and mother."[81] Not counting a short interlude of the chorus of the foremothers (85), Rainbow Grandmother is the last of the narrator's foremothers to speak (79). The remainder of the poem is filled with a long conversation that the narrator has with her father and, finally, with her mother. Yet, even though these conversations are intimate, the narrator repeatedly refuses to name her parents because they are "many fathers" (80) and "everyone's / mother" (86). Thus, in the end, the narrator's personal story is also the story of many other contemporary Indigenous women. More importantly, when the narrator realizes that she has become "Grandmother, the Woman in me" (99), she has connected her own story to the opening of her narrative and to all the Indigenous women listed there.

The first traces of a narrative closing are already visible in the narrator's dialogue with her father, whom the narrator introduces to readers as looking with his "**dubious eye**" (80). This reference to his outward appearance could be incidental, but her choice to speak of his "eye," rather than his "eyes," points back to her vision in the opening, where each of *nôhkom*'s many faces displays "one large eye" (2). Other intratextual elements in the narrator's dialogue with her father include a number of references to the metaphor of the journey. Indian Affairs took the narrator away from her father and "**Gave me a one-way / ticket**." She ended up going to residential school, and when she left she "**Filled my fist with my father's / walk**" (85). "**For miles my father and I / walked**," while "**Mother and I / held our breath a hundred miles / across the *sôhkêciwani-sîpiy*—/ the Fast Flowing River**" (86). These references to the narrator walking call to mind the walk that she decides to undertake for her ancestors after having had her vision (see 1–3).

When her mother's memory stirs, the narrator joins her mother "in a clear and mournful chant" (87):

waniskâ
Arise

pê-wâpan ôma
dawn has come

âsay piyêsîsak
already the birds

nikamowak
sing

miyohtâkwan.
the beautiful song

kitaskînaw.
our land. (87)[82]

CHAPTER 5

With its references to song and to the land that evoke the ideas in the poem's opening—*okâwîmâwaskiy*, *nôhkom âtayôhkan*, and *pawâkan*—this Cree morning song becomes an allegory of the narrator's vision. As her mother speaks about her grandchildren, the narrator starts to remember how she would "**walk the valley with my little ones, / picking chokecherries. I'd crush till / I burst all over my canvas**" (92)—berries that she also picked with *nôhkom* in the opening, "Crush[ing] them between the rocks" (2). Finally, after the narrator has finished her "We are collectors poem" (94–95), the end of the poem's closing is near. The final *âcimowinis* "small story" again points back to the poem's opening, thus completing its frame. The intratextual references are indicated by boldface type here:

> **Ram Woman**, we met for the first time.
> You stood on top of graves at White Rabbit,
> **large eye** staring.
> My legs wrapped my husband.
> Your head thumped those stones.
>
> Ram Woman, I stood **naked**
> **beneath the falls.**
> **Your hoofs pounded**
> **in that April rain.**
> [...]
>
> Ram Woman, Ram Woman
> in Kootenay Plains you sang,
> lured me to your grave,
> gave my heart a twist and
> sent me flying, gave me
> **your large eye**
> for my stepping stone.
>
> She came in a Vision, flipped **many faces**.
> **Stone-aged wrinkled**, creased like stretched drum,
> thin flesh, sharp nose. [...]
> Long ago Grandmother dances in glades,
> **woman crushed chokecherries**, saved the blood,
> [...].
> They **drummed, danced**, lifted their dreams.
> **Ribboned the Sky.**

> Raw-boned,
> they left their blood.
> In these moccasin gardens
> I pick my medicines. (96–97)

In this "Ram Woman poem," the narrator relives and retells her vision, but this time she directly addresses *nôhkom* (*âtayôhkan*) as Ram Woman (perhaps a reference to the Ram River that drains the Kootenay Plains) and refers to their meeting as "a Vision" (97). When the narrator describes Ram Woman as "stone-aged wrinkled," this description underlines her age and further supports a reading of her as the *nôhkom* (*âtayôhkan*) of the opening, but this description can also be read as a reference to the Stoney people, who originally called the Kootenay Plains their home. Like *nôhkom* (*âtayôhkan*) (2), Ram Woman stares with one "**large eye**" (96, 97), a symbol of her vision and wisdom, and sings to the narrator (2, 97). As in the opening, the narrator stands "**naked beneath the falls**" (96; also see 1), exposed and vulnerable. When the two meet, Ram Woman is pounding her hoofs as if to inscribe onto the narrator's body her duty to walk for her foremothers (96), but, as readers know by now, this hoofprint disappears the moment the narrator fulfills this duty (3). The "Ram Woman poem" also contains a reference to the northern lights of the opening, which "**Ribboned the Sky**," whereas "**Raw-boned / they left their blood**" (97) refers to the bones populating the prairie whose marrow, or blood, produces the stories (2) that the narrator is collecting: "**In these moccasin gardens / I pick my medicines**" (97). In other words, the "Ram Woman poem" in the closing fills in all those blanks in the opening; thus, the poem that is *Blue Marrow* is about to end (and might begin yet again).

In addition to these intratextual connections to the story of the narrator's vision told in its opening, the poem's closing picks up the metaphor of the narrator's storytelling as a journey, but a journey *on paper* ("Did they [the Grandmothers] know our memory, **our / talk would walk on paper**" [98]), thus underlining the complex nature of *Blue Marrow* as an account of the textualization of orature. Moreover, its closing points yet again to the importance of *okâwîmâwaskiy* and *nôhkom âtayôhkan*. The latter are evoked by way of an intertextual reference to *wîsahkêcâhk*, the Cree cultural hero, and the narrator's version of the Cree earth diver myth:

> We are Star People.
> *wîsahkêcâhk* sang to the Water People
> to bring back to Earth from where we dove.

> She pinched the mud from the exhausted Muskrat.
> Blew *yotin* ["wind"], Blew *iskotêw* ["fire"]. *iskwêw* ["woman"] was born.
> *pimâtisiwim* ["life"] fills woman.
> Man is born. (98)

This poem emphasizes both the life-giving force of Mother Earth and the significant role of woman in creation. Having thus recounted part of the Cree creation story, the narrator joins "Grandmother danc[ing] at Midnight," and then, as she realizes "Grandmother, the Woman in me," she closes—but does not end—her narrative with the words "**A pagan. Again. / All my relations.** *Ahâw*"[83] (99).

In that it moves from the vision to the prayer, the closing of *Blue Marrow* is its opening told backward and hence establishes a "mirror-image" or cyclical structure within the frame.[84] Still, there is a significant difference between the opening of Halfe's long poem and its closing: whereas in the former the narrator parodies Christian prayers to have them reflect Cree religious concepts, she does not use parody in her closing prayer. She does acknowledge that telling her foremothers' stories has turned her into "A pagan. Again." These words, however, are ironic because her embracing of the colonizer's evaluation of the colonized subject as non-Christian (pagan) and, hence, inferior, marks her self-discovery and self-affirmation as an Indigenous woman with strong ties to her Cree culture—a form of self-empowerment that she gains in the process of turning her ancestors' talk into a "walk on paper." As if to demonstrate this rather political statement, the narrator's last words in English are "All my relations" (99). Thomas King explains the meaning of this phrase in this way:

> "All my relations" is the English equivalent of a phrase familiar to most Native peoples in North America. It may begin or end a prayer or a speech or a story, and, while each tribe has its own way of expressing this sentiment in its own language, the meaning is the same.
>
> "All my relations" is at first a reminder of who we are and of our relationship with both our family and our relatives. It also reminds us of the extended relationship we share with all human beings. But the relationships that Native people see go further, the web of kinship extending to the animals, to the birds, to the fish, to the plants, to all the animate and inanimate forms that can be seen or imagined. More than that, "all my relations" is an encouragement for us to accept the responsibilities we have within this universal family by living our lives in a harmonious and moral manner [...].[85]

"All my relations," then, is a very appropriate way for the narrator to end her prayer/song in *Blue Marrow*; the phrase gains particular significance, though, because it points again to the importance of *okâwîmâwaskiy* (Mother Earth) and *nôhkom âtayôhkan* (Grandmother Keeper of Sacred Legends), which were first introduced in the opening and which pervade the narrator's composition. With two of the key notions of the collection thus evoked, the narrator is finally prepared to say *ahâw*, a formulaic discourse marker used to end a conversation in Cree and hence a marker of the oral. Her task has been fulfilled: she has walked for her foremothers and imparted their stories to the next generation, the generation that will eventually have to follow her footsteps. The survival of the tradition passed on to the narrator is assured, and her poem can begin anew.

The chunks of language that I have pointed out as featuring prominently in the closing of *Blue Marrow* establish intratextual references to the story of the narrator's vision told in the poem's opening. These phrases—

a. "dubious eye" (80; symbol),
b. "Gave me a one-way / ticket" (85; metaphor),
c. "Filled my fist with my father's / walk" (85; metaphor),
d. "For miles my father and I walked" (86; symbol),
e. "Mother and I / held our breath a hundred miles / across the *sôh-kêciwani-sîpiy*—/ the Fast Flowing River" (86; metaphor),
f. the Cree Morning Song (87; allegory),
g. "walk the valley with my little ones, / picking chokecherries. I'd crush till / I burst all over my canvas" (92; metaphor),
h. "Ram Woman" (96; symbol),
i. "large eye" (96; symbol),
j. "naked beneath the falls" (96; symbol)
k. "Ribboned the Sky" and "Raw-boned / they left their blood" (97; metaphor),
l. "In these moccasin gardens / I pick my medicines" (97; metaphor),
m. "our / talk would walk on paper" (98; metaphor), and
n. "A pagan. Again / All my relations. *ahâw*" (99; irony)[86]

—link the closing to the opening and thus complete the poem's frame. As figures of speech, which by definition form the core of a complex idea, and as the structural hinges of the closing, these chunks of language are equivalent in function to holophrases in Indigenous languages.

Together with the paraholophrases of the opening, these paraholophrases of the closing form the structural hinges of *Blue Marrow*. They reveal the author's involvement with her audience in the attempt to invite reader participation because they provide the interpretative context for the main part of the poem. With a night song—

> I turn to the Moon glade,
> turn up the sod,
> lift up my songs.
> Dream.
> Grandmother dances at Midnight.
> Grandmother Moon,
> my Shadow
> dreams the dark (98–99)

—the narrator closes the narrative that she opened with a prayer. Both comparatively oral genres, the prayer and song constitute the frame for the narrator's "walk on paper" that eventually becomes *Blue Marrow*. The narrative frame highlights the metafictional dimension of Halfe's long poem, but its real significance lies in stressing the cultural significance of the fore- and grandmothers' stories: these stories are not just told in writing but are also the ancestors' *offering* to readers through the medium of the narrator, who gratefully acknowledges their gift by giving tobacco in return—"I give you these offerings / from their *âcimowina* [stories] and tie tobacco / to their ribs" (61)—and by passing on their stories to others in the form of a prayer. That two of the paraholophrases constituting the poem's frame contain Cree words (*okâwîmâwaskiy, nôhkom âtayôhkan, pawâkan*) further establishes the proper cultural context for the poem.

The first edition of *Blue Marrow* lacks not only the invocation of "Voice Dancer *pawâkan*, the Guardian of Dreams and Visions" and the recitation of the Cree opening prayer but also the last two lines of the revised edition, "A pagan. Again. / All my relations. *ahâw*," ending instead with "Grandmother, the Woman in Me."[87] Indeed, the words "A pagan. Again. / All my relations. *ahâw*" make sense only in the revised edition, which opens with a prayer and must close with a prayer to come full circle, to give the narrative frame its cyclical shape. Like the comparison of the openings, a comparison of the closings in the two editions of *Blue Marrow* reveals the great significance of the paraholophrase as a narrative hinge and as a culturally specific strategy in textualizing orality.

Paraholophrases with Other Narrative Functions

Like the four texts discussed in the earlier chapters, *Blue Marrow* contains paraholophrases—in the form of personal names, intratextual references, and metafictionality—that are significant even though their narrative function lies in something other than constituting an opening and closing frame.

The poem's many personal names evoke Indigenous traditions of name giving and are based either on English or Cree or on a conflation of the two languages. Many of them are found in the opening frame, in the long list of the narrator's foremothers, but others are found in the main part of the poem. As discussed in previous chapters, these indigenized personal names all function as examples of synecdoche in that they use for a person's name that person's defining characteristic.[88]

The indigenized personal names in *Blue Marrow*, however, also have a political purpose. The names of the women whose voices we hear in the main part of the poem are particularly interesting because the stories that these women tell also reveal the stories behind their names. *Sîpi-kiskisiw Grandmother*—Long Term Memory Grandmother speaks of the times when her father *"fought with lance and arrow, / rotted behind bars / his treaty coat / a shredded ribbon"* (76). Grandmother Bargain explains in her confession how *"My father saw / my future husband—/ mounds of fur"* and thus tells the story of how she was sold by her father to a white man as part of a bargain to obtain the white man's provisions (54–56). Speaking herself into an angry fit, one woman *"put dem [white men] back / on dem big canoe. / Dem go home. / My big family / make dem go home"*—and so becomes Not So Long Ago Granny Wants to Get Even (64–65). Another woman, talking about her birth, tells the reader, *"I can't dell you where I waz born. / In a dent somewhere, / maybe in da bush"*; she becomes Born in a Dent Grandmudder (61).

Yet, though the narrator assigns indigenized personal names to the women speaking in the main part of her narrative, she claims that she does "not recognize who speaks" (18, 61). Her ignorance about who speaks to her might seem contradictory, but it makes sense when one considers that the indigenized personal names assigned to these women reduce their identities to those of female colonized objects conquered and ruled over by white men. This use of Indigenous traditions of name giving thus marks the narrative as one that carries an implicit political statement that "affronts the master narrative of imperialism and commodification by offering, in its place, a vivid account of the dispossessed who, though dead and buried, refuse to be silent."[89] As symbols of the stories of colonization, the women's names in the main part of *Blue Marrow* can be read, then, as "abbreviated texts":[90] they mark the women who bear these names as colonized objects. They have become unrecognizable for the narrator, yet their stories persist, and thus so do the women, ultimately, through the narrator's "walk on the page" that passes their stories on to future generations.

CHAPTER 5

As symbols, the indigenized personal names in the main part of *Blue Marrow* form the cores of complex ideas and thus carry a bundle of meaning. Introduced at the beginning of the women's stories, these names provide structural markers within the narrator's long "walk on the page" and function much like chapter titles in longer narratives, facilitating reader understanding. As figures of speech with significant narrative function, then, the indigenized personal names in the main part of Halfe's long poem are equivalent in function to holophrases in Indigenous languages and therefore qualify as paraholophrases.[91] Because they also evoke an Indigenous cultural tradition—name giving—these personal names weave Cree cultural contexts into Halfe's long poem and show her involvement with her readers by inviting their participation. Because they combine various words to form more complex chunks of language in the form of compounds, the indigenized personal names in the main part of *Blue Marrow* also mimic the structure of holophrases in Indigenous languages and thus can be regarded as direct holophrastic traces; this will be discussed in detail in the next section.

Another group of paraholophrases not involved in the construction of the narrative frame consists of intratextual references inside the main narrative that refer readers back to the poem's opening. The most direct evocation of the opening in the main narrative occurs about midway, when the first Mother Earth prayer is repeated nearly verbatim ("Holy Mother of all" is replaced with *nikâwiy* "my mother"), recalling *okâwîmâwaskiy* "Mother Earth" and her central importance in Cree religion (and in the construction of *Blue Marrow*) (3, 42). Although it encompasses a total of seven lines, I would still read this recitation of the prayer as a paraholophrase because it forms the core of a complex idea (i.e., a central notion in Cree religion and a synecdoche of the narrators' foremothers) and functions as a reminder of the fact that the main narrative is not just a concatenation of stories but also a concatenation of prayers and/or songs.

Other intratextual references pointing to the opening of the poem are formulaic. Such formulae include invocation of the voices of the foremothers—***kahkiyaw iskwêwak, nôtokwêsiwak, câpânak, êkwa ohkomipanak*** (22, 30, 34, 49, 54, 59, 63, 67, 72, 77, 85)—and those of the forefathers—***kahkiyaw nâpêwak, kisêyiniwak, câpânak, êkwa omosômipanak*** (77, 78, variations at 37, 70). An evocation of the ancestors' dancing in the sky in front of the narrator, these formulae inscribe the main part of the poem with reminders of the context that was established in the poem's opening. As intratextual references with significant narrative function, then, the formulaic invocations of the narrator's foremothers and forefathers are equivalent in function to holophrases in Indigenous languages and can thus be read as paraholophrases.⁹² The evocation of the ancestors' dancing not only creates context (cultural and interpretative) but also reveals the author's attempt to engage her readers in the composition of the poem; these formulaic clusters also function, then, as strategies in textualizing orality.

Another formulaic cluster—"*pê-nîhtaciwêk, nôhkomak.* / **Climb down, my Grandmothers**" (17)—opens the bilingual recitation of the "Climb down prayer," which is told in Cree before it is repeated in a conflation of Cree and English (clearly emphasizing the importance of this poem). Over thirty pages later (54), this formulaic cluster is repeated but is not followed by the rest of the prayer.⁹³ The formula alone is sufficient to evoke the whole prayer—"Before the thought is done / they know my prayers" (54)—and to act as a reminder that the stories narrated by the narrator are *prayers* in print. The formulaic cluster in the "Climb down prayer" ultimately describes the communication between the narrator and her ancestors dancing in the sky as the northern lights and thus points back to the opening of the poem. As a metaphor of the narrator's vision, the phrase "*pê-nîhtaciwêk, nôhkomak.* / Climb down, my Grandmothers" forms the core of a complex idea; as a reminder of the poem's cultural and interpretative contexts, it performs a significant narrative function. Equivalent in function to holophrases in Indigenous languages, this phrase qualifies as a paraholophrase whose textualization of orality lies in creating context (cultural and interpretative) as well as author involvement and reader participation through the use of figurative language.

Other references to the northern lights in the main narrative of *Blue Marrow* establish metafictional moments in the poem, either in the narrator's description of her ancestors' spirits—"The women's blankets spiral / into the Northern Lights" (27); "The Sky Dancers circle / my head" (32); "We dance / and dance and dance" (59)—or in the foremothers' conversations with the narrator—"*My mouth a wind of souls / dancing the empty night*" (40); "We do not exist / except in the open mouth / of sky. No voices / dream our Visions" (72). Other metafictional moments include the foremothers speaking directly to the narrator, thus recalling the role of the ancestors in the narrator's vision as the sources for what will become *Blue Marrow*;⁹⁴ still others include the narrator describing the transcription of the voices' messages,⁹⁵ thus bringing to mind the narrator's vision, as narrated in the poem's opening.

I have already noted that the frequent metafictional moments repeatedly remind readers that what they witness as they are reading *Blue Marrow* is *an account of textualizing orature*. These metafictional moments also textualize orality by helping to disrupt the linearity of the narrative, thus making it more fluid. More importantly, however, metafictionality in *Blue Marrow* establishes connections between the main narrative and its opening.

CHAPTER 5

By repeatedly emphasizing that what she is passing on she has received from her ancestors, the narrator re-evokes the religious concepts in the poem's opening. Her "**Cree-ing loud into my night**" (16), for example, is a metaphor of taking dictation from her ancestors as they dance in the night sky. That the narrator can see their voices in the sky and "cree" out their bones' marrow—that is, carry on their stories in a culturally appropriate form—is possible only because *pawâkan* and *nôhkom âtayôhkan* are guiding her. The most immediate re-enactment of the poem's "birth" (as found in the opening) is in this passage from the main narrative:

> *Sage Woman Eyes with Spirits.*
> *When Thunder speaks,*
> *Lightning flashes from them.*
> I sit with her in her Lodge.
> *We cling to our Pipes* and weep.
> When we weep her tears get up,
> become Blue Butterflies.
> *Mine become Little People*
> *beating their drum.*
> Butterflies dance.
> *The Morning Robins lay*
> *their heads to one side*
> *then to the other.*
> Lift their bustles,
> War Dance around our Lodge,
> Neither one of us want to brush away
> our tears. (35; emphasis added)

In this poem, the narrator takes up the main elements that led to her vision as described in the opening (the ancestors as northern lights, the sacred pipe, the Little People's drumming, the robins) and elaborates on them, thus giving the reader a more detailed image of her encounter with the ancestors' spirits.

These are but a few of the many metafictional passages in *Blue Marrow*. Although discussing all of them in detail isn't practical, let me say that, by pointing to the narrator's vision as well as to the process of composition underlying the poem, these instances of metafictionality not only express the cores of complex ideas but also serve a significant narrative function because they evoke the prayer-like nature of the poem as introduced in its opening. The various examples of metafictionality in *Blue Marrow* can thus be regarded as paraholophrases, which textualize orality by making the narrative more fluid and by creating context (cultural and interpretative) as well as author involvement and reader participation. After all, the connections between these various examples of paraholophrases and the opening of the poem are not explicitly stated in the text but must be drawn by readers themselves.

To summarize, paraholophrases in *Blue Marrow* that do not constitute the poem's frame take the form of indigenized personal names, intratextuality, or metafictionality. These paraholophrases perform significant narrative functions either by providing structural markers that divide the long poem into sections, thus facilitating reader understanding (indigenized personal names), or by ensuring that the cultural and interpretative contexts of the poem do not get lost once readers have been led into its main part (intratextuality, metafictionality).

Holophrases and Holophrastic Traces

Formal manifestations of the holophrase in *Blue Marrow* are abundant—about one-quarter of all the entries in its glossary are Cree holophrases. These manifestations are not restricted to code switching alone, however, but also involve a pervasive use of holophrastic traces, notably compounding and, invited by the choice of genre, subject dropping and pronoun copying.

The revised edition of *Blue Marrow* includes a Cree glossary and, more often than the first edition, gives immediate translations of Cree words in the text. True, the lack of a glossary in the first edition further increases the estranging effect that Cree words in the English text have on non-Cree readers. Without a glossary, such readers are kept at a certain distance from the text and its meanings. When *Blue Marrow* uses Cree phrases and what seem to be their English translations in the same line or in alternating lines, giving "the appearance of a bilingual text,"[96] the reader is allowed to guess the meaning of the Cree words, such as in the "Climb down prayer" or in the following passage:

> sôhkêyimo. sôhkêyimo.
> pimâtisi. âcimostawinân.
> *Strive in boldness. Strive in strength.*
> *Live.*
> âcimo. (30–31)

When no such in-line translations are provided, however, non-Cree readers are forced to research the meanings of the Cree words in the text, a complicated undertaking given that the use of polysynthetic dictionaries presupposes at least a basic knowledge of polysynthetic language structures. The meanings of the Cree words in "*Glory be to* okâwîmâwaskiy / *To the* nôhkom âtayôhkan / *To* pawâkan" (1) can be found rather easily using a Cree-English dictionary. The sentence "namôya ê-kaskihtâyân / kîkway" (48), however, is not so easily translated, since *ê-kaskihtâyân* means "I know" and hence is already a conjugated form of the verb's infinitive, which begins with a *k*, not an *e*. The polysynthetic morphology of the Cree language thus can multiply the estranging effect of the poem on non-Cree readers, an effect that is further complicated because there are regional variations within the Plains Cree dialect that Halfe uses in *Blue Marrow*. In the case of *ê-kaskihtâyân*, for example, the Cree word for the verb *know* given in the *Alberta Elders' Cree Dictionary* is *kiskeyitam*, "S/he knows."[97]

However, even though a glossary, an act of editorial intervention, is provided at the end of the revised edition of *Blue Marrow*, the translation of the Cree words and phrases into English does not automatically ensure that non-Cree readers will understand their meanings. Ignorant of the *contexts* of the words and phrases listed in the glossary, non-Cree readers might be compelled to do research to understand the Cree words used in *Blue Marrow*. The words *okâwîmâwaskiy*, *nôhkom âtayôhkan*, and *pawâkan*, for example, are translated in the glossary, but these translations merely give the words' approximate equivalents in English, not their cultural contexts. This problem of translation not only concerns words with spiritual meanings but also affects Cree toponyms and kinship terms.

Blue Marrow includes four traditional Cree toponyms: "âyimani-sîpiy—*Difficult River*" (43); "*mistasinîwi-sîpiy*—the Big Stone River" (72); *oskana kâ-asastêki* (51), the Cree name for Regina;[98] and *sôhkêciwani-sîpiy* (45, 63, 86).[99] Although *Blue Marrow* gives the translation of each toponym either in the text or in the glossary, non-Cree readers can only guess the stories attached to these names and are thus not able to gather fully the cultural importance of the places mentioned. Similarly, kinship terms in Cree culture, such as *nôhkom*, "carry much broader social connotations in Cree society."[100] That "English, as opposed to Indigenous languages, is a concrete signifying system too limited to communicate adequately the emotional ties between people" is, as Cook has concluded in a reading of a short story by the Oneida writer Roberta J. Hill, "a familiar construct in First Nations writing."[101] As familiar as it might be, this construct becomes one of the main pillars of *Blue Marrow*, whose code switching greatly resembles that of Halfe's *Bear Bones and Feathers*, in which "Cree words are largely, although not exclusively, from the parts of the Cree lexicon relating to kinship or spiritual matters, and, thus, work as synecdoches for the values against which the impoverished and sexist values and the hypocritical behaviours of the agents of the Roman Catholic church and other Western institutions are measured."[102] Thus, the more code switching an Indigenous text contains, and the more this code switching concerns notions tied to specific cultural, religious, or social contexts, the less accessible the text is to non-Indigenous readers.

Whether through a "dialectic separation of Cree and English" in the form of "dialogic parallelisms,"[103] or through its inclusion of a glossary, *Blue Marrow*'s use of the Cree language and particularly of Cree holophrases marks non-Cree readers as cultural outsiders and does so more vigorously than any of the other Indigenous texts discussed in previous chapters. The abundance of Cree in *Blue Marrow* might scare off some readers because it makes them feel excluded, but it does not entail exclusion per se. As Thomas King once noted when asked by Jennifer Andrews about the "insider/outsider phenomenon" in his own writing, "Books that make you feel like an outsider may get you to examine what you do and who you are in a greater fashion."[104] King's observation applies to any Indigenous literary text, but it seems to fit particularly well in the case of *Blue Marrow*: Halfe's persistent use of Cree words and holophrases not only marks the text as Cree but also "promotes bicultural awareness and participation."[105]

The readers' participation is also invited through the poem's elaborate use of compounding. As I have already noted, *Blue Marrow* contains an abundance of personal names that evoke Indigenous traditions of name giving. Most of these names are compound nouns using "grandmother" or "woman" as their head. While some of the personal names take the form of (A/N) N N compounds, such as Horse Dance Woman (4), Gopher Grandmother (51), Grandmother Bargain (54), Petticoat Grandmother (68), Rainbow Grandmother (79), or Old Pelt Man (43, 44), most other personal names in *Blue Marrow* qualify more clearly as direct holophrastic traces because they are either deverbal compound nouns or quotation compounds.

Deverbal A N compounds in Halfe's long poem derive their modifiers by affixation of a verb, as in

- Lightning Woman (3) and
- Wailing Woman (5).

Often, however, compounds in *Blue Marrow* feature modifiers that contain an affixed verb that becomes an adjective and is combined with a noun before it is compounded with the head to form a deverbal A N N compound, as in

- Dodging Horse Woman (5),
- Frying Pan Woman (3),

- Sparkling Eyes Woman (6),
- Melting Tallow Woman (6),
- Kicking Horse Woman (6), and
- Rolling Head Woman (5).[106]

All of the above compounds take the form of $[[x_1\ x_2]\ x_3]$: that is, they take "Woman" as their head. The same structure can be assumed for the following deverbal A N N compounds:

- Wandering Stone Grandmother (42, 43, 44, 45, 48),
- Starved Gopher Grandmother (52),
- Sitting Weasel Woman (4), and
- Whistling Eagle Woman (5).

Although one could analyze these compounds also in terms of $[x_1\ [x_2\ x_3]]$—that is, as the first noun combining with the second noun (either "Grandmother" or "Woman") to form the head—such an analysis seems incongruous given the number of deverbal A N N compounds in *Blue Marrow* whose head is without doubt formed by the second noun alone.

When compounds in *Blue Marrow* include affixed verbs, these verbs take the form of participles (*-ing* or *-ed*), but there are also examples of deverbal compound nouns in which the verbs are given the suffix *-er* to be deverbalized, as in Fiddler Woman (4), Hunter Woman in Little Hunter Woman (5), and arguably Kingfisher Woman (4) (though the first noun in this particular compound denotes a specific kind of bird). *Blue Marrow* also features compounds that include components that can function as both verbs and nouns, such as

- Thunder Child Woman (6),
- Fire Thunder Woman (6), and
- Thunder Woman (5).

Since both of these sorts of verbs—that is, verbs that become nouns through affixation and verbs that can also function as nouns—are always combined to form a compound with another noun, these "verbs" are more likely perceived as nouns. Synthetic compounds are rarely encountered in *Blue Marrow*. The only examples of which I am aware are the complex N N compounds Watchmaker Woman (5), Night Traveller Woman (5), and Lip Pointing Woman (6). The compounds are partly synthetic since their modifiers ("watchmaker," "night traveller," and "lip pointing") are derived by combining an affixed verb ("make," "travel," and "point") with a noun ("watch," "night," and "lip") that functions as complement to the verb.

While these personal names based on deverbal compound nouns already evoke the highly synthetic nature of polysynthetic language, the personal names in *Blue Marrow* that qualify as quotation compounds come still closer to the structure of holophrases in Indigenous languages. They include

- She Has Strong Back Strong Wings Woman (4),
- She Flies Strong and Swift Woman (4),
- Count My Blessings Grandmother (57),
- Born in a Dent Grandmudder (61) or Born in Tent Grandmother (63), and
- Not So Long Ago Granny in the lexical phrase "Not So Long Ago Granny Wants to Get Even" (64).

These quotation compounds create the *illusion* of English loan translations because they evoke the descriptiveness and highly synthetic nature of traditional Indigenous names.

Blue Marrow also contains examples of quotation compounds that involve the use of Cree and are even more evocative of traditional Indigenous personal names than those personal names involving only the illusion of loan translations:

- *kâ-itwêhât*—She Who Says So Woman (6),
- *wâpâsôs*—Up at Dawn Woman (3), and
- *sîpi-kiskisiw Grandmother*—Long Term Memory Grandmother (76).

Putting Cree personal names and their English renderings side by side in this way explicitly marks them as *attempts* to translate the structure of holophrases into English grammar—but it is always a failed attempt. In fact, providing English renderings of personal names in Cree serves only to underline the inability of English to construct holophrases: a single Cree word corresponds to three, four, or even five words in the English renderings of the Cree names. To put it another way, quotation compounds in *Blue Marrow* that involve the use of Cree, however evocative of the structure of holophrases, are always explicitly marked as being mere *traces* of holophrases from Indigenous languages.

As we have seen, compounding in *Blue Marrow* creates a strong textual marker: it is not restricted to N N compounds but includes examples of deverbal compound nouns, traces of synthetic compounds, and examples of quotation compounds, the last of which are particularly evocative of the structure of holophrases. Regardless of their respective morphological structure, all kinds of compounds featured in *Blue Marrow*, and particularly the quotation compounds, are semantically dense and therefore demand that readers invest their attention in deciphering the full meanings of these compounds. Compounding in Halfe's long poem, then, serves as a culturally specific strategy in textualizing orality because it is indicative of author involvement and invites reader participation.

The choice of genre in *Blue Marrow* adds to the poem's textualization of orality. The arrangement of the text in short lines serves to textualize the oral through a number of strategies: by imitating the intonation units of oral discourse, by imitating polysynthetic grammars by emphasizing verbs, and through subject dropping and pronoun copying. The poem's short lines reflect closely the prosody of speech and hence inscribe an oral characteristic into the poem:

> Grandmothers hold me.
> I must pass all that I possess,
> every morsel to my children.
> These small gifts. (7)

The length of these lines approximates intonation units in speech, making the poem fragmented and prosodic and thus mirroring the information flow in oral discourse. The arrangement in these shorter lines, then, clearly serves as a strategy in textualizing orality; this strategy is culturally *un*specific, but it also promotes the use of features of discourse that can be associated with polysynthesis in Indigenous languages.

The arrangement of text in lines enables the author to emphasize specific words, particularly verbs, by placing them at the beginning of a new line rather than within a longer line:

> I sit by the window
> Thick woodsmoke lets the moon shine in.
> I take my finger and walk it,
> **leave** mice-size tracks.
> The cabin is warm with the smell of bannock.
> This long bone I hold
> **leaves** me calloused and cold. (13)

> *Let them flog.*
> **Enter** *my parched land.*

> *I am rich. Five dollar every year until I die.*
> *Until the grass die. Until the river die.*
> *Until the sun die. Until*
> *the wind*
> ***die****.* (21)
>
> *Bitterness*
> ***eats*** *me. I left too early,*
> ***was*** *with him for five winters*
> *before the talk of going over the waters.*
> *One night*
> *I felt the axe*
> *I watched him*
> ***bury*** *me.* (48)

In some cases, these initial verbs are further emphasized through subject dropping:

> They thought they could have as many
> as they pleased and we, wanting their flesh,
> tasted them. Some took us in our sleep.
> **Spread** us with their hands.
> Many bodies tight. We scratched,
> **lifted** our hatches
> while our men lay like death,
> foul winds grunting,
> their spirits trickling. (49–50)
>
> *I'll have a bunch of dem,*
> *hus'been, wives.*
> *As many as my fingers.*
> ***Kill*** *lotsa deer,*
> ***have*** *lotsa baby.*
> *Dat'll put dem back*
> *on dem big canoe.*
> *Dem go home.*
> *My big family*
> *make dem go home.*
> *Yes.* (64–65)

> For miles my father and I
> walked. Cans, beer bottles,
> filled a jalopy full of pennies.
> **Drank** spirits. Mother and I
> held our breath a hundred miles
> across the *sôhkêciwani-sîpiy*—
> the Fast Flowing River.
> A brewing storm of metal boots
> broke mother's bones,
> set my stomach heaving. (86)

Thus, the initial positioning of verbs here creates the illusion of a more verb-centred discourse, which is further emphasized by instances of subject dropping. By highlighting verbs, the basic component in polysynthetic grammars, *Blue Marrow* imitates a feature of discourse that is associated with polysynthesis: the independence of holophrases that can produce full grammatical sentences or clauses without the use of independent noun phrases. Furthermore, the ellipses implicit in subject dropping are indicative of a colloquial use of language that imitates more clearly the intonation units in oral speech; at the same time, ellipses indicate author involvement and invite reader participation. The emphasizing of verbs in *Blue Marrow* hence textualizes orality by recourse to a strategy that is culturally specific.

The arrangement of the text in verse form also invites the use of *pronoun copying*, as can be seen in the following:

> *ê-pêcimakik.*
> I haunt them.
> My wailing stories. (52)

Pronoun copying and verb emphasis are also found in *Blue Marrow*'s prose poems:

- "*nôhkomak*, the four of them. How well I remember them."
- "*nôhkom* Emma. She always arrived late in the evening [...]."
- "*nôhkom* Bella, she's the one who loved to laugh."
- "Guess you can say that about my father too, white-skinned Indian [...]." (all 8)

Pronoun copying in English reflects the "repetitive" structure of discourse in Indigenous languages, which is invited in part by the holistic nature of polysynthetic verbs. At the same time, pronoun copying makes the discourse increasingly prosodic, redundant, and fragmented. It therefore marks not only an indirect holophrastic trace but also a strategy in textualizing orality that is culturally specific.

As noted in my introductory chapter, *evidentials* are an important component of conventions of discourse in many Indigenous languages, but *Blue Marrow* features only rare examples of this indirect holophrastic trace, despite the poem's reliance on source citing. The citing of sources is particularly significant for *Blue Marrow* since the poem forms a spider-web of stories told by various first-person narrators. The poem's master narrator can orchestrate the poem's many voices only by identifying who is speaking at any particular point in the poem[107] or by having the next speaker in the poem identify him- or herself.[108] Source citing in *Blue Marrow*, then, serves primarily as a structural device without which the poem would fall apart entirely. However, in order not to interfere with the storytelling of other narrators, the master narrator typically does not interrupt their stories by adding quotatives. The source citing in Halfe's long poem hence reflects only palely the frequent use of evidentials in traditional Cree storytelling.[109]

Let me close this linguistic analysis of *Blue Marrow* by commenting briefly on its use of language more generally. *Blue Marrow* diverges from the language of most prose fiction in its *frequent use of figurative language*, which it features in both its prose and its free verse poems. As noted in the discussion of figurative language in Richard Van Camp's *The Lesser Blessed* in Chapter 3 of this volume, however, not every figure of speech necessarily functions as a paraholophrase. In fact, most figures in *Blue Marrow* lack any significant narrative function and hence function only as indirect holophrastic traces: they reflect the often figurative use of language in Indigenous tongues, and they textualize orality by creating a text whose composition relies considerably on readers' participation—as Gérard Genette has noted, no figure of speech comes into being without a reader recognizing it as such.[110] Genette's observation naturally applies to the use of figures in any kind or form of discourse, language, or tradition. In other words, though the multiple figures of Halfe's *Blue Marrow* evoke the prominent role that figurative uses of language play in Cree, it is important to remember that their presence in this long poem is not as evocative of Cree language structures as its use of subject dropping and pronoun copying, which are not ordinarily found in written English but are invited in *Blue Marrow* through the presentation of text in the form of verse.

CHAPTER 5

SUMMARY

Blue Marrow showcases a creative conflation not only of discourse modes (the written and the oral) but also of languages (Cree and English), genres (lyric and epic), and literary traditions (Indigenous and Euro-Western). This complex conflation turns Halfe's long poem into a significant site for holophrastic analysis. As an *account of the textualization of orature*—the narrator is taking dictation from her ancestors—*Blue Marrow* lets readers witness the intimate event of the passing on of a tradition and the reception of this tradition, thus demonstrating the extent to which oral traditions bridge generations.

The extensive and elaborate conflation of Cree and English provides *Blue Marrow* with textual markers that render the narrator's crying out of her ancestors' stories in writing into a "cree-ing loud into my night," thus inscribing into the poem its proper *linguistic context*. Because her code switching is deeply ingrained in the poem, Halfe's use of Cree—far more than the code switching in the other four Indigenous texts discussed in this study—promotes bicultural awareness, shows *author involvement*, and invites *reader participation*. The demand for reader participation is further heightened by wide-ranging compounds (N N compounds, deverbal N compound nouns, quotation compounds, and, though slightly less so, synthetic compounds) that are used as indigenized personal names. In some cases, they are explicitly marked as English loan translations through code switching; in other cases, they create the *illusion* of English loan translations through their descriptiveness and semantic density. Further author involvement and reader participation are suggested by the incorporation of lyrical moments into the narrative, particularly in the revised edition. Halfe's turn to the lyric, however, goes beyond the mere use of figurative language and textual silences. Through its verse form—which, according to Dell Hymes and other scholars involved in ethnopoetics, is the most appropriate mode of presenting Indigenous oratures—*Blue Marrow* particularly invites those kinds of indirect holophrastic traces that are close to polysynthesis in Indigenous languages and that involve strategies of conceptual orality that result from the context of language production: namely, pronoun copying and subject dropping. The textualization of orality achieved through the use of holophrastic traces in Halfe's long poem, then, is invited in part by her choice of genre.

In fact, genre is also the reason why the paraholophrase turns into such a significant strategy of discourse in *Blue Marrow*. Long poems conflate epic with lyric. Given its holistic nature, the paraholophrase functions on the levels of both content and form. To put it differently, paraholophrases lend themselves to the composition of long poems because, as has become apparent in the preceding discussions, they can involve the figurative use of language (lyric), all the while taking over significant narrative functions, such as the weaving together of various poems into a longer series of poems (epic). As noted above, the double voicing in *Blue Marrow* is twofold: the text is a long poem conflating lyrical and epic moments; taking the form of two elements traditionally accompanying Plains Cree ceremonies (i.e., prayer and song[111]), this long poem also conflates Euro-Western and Indigenous literary traditions, at times involving the use of parody. To achieve this conflation, *Blue Marrow* relies heavily on the use of paraholophrases, without which the poem's opening and closing frame could not exist. Like any other narrative frame in Indigenous works composed in English, the frame in Halfe's long poem serves to guide readers *into* as well as *out of* the poem by providing them with the *interpretative context* needed to make sense of the poem. To uncover this context, however, readers must make out the frame and, ultimately, the paraholophrases constituting it. By closing, but not *ending*, the poem, the frame helps to create a cyclical narrative structure for *Blue Marrow*, thus evoking one of the generic conventions of Indigenous oratures. To ensure that the *cultural context* established in the opening is maintained throughout the poem, paraholophrases in the main part of *Blue Marrow* serve to provide links to the opening and take the form of either intratextual or metafictional references.

With its many different female voices floating into each other, *Blue Marrow* not only provides a multitude of lyrical moments but also creates a narrative that suggests the fluidity of stories in Indigenous oratures. To ensure that the narrative does not fall apart in the face of all this fluidity, readers are guided through the main part of the narrative by way of paraholophrases that take the form of Indigenous personal names and function as structural markers. By creating context, showing *author involvement*, and creating *reader participation*, paraholophrases are a crucial strategy in textualizing orality in *Blue Marrow*. However, their significance also lies in the fact that they establish this text's double voicing: they help to conflate epic and lyric, all the while continuing Indigenous literary traditions in a rather Euro-Western literary genre. As such, paraholophrases in Halfe's long poem function as *dynamic equivalents to holophrases* in Indigenous languages. They are formally (i.e., grammatically) very different from actual holophrases, but their function is the same: paraholophrases form the very grid of Halfe's long poem, just as much as holophrases form the grid of Indigenous discourse composed in Indigenous languages.

CONCLUSION

Contemporary Indigenous Literatures, Textualized Orality, and Rhetorical Sovereignty

At the beginning of this study, I argued that the (para)holophrase functions as a culturally specific signifier of textualized orality in contemporary Indigenous literatures composed in English. That is, I proposed to read these literatures' textualization of orality from inside rather than outside Indigenous languages and cultures. Demonstrating on both formal (i.e., grammatical) and functional levels language uses in Indigenous literatures in English that "make its 'English' on the page a translation in which traces of the 'foreign tongue,' the 'Indian,' can be discerned,"[1] my discussion has thus moved beyond the mere idea of a culturally specific form of code switching. The holophrastic readings in Chapters 1 to 5 reveal a widespread use of paraholophrases as discourse devices that help to re-create generic conventions of Indigenous oratures. These readings also show how the texts discussed employ paraholophrases along with holophrastic traces and holophrases proper as culturally specific strategies in textualizing orality in contemporary Indigenous literatures in English.

PARAHOLOPHRASES

Paraholophrases in the Indigenous works discussed produce functions of language in Indigenous literatures in English that are equivalent to (though never identical with) those of holophrases in Indigenous languages because

1. they create semantic density in the form of figures of speech, formulae or formulaic clusters, as well as inter- and intratextual references (i.e., they form the cores of complex ideas), and because
2. they mimic generic conventions of Indigenous oratures by creating narrative frames, cyclical narrative structures, and a comparatively open and fluid discourse (i.e., they function as significant narrative units).

Paraholophrases thus come into being once a concatenation of ideas does both—carry a bundle of meaning and serve significant narrative functions. As far as their semantic density is concerned, paraholophrases take advantage of all those literary devices that are semantically dense and whose meanings are not explicitly stated in the text but are left for readers to uncover. That such devices include figures of speech is significant, given the tendency of polysynthetic languages for figurative uses of language. The use of formulae (or formulaic clusters) and inter- and intratextual references is equally interesting, however. As creative and ordered concatenations of signs that express an essential idea and that are repeatedly used throughout a narrative, thus functioning as a significant narrative unit, paraholophrases in Indigenous literatures in English at times take the form of formulae— defined by Milman Parry as "*a group of words which is regularly employed under the same metrical conditions to express a given essential idea.*"[2] Formulae are strongly associated with orature, even if they are not found in every oral tradition. As inter- and intratextual references, paraholophrases in Indigenous literatures composed in English are used to open up the narratives and thus to break away some of the fixity implied in writing. As intertextual references, paraholophrases also point to what Robin Ridington calls Indigenous "narrative technology":

> In the technology of storied experience, each performer's speech and action evoke and are meaningful in relation to everything that is known but, for the moment, unstated. Each story contains every other story. Each person's life is an example of the mythic stories that people know to exist in a time out of time. As in post-structuralist semiotic theory, in which a sign is meaningful in relation to what it is not [...], experience within a closely contexted oral tradition is meaningful in relation to an unstated but mutually understood totality. Storied speech is an example of that totality, not simply a part of it.[3]

CONCLUSION

Although the references to intertexts in Indigenous oral traditions usually serve to re-create the cultural context of the respective narrative, *Arctic Dreams and Nightmares*, *Green Grass, Running Water*, and *Blue Marrow* also showcase the use of paraholophrases as parodic strategies.

The significant narrative function of paraholophrases lies not in their construction of just any narrative structure but in their construction of those narrative structures that carry on generic conventions of Indigenous oratures. Opening and closing frames are found in all five of the Indigenous texts chosen for analysis in this study. Although these narrative frames are generally not formulaic and are rather elaborate compared with traditional opening and closing frames in Indigenous oratures, they nonetheless perform the same narrative function as these traditional frames. Richard Bauman has pointed out, with reference to Gregory Bateson, that "All framing [...] is accomplished through the employment of culturally conventionalized metacommunication."[4] One central device used in contemporary Indigenous literatures to achieve this "culturally conventionalized metacommunication" is the paraholophrase. Framing is as much an indication of author involvement as it is an invitation for reader participation. Containing the narratives' interpretative contexts, the frames in the texts discussed indicate to readers the lines along which to understand these texts. None of the frames discussed in these holophrastic readings, however, readily gives away the text's message(s); instead, readers must first make out the text's opening and closing, which are never explicitly marked but must always be inferred from a web of interrelated paraholophrases, to uncover the text's interpretative context before being able to consider the text's meaning(s).[5]

When paraholophrases in the Indigenous texts discussed are used to create cyclical structures or a comparatively open and fluid discourse, they constitute narrative structures that are just as indicative of author involvement and reader participation as opening and closing frames. Like the latter, cyclical structures and open and fluid discourse are so constructed that they come into existence only through readers' recognition of them. As Kenneth Burke has noted in *A Rhetoric of Motives*, "we know that many purely formal patterns can readily awaken an attitude of collaborative expectancy in us."[6] Bauman has therefore argued with reference to Burke that narrative frames are indicative of author involvement because they bind an audience to its performer and induce participation.[7] The same bond between author and reader is created in the opening and closing frames in Indigenous literatures as well as in their cyclical structures and their use of open and fluid discourse. In the meantime, the various narrative structures employed in Indigenous literatures also happen to carry much of the texts' literary and cultural contexts.

Thus, paraholophrases in the works discussed create author involvement and reader participation not solely through semantic density (content) but also through the very structures that these paraholophrases help to constitute in the texts (form). The textualization of orality achieved by paraholophrases thus concerns verbal strategies that result from the context of language use (context, involvement, and participation) rather than the context of language production (prosody, redundancy, fragmentation, and fuzziness).

HOLOPHRASES

Holophrases in the Indigenous texts discussed in this study mark a culturally specific kind of code switching in contemporary Indigenous literatures. They serve as textual markers that provide the texts with the linguistic context of Indigenous oratures and indicate the author's involvement with his or her readers by marking their relationship to the text and thus defining the terms of their participation with it. In other words, holophrases in the texts discussed also employ strategies of conceptual orality that result from the context of language use. As such, holophrases used in Indigenous literatures composed in English complement the textualization achieved by the use of paraholophrases. The more code switching an Indigenous text includes, the more difficult it becomes for both non-Indigenous readers and Indigenous readers without any knowledge of the respective Indigenous language to access the cultural and linguistic contexts of the text.[8] The extent to and the ways in which holophrases are used in Indigenous literatures composed in English are hence always influenced by the authors' need to cater at least partially to their audiences.

Holophrases are employed primarily by Indigenous writers who are either fluent in or still have considerable knowledge of an Indigenous language—though the purposes, forms, and degrees of their code switching can differ notably. Whereas Ishmael Alunik's and Alootook Ipellie's code switching only occasionally involves the use of actual Inuktitut holophrases, Louise Halfe's use of Cree is far more extensive and consists of about one-quarter Cree holophrases. Ipellie's use of Inuktitut to invent personal names, which evoke Indigenous traditions of name giving, not only is holophrase-like in its application of synecdoche but also, by emphasizing the importance of personal names, further emphasizes the role of Inuit shamanism in the text as well as in Inuit society. Alunik's use of Inuvialuktun/Inupiaq is concerned with the passing on of traditional terminology, particularly concerning the land and Inuvialuit/Inupiat material culture. However, the use of holophrases as a strategy in textualizing orality is also encountered in the works of Indigenous authors without any knowledge of an Indigenous language, as suggested by Thomas King's use of Cherokee in *Green Grass, Running Water*. Naturally, though, holophrases occur far less frequently in the writing of Indigenous authors who do not speak an Indigenous language than in the writing of Indigenous authors who still speak their tribal languages.

HOLOPHRASTIC TRACES

Holophrastic traces in the Indigenous texts discussed in this study re-create some of the linguistic context of Indigenous oratures on the level of discourse. However, compared with that created by the use of holophrases, the linguistic context created by holophrastic traces often proves to be moved even further away from its originary source since the holophrastic traces used in the Indigenous texts discussed cannot always be associated with polysynthesis alone. Although the extensive use of figurative language and textual silences is indicative of additional author involvement and can create additional reader participation in Indigenous texts, such as in Van Camp's *The Lesser Blessed* or Halfe's *Blue Marrow*, figurative language and textual silences, of course, mark discourse strategies found universally in literature. At the same time, however, the presentation of text in the form of verse in *Blue Marrow* demonstrates how the choice of genre can increase the use of those indirect holophrastic traces that can more readily be associated with polysynthesis and mark oral strategies that result from the context of language production (prosody, redundancy, and fragmentation): namely, pronoun copying and subject dropping. The choice of genre might foster the use of particular holophrastic traces—*The Lesser Blessed* and *Blue Marrow* contain more instances of figures of speech than, for example, *Call Me Ishmael* and *Arctic Dreams and Nightmares*—but genre is not the only factor influencing the use of holophrastic traces. *Green Grass, Running Water*, for example, uses just as much subject dropping and pronoun copying as *Blue Marrow*. How often and how widely holophrastic traces are used in Indigenous literatures, then, appears to depend also on the specific demands and interests of the work and author in question.

The most diverse and extensive use of holophrastic traces has been found in Alunik's *Call Me Ishmael*, the most traditional of the Indigenous texts discussed in this study. Holophrastic traces in his narrative include not just compounding, pronoun copying, and subject dropping but also repetitions and evidentials, which have a more immediate effect on readers because they are even less compliant with standard uses of English than other holophrastic traces. The least diverse and least extensive use of holophrastic traces is exhibited in *Arctic Dreams and Nightmares*; Ipellie's story cycle, however, compensates for its relative lack of holophrastic traces through the use of pen-and-ink drawings as visualized holophrases, which reflect both the significance of illustrations in Inuit culture and the highly figurative use of language in Inuktitut and its variants.

While compounding is found in all five of the Indigenous texts selected for analysis in this study, it appears as a particularly noteworthy direct holophrastic trace in *Call Me Ishmael,* where the use of synthetic compounds is comparatively well developed, as well as in *The Lesser Blessed* and *Blue Marrow,* both of which showcase an interesting use of quotation compounds. In the case of *The Lesser Blessed,* these compounds can even involve the use of a single signifier. As a rule, however, compounding in the texts discussed is usually polylexical. Except for *Call Me Ishmael,* each text discussed also evokes Indigenous traditions of name giving, usually involving the use of synecdoche. In the case of *Arctic Dreams and Nightmares,* indigenized personal names are monolexical, involve code switching, and are holophrase-like. In the other three texts, however, Indigenous personal names take the form of compounds (*The Lesser Blessed, Blue Marrow,* and *Green Grass, Running Water*) or idiom-like lexical phrases (*Green Grass, Running Water*) and, in their descriptiveness, create the illusion of English loan translations. Repetitions and evidentials—holophrastic traces that have a more immediate effect on (Western) readers than others—are found primarily in *Call Me Ishmael,* but *Green Grass, Running Water* also displays an interesting use of evidentials in its frame narrative. The latter text also demonstrates a comparatively pervasive use of pronoun copying and subject dropping in its realistic narrative strand.

On the whole, we can conclude that the significance of holophrastic traces in the Indigenous texts chosen for this study lies in their function rather than in their quantity, which is relatively low. Although they are not formally (i.e., grammatically) equivalent to holophrases in Indigenous languages, holophrastic traces serve as textual markers that re-create at least some of the linguistic context of Indigenous oratures, thus providing an English-language discourse with snippets of holophrases proper. At the same time, holophrastic traces complement the textualization of orality achieved through the use of paraholophrases and holophrases by using strategies of conceptual orality that result from the context of language production, the context of language use, or both.

HOLOPHRASTIC READING AND RHETORICAL SOVEREIGNTY

There are notable differences, then, among the texts chosen for this study concerning their use of holophrases and holophrastic traces, in terms of both degree and scope. At the same time, I have not been able to detect any significant differences in their use of paraholophrases. Regardless of the authors' respective tribal affiliation, age, linguistic background, or choice of genre, each of the five works discussed here has pointed to the paraholophrase as a strategy in textualizing orality that helps to continue Indigenous verbal traditions in the colonizers' language and their preferred mode of discourse. Naturally, oral strategies in contemporary Indigenous literatures are not any more or any less significant than those found in other literatures. What is significant, however, is that the textualization of the oral in Indigenous literatures composed in English is also achieved through strategies that are *culturally specific* because they can be traced back to an Indigenous language structure, the holophrase. The method of holophrastic reading, then, defines a reading strategy for textualized orality that supports claims made by Indigenous authors, such as Jeannette Armstrong, about the relevance of ancestral languages for Indigenous peoples today. Contemporary Indigenous authors may be writing in English, but they have successfully incorporated this language and the written word into their own traditions of using language. The empowerment of Indigenous peoples achieved in the writings of Ishmael Alunik, Alootook Ipellie, Richard Van Camp, Thomas King, and Louise Halfe is also mirrored in the very ways that these writers employ language for the purpose of decolonization: their use of (para)holophrases empowers Indigenous peoples in their own traditions and on their own terms; it is an expression of Indigenous rhetorical sovereignty, which Scott Richard Lyons (Anishinaabe/Mdewakanton Dakota) has defined as the "inherent right and ability of *peoples* to determine their own communicative needs and desires in this pursuit [of sovereignty], to decide for themselves the goals, modes, styles, and languages of public discourse."[9]

The method of holophrastic reading, as proposed here, is naturally based on generalizations. First, not every North American Indigenous language is holophrastic; some are "only mildly synthetic."[10] Second, North America is well known for its linguistic diversity; thus, two Indigenous languages can differ extensively even if both are holophrastic. And third, arguing that the (para)holophrase is a culturally specific signifier of textualized orality in Indigenous literatures composed in English—based on the five holophrastic readings contained in this study—is a generalizing statement. Not every Indigenous story cycle, novel, or long poem ultimately textualizes orality to the same degree and in the same ways as the texts that I have analyzed here. Nor is every Indigenous story cycle, novel, or long poem engaged in the same holophrastic play as these texts; even these five works show notable differences in their holophrasticizing of the English language.

Yet, even if "holophrastic reading" is an academic construct, it allows us to read textualized orality in Indigenous literatures in the context of Indigenous rhetorical sovereignty. As such, holophrastic reading also helps to build the grounds for further and more specialized research. One such area of research points to the question of how far the holophrastic use of language in Indigenous literatures is tribal and/or ancestral language specific. Closely tied to this question is another matter: namely, how ancestral language influences more generally contribute to the preservation of *tribal* intellectual sovereignty, a question that can also take into account all those Indigenous traditions based in languages that are synthetic rather than holophrastic. The very term "holophrastic reading" also needs further scrutiny, particularly given that it is based on descriptions of Indigenous languages that grow out of linguistics, a Euro-Western-informed discipline.

In selecting texts for analysis in this study, I have focused on narrative genres because many Indigenous oratures are narrative. Another area of future holophrastic research thus consists of extending holophrastic research to other genres, particularly to Indigenous drama—which should provide interesting insights given the oral roots of this genre—and Indigenous writing more generally (non-fiction, political, journalistic, feminist, etc.). The discussions of holophrastic traces in the holophrastic readings in this study do not contain quantitative analyses. Another possible area of future holophrastic research thus lies in conducting comparative quantitative analyses of compounding, as well as of pronoun copying and subject dropping, in Indigenous and non-Indigenous literatures to arrive at more differentiated results.

Having its basis in language, or grammar, the paraholophrase primarily concerns *logos*: that is, that type of artificial proof identified by Aristotle in his *Rhetoric* as produced by speech itself.[11] As the examples of paraholophrases that I discuss in this book suggest, the paraholophrase marks an enhanced use of language that functions on the levels of both content ("core of a complex idea") and form ("significant narrative unit"). More specifically, a paraholophrase can be described as a figure with significant narrative function that is combined with other such figures to form the text's narrative grid, thus functioning as synecdoche (*narrative grid pro narrative*). The significance of the paraholophrase, then, goes beyond serving as a culturally specific signifier of textualized orality in Indigenous writing and concerns Indigenous rhetorics more generally. A more straightforward term to describe this category would be "holoscheme"[12]—from the Greek *holos* "whole" and *schema* "figure." What the rhetorical structure of the paraholophrase/holoscheme looks like exactly, how its use relates to tribal intellectual sovereignty, Indigenous rhetorics, and Indigenous notions of peoplehood, as well as how the term could better reflect the origin of the language structure that this holistic figure derives from—these are questions that will be explored in detail at another time.

APPENDIX

The Narrative Function of Holophrases in Indigenous Languages

Table App.1 illustrates the significant narrative function of holophrases in Indigenous discourse, in this case in Cree. For this purpose, an excerpt of an autobiographical story by Glecia Bear (Cree, b. 1913) from *kwâkopîwi-sâkahikanihk* (Green Lake, Saskatchewan) was chosen. Bear told this story to Freda Ahenakew (Cree) in 1988. Ahenakew, who also speaks Cree as a mother tongue and has known Bear since early in her life,[1] recorded Bear's story and later transcribed, translated, and edited it with H. Christoph Wolfart. The story first appeared as a bilingual and illustrated children's book under the title *wanisinwak iskwêsisak* (1991). This children's book version of Bear's story is an adaptation from a version of the story published (a year later) in a bilingual collection of personal narratives by Cree women, *kôhkominawak otâcimowiniwâwa*.[2] As noted by Wolfart, the children's book lacks two paragraphs that serve as "an afterthought not essential to the plot." It also omits false starts in Bear's telling.[3] The translation in the children's book, then, is slightly smoother than in the other published version, but it can still be said to have chosen "fidelity to the original over elegance in English," the approach taken to translating the stories collected in *kôhkominawak otâcimowiniwâwa*.[4]

To illustrate the narrative significance of holophrases, an interlinear translation of an excerpt of Bear's story in Cree was undertaken (see Table App.1).[5] For these purposes, the children's book version of Bear's story was chosen as it omits false starts and the like, which would have unnecessarily complicated the reading of this translation for native speakers of English.

Line breaks in Table App.1 follow the punctuation used in the Cree original. Holophrases are marked **boldface** in the original and in the interlinear translation, with no distinction drawn between verbs in the independent mode and verbs in the conjunct mode.[6]

APPENDIX

Cree Original (Bear)	Interlinear Translation (Neuhaus)	Published Translation (Ahenakew/Wolfart)
nisîmis awa,	[my younger sister] [this one]	My little sister
"*Gigi*" isiyîhkâsow,	[Gigi] [**she is called**]	is called *Gigi*,
kwâkopîwi-sâkahi-kanihk,	[at Green Lake]	we lived at Green Lake,
ayinânêw **ê-itahtopiponêt**,	[eight] [**she is ... years old**]	she was eight years old,
pêyakosâp niya **ê-itahtopiponêyân**.	[eleven] [I] [**I am ... years old**]	and I, I was eleven years old.
êkwa **nikî-nitawi-ayamihân**	[and] [**I went and prayed/attended mass**]	And I had been to church
êwako anima kîkisêpâ **ê-nitawi-sask-amoyân**,	[and so] [after that] [in the morning; this past morning] [**I am going to take holy communion**]	early that morning to take communion,
nimâmâ awa ê-**wîcêwak ê-nitawi-saskamoyân** anima.	[my mother] [this one] [**I am going with her**] [**that I am going to take holy communion (i.e., to go and take communion)**] [that one]	I had gone with my mom to take communion.
ê-pê-kîwêyâhk êkwa,	[**we are coming to go home**] [and]	On our way home,
nipâpâ êkwa—	[my father] [and]	my dad—
nikî-wîhtamâkonân sâsay,	[**he told us**] [already, yet]	he had told us,
otâskosihk isi **ê-wîhtamâkoyâhk**,	[yesterday] [like this] [**he is telling us**]	telling us the previous evening already,
mostos awa **ê-wî-otawâsimisit** nânitaw ôtê sakâhk;	[cow] [this one] [**she is going to be having a child**] [approximately, about; simply] [here] [in the woods]	that one cow would be calving somewhere in the bush over here;

Cree Original (Bear)	Interlinear Translation (Neuhaus)	Published Translation (Ahenakew/Wolfart)
êkwa, "**aswahohk!**"	[and] [**be on her guard**]	so he had said,
itwêw,	[he says]	"Watch out for her
"atisamânihk;"	[at the smudge]	at the smudge!"
(kayâs mâna kî-atisamânihkêwak	[a long time ago] [habitually] [**they made smudges**]	(they used to make smudges long ago,
êkota mostoswak **ê-asikâpawicik**),	[there] [the cows] [**they stand up as a crowd**]	with the cows standing out there),
"**asawâpamihk** êwako ana onîcâniw!"	[**guard someone/ something**] [that one] [that one] [cow (that never had a calf)]	"Look out for that female!"
itwêw,	[he says]	he had said,
"**sêskisici,**	[**she leaves the prairie to enter the forest**]	"When she goes into the bush,
pimitisahwâhkêk!"	[**follow her**]	then you all follow her!"
nititik awa nipâpâ;	[**he says to me**] [this one] [my father]	my dad had said to me;
"**ka-pimitisahwâwâw,**	[**you will follow her**]	"you follow her,
mâka êkâya cîki ohci **ka-pimitisahwâyêk,**	[but] [not] [near] [from, for] [**when you are following her**]	but you should not follow her too closely,
nâh-nakîci,	[**she stops now and then**]	for when she stops now and then,
ka-kiskêyihtam ê-pimitisahwâyêk,	[**she will know**] [**you are following her**]	she will know that you are following her,
piko wâhyawês ohci piko **ka-pimitisahwâyêk,**	[only] [far, far away] [from, for] [only] [**you are following her**]	you have to follow her from a little distance,
êkâ **ka-wâpamikoyêk,**"	[not] [**that she will see you**]	so that she will not see you,"
itwêw.	[he says]	he had said.

Table App.1 Narrative Function of Holophrases

Glossary

A N compounds: adjective-noun compounds: that is, compounds that are derived from combining an adjective and a noun, with the latter serving as the head (e.g., Changing Woman,[1] which uses a deverbal adjective).

code switching: "the use of more than one language in the course of a single communicative episode."[2]

conceptual orality: (based on Peter Koch and Wulf Oesterreicher[3]) a type of orality that is independent of the medium; it is characterized by a *language of immediacy*.

dynamic equivalence: an approach to translation that was introduced by Eugene Nida and Charles Taber[4] and strives for an equivalence of effect or response; here modified to encompass primarily function, which has certain, if however non-specifiable, effects. Also see *formal equivalence*.

evidentiality: (in linguistics) the marking of the information source on which a given statement is based.

formal equivalence: an approach to translation that strives for an equivalence of form. Also see *dynamic equivalence*.

head: that part of a compound that determines its semantic category (e.g., "driver" in "truck driver").

holophrase: a single word expressing a complete sentence (e.g., *sîpi-kiskisiyân*, Cree for "I stretch my memory"[5]); for the purposes of this study defined as *a productive and ordered concatenation of signs in polysynthetic languages that forms the core of a substantive polysynthetic idea unit and functions as a significant narrative unit in a given polysynthetic discourse.*

holophrasis: "The expression of a whole phrase or combination of ideas by one word";[6] (in morphology) the process of joining both lexical and grammatical morphemes into one word to form what in Indo-European languages corresponds to a complete sentence.[7] Also see *polysynthesis*.

holophrastic trace: traces of the *holophrase* on the level of form (i.e., grammar); direct holophrastic traces are traces of the morphological structure of the holophrase, whereas indirect holophrastic traces are traces of features of discourse invited by the use of holophrases.

language of immediacy: (based on Koch and Oesterreicher) a language that is characterized by a high degree of immediacy between speaker/author and listener/reader; it is characterized by low degrees of information density, compactness of language, integration, complexity, elaborateness, and planning.[8]

language use: "the occasion on which [a] text is actually processed by the hearer or reader."[9] Also see *language production*.

language production: "the moment and situation of [a] text's creation by speaker or writer."[10] Also see *language use*.

langue: the abstract system of language; the term is used by Ferdinand de Saussure in his *Course in General Linguistics* to distinguish the system of language (*langue*) from the actual utterances that are produced based on this system (*parole*).[11]

N N compounds: noun-noun compounds: that is, compounds that are derived from a concatenation of nouns (e.g., "cat house").

oral strategies: strategies associated with the *language of immediacy*; markers of *conceptual orality*.

paraholophrase: a creative and ordered concatenation of signs that forms the core of a complex idea and functions as a significant narrative unit in a given discourse; an object dynamically equivalent to the *holophrase*.

(para)holophrase: the two kinds of manifestation of the *holophrase* in English discourse: that is, both its functional manifestations in the form of *paraholophrases* and its formal (i.e., grammatical) manifestations in the form of *code switching* and *holophrastic traces*. Also see Fig. 0.2.

parole: (from French meaning "speech") the actual utterances produced by an individual; the term is used by Ferdinand de Saussure in his *Course in General Linguistics* to distinguish actual speech acts (*parole*) from the system of language that they are derived from (*langue*).[12]

polysynthesis: (in morphology) the process of joining both lexical and grammatical morphemes into one word to form what in Indo-European languages corresponds to a complete sentence.[13] Also see *holophrasis*.

productivity: "the possibility to coin new complex words according to the word formation rules of a given language."[14]

quotation compounds: phrases or sentences that are analyzed as single words[15] (e.g., "'dontwasteit' grip"[16]).

root compounds: "concatenated words"[17] (e.g., "houseboat").

synthetic compounds: compounds "formed from deverbal heads[,] and the non-head fulfils the function of the argument of the verb from which the head is derived"[18] (e.g., "truck driver").

textualized orality: the use of *oral strategies* in written discourse.

textualized orature: an oral discourse that has been put into writing or print; the transcription of an example of orature.

V N compounds: compound nouns with a verbal modifier: that is, compounds that are derived from combining a verb stem and a noun, with the latter serving as the head (e.g., "pickpocket").

Notes

INTRODUCTION

1. Jeannette C. Armstrong, "Land Speaking," in *Speaking for the Generations: Native Writers on Writing*, ed. Simon J. Ortiz (Tucson: University of Arizona Press, 1998), 175.
2. See Marianne Mithun, *The Languages of Native North America* (Cambridge, UK: Cambridge University Press, 1990).
3. For the purpose of this study, I rely on traditions of Euro-Western terminology but not without noting that this terminology, particularly when it comes to the description of Indigenous languages, is flawed because it is based on describing these languages from the perspective of Indo-European tongues. Although I am aware of the need to derive more appropriate terms that account for the cultural and linguistic specificity of Indigenous languages and literatures, such a task goes well beyond the goals and scope of this study.
4. Armstrong, "Land Speaking," 189–90.
5. Bernard Comrie, *Language Universals and Linguistic Typology: Syntax and Morphology*, 2nd ed. (Oxford: Basil Blackwell, 1989), 45.
6. Armstrong, "Land Speaking," 190; emphasis added.
7. See ibid., 190–94.
8. Polysynthetic languages are also encountered in Meso-America, Siberia, northern Australia, and Papua New Guinea; see Nicholas Evans and Hans-Jürgen Sasse, "Introduction: Problems of Polysynthesis," in *Problems of Polysynthesis*, ed. Nicholas Evans and Hans-Jürgen Sasse (Berlin: Akademie Verlag, 2002), 1.
9. David S. Rood, "North American Languages," in *International Encyclopedia of Linguistics*, ed. William J. Frawley, 2nd ed., vol. 3 (Oxford: Oxford University Press, 2003), 170.
10. Mithun, *Languages*, 38.
11. Evans and Sasse, "Introduction," 3.
12. See Mark C. Baker, *The Atoms of Language* (New York: Basic Books, 2001), 112.
13. Wallace L. Chafe, "Discourse Effects on Polysynthesis," in *Discourse across Languages and Cultures*, ed. Carol Lynn Moder and Aida Martinovic-Zic (Amsterdam: Benjamins, 2004), 44.
14. Ibid., 45.
15. See ibid., 45–51, for a detailed linguistic discussion of the discourse patterns resulting from holistic verbs in Seneca.
16. According to Chafe, an idea unit expresses "focuses of consciousness" present at the time of language production; Wallace L. Chafe, "The Deployment of Consciousness in the Production of a Narrative," in *The Pear Stories: Cognitive, Cultural, and Linguistic Aspects of Narrative Production*, ed. Wallace L. Chafe (Norwood, NJ: Ablex Publishing, 1980), 15. The assumption is that a speaker "does not, or cannot, focus attention on more information than can be expressed in about six words"; Wallace L. Chafe and Jane Danielewicz, "Properties of Spoken and Written Language," in *Comprehending Oral and Written Language*, ed. Rosalind Horowitz and S. Jay Samuels

(San Diego: Academic, 1987), 95. Hence, Chafe posits what he calls a "'one new concept at a time' constraint," meaning that every idea unit always carries only one new idea at a time; Wallace L. Chafe, "Writing in the Perspective of Speaking," in *Studying Writing: Linguistic Approaches*, ed. Charles R. Cooper and Sidney Greenbaum (Beverly Hills: Sage Publications, 1986), 25.

17. Wallace L. Chafe, *Discourse, Consciousness, and Time: The Flow and Displacement of Conscious Experience in Speaking and Writing* (Chicago: University of Chicago Press, 1994), 63.
18. Roland Barthes, "An Introduction to the Structural Analysis of Narrative," *New Literary History* 6.2 (1975): 246–50. Barthes' distinction between functions and indices is based on the assumption that "the former are functional in terms of action, the latter in terms of being" (247). Thus, cardinal functions serve as narrative hinges; catalyses fill the narrative space; indices proper provide information regarding personality traits, feeling, or atmosphere; and informants give temporal as well as spatial information (247–49).
19. Ibid., 250, 251.
20. Ibid., 268.
21. Ibid., 246–48.
22. See Baker, *Atoms*, 88, for Mohawk.
23. Ronald Lowe, introduction to *Siglit Inuvialuit Uqausiita Kipuktirutait/Basic Siglit Inuvialuit Eskimo Dictionary*, comp. Ronald Lowe (Inuvik, NWT: Committee for Original Peoples Entitlement, 1984), xxvii.
24. Although "there is still no consensus about the nature of productivity" despite the centrality of the concept in morphology, linguists usually describe productivity as "the possibility to coin new complex words according to the word formation rules of a given language"; Ingo Plag, *Morphological Productivity: Structural Constraints in English Derivation* (Berlin: Mouton de Gruyter, 1999), 6.
25. Holophrases are restricted to verbal language, but even the writing systems used in precontact North America, such as pictographs or wampum belts, can be regarded as "holophrastic" insofar as they communicate complex ideas in the form of "visualized holophrases." Also see Ipellie's use of "visualized holophrases" discussed in Chapter 2 of this volume (pp. 102–04)
26. Craig S. Womack, "Theorizing American Indian Experience," in *Reasoning Together: The Native Critics Collective*, ed. Craig S. Womack, Daniel Heath Justice, and Christopher B. Teuton (Norman: University of Oklahoma Press, 2008), 404.
27. Ibid., 405.
28. Guillermo Bartelt, *Socio- and Stylolinguistic Perspectives on American Indian English Texts* (Lewiston, NY: Edwin Mellen Press, 2001), 131.
29. Anthony Mattina, "North American Indian Mythography: Editing Texts for the Printed Page," in *Recovering the Word: Essays on Native American Literature*, ed. Brian Swann and Arnold Krupat (Berkeley: University of California Press, 1987), 139.
30. William L. Leap, *American Indian English* (Salt Lake City: University of Utah Press, 1993), 110.
31. Ibid., 91.
32. Guillermo Bartelt, "American Indian English in Momaday's *House Made of Dawn*," *Language and Literature* 19 (1994): 38.

33. See Leap, *American Indian English*, 44–89.
34. Ibid., 278.
35. Ibid., 279.
36. Allison Adelle Hedge Coke, "Seeds," in *Speaking for the Generations: Native Writers on Writing*, ed. Simon J. Ortiz (Tucson: University of Arizona Press, 1998), 108.
37. Figures vary but are alarming: according to Frederick H. White, of the about 200 Indigenous languages still alive in North America today, "only 10 percent have a chance of enduring beyond the second decade in the new millennium"; Frederick H. White, "Language Reflection and Lamentation in Native American Literature," *Studies in American Indian Literatures*, 2nd ser., 18.1 (2006): 95.
38. Thomas King, in Peter Gzowski, "Peter Gzowski Interviews Thomas King on *Green Grass, Running Water*," *Canadian Literature* 161–62 (1999): 72.
39. I prefer "orature" to the still more common but contradictory and ethnocentric "oral literature," for, as Terry Goldie has argued, "'orature' [...] unlike 'oral literature' or 'oral poetry' does not denote the oral as inferior to the formally written"; Terry Goldie, "Two Voices," preface to the 1st ed. of *An Anthology of Canadian Native Literature in English*, ed. Daniel David Moses and Terry Goldie, 3rd ed. (Toronto: Oxford University Press, 2005), xix. "Orature" also "allows this body of knowledge its own validity"; Daniel David Moses and Terry Goldie, "Traditional Orature: Southern First Nations," in *An Anthology of Canadian Native Literature in English*, ed. Daniel David Moses and Terry Goldie, 3rd ed. (Toronto: Oxford University Press, 2005), 1.
40. Arnold Krupat, *The Turn to the Native: Studies in Criticism and Culture* (Lincoln: University of Nebraska Press, 1996), 36.
41. Margery Fee, "Writing Orality: Interpreting Literature in English by Aboriginal Writers in North America, Australia, and New Zealand," *Journal of Intercultural Studies* 18.1 (1997): 31.
42. Francis Lieber, "On the Study of Foreign Languages," *Southern Literary Messenger* 3 (1837): 162–72.
43. See, for example, Geraldine Balzer, "'Bring(ing) Them Back from the Inside Out': Coming Home through Story in Richard Wagamese's *Keeper 'n Me*," in *Textualizing Orature and Orality*, ed. Susan Gingell, special issue, *Essays on Canadian Writing* 83 (2004): 222–39; Méira Cook, "Bone Memory: Transcribing Voice in Louise Bernice Halfe's *Blue Marrow*," *Canadian Literature* 166 (2000): 85–110; Teresa Gibert, "Narrative Strategies in Thomas King's Short Stories," in *Telling Stories: Postcolonial Short Fiction in English*, ed. Jacqueline Bardolph (Amsterdam: Rodopi, 2001), 67–76; Susan Gingell, "When X Equals Zero: The Politics of Voice in First Peoples Poetry by Women," *ESC: English Studies in Canada* 24.4 (1998): 447–66; and Shelley Stigter, "The Dialectics and Dialogics of Code-Switching in the Poetry of Gregory Scofield and Louise Halfe," *American Indian Quarterly* 30.1–2 (2006): 49–60.
44. See Susan Gingell, "Lips' Inking: Cree Writings of the Oral in Canada and What They Might Tell Educators," paper presented at Celebrating the Local, Negotiating the School: Symposium on English Language and Literacy in Aboriginal Communities, Aboriginal Education Research Centre, University of Saskatchewan, Saskatoon, 7–8 November 2008, aerc.usask.ca/downloads/GingellDRAFTpager.pdf.
45. Daniel Heath Justice, *Our Fire Survives the Storm: A Cherokee Literary History* (Minneapolis: University of Minnesota Press, 2006), 210.

46. The linguistic evidence for the oral qualities of literature is, in fact, extensive. Elinor Ochs has pointed to "the self-conscious expression of unplanned [i.e., informal oral] discourse features" used by novelists in their attempts "to recreate a casual situational context"; Elinor Ochs, "Planned and Unplanned Discourse," in *Discourse and Syntax*, ed. Talmy Givón (New York: Academic, 1979), 77. Robin Tolmach Lakoff has discussed how contemporary novelists transfer "real" oral discourse into writing, using quotation marks, italics, capitalization, and non-fluencies; Robin Tolmach Lakoff, "Some of My Favorite Writers Are Literate: The Mingling of Oral and Literate Strategies in Written Communication," in *Spoken and Written Language: Exploring Orality and Literacy*, ed. Deborah Tannen (Norwood, NJ: Ablex Publishing, 1982), 244–52. Wallace L. Chafe's analysis of Thomas Tyron's novel *The Other* (1971) has shown "indices of integration and involvement not significantly different from those of spoken language"; Wallace L. Chafe, "Integration and Involvement in Spoken and Written Language," in *Semiotics Unfolding*, vol. 2 of *Proceedings of the Second Congress of the International Association for Semiotic Studies, Vienna, July 1979*, ed. Tasso Borbé (Berlin: Mouton Publishers, 1979), 1101. Douglas Biber, too, has noted a relatively high degree of involvement in fiction; Douglas Biber, *Dimensions of Register Variation: A Cross-Linguistic Comparison* (Cambridge, UK: Cambridge University Press, 1995), 149–51. Deborah Tannen has shown at length "that ordinary conversation is made up of linguistic strategies that have been thought quintessentially literary"—namely, repetition, dialogue, and imagery—and that the construction of dialogue can thus be read as "an example of the poetic in everyday conversation"; Deborah Tannen, *Talking Voices: Repetition, Dialogue, and Imagery in Conversational Discourse*, 2nd ed. (Cambridge, UK: Cambridge University Press, 2007), 1, 132. Similarly, Livia Polanyi argues that "literary texts do not have a monopoly on phenomena such as indirect free style, and complexities of point of view, and ambiguity, such as many literary theorists appear to believe"; Livia Polanyi, "Literary Complexity in Everyday Storytelling," in *Spoken and Written Language: Exploring Orality and Literacy*, ed. Deborah Tannen (Norwood, NJ: Ablex Publishing, 1982), 169.
47. See Jacques Derrida, *Of Grammatology*, trans. Gayatri Chakravorty Spivak (Baltimore: Johns Hopkins University Press, 1976).
48. In *Recovering the Word: Essays on Native American Literature*, ed. Brian Swann and Arnold Krupat (Berkeley: University of California Press, 1987).
49. N. Scott Momaday, *The Man Made of Words: Essays, Stories, Passages* (New York: St. Martin's Press, 1997), 114.
50. Boris M. Éjchenbaum, "The Illusion of *Skaz*," translated by Martin P. Rice, *Russian Literature Triquarterly* 12 (1975): 233.
51. Ibid., 235.
52. John Willinsky, "The Paradox of Text in the Culture of Literacy," in *After Literacy: Essays* (New York: Peter Lang, 2001), 61.
53. Robert Kellogg, "Oral Narrative, Written Books," *Genre* 10 (1977): 655.
54. Paul Goetsch, "Fingierte Mündlichkeit in der Erzählkunst entwickelter Schriftkulturen," *Poetica* 17.3–4 (1985): 218; my translations.
55. Susan Berry Brill de Ramírez, *Contemporary American Indian Literatures and the Oral Tradition* (Tucson: University of Arizona Press, 1999), 2.

56. Despite studies such as Dennis Cooley's *The Vernacular Muse* (Winnipeg: Turnstone Press, 1987) and David Williams' *Imagined Nations* (Montreal: McGill-Queen's University Press, 2003), most critical attention paid to aspects of the oral in writing in Canada still concerns Aboriginal literatures. Susan Gingell thus notes correctly at the end of her introduction to *Essays on Canadian Writing*'s special issue on textualized orature and textualized orality that "What is most problematically absent from the scholarship gathered in this issue is any consideration of Euro-Canadian oral traditions and orality being brought to page"; Susan Gingell, introduction to *Textualizing Orature and Orality*, ed. Susan Gingell, special issue, *Essays on Canadian Writing* 83 (2004): 14; emphasis added.
57. Carol Fleisher Feldman, "Oral Metalanguage," in *Literacy and Orality*, ed. David R. Olson and Nancy Torrance (Cambridge, UK: Cambridge University Press, 1991), 47.
58. J. Edward Chamberlin, "From Hand to Mouth: The Postcolonial Politics of Oral and Written Traditions," in *Reclaiming Indigenous Voice and Vision*, ed. Marie Battiste (Vancouver: UBC Press, 2000), 138. Referring to the reading and interpreting of natural and supernatural signs and of cultural artifacts, Chamberlin joins other scholars such as Gordon Brotherston, *Book of the Fourth World: Reading the Native Americas through Their Literature* (Cambridge, UK: Cambridge University Press, 1992); Walter D. Mignolo, *The Darker Side of the Renaissance: Literacy, Territoriality, and Colonization* (Ann Arbor: University of Michigan Press, 1995); and Richard Daly, "Writing on the Landscape: Protoliteracy and Psychic Travel in Oral Cultures," in *They Write Their Dream on the Rock Forever: Rock Writings of the Stein River Valley of British Columbia*, by Annie York, Richard Daly, and Chris Arnett (Vancouver: Talonbooks, 1993), 223–60. These scholars "have cast doubt on the exclusion of nonphonetic writing systems from the canons of literacy"; Germaine Warkentin, "In Search of 'The Word of the Other': Aboriginal Sign Systems and the History of the Book in Canada," *Book History* 2.1 (1999): 5. Such exclusion has been commonly practised by linguists who, with the exception of Archibald A. Hill, "The Typology of Writing Systems," in *Papers in Linguistics in Honor of Leon Dostert*, ed. William M. Austin (The Hague: Mouton, 1967), 92–99, view North American Indigenous pictographs as not representing a writing system.
59. Previous studies on oral dimensions in Anglo-American literatures have either analyzed the work of specific authors (e.g., Charles Dickens, Thomas Hardy, Joseph Conrad, William Faulkner, and James Joyce) or discussed specific thematic questions (e.g., the function of fictive oral storytelling, of fictional dialogue, or of dialect and foreign languages; receptions of oral traditions; implications and evaluations of literacy). For the former, see, for example, Ian Watt, "Oral Dickens," *Dickens Studies Annual* 3 (1974): 165–81; Paul Goetsch, *Hardys Wessex-Romane: Mündlichkeit, Schriftlichkeit, kultureller Wandel* (Tübingen: Gunter Narr Verlag, 1994); Julika Griem, *Brüchiges Seemannsgarn: Mündlichkeit und Schriftlichkeit im Werk Joseph Conrads*, PhD diss., Universität Freiburg i. Br., 1995 (Tübingen: Gunter Narr Verlag, 1995); Helen Swink, "William Faulkner: The Novelist as Oral Narrator," *The Georgia Review* 26.2 (1972): 183–209; and Willi Erzgräber, *James Joyce: Oral and Written Discourse as Mirrored in Experimental Narrative Art* (Frankfurt am Main: Peter Lang, 2002). For the latter, see, for example, Norman Page, *Speech in the English Novel* (London: Longman, 1973); Willi Erzgräber and Paul Goetsch, eds., *Mündliches Erzählen im Alltag*,

fingiertes mündliches Erzählen in der Literatur (Tübingen: Gunter Narr Verlag, 1987); Sumner Ives, "A Theory of Literary Dialect," *Tulane Studies in English* 2 (1950): 137–82; Paul Goetsch, ed., *Dialekte und Fremdsprachen in der Literatur* (Tübingen: Gunter Narr Verlag, 1987); Renate Mace, *Funktionen des Dialekts im regionalen Roman von Gaskell bis Lawrence*, PhD diss., Universität Freiburg i. Br., 1986 (Tübingen: Gunter Narr Verlag, 1987); Paul Goetsch, ed., *Mündliches Wissen in neuzeitlicher Literatur* (Tübingen: Gunter Narr Verlag, 1990); and Paul Goetsch, *The Oral and the Written in Nineteenth-Century British Fiction* (Frankfurt am Main: Peter Lang, 2003).

60. Also see Thomas King, who applies the term "interfusional literature"—the fusing of oral with written traditions—not to the body of contemporary Indigenous literatures as a whole but to a particular portion of it; Thomas King, "Godzilla vs. Post-Colonial," *World Literature Written in English* 30.2 (1990): 13–14.

61. Fee, "Writing Orality," 33.

62. Kimberly M. Blaeser, "Writing Voices Speaking: Native Authors and an Oral Aesthetic," in *Talking on the Page: Editing Aboriginal Oral Texts*, ed. Laura J. Murray and Keren Rice (Toronto: University of Toronto Press, 1999), 65; emphasis added.

63. Blanca Schorcht, *Storied Voices in Native American Texts: Harry Robinson, Thomas King, James Welch, and Leslie Marmon Silko*, PhD diss., University of British Columbia, 1999 (New York: Routledge, 2003), 17.

64. Brill de Ramírez, *Contemporary American Indian Literatures*, 2.

65. Ibid., 6–7.

66. Ibid., 134.

67. Kimberly M. Blaeser, *Gerald Vizenor: Writing in the Oral Tradition* (Norman: University of Oklahoma Press, 1996), 30.

68. Ibid., 32–33.

69. See Lester A. Standiford, "Worlds Made of Dawn: Characteristic Image and Incident in Native American Imaginative Literature," in *Three American Literatures: Essays in Chicano, Native American, and Asian-American Literature for Teachers of American Literature*, ed. Houston A. Baker, Jr. (New York: Modern Language Association of America, 1982), 185, 188.

70. Blaeser, *Gerald Vizenor*, 33; emphasis added. Standiford was not the first to note the influence of Indigenous language structures on Indigenous compositions. As early as 1923, Mary Austin pointed out in *The American Rhythm* the holophrastic nature of Indigenous languages and its effect on Indigenous discourse practices (new and enlarged ed. 1930; reprint, New York: Cooper Square Publishers, 1970, 59–61).

71. Blaeser, "Writing Voices Speaking," 57; emphasis added.

72. Monica Heller, introduction to *Codeswitching: Anthropological and Sociolinguistic Perspectives*, ed. Monica Heller (Berlin: Mouton de Gruyter, 1988), 1.

73. Eugene Nida and Charles A. Taber, *The Theory and Practice of Translation* (Leiden: E.J. Brill, 1969), 1, 22.

74. Eugene A. Nida, *Toward a Science of Translating: With Special Reference to Principles and Procedures Involved in Bible Translating* (Leiden: E.J. Brill, 1964), 159.

75. Old English (450–1150 C.E.), belonging to the West Germanic branch of the Indo-European language family, was a synthetic language whose resourcefulness involved the use of affixes and self-explaining compounds; Albert C. Baugh and Thomas Cable, *A History of the English Language*, 5th ed. (London: Routledge, 2002), 64–66,

181–83. With its development into Middle English (c. 1150 C.E.), however, English started losing its inflections, a process that was completed around 1500 C.E., which marks the "birth" of Modern English; ibid., 52.

76. No translation is ever complete in the sense that it can never be identical but only equivalent to the original. In the case of translating the holophrase into English, aiming at an equivalence of form, the product of translation, however, is neither identical nor equivalent to the holophrase, and it is for this reason that I describe this translation as unsuccessful.

77. Also see Baker, *Atoms*, 114: "if one thinks of languages as I-languages—as sets of principles and constraints that determine the structure of sentences—then Mohawk and English turn out to be very similar. They have (at least) eight principles in common and only one that is different [what Baker calls the polysynthesis parameter], making them roughly 89 percent the same in terms of their recipes."

78. Andrew Spencer, *Morphological Theory: An Introduction to Word Structure in Generative Grammar* (Oxford: Basil Blackwell, 1991), 319.

79. Ishmael Alunik, *Call Me Ishmael: Memories of Ishmael Alunik, Inuvialuk Elder* (Inuvik: Kolausok Ublaaq Enterprises, 1998), 35.

80. Alootook Ipellie, *Arctic Dreams and Nightmares* (Penticton, B.C.: Theytus Books, c. 1993), 42, 120.

81. Thomas King, *Green Grass, Running Water* (1993; reprint, Toronto: HarperPerennialCanada, 1999), 109.

82. Richard Van Camp, *The Lesser Blessed* (1996; reprint, Vancouver: Douglas and McIntyre, 2004), 37.

83. King, *Green Grass*, 349.

84. As the holophrastic readings in Chapters 1 to 5 will show, the creation of loan translations into English is sometimes also achieved by way of non-phrasal compounds, such as synthetic or root compounds.

85. Deborah James, Sandra Clarke, and Marguerite MacKenzie, "The Encoding of Information Source in Algonquian: Evidentials in Cree/Montagnais/Naskapi," *International Journal of American Linguistics* 67.3 (2001): 229.

86. Chafe, "Discourse Effects," 42.

87. James, Clarke, and MacKenzie, "Encoding of Information," 229; Thomas Willett, "A Cross-Linguistic Survey of the Grammaticization of Evidentiality," *Studies in Language* 12.1 (1988): 51.

88. Wallace L. Chafe and Johanna Nichols, introduction to *Evidentiality: The Linguistic Coding of Epistemology*, ed. Wallace L. Chafe and Johanna Nichols (Norwood, NJ: Ablex Publishing, 1986), viii; emphasis added.

89. H. Christoph Wolfart and Janet F. Carroll, *Meet Cree: A Guide to the Cree Language*, rev. ed. (Edmonton: University of Alberta Press, 1981), 91.

90. See Willett, "Cross-Linguistic Survey," 57.

91. Xavier Sutherland, "cahkâpês nêsta mâka mistâpêskwêwak/Chahkabesh and the Giant Women," *âtolôhkâna nêsta tipâcimôwina/Cree Legends and Narratives from the West Coast of James Bay*, ed. and trans. C. Douglas Ellis (Winnipeg: University of Manitoba Press, 1995), 104; emphasis added.

92. Ibid., 105; emphasis added.

93. M. Dale Kinkade and Anthony Mattina, "Discourse," in *Languages*, ed. Ives Goddard, vol. 17 of *Handbook of North American Indians*, gen. ed. William C. Sturtevant (Washington, DC: Smithsonian Institution Press, 1996), 262–63.
94. Ibid., 262.
95. Harry Robinson, *Write It on Your Heart: The Epic World of an Okanagan Storyteller*, comp. and ed. Wendy Wickwire (Vancouver: Talonbooks, 1989), 45; emphasis added.
96. Bartelt, *Socio- and Stylolinguistic Perspectives*, 110.
97. Baker, *Atoms*, 102.
98. Maria Campbell, trans., *Stories of the Road Allowance People* (Penticton, B.C.: Theytus Books, 1995), 11; emphasis added. For a discussion of other ancestral language influences in *Stories of the Road Allowance People*, see Mareike Neuhaus, "The Marriage of Mother and Father: Michif Influences as Expressions of Métis Intellectual Sovereignty in *Stories of the Road Allowance People*," *Studies in American Indian Literatures*, 2nd ser., 22.1 (2010): 20–48.
99. Bartelt, *Socio- and Stylolinguistic Perspectives*, 110, has noted that pronoun copying has also been found in other New English codes besides Indigenous English.
100. Campbell, *Stories*, 29.
101. Robert Arthur Alexie, *Porcupines and China Dolls* (Toronto: Stoddart Publishing, 2002), 12.
102. *The Oxford English Dictionary Online*, draft rev. March 2009, s.v. "Para" (def. A1).
103. I owe this term to Martin Kuester.
104. Linda Hutcheon, *A Theory of Parody: The Teachings of Twentieth-Century Art Forms* (New York: Methuen, 1985), 32.
105. As an object whose significance lies in the functions of language that it produces, rather than in its linguistic structure, the paraholophrase is no longer language specific.
106. King, *Green Grass*, 391; emphasis added.
107. Ibid., 349; emphasis added.
108. See John 6.16–21, Matthew 14.22–31, and Mark 6.45–52.
109. Leo J. O'Donovan, "Mutual Teachers," *America: The National Catholic Weekly*, 29 August 2005, www.americamagazine.org/content/article.cfm?article_id=4325; emphasis added.
110. Bronisław Malinowski, *The Language of Magic and Gardening*, vol. 2 of *Coral Gardens and Their Magic: A Study of the Methods of Tilling the Soil and of Agricultural Rites in the Trobriand Islands* (London: Allen and Unwin, 1935), 22.
111. King, *Green Grass*, 3.
112. Armstrong, "Land Speaking," 190; emphasis added.
113. Gérard Genette, *Figures of Literary Discourse*, trans. Alan Sheridan (New York: Columbia University Press, 1982), 49, 54.
114. I owe this reference to Susan Gingell.
115. Maria Campbell, in Susan Gingell, "'One Small Medicine': An Interview with Maria Campbell," in *Textualizing Orature and Orality*, ed. Susan Gingell, special issue, *Essays on Canadian Writing* 83 (2004): 200.
116. One thing that needs to be explored further to determine how closely related these two concepts really are is whether or not Campbell assigns narrative function to the word bundle.

117. See Roland Barthes, *Elements of Semiology*, trans. Annette Lavers and Colin Smith (London: Cape, 1967), 89–94.
118. Barthes, *Elements*, 91.
119. Neal McLeod, *Songs to Kill a Wîhtikow* (Regina: Hagios Press, 2005), 42.
120. Roland Barthes, *Mythologies*, selected and trans. Annette Lavers (New York: Hill and Wang, 1972), 114.
121. Ibid., 126, 127, 120.
122. Susan Gingell, "Teaching the Talk that Walks on Paper: Oral Traditions and Textualized Orature in the Canadian Literature Classroom," in *Home-Work: Postcolonialism, Pedagogy, and Canadian Literature*, ed. Cynthia Sugars (Ottawa: University of Ottawa Press, 2004), 286. Also see Gingell, introduction to *Textualizing Orature and Orality*, 3–4.
123. Peter Koch and Wulf Oesterreicher, "Sprache der Nähe—Sprache der Distanz: Mündlichkeit und Schriftlichkeit im Spannungsfeld von Sprachtheorie und Sprachgeschichte," *Romanistisches Jahrbuch* 36 (1985): 17–18.
124. Martin Nystrand, "The Role of Context in Written Communication," in *Comprehending Oral and Written Language*, ed. Rosalind Horowitz and S. Jay Samuels (San Diego: Academic, 1987), 206.
125. Koch and Oesterreicher, "Sprache der Nähe," 19–24. Adopting immediacy and distance, I am following the translation suggested by Sabine Habermalz in "'Signs on a White Field': A Look at Orality in Literacy and James Joyce's *Ulysses*," *Oral Tradition* 13.2 (1998): 290n11.
126. See, for example, Biber, *Dimensions*, 238.
127. See Khosrow Jahandarie, *Spoken and Written Discourse: A Multi-Disciplinary Perspective* (Stamford, CT: Ablex Publishing, 1999), 131–49, for a summary of the linguistic research conducted on the nature of speech and writing and their relationship. Empirical research by linguists is largely based on comparing examples of discourses composed in English. Although the results are usually thought to apply to any other language (Jahandarie, *Spoken and Written Discourse*, 149; also see Koch and Oesterreicher, "Sprache der Nähe," 27), future research, including research concerning Indigenous and other non-Indo-European languages, still needs to confirm this claim. For a history of the linguistic research conducted on the relationship between speech and writing, see Wallace L. Chafe and Deborah Tannen, "The Relation between Written and Spoken Language," *Annual Review of Anthropology* 16 (1987): 383–407.
128. Koch and Oesterreicher, "Sprache der Nähe," 21.
129. This list is based mainly on the discussion in Jahandarie, *Spoken and Written Discourse*, 131–49. Linguists do not usually list "participatory" when discussing oral strategies of language use; audience participation, however, is as much a feature of spontaneous conversation as involvement, which linguists reserve for speakers only.
130. Even if the first part of the term suggests otherwise, neither use of "textualized orality," Gingell's or mine, implies a narrow definition of the word *text*; such a definition would only reinforce the notion of the great divide between the oral and the written; Karin Barber, *The Anthropology of Texts, Persons, and Publics* (Cambridge, UK: Cambridge University Press, 2007), 21. Using "text" in a broad sense as applying to all kinds of verbal discourse, regardless of their medium, I differ from Koch and Oesterreicher, who suggest that, based on their discussion, a distinction between

"discourse" (an expression using a language of immediacy) and "text" (an expression using a language of distance) might be both necessary and illuminating; see "Sprache der Nähe," 21–22.
131. Ruth Finnegan, "What Is Orality—If Anything?" *Byzantine and Modern Greek Studies* 14 (1990): 146.
132. Ibid., 148.
133. To facilitate reading, uses of boldface in quotations are explicitly marked as emphases only when they are not my own emphases.
134. Van Camp, *The Lesser Blessed*, 14, 22, 29, 31.

CHAPTER 1

1. Uluksuk, "A Brief History," introduction to *Call Me Ishmael: Memories of Ishmael Alunik, Inuvialuk Elder*, by Ishmael Alunik (Inuvik, NWT: Kolausok Ublaaq Enterprises, 1998), 12.
2. Presenting some of his stories in front of a class of students at Aurora College, Inuvik, Alunik, fiddling with some pieces of handwritten paper, pointed to the writing as his stories and said that he had a lot more stories to tell that Kolausok had not allowed him to include in *Call Me Ishmael*; Ted Dyck, personal communication.
3. Ishmael Alunik, Eddie D. Kolausok, and David Morrison, *Across Time and Tundra: The Inuvialuit of the Western Arctic* (Vancouver: Raincoast Books; Seattle: University of Washington Press; Gatineau, QC: Canadian Museum of Civilization, 2003), 34, 35, 219n53, 219n54. While Morrison's first citation from *Call Me Ishmael* is not entirely verbatim, his second citation is (with the exception of two words).
4. Ibid., vi.
5. Simon Bennett, "Simon Bennett Stories," *Inuvialuit* (summer 1981): 16–17.
6. According to the copyright page in Alunik's collection, its illustrations are by Heidi Willkommen and are based on drawings by Alunik himself. The two illustrations in its Tulugak stories (29, 33) are, however, remarkably similar to the illustrations by John Antaya published with the stories in *Inuvialuit*; ibid., 13, 16.
7. Agnes Grant, introduction to *Our Bit of Truth: An Anthology of Native Canadian Literature*, ed. Agnes Grant (Winnipeg: Pemmican Publications, 1990), ix.
8. Alexander Wolfe, introduction to *Earth Elder Stories: The Pinayzitt Path* (Saskatoon: Fifth House Publishers, 1989), xiv.
9. Lenore Keeshig-Tobias, "Stop Stealing Native Stories," *Globe and Mail*, 26 January 1990, A7.
10. David Morrison, "Time and Tundra," e-mail message to Ted Dyck, 9 August 2004.
11. Robin McGrath, *Canadian Inuit Literature: The Development of a Tradition* (Ottawa: National Museums of Canada, 1984), 80–81.
12. Ibid., 80.
13. Ibid., 84.
14. For the four ways in which things can be said to be opposed to each other, see Aristotle, *Categories*, in *The Complete Works of Aristotle: The Revised Oxford Translation*, ed. Julian Barnes, vol. 1 (Princeton, NJ: Princeton University Press, 1983), 11b18–11b23.

15. Based on the motivation that Alunik outlines in Chapter 1, one can assume that *Call Me Ishmael* is directed primarily at an Inu(vialu)it audience. However, the way in which *Call Me Ishmael* plays with readers' expectations, together with Uluksuk's introduction to the text (which provides much historical and cultural context that Inuvialuit and Inupiat readers would be familiar with), suggests that *Call Me Ishmael* is also intended to reach a non-Inu(vialu)it audience.
16. Also see the penultimate chapter of *Call Me Ishmael*, "Navigating the Tundra by Stars, Moon, and Snowdrifts" (90–96).
17. McGrath, *Canadian Inuit Literature*, 92.
18. Ibid., 93.
19. Wendy Rodgers, "Circumscribing Silence: Inuit Writing Orature," *Northern Review* 17 (1996): 54.
20. The narrative's title can also be seen as an intertextual reference to the Bible; see also the discussion that follows (pp. 42–43) about Chapter 4 of *Call Me Ishmael*.
21. Whales were one of the main sources of subsistence for the Inuit in the precontact era. Unlike Ahab in Melville's novel, the Inuit show deep respect for the animals that they hunt. In fact, this respect forms "an important part of Inuvialuit spiritual beliefs," as the animals were believed to have "souls or spirits, which were offended if not treated properly" (Morrison in Alunik, Kolausok, and Morrison, *Across Time and Tundra*, 24). See also my survey of Inuit spirituality and religion in Chapter 2 (pp. 72–79) of this volume.
22. It is not clear why Alunik gives the self-designation for Inuit living in a particular region of Nunavut (Kitikmeot) rather than Nunavut as a whole.
23. A more accurate way of spelling the Inuktitut word for "raven" using standard Roman orthography is *tulugaq*; Peter Irniq, "Inuit Names," e-mail communication, 15 January 2007. According to Jarich Oosten and Frédéric Laugrand, *tulugaq* derives from *tulu*, meaning "to hit." Unlike other birds, the raven can bite and hit—an ability that it shares with the bear; Jarich Oosten and Frédéric Laugrand, "The Bringer of Light: The Raven in Inuit Tradition," *Polar Record* 42.3 (2006): 191.
24. The Crees, for example, distinguish between *âtayohkewina* or sacred stories, on the one hand, and *âcimowina*, stories that are concerned with the present world, on the other hand. See Chapter 5 (pp. 181–82) of this volume.
25. Zebedee Nungak and Eugene Arima, "A Review of Central Eskimo Mythology," in *Unikkaatuat sanaugarngnik atyingualiit Puvirngniturngmit/Eskimo Stories from Povungnituk, Quebec, Illustrated in Soapstone Carvings*, ed. Zebedee Nungak and Eugene Arima (Ottawa: National Museum of Canada, 1969), 113, 115.
26. Nelson generally avoids the use of Tulugak and speaks instead of Raven Father (*Tu-lu'-kau-gûk*) or simply Raven; Edward William Nelson, *The Eskimo about Bering Strait* (1899; reprint, New York: Johnson Reprint, 1971), 425. Nelson's transcriptions and translations of Tulugak legends include the following: the extensive "Raven Creation Myth" (452–62) and the much shorter stories "Raven Takes a Wife" (462–64), "The Raven, the Whale, and the Mink" (464–67), "The One-Who-Finds-Nothing" (474–75), "The Raven and the Marmot" (514–15), and "The Bringing of the Light by Raven" (483–85), a story that resembles both Alunik's first Tulugak story and the ending of Nelson's "Raven Creation Myth."
27. Ibid., 452–62.

28. Oosten and Laugrand, "Bringer of Light," 189.
29. Nelson, *Eskimo*, 425.
30. Robert F. Spencer, *The North Alaskan Eskimo: A Study in Ecology and Society* (Washington, DC: Smithsonian Institution Press, 1959), 257.
31. As pointed out by Oosten and Laugrand, "Bringer of Light," 201, 191, the raven also features in the eastern Arctic, albeit neither as creator/cultural hero nor in the form of elaborate mythological cycles. Yet, they argue, the raven is still regarded as the bringer of light in the eastern Arctic (201). While Oosten and Laugrand avoid "historical speculation on the development and disintegration of the raven complex" in the eastern Arctic (188), William Thalbitzer believes that the notion of the raven as creator might also have been found originally among eastern Arctic Inuit; William Thalbitzer, "Die kultischen Gottheiten der Eskimos," *Archiv für Religionswissenschaft* 26.3–4 (1928): 411n1. Åke Hultkrantz, however, doubts any connection between the still-existing eastern Arctic raven material with the western Arctic notion of the raven; Åke Hultkrantz, "Die Religion der amerikanischen Arktis," in *Die Religionen Nordeurasiens und der amerikanischen Arktis*, by Ivar Paulson, Åke Hultkrantz, and Karl Jettmar (Stuttgart: W. Kohlhammer, 1962), 377n24.
32. Thalbitzer, "Die kultischen Gottheiten der Eskimos," 411n1. Given the migration of many Inupiat into the Mackenzie Delta in the early twentieth century—and the cultural interplay that we can assume between these two Inuit groups throughout history—the presence of Tulugak in Inuvialuit culture is not surprising. For Inuvialuit stories of Raven as cultural hero, see Knud Rasmussen, *The Mackenzie Eskimos: After Knud Rasmussen's Posthumous Notes*, ed. H. Ostermann (Copenhagen: Gyldendal, 1942), 61–65, 70–71, 73–74, 106–10; and Herbert T. Schwarz, *Elik, and Other Stories of the MacKenzie Eskimos* (Toronto: McClelland and Stewart, 1970), 11–14, 43–45.
33. Knud Rasmussen, *Across Arctic America: Narrative of the Fifth Thule Expedition* (1927; reprint, Fairbanks: University of Alaska Press, 1999), 356; Hultkrantz, "Religion," 369, 377; Spencer, *North Alaskan Eskimo*, 257. Unlike Rasmussen, who believes the western Arctic Inuit to have adopted the Tulugak cycle from the Tlingit (*Across Arctic America*, 356), Oosten and Laugrand argue that this cycle is too complex and too much "a structural feature of Inuit culture" to be "a recent phenomenon" borrowed from other cultures ("Bringer of Light," 188).
34. Sam D. Gill and Irene F. Sullivan, comps., *Dictionary of Native American Mythology* (Santa Barbara: ABC-CLIO, 1992), sv. "Culture Hero(es)."
35. For a discussion of tricksters in Indigenous traditions, including ethnocentric readings of this figure by Euro-Western scholars, see Chapter 4 (pp. 145–47) of this volume.
36. Toward the end of *Call Me Ishmael*, Alunik tells the story of a shaman who transforms into a raven in the darkness of a sod house. This story provides an intratextual reference to the first Tulugak story in *Call Me Ishmael*; but it is also part of what may be read as a critique of the Christian misreading of shamanism as devilish (see further discussion on pp. 46–50).
37. Hultkrantz, "Religion," 377n27, finds that what he calls the mischievous nature of Raven is less pronounced in Inuit traditions than in the traditions of First Nations people. Oosten and Laugrand, "Bringer of Light," 190, understand Raven to be both creator and trickster and point to two stories collected by Nelson,

"The One-Who-Finds-Nothing" (*Eskimo*, 474–75) and "The Raven, the Whale, and the Mink " (*Eskimo*, 464–67), in which Raven behaves like "a devious trickster." Mac Linscott Ricketts' reading of the shaman and the trickster as "represent[ing] two diametrically opposite poles of spirituality"—the former worshipping the spirits, the latter ignoring, overcoming, and finally mocking them—might provide an explanation for the seemingly greater significance of the shaman in Inuit traditions. Shaman and trickster, Ricketts argues, offer Indigenous peoples "two very different religious options that served the needs of different temperaments and different times"; Mac Linscott Ricketts, "The Shaman and the Trickster," in *Mythical Trickster Figures: Contours, Contexts, and Criticisms*, ed. William J. Hynes and William G. Doty (Tuscaloosa: University of Alabama Press, 1993), 87–88. The need to overcome "the weaknesses of the human condition" might arguably have been more significant among Inuit groups than the need to overcome "the absurdity of human existence" (105).

38. Shamans in Inuit cultures were believed to have "the power of bringing people back from death if their time was not yet up"; such people were called *angirraqtut*; Mariano Aupilaarjuk et al., *Cosmology and Shamanism*, ed. Bernard Saladin d'Anglure, vol. 4 of *Interviewing Inuit Elders* (Iqaluit: Language and Culture Program, Nunavut Arctic College, 2001), 10.
39. Susan Gingell, "When X Equals Zero: The Politics of Voice in First Peoples Poetry by Women," *ESC: English Studies in Canada* 24.4 (1998): 464n17.
40. Melville Jacobs, *The Content and Style of an Oral Literature: Clackamas Chinook Myths and Tales* (1959; reprint, Chicago: University of Chicago Press, 1971), 220–24.
41. Dennis Tedlock, *The Spoken Word and the Work of Interpretation* (Philadelphia: University of Pennsylvania Press, 1983), 160–62.
42. Richard Bauman, *Verbal Art as Performance*, with essays by Barbara A. Babcock et al. (Prospect Heights, IL: Waveland Press, 1984), 9, 11, 9.
43. Ibid., 15.
44. With its twenty pages, the introduction takes no less than one-quarter of the entire text. Its main function is to introduce outsiders to the Inuvialuit, their history, and their traditions. Dressed as an essay, it is presented in a genre that Euro-Western readers know how to read. That the introduction is not written by Alunik further underlines that it is better read separate from his narrative.
45. The opening comprises fourteen pages of a total of seventy-six pages (not including the introduction by Uluksuk).
46. Thomas King, *The Truth about Stories: A Native Narrative* (Toronto: House of Anansi Press, 2003), 153–54.
47. Gérard Genette, *Figures of Literary Discourse*, trans. Alan Sheridan (New York: Columbia University Press, 1982), 49.
48. The last two phrases are also part of a microframe established within Chapter 4.
49. Jacobs' and Tedlock's analyses, for example, suggest that opening and closing frames among the Clackamas Chinook and Zuni traditionally consist of just a few formulae.
50. As noted by Ives Goddard, the word *Eskimo* means "eaters of raw meat" in some Algonquian languages, such as Plains Ojibwa and Cree; some linguists, however, believe that *Eskimo* or *Esquimaux*, as it was spelled in its earliest English uses, derives

from another word with a completely different meaning; Ives Goddard, "Synonymy," in *Arctic*, ed. David Damas, vol. 5 of *Handbook of North American Indians*, gen. ed. William C. Sturtevant (Washington, DC: Smithsonian Institution, 1984), 5–6. While Goddard assumes that *Eskimo* originated from a Montagnais word, meaning "snowshoe-netter" (6), José Mailhot proposes that *Eskimo*, as used in various proto-Algonquian languages, translates as "parlant la langue d'une terre étrangère"; José Mailhot, "L'étymologie de 'esquimau' revue et corrigée," *Études Inuit/Inuit Studies* 2.2 (1978): 66.

51. The word *angakkuq* is common among Polar, Baffin, and Iglulik Inuit, whereas among Caribou, Netsilik, and Copper Inuit the shaman is commonly referred to as *angatkuq*. The spelling used throughout this study, unless in quoted matter, is *angakkuq*.

52. Peter Irniq, "Speaking Notes: Inuit Spirituality," address, 31st Annual Saskatchewan Prayer Breakfast, Regina, 4 April 2001.

53. Bernard Saladin d'Anglure, "An Ethnographic Commentary: The Legend of Atanarjuat, Inuit, and Shamanism," in *Atanarjuat, the Fast Runner: Inspired by a Traditional Inuit Legend of Igloolik*, by Paul Apak Angilirq (Toronto: Coach House Books and Isuma Publishing, 2002), 225, 209.

54. Ibid., 203.

55. Harold Seidelman and James Turner, *The Inuit Imagination: Arctic Myth and Sculpture* (Vancouver: Douglas and McIntyre, 1993), 51, 56.

56. Aupilaarjuk in Aupilaarjuk et al., *Cosmology*, 26.

57. Nutaraaluk in Aupilaarjuk et al., *Cosmology*, 10.

58. Aupilaarjuk et al., *Cosmology*, 246.

59. See, for example, Peter Pitseolak, *People from Our Side: A Life Story with Photographs*, oral biography by Dorothy Harley Eber (1975; reprint, Montreal: McGill-Queen's University Press, 1993), 40; and Salome Qalasiq in *Representing Tuurngait*, by Frédéric Laugrand, Jarich Oosten, and François Trudel, Inuktitut text trans. and ed. Alexina Kublu (Iqaluit: Nunavut Arctic College, 2000), 50.

60. The Christianization of Inuit started in the late eighteenth century in western Greenland and eastern Siberia and Alaska; Saladin d'Anglure, "Ethnographic Commentary," 205. One of the first missions in the Canadian Arctic was located on the east coast of Labrador and was founded by German Moravians in 1771; Inge Kleivan and Birgitte Sonne, *Eskimos: Greenland and Canada* (Leiden: E.J. Brill, 1985), 2. The central Arctic was Christianized only in the late nineteenth century; Saladin d'Anglure, "Ethnographic Commentary," 205.

61. Saladin d'Anglure, "Ethnographic Commentary," 225, 227.

62. The following discussion of Inuit terminology regarding spirits and the devil involves to a certain extent a conflation of various dialects of the Inuit language. Due to a lack of Inuvialuit informants, my only option for discussing the issue has been recourse to material from other Inuit groups; however, given the linguistic and cultural similarities among the various Inuit groups in the Arctic, such a conflation should not distort the overall analysis to a significant degree.

63. Ronald Lowe, comp., *Siglit Inuvialuit Uqausiita Kipuktirutait/Basic Siglit Inuvialuit Eskimo Dictionary* (Inuvik: Committee for Original Peoples Entitlement, 1984), sv. "devil" (246).

64. Peter Irniq, "Question," e-mail communication, 7 November 2006.
65. Aupilaarjuk et al., *Cosmology*, 255.
66. Kleivan and Sonne, *Eskimos*, 23.
67. Ibid.
68. Aupilaarjuk et al., *Cosmology*, 255. For another reading of *tupilait* as the unsatisfied souls of the dead, see an observation made by Edward Peck, an Anglican missionary on South Baffin Island: "They (the Tupelât) are the souls of the unforgiven ones who are rejected by Sedna and sent back to have their sins taken away"; Edward Peck in Laugrand, Oosten, and Trudel, *Representing Tuurngait*, 38.
69. Among the Inuit in Greenland, *tupilak* refers to a living creature fashioned out of the bones of dead animals and brought to life by the use of magic formulae with the intention of killing an enemy; Kleivan and Sonne, *Eskimos*, 23.
70. Alex Spalding, comp., *Inuktitut: A Multi-Dialectal Outline Dictionary* (Iqaluit: Nunavut Arctic College, 1998), sv. "tuurngaq."
71. Tungilik in Laugrand, Oosten, and Trudel, *Representing Tuurngait*, 18.
72. See, for example, Spalding, *Inuktitut*, sv. "tuurngaq"; Laugrand, Oosten, and Trudel, *Representing Tuurngait*, 2; and Aupilaarjuk et al., *Cosmology*, 255.
73. Peter Irniq, "Question," e-mail communication, 7 November 2006.
74. Tungilik in Laugrand, Oosten, and Trudel, *Representing Tuurngait*, 18.
75. Spalding, *Inuktitut*, sv. "tuurngaaluk."
76. My reading of the etymology of *tuurngaq* is supported by Saladin d'Anglure, "Ethnographic Commentary," 211, who gives "the powerful spirit" as the original meaning of *tuurngarjuaq*, the word that, he notes, "certain missionaries gave to the devil." Similarly, Spalding's Inuktitut dictionary includes the holophrase *tuurngijuq*, meaning "he shamanizes or invokes spirits or helping spirits; calls upon helping spirits for aid"; Spalding, *Inuktitut*, sv. "tuurngijuq."
77. Kleivan and Sonne, *Eskimos*, 8.
78. John Bennett and Susan Rowley, comp. and ed., *Uqalurait: An Oral History of Nunavut* (Montreal: McGill-Queen's University Press, 2004), 194.
79. Laugrand, Oosten, and Trudel, *Representing Tuurngait*, 48, 50.
80. The practice of *ilisiinneq* among Inuit, often falsely translated as witchcraft, might have invited the one-sided and prejudiced interpretation of Inuit religion. *Ilisiinneq*, translated literally as to "have got rid of one's ignorance," was used in Inuit cultures only in the case of social concern in order to "exterminat[e] an individual detrimental to society, if no one had the courage and strength to overpower him in any other way"; Kleivan and Sonne, *Eskimos*, 10.
81. Seidelman and Turner, *Inuit Imagination*, 150.
82. McGrath, *Canadian Inuit Literature*, 103.
83. See Gill and Sullivan, *Dictionary of Native American Mythology*, sv. "Flood(s)."
84. Lela Kiana Oman, *The Epic of Qayaq: The Longest Story Ever Told by My People*, ed. Priscilla Tyler and Maree Brooks (Ottawa: Carleton University Press; Seattle: University of Washington Press, 1995), 24–28.
85. Ann Chandonnet, preface to ibid., viii. For yet other versions of the epic of Qayaq, see Catherine Attla, *K'etetaalkkaanee, the One Who Paddles among the People and Animals: The Story of an Ancient Traveller*, trans. Eliza Jones (Nenana: Yukon Koyukuk School District; Fairbanks: Yukon Koyukuk School District, Alaska Native

Language Center, 1990); and Ticasuk, *The Longest Story Ever Told: Qayaq, the Magical Man*, 2nd ed. (Fairbanks: University of Alaska Press, 2008).
86. Priscilla Tyler and Maree Brooks, introduction to *The Epic of Qayaq*, by Lela Kiana Oman, xiii.
87. A variation of Oman's and Alunik's stories of the flood that also features Raven as a cultural hero is found in Schwarz's *Elik*. "The MacKenzie Land" recounts the events of a flood that took place in what is now the Mackenzie Delta, which, according to this story, owes its topography to the way in which the water receded after Raven harpooned the land to prevent it from always disappearing into the water; Schwarz, *Elik*, 11–14.
88. In a north Alaskan, that is, Inupiat, creation story collected by Spencer, *North Alaskan Eskimo*, 384–85, Tulugak also fixes the land with a spear, and Spencer compares this story to the earth-diver myth (385), a type of creation story often found among Indigenous peoples in North America. For Thomas King's discussion of Indigenous creation stories as well as a discussion of his use of the earth-diver myth in his *Green Grass, Running Water*, see Chapter 4 of this volume (pp. 143–145).
89. Oman, *Epic*, 13.
90. In traditional Inuit poetry, "derisive poems" are known for their satirical or ironic component; McGrath, *Canadian Inuit Literature*, 48.
91. Leslie Marmon Silko, "Language and Literature from a Pueblo Indian Perspective," in *English Literature: Opening up the Canon*, ed. Leslie A. Fiedler and Houston A. Baker, Jr. (Baltimore: Johns Hopkins University Press, 1981), 54.
92. As Peter Irniq has pointed out to me, the Inuit Cultural Institute standardized the Roman orthography for spelling Inuktitut in 1976 to reflect pronunciation. Kugluktuk is thus spelled properly *Qurluqtuq*. However, when Coppermine was renamed, the anglicized version was chosen over the correct spelling following proper pronunciation. The meaning of the place name Kugluktuk is sometimes wrongly given as "startled," which in the Nattilingmiut dialect is *qugluktuq* rather than *qurluqtuq*, meaning "water falling down." The improper spelling of Inuit words hence fosters misunderstanding and a loss of meaning and, ultimately, of the language itself; Peter Irniq, "Question," e-mail communication, 6 November 2006.
93. Lowe, *Siglit Inuvialuit Uqausiita Kipuktirutait*, svv. "qurluqtuq" (52), "water is falling down" (300).
94. Peter Irniq, "Ulu," e-mail communication, 8 August 2007.
95. Reading is usually a silent act, but knowing how to pronounce words helps readers to scan and make sense of a text. The more words in a text that a reader does not know how to pronounce, the less intelligible the text becomes for that reader.
96. For example, "He was very hungry, *and oh*, he just could not resist the smell" (31; emphasis added); "I wish we had a tape recorder in *them years*" (39; emphasis added); or "In the dark *he turn* into a Raven" (96; emphasis added).
97. Rodgers, "Circumscribing Silence," 50.
98. McGrath, *Canadian Inuit Literature*, 81.
99. Ibid., 92. For example, Alunik explains the meaning of *ulu* by translating it as "women's knife" and adding an illustration showing a semi-circular knife (52, 60).
100. During a storytelling performance at Aurora College in Inuvik that was broadcast to Yellowknife via audio-video, Alunik, who was telling the story of "How William

Kuptana Hunted Polar Bears," left the microphone to illustrate how to carry a dead polar bear. The audience in Yellowknife was left out of the performance for several minutes; Ted Dyck, personal communication.
101. McGrath, *Canadian Inuit Literature*, 16.
102. Ibid., 17.
103. Ibid., 18.
104. Ibid., 81.

CHAPTER 2

1. Markoosie's *Harpoon of the Hunter* (Montreal: McGill-Queen's University Press, 1970) was the first Inuit novel ever published.
2. Robin McGrath, *Canadian Inuit Literature: The Development of a Tradition* (Ottawa: National Museums of Canada, 1984), 81.
3. Michael P.J. Kennedy, "Alootook Ipellie: The Voice of an Inuk Artist," *Studies in Canadian Literature/Études en litterature canadienne* 21.2 (1996): 163.
4. Valerie Alia, "Ipellie's Interior Visions," *Up Here* 5.5 (1989): 59.
5. Maggie Dunn and Ann Morris, *The Composite Novel: The Short Story Cycle in Transition* (New York: Twayne Publishers; Toronto: Maxwell Macmillan Canada; New York: Maxwell Macmillan International, 1995).
6. Harold Seidelman and James Turner, *The Inuit Imagination: Arctic Myth and Sculpture* (Vancouver: Douglas and McIntyre, 1993), 84, 150–51.
7. Mariano Aupilaarjuk et al., *Cosmology and Shamanism*, ed. Bernard Saladin d'Anglure, vol. 4 of *Interviewing Inuit Elders* (Iqaluit: Language and Culture Program, Nunavut Arctic College, 2001), 9, 19. Seidelman and Turner, *Inuit Imagination*, 36, also give "soul" as a possible translation of *anirniq*. In fact, *anirniq* also serves as the root word for *anirnialuk*, meaning "Holy Ghost"; see Alex Spalding, comp., *Inuktitut: A Multi-Dialectal Outline Dictionary* (Iqaluit: Nunavut Arctic College, 1998), svv. "anirniq" and "anirnialuk."
8. Seidelman and Turner, *Inuit Imagination*, 36.
9. Aupilaarjuk et al., *Cosmology*, 10.
10. Ibid., 9, 19.
11. For a discussion of helping spirits or *tuurngait*, also see Chapter 1 (pp. 48–49) in this volume.
12. Frédéric Laugrand, Jarich Oosten, and François Trudel, *Representing Tuurngait*, Inuktitut text trans. and ed. Alexina Kublu (Iqaluit: Nunavut Arctic College, 2000), 22. See also Åke Hultkrantz, "Die Religion der amerikanischen Arktis," in *Die Religionen Nordeurasiens und der amerikanischen Arktis*, by Ivar Paulson, Åke Hultkrantz, and Karl Jettmar (Stuttgart: W. Kohlhammer, 1962). Hultkrantz argues with reference to the lack of secret shamanic societies that shamanic language was not a secret, sacral language and notes that it was used by shamans to communicate with their helping spirits rather than among each other (402). Inuit elders often point out that the shamans' helping spirits had a language of their own, but, as Laugrand, Oosten, and Trudel note (24), Inuit did not clearly distinguish between the language of the *tuurngait* and that of Inuit shamans; *tuurngait* were believed to speak through the

angakkuit's voice. Not all shamans made use of shamanic language, however; *angakkuit* of the interior, for example, did not have a shamanic language because they believed that it was unnecessary. See Ibjugaarjuk in John Bennett and Susan Rowley, comps. and eds., *Uqalurait: An Oral History of Nunavut* (Montreal: McGill-Queen's University Press, 2004), 187.

13. Seidelman and Turner, *Inuit Imagination*, 36.
14. See the Introduction (pp. 15–16) and Chapter 1 (pp. 59–61) in this volume for a discussion of compounds.
15. Knud Rasmussen, *Across Arctic America: Narrative of the Fifth Thule Expedition* (1927; reprint, Fairbanks: University of Alaska Press, 1999), 132.
16. Aupilaarjuk et al., *Cosmology*, 9.
17. Inge Kleivan and Birgitte Sonne, *Eskimos: Greenland and Canada* (Leiden: E.J. Brill, 1985), 15.
18. Bennett and Rowley, *Uqalurait*, 3.
19. Bernard Saladin d'Anglure, "From Foetus to Shaman: The Construction of an Inuit Third Sex," in *Amerindian Rebirth: Reincarnation Belief among North American Indians and Inuit*, ed. Antonia Mills and Richard Slobodin (Toronto: University of Toronto Press, 1994), 96–97. As Saladin d'Anglure notes, Inuit traditionally held the belief that children could change their sex at birth, most often from boy to girl, but accounts of changes from girl to boy were also believed to be true. Inuit accounts of sex changes at birth collected by Saladin d'Anglure include details that can be associated with "genital anomalies" (105n1).
20. Bernard Saladin d'Anglure, "The 'Third Gender' of the Inuit," *Diogenes* 52.4 (2005): 143.
21. Ibid., 144n3.
22. Knud Rasmussen, *Fra Grønland til Stillehavet: Rejser og Mennesker fra 5. Thule-Ekspedition 1921–24*, 2 vols. (Kobenhavn: Gyldendalske boghandel, 1925–26), 1: 351.
23. Hultkrantz, "Religion," 383.
24. Nuligak (Bob Cockney), *I, Nuligak*, trans. and ed. Maurice Metayer (1966; reprint, Richmond Hill, ON: Pocket Books, 1971), 134.
25. Kleivan and Sonne, *Eskimos*, 7.
26. Seidelman and Turner, *Inuit Imagination*, 38.
27. Kleivan and Sonne, *Eskimos*, 20.
28. Hultkrantz, "Religion," 385. Hultkrantz further notes that the strict separation of sea animals and land animals formed the overarching principle in Inuit hunting rituals (384).
29. Kleivan and Sonne, *Eskimos*, 7.
30. Rasmussen, *Across Arctic America*, 195.
31. Ibid., 130–31.
32. Seidelman and Turner, *Inuit Imagination*, 154.
33. Kleivan and Sonne, *Eskimos*, 32–33.
34. Hultkrantz, "Religion," 368.
35. Peter Irniq, two e-mails entitled "Inua and Anirniq," 12 and 13 December 2006.
36. Daniel Merkur, *Becoming Half Hidden: Shamanism and Initiation among the Inuit* (New York: Garland Publishing, 1992), 301–02.
37. See also Chapter 1 (pp. 46–50) of this volume for a discussion of Christian misreadings of Inuit shamanism as the work of the devil.

38. Kleivan and Sonne, *Eskimos*, 8.
39. Laugrand, Oosten, and Trudel, *Representing Tuurngait*, 42, 44, 46.
40. Zebedee Nungak and Eugene Arima, "A Review of Central Eskimo Mythology," in *Unikkaatuat sanaugarngnik atyingualiit Puvirngniturngmit/Eskimo Stories from Povungnituk, Quebec, Illustrated in Soapstone Carvings*, ed. Zebedee Nungak and Eugene Arima (Ottawa: National Museum of Canada, 1969), 124. Nungak and Arima refer to Diamond Jenness and Knud Rasmussen, who reported that the Copper Inuit were vague in their description of an afterlife; Rasmussen, however, assumed that they must have shared beliefs similar to those of other central Inuit groups.
41. Hultkrantz, "Religion," 407–08.
42. The northern lights were read by some—for example, the Inuit on the Ungava Peninsula (Nunavik, Quebec)—as torches guiding the recently deceased. See ibid., 380.
43. Rasmussen, *Across Arctic America*, 28–30.
44. Nungak and Arima, "Review," 123.
45. Aupilaarjuk et al., *Cosmology*, 74.
46. Merkur, *Becoming Half Hidden*, 8.
47. Spalding, *Inuktitut*, svv. "ikumaaluk" and "kappianakturvik."
48. Kleivan and Sonne, *Eskimos*, 6.
49. See Bernard Saladin d'Anglure, "Nanook, Super-Male: The Polar Bear in the Imaginary Space and Social Time of the Inuit of the Canadian Arctic," in *Signifying Animals: Human Meaning in the Natural World*, ed. Roy Willis (London: Unwin Hyman, 1990), 178–83.
50. Seidelman and Turner, *Inuit Imagination*, 109.
51. Nungak and Arima, "Review," 115.
52. See, for example, Seidelman and Turner, *Inuit Imagination*, 71.
53. Kleivan and Sonne, *Eskimos*, 27.
54. Paul Apak Angilirq, *Atanarjuat, the Fast Runner: Inspired by a Traditional Inuit Legend of Igloolik* (Toronto: Coach House Books and Isuma Publishing, 2002), 229.
55. For a version of this conflated Sedna story, see Angilirq, *Atanarjuat*, 229. Here *Uinigumasuittuq* "the one who did not wish to marry" eventually turns into *Kannaaluk* "the great one down below."
56. The conflated Sedna story bears some resemblance to the Dogrib creation story retold in Richard Van Camp's *The Lesser Blessed* (discussed in Ch. 4 of this volume).
57. Nungak and Arima, "Review," 115.
58. Rasmussen, *Across Arctic America*, 195.
59. Seidelman and Turner, *Inuit Imagination*, 81.
60. Ibid., 81–83.
61. Merkur, *Becoming Half Hidden*, 6, 7.
62. Kleivan and Sonne, *Eskimos*, 8.
63. Aupilaarjuk et al., *Cosmology*, 73.
64. Åke Hultkrantz, "A Definition of Shamanism," *Temenos* 9 (1973): 34.
65. Mircea Eliade, *Shamanism: Archaic Techniques of Ecstasy*, trans. Willard R. Trask (London: Routledge and Kegan Paul, 1970), 5.
66. Merkur, *Becoming Half Hidden*, 63. In *Inuit Imagination*, 48, Seidelman and Turner translate "shaman" as "one who commands respect." The root word *anga* also appears in *angak*, the Inuktitut word for "maternal uncle"; Angilirq, *Atanarjuat*, 231.

Aupilaarjuk, a native speaker of Inuktitut, has noted, however, that "The word *angakkuq* has nothing to do with *angak*"; in Aupilaarjuk et al., *Cosmology*, 10.
67. Merkur, *Becoming Half Hidden*, 3, 129.
68. Laugrand, Oosten, and Trudel, *Representing Tuurngait*, 22.
69. Robert G. Williamson, "Eskimo Underground: Socio-Cultural Change in the Canadian Central Arctic" (PhD diss., Uppsala University, 1974), 21.
70. See, for example, Hanne Birk, "Kulturspezifische Inszenierungen kollektiver Gedächtnismedien in autochthonen Literaturen Kanadas: Alootook Ipellies *Arctic Dreams and Nightmares* und Ruby Slipperjacks *Weesquachak and the Lost Ones*," in *Medien des kollektiven Gedächtnisses: Konstruktivität, Historizität, Kulturspezifität*, ed. Astrid Erll and Ansgar Nünning (Berlin: Walter de Gruyter, 2004), 225.
71. Spalding, *Inuktitut*, sv. "qakurturjuaq."
72. Saladin d'Anglure, "Nanook," 183.
73. Variations of this paraholophrase are "my own image as the Satan of Hell" (7) and "Satan incarnate" (8).
74. These two phrases are later interwoven as "the image of myself as the Satan of Hell's Garden of Nede" (8), thus enforcing their effect.
75. Nuligak, *I, Nuligak*, 159.
76. McGrath, *Canadian Inuit Literature*, 104.
77. These include "**incarnation** of myself" (5; boldface in original) as well as "Garden of Nede" (7), "Hell's Garden of Nede" (5, 6, 8), and "Satan's Garden of Nede" (11).
78. The phrase "Great White Arctic" also evokes one of the paraholophrases constituting the narrative's opening: that is, the shamanic circumlocution for *nanuq* "the great White Ghost."
79. The phrase "the incredible shrinking man" can also be read as an intertextual reference to Jonathan Swift's *Gulliver's Travels* (vol. 3 of *Works*, Dublin: George Faulkner, 1735). Given the Inuit cultural context of *Arctic Dreams and Nightmares*, the Inuit intertext appears to be more significant, however.
80. Edward William Nelson, *The Eskimo about Bering Strait* (1899; reprint, New York: Johnson, 1971), 457.
81. Tulugak is not featured in *Arctic Dreams and Nightmares*. The Inupiaq and Inuvialuit blanket toss, a practice that seems to be found in the western Arctic only (Peter Irniq, "Inuit Blanket Toss and Inuit Personal Names," e-mail communication, 3 January 2007), is referred to in "Trying to Get to Heaven," however (story nine, 68–74).
82. Daniel Merkur, "Eagle, the Hunter's Helper: The Cultic Significance of Inuit Mythological Tales," *History of Religions* 27.2 (1987): 173–75.
83. Bernard Saladin d'Anglure, "An Ethnographic Commentary: The Legend of Atanarjuat, Inuit, and Shamanism," in *Atanarjuat, the Fast Runner: Inspired by a Traditional Inuit Legend of Igloolik*, by Paul Apak Angilirq (Toronto: Coach House Books and Isuma Publishing, 2002), 223.
84. See Makka Kleist, "Pre-Christian Inuit Sexuality," in *Me Sexy: An Exploration of Native Sex and Sexuality*, ed. Drew Hayden Taylor (Vancouver: Douglas and McIntyre, 2008), 16. In fact, the drawing "Hunting for Skins and Fur" caught particular criticism by visitors to an exhibition of Ipellie's drawings in 1994 (see note 111 below).
85. See Chapter 1 (pp. 48–49) of this volume for a discussion of *tupilait* (pl.).

86. *Guti*, or *Guuti*, is the Anglican Inuktitutized version of God. The Roman Catholic missionaries usually referred to God as *nunaliurti* "earth maker"; Peter Irniq, "Guti," e-mail communication, 19 January 2007.
87. Spalding, *Inuktitut*, sv. "kappianaktuq."
88. Peter Irniq, "Inuit Blanket Toss and Inuit Personal Names," e-mail communication, 3 January 2007.
89. Saladin d'Anglure, "Ethnographic Commentary," 225.
90. McGrath, *Canadian Inuit Literature*, 111, has pointed out the significance of satire in contemporary Inuit literature "as a continuation of a traditional practice" that helps to heal a colonized people, or what she refers to as a "group suffering from severe culture shock."
91. The inversion of the Garden of Eden in this first story is mirrored also in Kappia's name.
92. Peter Irniq, "Inuit Names," e-mail communication, 17 January 2007.
93. *Arctic Dreams and Nightmares* contains two other stories that evoke the Inuit notion of a third gender, this time in connection with shamanism. In "Public Execution of the Hermaphrodite Shaman" (story five, 26–32), the shaman is executed by fellow Inuit after it is discovered that he is a hermaphrodite—an act that may be read as signalling internalized colonialism. In "Walrus Ballet Stories" (story fourteen, 114–23), however, homosexuality is embraced, as the first-person narrator, in his attempt to provide food for his community, takes the disguise of a famous ballet dancer who is obviously homosexual: "I mean, what can one do with a heterosexual?" (121).
94. Edward H. Schafer, "The Sky River," *Journal of the American Oriental Society* 94.4 (1974): 401.
95. Ibid., 402.
96. The blanket toss was a method used in the Mackenzie River Delta and along the western Arctic coast to locate caribou and other animals: the hunter was tossed into the air using a blanket hide held by members of the community. According to elders, the ceremony marking the end of a successful whaling season also included the blanket toss. See "Northern Games," Inuvialuit Regional Corporation, www.irc.inuvialuit.com/culture/northerngames.html. See also Ishmael Alunik, Eddie D. Kolausok, and David Morrison, *Across Time and Tundra: The Inuvialuit of the Western Arctic* (Vancouver: Raincoast Books; Seattle: University of Washington Press; Gatineau, QC: Canadian Museum of Civilization, 2003), in which Kolausok notes that the blanket toss was also part of the Northern Games, a cultural event that celebrated games reflecting the traditional ways of the Inuvialuit. The Northern Games vanished almost completely in the first half of the twentieth century but were reintroduced in the 1970s (208).
97. Peter Pitseolak, *People from Our Side: A Life Story with Photographs*, oral biography by Dorothy Harley Eber (1975; reprint, Montreal: McGill-Queen's University Press, 1993), 40.
98. Ibid., 41.
99. McGrath, *Canadian Inuit Literature*, 107–09.
100. Semantically speaking, "soap bubble" and perhaps "huge bubble" function as compounds, not phrases.

101. This personal name is spelled Tookeetooq (73) in the text but Tootkeetooq in the glossary (183).
102. Inuktitut words marked in **boldface** are holophrases proper.
103. In the case of Ukjuarlak, another figure is involved: namely, metaphor. In a similar fashion, the personal names of the three protagonists in "Love Triangle" become a metaphor of the triangular relationship of Aqaqa, Nalikkaaq, and Ossuk.
104. David H. French and Kathrine S. French, "Personal Names," in *Languages*, ed. Ives Goddard, vol. 17 of *Handbook of North American Indians*, gen. ed. William C. Sturtevant (Washington, DC: Smithsonian Institution Press, 1996), 214.
105. See Elke Nowak, "Is Inuktitut a Morphological Argument Language?" TS, 1999, ling.kgw.tu-berlin.de/staff/Nowak/HALLE-AU.doc. For the lack of copulae in Cree, see Lorna L'Hirondelle et al., eds., *Plains Cree Grammar Guide and Glossary* (Edmonton: School of Native Studies, University of Alberta, 2001), 22; for Seneca, see Wallace L. Chafe, "Discourse Effects on Polysynthesis," in *Discourse across Languages and Cultures*, ed. Carol Lynn Moder and Aida Martinovic-Zic (Amsterdam: John Benjamins Publishing, 2004), 38–39.
106. Even though the narrator proclaims Sattaanassee as an "Inuktitut name" (46), it is obviously an Inuktitutized version of Satan.
107. Linguists usually distinguish between three types of involvement in spoken language: the speaker's involvement *with the listener(s)*, his or her involvement with *himself or herself*, and his or her involvement *with reality*; Wallace L. Chafe and Jane Danielewicz, "Properties of Spoken and Written Language," in *Comprehending Oral and Written Language*, ed. Rosalind Horowitz and S. Jay Samuels (San Diego: Academic Press, 1987), 105. Hence, involvement characterizes the speaker's actions, not those of the listener, but involvement always *results in* audience participation.
108. M. Dale Kinkade and Anthony Mattina, "Discourse," in *Languages*, ed. Ives Goddard, vol. 17 of *Handbook of North American Indians*, gen. ed. William C. Sturtevant (Washington, DC: Smithsonian Institution Press, 1996), 265.
109. Edmund Carpenter, "Image Making in Arctic Art," in *Sign, Image, Symbol*, ed. Gyorgy Kepes (New York: G. Braziller, 1966), 218; emphasis added. Carpenter's article happens to be one of two sources that substantially influenced Canadian poet Pat Lowther in the composition of her poem "Woman on/against Snow," in which she attempted, as Christine Wiesenthal has put it, "to acknowledge and inflect what she had been able to learn about the existence of that Native tongue," Inuktitut; Christine Wiesenthal, *The Half-Lives of Pat Lowther* (Toronto: University of Toronto Press, 2005), 264.
110. Carpenter, "Image Making," 218; emphasis added.
111. At an exhibition of the drawings at the Manx Pub on Elgin Street in Ottawa in 1994, some observers "wrote comments in a guest book that he [Ipellie] was portraying women in a sexist way," a reaction that Ipellie "expected"; Paul Gessell, "Dreaming in the Arctic," *Ottawa Citizen*, 6 February 1994, D5.
112. Alia, "Ipellie's Interior Visions," 59. In fact, the drawing's full title is "Self-Portrait: Inverse Ten Commandments."
113. In Bennett and Rowley, *Uqalurait*, 121.
114. Seidelman and Turner, *Inuit Imagination*, 116. In fact, as Seidelman and Turner further note, "storyteller" has recently become a circumlocution used by contemporary Inuit shying away from discussing shamanism.

115. Birk, "Inszenierungen," 226; my translation.
116. In Alia, "Ipellie's Interior Visions," 59.
117. That Ipellie's drawings and stories are sexually explicit might be regarded as controversial by some people, but this explicitness is only in line with the purpose of *Arctic Dreams and Nightmares* to reinvent Inuit cultural traditions; Inuit groups were traditionally very open about sexual matters. As Robert F. Spencer has noted about Inupit (north Alaskan Inuit), "There were no well-defined restrictions as to sexual behavior; a girl, as noted, was not expected to remain chaste. The child saw others in the household engaging in sexual relations and there were hence no secrets to him. Should he ask where a new sibling came from, he was told at once that it came out of the mother's body. This is quite in contrast to the situation today, where under Euro-American influence, the frankness relating to sexual matters has vanished"; Robert F. Spencer, *The North Alaskan Eskimo: A Study in Ecology and Society* (Washington, DC: Smithsonian Institution Press, 1959), 244–45. For a recent article discussing Inuit sexuality, see Kleist, "Pre-Christian Inuit Sexuality."

CHAPTER 3

1. Richard Van Camp in Junko Muro, "Living in a Time for Celebration: An Interview with Richard Van Camp," in *Across Cultures/Across Borders: Canadian Aboriginal and Native American Literatures*, ed. Paul DePasquale, Renate Eigenbrod, and Emma LaRocque (Peterborough: Broadview Press, 2010), 302.
2. Van Camp in Muro, "Living in a Time for Celebration," 301.
3. Nicole Nicosia, "May I Suggest," review of *The Lesser Blessed*, by Richard Van Camp, *Indian Country Today*, 22 December 2004, www.indiancountrytoday.com/archive/28172764.html.
4. Geary Hobson, review of *The Lesser Blessed*, by Richard Van Camp, *Studies in American Indian Literatures*, 2nd ser., 10.4 (1998): 79.
5. Van Camp in Judi Saltman, "Richard Van Camp Interview," 29 September 2003, www.hanksville.org/storytellers/VanCamp/JSaltman.html.
6. William Bevis, "Native American Novels: Homing In," in *Recovering the Word: Essays on Native American Literature*, ed. Brian Swann and Arnold Krupat (Berkeley: University of California Press, 1987), 580–620.
7. Hobson, 79.
8. This remark is repeated almost verbatim a few chapters later: "Like I said, I'm Dogrib: I gotta watch it" (32).
9. Van Camp in Muro, "Living in a Time for Celebration," 307.
10. Kerry Abel, *Drum Songs: Glimpses of Dene History* (Montreal: McGill-Queen's University Press, 1993), xvi.
11. June Helm, "Dogrib," in *Subarctic*, ed. June Helm, vol. 6 of *Handbook of North American Indians*, gen. ed. William C. Sturtevant (Washington, DC: Smithsonian Institution Press, 1981), 291.
12. Abel, *Drum Songs*, xv, 9.
13. Helm, "Dogrib," 293; also see Abel, *Drum Songs*, xvii.

14. June Helm, "Tlicho (Dogrib)," in *The Canadian Encyclopedia*, rev. Thomas D. Andrews, www.thecanadianencyclopedia.com/index.cfm?PgNm=TCE&Params=A1ARTA0002332.
15. Helm, "Dogrib," 306.
16. Ibid., 303, 305.
17. Nancy LeClaire and George Cardinal, comps., *Alberta Elders' Cree Dictionary/alperta ohci kehtehayak nehiyaw otwestamâkewasinahikan*, ed. Earle Waugh (Edmonton: University of Alberta Press, 1998), svv. "atim," "dogrib," "rib"; also see Abel, *Drum Songs*, 45. Cf. Helm, "Dogrib," 303, 305, who translates *atimospikay* as "dog side."
18. Helm, "Dogrib," 305.
19. Ibid., 302, 305.
20. Abel, *Drum Songs*, 131.
21. See June Helm and Vital Thomas, "Tales from the Dogribs [Part I]," *The Beaver* 47.3 (1966): 17–18.
22. Helm, "Dogrib," 302.
23. Alexander Mackenzie, *The Journals and Letters of Sir Alexander Mackenzie*, ed. W. Kaye Lamb (Toronto: Macmillan of Canada, 1970), 149.
24. "Les *Dènè Étcha-Ottinè* ou Esclaves, les *Dounié Espa-tpa-Ottinè* ou gens de chèvres, et les *Éta-Gottinè* ou gens des montagnes, qui tous s'attribuent la même origine, poussent plus loin encore cet amour du chien"; Émile Petitot, *Autour du Grand Lac des Esclaves* (Paris: A. Savine, 1891), 301, Early Canadiana Online, www.canadiana.org/ECO/ItemRecord/11181?id=c916b31f945a8bf2; my translation.
25. "toutes les variantes de la fable des *Hommes-Chiens*, chez les Danites"; ibid.; my translation. For these stories, see Émile Petitot, *Traditions indiennes du Canada nord-ouest* (Paris: Maisonneuve et C. Leclerc, 1886), 56, 170, 204, 239, 311, 431, Early Canadiana Online, www.canadiana.org/ECO/ItemRecord/15869?id=c916b31f945a8bf2.
26. Petitot, *Grand Lac*, "Légende nationale des Flancs-de-Chien," 296–301; Petitot, *Traditions indiennes*, "Origine des indiens flancs-de-chiens d'après eux-mêmes," 311–16.
27. That Larry is told this story by Jed, who is Slavey (3), can hardly turn this creation story into a Slavey story.
28. George Blondin, *Trail of the Spirit: The Mysteries of Medicine Power Revealed* (Edmonton: NeWest Press, 2006); George Blondin, *When the World Was New: Stories of the Sahtú Dene* (Yellowknife: Outcrop, the Northern Publisher, 1990); George Blondin, *Yamoria, the Lawmaker: Stories of the Dene* (Edmonton: NeWest Press, 1997).
29. Dene Wodih Society, comp., *Wolverine Myths and Visions: Dene Traditions from Northern Alberta*, ed. Patrick Moore and Angela Wheelock (Edmonton: University of Alberta Press, 1990).
30. Émile Petitot, *The Book of Dene: Containing the Traditions and Beliefs of Chipewyan, Dogrib, Slavey, and Loucheux Peoples* (Yellowknife: Department of Education, Government of the Northwest Territories, 1976), 17–25.
31. Evalyn Gautreau, *Tale Spinners in a Spruce Tipi* (Ottawa: Borealis Press, 1981).
32. June Helm, *Prophecy and Power among the Dogrib Indians* (Lincoln: University of Nebraska Press, 1994), 121–45.
33. Armin Wiebe, *Tatsea* (Winnipeg: Turnstone Press, 2003), 149–50.
34. Petitot, *Book of Dene*, 17–19; Gautreau, *Tale Spinners*, 2–9; Wiebe, *Tatsea*, 149–50.

35. Richard Van Camp, "Message from Richard Van Camp," e-mail communication, 28 March 2007.
36. Gautreau, *Tale Spinners*, 8.
37. Petitot, *Book of Dene*, 18; Gautreau, *Tale Spinners*, 7–8; Wiebe, *Tatsea*, 149–50.
38. Also see Petitot, *Traditions indiennes*, 316.
39. Larry never explicitly says that he wants to do it doggy-style with Juliet, but his frequent references to "doing it doggy-style" suggest it. These asides remain ambiguous, however; given his retelling of the Dogrib creation story and the implications of his eventual lovemaking with Juliet, they can also be read as his interpretation of the Dogrib story of tribal creation (see also the discussion of the novel's ending on pages 120–123).
40. Hobson, 78.
41. Darcy McMannus is one of Larry's fellow students. He usually hangs out with Juliet and once beat up Larry for letting a husky kill Darcy's puppy, which Larry had promised to take care of.
42. Except for "weakdizzydemented," an appositional compound, all these chunks of language are phrasal.
43. The metaphor echoes both the notion of the *nephilim*—the fallen angels referred to in the novel's epigraph—and Juliet's description as an angel: "She had the face of an angel" (27).
44. John Burns, review of *The Lesser Blessed*, by Richard Van Camp, *Georgia Straight*, 28 November 1996.
45. See, for example, Blondin, *When the World Was New*, 5.
46. Tom Holm, J. Diane Pearson, and Ben Chavis, "Peoplehood: A Model for the Extension of Sovereignty in American Indian Studies," *Wicazo Sa Review* 18.1 (2003): 7–24.
47. "Cornmeal snow" brings to mind what Geoffrey K. Pullum calls "The Great Eskimo Vocabulary Hoax," "the notion that Eskimos have bucketloads of different words for snow"; Geoffrey K. Pullum, "The Great Eskimo Vocabulary Hoax," in *The Great Eskimo Vocabulary Hoax and Other Irreverent Essays on the Study of Language* (Chicago: University of Chicago Press, 1991), 160. This notion, according to Pullum, is problematic not just because of the question of how to interpret "Eskimo" and "for snow" but also because of the question of what counts as a word—unanalyzable roots or inflected word forms (168–69). If not for its polysynthetic morphology, which lends Inuktitut a very productive word-building capability, it would likely have as many, or as few, words for snow (or any other word) as English and most other Indo-European languages.
48. See Patricia O. Afable and Madison S. Beeler, "Place-Names," in *Languages*, ed. Ives Goddard, vol. 17 of *Handbook of North American Indians*, gen. ed. William C. Sturtevant (Washington, DC: Smithsonian Institution Press, 1996), 185.
49. Thomas D. Andrews and John B. Zoe, "The Dogrib Birchbark Canoe Project," *Arctic* 51.1 (1998): 79.
50. "Hose Cock" is clearly a typographical error, for Darcy is described as always wearing "grey track pants and never any ginch. His *horse* cock would jiggle through the cotton as he limped down the main hallway" (20; emphasis added).
51. "The skin on my back dries. Cracks" (1) appears to be the only exception.

52. See Wolfgang Iser, *Der Akt des Lesens: Theorie ästhetischer Wirkung* (Munich: Wilhelm Fink Verlag, 1976).
53. As noted in Chapter 2 of this volume, linguists usually distinguish between a speaker's involvement with the listener(s), his or her involvement with himself or herself, and his or her involvement with reality; Wallace L. Chafe and Jane Danielewicz, "Properties of Spoken and Written Language," in *Comprehending Oral and Written Language*, ed. Rosalind Horowitz and S. Jay Samuels (San Diego: Academic Press, 1987), 105. Historical present is a common indicator of involvement with reality; see Gisela Redeker, "On Differences between Spoken and Written Language," *Discourse Processes* 7.1 (1984): 48.
54. Wagamese, *Keeper 'n Me*, 4.
55. Thomas King, *The Truth about Stories: A Native Narrative* (Toronto: House of Anansi Press, 2003), 29; also see 60, 89, 119, 151, 167.
56. Hobson, 77–78.
57. Hartmut Lutz, "First Nations Literature in Canada and the Voice of Survival," *London Journal of Canadian Studies* 11 (1995): 66.

CHAPTER 4

1. Thomas King in Peter Gzowski, "Peter Gzowski Interviews Thomas King on *Green Grass, Running Water*," *Canadian Literature* 161–62 (1999): 71.
2. Thomas King in Constance Rooke, "Interview with Tom King," *World Literature Written in English* 30.2 (1990): 74.
3. Thomas King in Hartmut Lutz, "Thomas King," in *Contemporary Challenges: Conversations with Canadian Native Authors* (Saskatoon: Fifth House Publishers, 1991), 107.
4. See, for example, Arnold E. Davidson, Priscilla L. Walton, and Jennifer Andrews, *Border Crossings: Thomas King's Cultural Inversions* (Toronto: University of Toronto Press, 2003).
5. Thomas King in Jace Weaver, *That the People Might Live: Native American Literatures and Native American Community* (New York: Oxford University Press, 1997), 149.
6. Thomas King in Jeffrey Canton, "Coyote Lives: Thomas King," in *The Power to Bend Spoons: Interviews with Canadian Novelists*, ed. Beverley Daurio (Toronto: Mercury Press, 1998), 91.
7. Daniel Heath Justice, *Our Fire Survives the Storm: A Cherokee Literary History* (Minneapolis: University of Minnesota Press, 2006), 170.
8. Ibid., 169.
9. Thomas King in Gerald R. Vizenor, *Manifest Manners: Postindian Warriors of Survivance* (Hanover, NH: Wesleyan University Press, 1994), 174.
10. King in Canton, "Coyote Lives," 92.
11. Thomas King in Jennifer Andrews, "Border Trickery and Dog Bones: A Conversation with Thomas King," *Studies in Canadian Literature/Études en littérature canadienne* 24.2 (1999): 162.
12. All subsequent references are to the 1999 edition by HarperPerennialCanada.
13. Lutz, "First Nations Literature," 64.

14. Stacey Curry Gunn, "King Novel Popular in Canadian Literature Courses," *@Guelph* 46.4 (27 February 2002), University of Guelph, www.uoguelph.ca/atguelph/02-02-27/articles/king.html.
15. Thomas King, *Inventing the Indian: White Images, Native Oral Literature, and Contemporary Native Writers* (Ann Arbor, MI: University Microfilms International, 1986).
16. George Gibbs in Arlene Hirschfelder and Paulette Molin, comps., *Encyclopedia of Native American Religions: An Introduction*, updated ed. (New York: Checkmark Books, 2001), sv. "Creation Accounts."
17. Sam D. Gill and Irene F. Sullivan, comps., *Dictionary of Native American Mythology* (Santa Barbara, CA: ABC-CLIO, 1992), sv. "Creation."
18. King, *Inventing the Indian*, 69.
19. The first group of creation stories contains single creators (King, *Inventing the Indian*, 78–83), of which some are omnipotent and in charge of creation (79–80), whereas others share their responsibility with other beings (80–83). The second group of creation stories includes primary creators on whom most of the creative power is bestowed but who are assisted by other characters or helpers (83–86). Finally, the third group of creation stories features a multitude of creators who share the responsibility of creation (87–89). King's typology is thus based on the question of *who* creates the world. For a typology of creation stories (earth diver story, emergence story, world parent myth, creator twin story) that focuses on *how* the world is created, see Gill and Sullivan, *Dictionary of Native American Mythology*, sv. "Creation."
20. King, *Inventing the Indian*, 70, 89.
21. Ibid., 71.
22. Ibid., 90.
23. Ibid., 71.
24. Ibid., 92.
25. Ibid., 72.
26. Ibid., 93.
27. Ibid., 122.
28. The Four Women featured in the mythological narrative strand of *Green Grass, Running Water* are encountered in the traditions of the Navajo (First Woman, Changing Woman), the Pueblo (Thought Woman), and the Blackfoot and Dunne-za (Old Woman), but there are also various other tribes whose creation stories feature these women, always in a slightly different fashion; Blanca Chester, "*Green Grass, Running Water*: Theorizing the World of the Novel," *Canadian Literature* 161–62 (1999): 46, 60n5. Found among Indigenous tribes in California, the Great Basin, the Plains, the Eastern Woodlands, and the Atlantic coast, the earth diver story is the "most widely distributed of all North American origin myths"; Erminie W. Voegelin, "Creation," in *Funk and Wagnalls Standard Dictionary of Folklore, Mythology, and Legend*, ed. Maria Leach, 2 vols (New York: Funk and Wagnalls, 1949–50), 1: 260.
29. King in Gzowski, "Peter Gzowski Interviews Thomas King," 71.
30. Thomas King, "Godzilla vs. Post-Colonial," *World Literature Written in English* 30.2 (1990): 14.
31. "[T]he trickster tends to be of uncertain sexual status"; Barbara Babcock, "'A Tolerated Margin of Mess': The Trickster and His Tales Reconsidered," in *Critical Essays on*

Native American Literature, ed. Andrew Wiget (Boston: G.K. Hall, 1985), 163. For the sake of convenience, however, the trickster will be referred to in the following as male.

32. William Bright, *A Coyote Reader* (Berkeley: University of California Press, 1993), xi.
33. Erminie W. Voegelin, "Coyote," in *Funk and Wagnalls Standard Dictionary of Folklore, Mythology, and Legend*, ed. Maria Leach, 2 vols. (New York: Funk and Wagnalls, 1949–50), 1: 257; Gill and Sullivan, *Dictionary of Native American Mythology*, sv. "Trickster(s)."
34. Gill and Sullivan, *Dictionary of Native American Mythology*, sv. "Coyote."
35. Bright, *Coyote Reader*, 19–20; Kimberly M. Blaeser, "Trickster: A Compendium," in *Buried Roots and Indestructible Seeds: The Survival of American Indian Life in Story, History, and Spirit*, ed. Mark A. Lindquist and Martin Zanger (Madison: University of Wisconsin Press, 1994), 50.
36. Gill and Sullivan, *Dictionary of Native American Mythology*, sv. "Creator(s)."
37. Ibid., sv. "Coyote."
38. Anne Doueihi, "Inhabiting the Space between Discourse and Story in Trickster Narratives," in *Mythical Trickster Figures: Contours, Contexts, and Criticisms*, ed. William J. Hynes and William G. Doty (Tuscaloosa: University of Alabama Press, 1993), 195, 197; emphasis added.
39. Craig S. Womack, "A Single Decade: Book-Length Native Literary Criticism between 1986 and 1997," in *Reasoning Together: The Native Critics Collective*, ed. Craig S. Womack, Daniel Heath Justice, and Christopher B. Teuton (Norman: University of Oklahoma Press, 2008), 19.
40. Ibid., 70.
41. Neal McLeod, *Cree Narrative Memory: From Treaties to Contemporary Times* (Saskatoon: Purich Publishing, 2007), 97.
42. Ibid.
43. Kristina Fagan, "What's the Trouble with the Trickster? An Introduction," in *Troubling Tricksters: Revisioning Critical Conversations*, ed. Deanna Reder and Linda M. Morra (Waterloo: Wilfrid Laurier University Press, 2010), 14.
44. Ibid., 12.
45. King in Canton, "Coyote Lives," 96.
46. Patricia Linton, "'And Here's How It Happened': Trickster Discourse in Thomas King's *Green Grass, Running Water*," *Modern Fiction Studies* 45.1 (1999): 220.
47. There is only one moment in the novel when the conversation between "I" and Coyote does not form a paragraph on its own and seems to blur into one of the other narrative strands. In this instance, however, Coyote talks to the four old Indians in the realist narrative strand before he returns to "I," who then shifts attention to the mythological narrative strand (293). It may be assumed, then, that the four old Indians are not aware of the conversation between "I" and Coyote. Their continuous dialogue hence clearly forms a third and completely independent narrative strand in the novel and acts as its frame
48. Linton, "And Here's How It Happened," 220.
49. Dr. Hovaugh's story about his "great-grandfather and his vision" (95–96), for example, suggests that his great-grandfather established Dr. Hovaugh's hospital in Fort Marion in 1876.

50. Marlene Goldman, "Mapping and Dreaming: Native Resistance in *Green Grass, Running Water*," *Canadian Literature* 161–62 (1999): 21–23.
51. First Woman's story is a conflation of the earth diver story and the Haudenosaunee tale of the Woman Who Fell from the Sky; Laura E. Donaldson, "Noah Meets Old Coyote; Or Singing in the Rain: Intertextuality in Thomas King's *Green Grass, Running Water*," *Studies in American Indian Literatures*, 2nd ser., 7.2 (1995): 32. First Woman is also featured in a Crow creation story; Gill and Sullivan, *Dictionary of Native American Mythology*, sv. "Old Man Coyote."
52. In Navajo tradition, Changing Woman appears in the fifth world of the emergence of mankind; John R. Hinnells, ed., *The Penguin Dictionary of Religions* (Harmondsworth, UK: Penguin Books, 1984), sv. "Navajo." She "is synonymous with life and the power of creation"; Gill and Sullivan, *Dictionary of Native American Mythology*, sv. "Changing Woman."
53. In Navajo tradition, Thought Woman thinks the world into being; Jane Flick, "Reading Notes for Thomas King's *Green Grass, Running Water*," *Canadian Literature* 161–62 (1999): 159.
54. Old Woman appears as helper of the primary creator, Old Man, in Blackfoot tradition; see the stories "Order of Life and Death" and "Why People Die Forever" in Clark Wissler and D.C. Duvall, eds., *Mythology of the Blackfoot Indians* (1908; reprint, Lincoln: University of Nebraska Press, 1995), 19–21. In a Cherokee creation story, it is Star Maiden/Star Woman who digs under a tree and falls from the sky; Flick, "Reading Notes," 161.
55. As Donaldson has noted with reference to Paula Gunn Allen, "most Indian cultures affirm that sacred beings inhabit the same space as humans and frequent interchanges with them form a necessary part of both individual and tribal experience"; Donaldson, "Noah," 31–32.
56. Paula Gunn Allen, *Grandmothers of the Light: A Medicine Woman's Sourcebook* (Boston: Beacon Press, 1991), 22.
57. Shifts in the frame narrative from a narration of verbal events to a narration of nonverbal events include "And that one [GOD] jumps into the garden" (41); "And that one [Coyote] dances around and jumps around and stands around" (238); "And that one [Coyote] dances back into this story" (293); and "Coyote dials the number several times. Busy. So that Coyote dials that number again" (300). Interestingly, with one exception (41), these narrative shifts are an indication of how Coyote, by jumping into the other narrative strands, influences the story told by the master narrator.
58. Dee Horne, *Contemporary American Indian Writing: Unsettling Literature* (New York: Peter Lang, 1999), 27.
59. Strictly speaking, the first episode in the realistic narrative strand focuses on Lionel and Norma driving back to the reserve (7–8) and is followed by discussions among the four old Indians relating to the correct beginning of their story (9–15); only then does the narration shift to Dr. Hovaugh contemplating his garden. Hence, the realistic narrative strand does not actually *begin* with the first Dr. Hovaugh garden scene, which mentions the escape of the four old Indians for the first time. Still, the first episode in the realistic narrative strand contains references to their escape; after all, the four old Indians' reason for escaping is their mission to fix up Lionel's life. These references, of

course, become obvious to readers only after Lionel picks up the "four old Indians standing by the side of the road" (97) to give them a ride to Blossom (121–22).

60. Flick, "Reading Notes," 164.

61. Movement and growth exist even though the stories of First Woman, Changing Woman, Thought Woman, and Old Woman are "the same story" (147, 329) or, to use Mieke Bal's three-layer model of narrative (fabula-story-text), are based on the same fabula, the logical and chronological sequence of events that is given colour on the story-level; see Mieke Bal, *Narratology: Introduction to the Theory of Narrative*, 3rd ed. (Toronto: University of Toronto Press, 2009), 5–10. In every creation story, a woman falls from the sky (39, 105, 269, 329) and meets a figure from the Bible (God, Noah, Gabriel, Jesus), and then—with the exception of First Woman—a figure from the English/Anglo-American literary tradition (Herman Melville, Daniel Defoe, James Fenimore Cooper). Each of the women assumes the identity of another person, either because someone gives her a new name (Lone Ranger, 71, 100; Hawkeye, 395–96) or because she chooses one herself (Ishmael, 195, 225; Robinson Crusoe, 295, 324). At the end of the story, each woman is taken prisoner and is sent to Fort Marion, Florida, arrested for "Being Indian" (72), for being one of the "unruly Indians" (225), for being "another Indian" (324), or "For trying to impersonate a white man" (396). The larger themes and structures remain the same, but certain details, such as the various characters, vary from story to story. Hence, the four creation stories represent *multi-forms* of the same fabula: they are stories of Indigenous resistance against European forms of oppression and colonization.

62. The meaning of the directions and the colours displayed in Table 4.2 is based on the Northern Cheyenne interpretation of the Medicine Lodge; Albert Tall Bull in Peter J. Powell, *Sweet Medicine: The Continuing Role of the Sacred Arrows, the Sun Dance, and the Sacred Buffalo Hat in Northern Cheyenne History*, 2 vols. (Norman: University of Oklahoma Press, 1969), 2: 852n14; see below.

63. Goldman, "Mapping and Dreaming," 36, 20.

64. Ibid., 35–36.

65. Also see 93, 96, 100, 104, 431.

66. Also see 38, 90, 98, 431.

67. Also see 431.

68. Also see 105, 144, 349, 431.

69. Doueihi, "Inhabiting the Space," 200; emphasis added.

70. Also see the following instances: "'Well, for one thing, what happened to them?' / 'What happened to the trees?' said Hawkeye" (21–22); "'So,' said Ishmael. 'Are we lost again? Have we made another mistake?' / Lionel had made only three mistakes in his entire life" (29–30); "'You look like a smart fellow,' one of the officers told him. 'Get your life together. With your record, you're running out of options.' / There was the matter of children. Alberta wanted at least one, perhaps two. And, as she saw it, she had several options" (64–65); "'Forget November,' I says. 'Pay attention.' / Pay attention, says Ahab" (195).

71. Also see the following instances: "Eli took Sifton's hand and held it for a second with just the fingers, the way you would hold something fragile or dangerous. 'Okay,' he said, 'nothing personal.' / [...] Charlie munched on his sandwich and replayed the conversation. 'Hey, nothing personal, but you're not sleeping with the guy, are

you?'" (114–15); "This is a Christian ship, he shouts. I am a Christian man. This is a Christian journey. And if you can't follow our Christian rules, then you're not wanted on the voyage. [...] 'Silly Coyote,' I says. 'This story is just beginning.' / 'Initial here that you've read the rules, here that you don't want the special no-deductible insurance waiver, and sign at the bottom'" (148–49).

72. See above for a discussion of the four cardinal directions, the four seasons, the course of the sun, and the four stages of life.
73. Flick, "Reading Notes," 146, 164.
74. Donaldson, "Noah," 40.
75. William J. Hynes, "Mapping the Characteristics of Mythic Tricksters: A Heuristic Guide" in *Mythical Trickster Figures: Contours, Contexts, and Criticisms*, ed. William J. Hynes and William G. Doty (Tuscaloosa: University of Alabama Press), 42.
76. Penelope Hamer, "Beyond the Nineteenth Century: Thomas King's Decolonization of the Literary Image of the Native" (MA thesis, Concordia University, 1995), 49.
77. Flick, "Reading Notes," 147.
78. Ibid., 158–59.
79. Catherine Rainwater, *Dreams of Fiery Stars: The Transformations of Native American Fiction* (Philadelphia: University of Pennsylvania Press, 1999), 60.
80. Robin Ridington, "Theorizing Coyote's Canon: Sharing Stories with Thomas King," in *Theorizing the Americanist Tradition*, ed. Lisa Philips Valentine and Regna Darnell (Toronto: University of Toronto Press, 1999), 19. To the extent that they are parts standing for wholes, Indigenous stories are more accurately labeled synecdoches.
81. Robin Ridington, "Dogs, Snares, and Cartridge Belts: The Poetics of a Northern Athapaskan Narrative Technology," in *The Social Dynamics of Technology: Practice, Politics, and World Views*, ed. Marcia-Anne Dobres and Christopher R. Hoffman (Washington, DC: Smithsonian Institution Press, 1999), 179.
82. Ridington, "Theorizing Coyote's Canon," 20.
83. Rainwater, *Dreams*, 143.
84. Ibid., 142.
85. Davidson, Walton, and Andrews, *Border Crossings*, 197.
86. Ibid., 197.
87. Thomas King, *Truth and Bright Water* (New York: Grove Press, 1999), 87.
88. Davidson, Walton, and Andrews, *Border Crossings*, 198–203.
89. Intertextual references within King's work also include his short stories. Dr. J. Hovaugh, for example, first appears in "A Seat in the Garden" in *One Good Story, That One* (Toronto: HarperPerennial, 1993), 83–96, and the four women of *Green Grass, Running Water* show up again as Woman Who Fell From The Sky in "The Garden Court Motor Motel" in *A Short History of Indians in Canada* (Toronto: HarperCollins, 2005), 190–99.
90. King in Andrews, "Border Trickery," 163.
91. King in Gzowski, "Peter Gzowski Interviews Thomas King," 72–73.
92. Flick, "Reading Notes," 143.
93. Tall Bull in Powell, *Sweet Medicine*, 2: 852n14.
94. Goldman, "Mapping and Dreaming," 37.
95. Flick, "Reading Notes," 147.
96. Helen Hoy in ibid., 144.

97. Goldman, "Mapping and Dreaming," 31.
98. Alan Kilpatrick, *The Night Has a Naked Soul: Witchcraft and Sorcery among the Western Cherokee* (Syracuse: Syracuse University Press, 1997), 99.
99. Ibid., 100.
100. Ibid., 46.
101. King in Andrews, "Border Trickery," 181.
102. Kilpatrick, *Night*, 104–20.
103. Ibid., 46–62.
104. Ibid., 63–85.
105. Durbin Feeling, comp., *Cherokee-English Dictionary*, ed. William Pulte (Tahlequah: Cherokee Nation of Oklahoma, 1975).
106. Italicized lines indicate the translation. All mistakes contained in these translations, of course, are entirely my own.
107. See Kilpatrick, *Night*, 48.
108. See Flick, "Reading Notes," 147.
109. See Kilpatrick, *Night*, 50.
110. See ibid., 48, 50, 61.
111. See ibid., 61.
112. See ibid., 48, 50, 91. See also Feeling, *Cherokee-English Dictionary*, sv. "o^{4}sda."
113. Flick, "Reading Notes," 144.
114. Ibid.
115. Ibid., 150.
116. In the case of Charlie Looking Bear, the realistic narrative strand even includes a self-reflexive comment on the name's internal structure: "'I have a reservation. Charlie Looking Bear.' And Charlie handed the man the credit card.—'Is that one word or two?'—'Two. Looking and Bear'" (153).
117. Ibis Gómez-Vega, "Subverting the 'Mainstream' Paradigm through Magical Realism in Thomas King's *Green Grass, Running Water*," *Journal of the Midwest Modern Language Association* 33.1 (2000): 7.
118. "So, that Coyote is dreaming and pretty soon, one of those dreams gets loose and runs around. *Makes* a lot of noise" (1; emphasis added). "A yellow dog was sniffing at the rear tire. Go ahead, Babo thought, pee on it. *Won't hurt* a thing" (23; emphasis added).
119. As noted in previous chapters in this volume, linguists distinguish between the speaker's involvement with the listener, with himself or herself, and with reality; Wallace L. Chafe and Jane Danielewicz, "Properties of Spoken and Written Language," in *Comprehending Oral and Written Language*, ed. Rosalind Horowitz and S. Jay Samuels (San Diego: Academic Press, 1987), 105. First-person evidentials are a common indicator of involvement with oneself; see Gisela Redeker, "On Differences between Spoken and Written Language," *Discourse Processes* 7.1 (1984): 48.
120. Jennifer Andrews, "Reading Thomas King's *Green Grass, Running Water*: Border-Crossing Humour," *ESC: English Studies in Canada* 28.1 (2002): 103.
121. See Redeker, "On Differences," 48.
122. See, for example, a conversation between Lionel and his father in the first volume of the novel (80–82), which is almost completely untagged and runs over two pages.
123. For example, "flip, flip, flip" (200) or "scratch, scratch" (266).

124. The only, if important, instance is "GOD" (2).
125. See Flick, "Reading Notes," 144, 161.

CHAPTER 5

1. "Louise Halfe," Coteau Books, www.coteaubooks.com/index.php?p=Author&authorid=25.
2. See, for example, Susan Gingell, "When X Equals Zero: The Politics of Voice in First Peoples Poetry by Women," *ESC: English Studies in Canada* 24.4 (1998): 447–66, and Shelley Stigter, "The Dialectics and Dialogics of Code-Switching in the Poetry of Gregory Scofield and Louise Halfe," *American Indian Quarterly* 30.1–2 (2006): 49–60.
3. Susan Gingell, introduction to *Textualizing Orature and Orality*, ed. Susan Gingell, special issue, *Essays on Canadian Writing* 83 (2004): 4.
4. Méira Cook, "Bone Memory: Transcribing Voice in Louise Bernice Halfe's *Blue Marrow*," *Canadian Literature* 166 (2000): 93; Stigter, "Dialectics," 56–57.
5. "Blue Marrow," Coteau Books, www.coteaubooks.com/index.php?p=Books&listingid=27.
6. Louise Bernice Halfe, "Cree Glossary," in *Blue Marrow*, by Louise Bernice Halfe (Regina: Coteau Books, 2004), 103. Although not denoted as such on the copyright page, the 2004 edition of *Blue Marrow* is *de facto* a *revised edition* of the original work published by McClelland and Stewart in 1998.
7. The cover photograph of the first edition is inserted between Halfe's dedication and the text's first page in the revised edition. This photograph shows what appear to be a Cree man and woman and resembles Euro-Western family portraits popular at the turn of the nineteenth and twentieth centuries. The cover photograph chosen for the 2004 edition of *Blue Marrow*, on the other hand, communicates Cree culture on Cree terms (see my discussion below in note 76).
8. Cree words and phrases are never capitalized in the revised edition.
9. Macrons in the revised edition are displayed by a ^ instead of a ¯ and/or are added to words lacking macrons in the first edition.
10. The first paragraph of the first woman's confession, for example, originally contains two verbs (to dance, to bathe) in the present tense; Louise Bernice Halfe, *Blue Marrow*, 1st ed. (Toronto: McClelland and Stewart, 1998), 17; they are put into the past tense in the revised edition (18).
11. For example, "*I've gathered, the Bundles / given to* amisk, iskotwêw / *and the swan* (Halfe, *Blue Marrow*, 1st ed., 23) reads "*I've gathered, the Bundles / given to* amisk—*beaver*, iskotêw—*fire / and the swan*" in the revised edition (24).
12. The addition of line breaks renders, for example, the ending of the text's closing from poetic prose (Halfe, *Blue Marrow*, 1st ed., 90) to a free verse poem (98–99).
13. Cook, "Bone Memory," 96.
14. Ibid., 104. The eleven "sections" in the poem remain without titles, but the various passages attributed to the narrator are usually marked as *âcimowinis* "small story"—a circumstance that "stories" the narrator: her voice belongs to her, but most of all it carries a story, however small.

15. Cook, "Bone Memory," 85, has correctly pointed out the irony of the readers' appreciation of these oral stories in the form of writing rather than as actual voices.
16. Ibid., 106.
17. Ibid., 88, 86.
18. Ibid., 98.
19. Neal McLeod, *Cree Narrative Memory: From Treaties to Contemporary Times* (Saskatoon: Purich Publishing, 2007), 97.
20. Leonard Bloomfield, *Sacred Stories of the Sweet Grass Cree* (Ottawa: National Museum of Canada, 1930), 6.
21. H. Christoph Wolfart and Janet F. Carroll, *Meet Cree: A Guide to the Cree Language*, rev. ed. (Edmonton: University of Alberta Press, 1981), 92.
22. Cree sacred legends in *Blue Marrow* are evoked only through the figure of *nôhkom âtayôhkan*, the "Grandmother Keeper of the Sacred Legends," or through intertextual references, such as the Cree "elder brother," *wîsahkêcâhk* (82, 89, 98; see also Ch. 4 of this volume, pp. 145–47); Rolling Head Woman (5); or the cannibalistic figure *wîhtikow* (36–37, 76). For Cree *âtayohkewina*, see, for example, Edward Ahenakew, "Cree Trickster Tales," *Journal of American Folklore* 42 (1929): 309–53, and Bloomfield, *Sacred Stories*. When, toward the end of the poem, the narrator writes, "Did they [our ancestors] know our memory, our talk would walk on paper, legends told sparingly?" (98), she seems to allude not so much to the loss of tradition due to colonization as to the fact that telling *âtayohkewina* in writing would amount to a breaking of protocol.
23. Debra Dudek, "Begin with the Text: Aboriginal Literatures and Postcolonial Theories," in *Creating Community: A Roundtable on Canadian Aboriginal Literatures*, ed. Renate Eigenbrod and Jo-Ann Episkenew (Penticton, BC: Theytus Books, 2002), 103.
24. Frank M. Tierney and Angela Robbeson, preface to *Bolder Flights: Essays on the Canadian Long Poem*, ed. Frank M. Tierney and Angela Robbeson (Ottawa: University of Ottawa Press, 1998), 1.
25. Cook, "Bone Memory," 109n13.
26. Susan Stanford Friedman, "Craving Stories: Narrative and Lyric in Contemporary Theory and Women's Long Poems," in *Feminist Measures: Soundings in Poetry and Theory*, ed. Lynn Keller and Cristanne Miller (Ann Arbor: University of Michigan Press, 1994), 38.
27. Ibid., 15.
28. Gingell, "When X Equals Zero," 456; emphasis added.
29. See Dell Hymes, "Discovering Oral Performance and Measured Verse in American Indian Narrative," *New Literary History* 8.3 (1977): 431–57.
30. Gingell, "When X Equals Zero," 458.
31. Tierney and Robbeson, preface, 1.
32. Stephen Scobie, "Double Voicing: A View of Canadian Poetry," in *O Canada: Essays on Canadian Literature and Culture*, ed. Jørn Carlsen (Aarhus, Denmark: Aarhus University Press, 1995), 46.
33. Gingell, "When X Equals Zero," 452.
34. Wolfart and Carroll, *Meet Cree*, 93.

35. Nancy LeClaire and George Cardinal, comps., *Alberta Elders' Cree Dictionary/ alperta ohci kehtehayak nehiyaw otwestamâkewasinahikan*, ed. Earle Waugh (Edmonton: University of Alberta Press, 1998), sv. "okâwîmâw."
36. Ibid., sv. "askîy."
37. Halfe herself, in an article co-written with Linda Jaine (Cree), describes the wake in Cree culture as a "ceremony for delivering the body back to *Mother Earth*"; Linda Jaine and Louise Halfe, "Traditional Cree Philosophy: Death, Bereavement, and Healing," *Saskatchewan Indian* (March 1989): 11, www.sicc.sk.ca/saskindian/a89mar11.htm; emphasis added. The widespread notion of Mother Earth as a major figure in Indigenous mythology has been questioned by Sam D. Gill, who argues that "Mother Earth has come into existence in America largely during the last one hundred years and that her existence stems primarily from two creative groups: scholars and Indians"; Sam D. Gill, *Mother Earth: An American Story* (Chicago: University of Chicago Press, 1987), 7. Although Jace Weaver (Cherokee) admits that not necessarily every Indigenous tribe viewed the earth as female and that Indigenous notions of Mother Earth changed over time, he criticizes Gill's analysis for "ignor[ing] evidence that the fundamental notion is both ancient and widespread" in North America; Jace Weaver, "Notes from a Miner's Canary," introduction to *Defending Mother Earth: Native American Perspectives on Environmental Justice*, ed. Jace Weaver (Maryknoll, NY: Orbis Books, 1996), 10. Similarly, Christopher Vecsey finds it plausible "that in the last century a more unified, major Mother Earth concept has coalesced as part of pan-Indian religious culture," but he doubts "that American Indians had no notion of an Earth Mother until Christian Anglos gave them one"; Christopher Vecsey, review of *Native American Religious Action: A Performance Approach to Religion*, and *Mother Earth: An American Story*, by Sam D. Gill, *American Indian Quarterly* 12.3 (1988): 256. What should concern us most, then, is that the Cree people today honour Mother Earth as a life-giving force.
38. The narrator in *Blue Marrow* also captures male voices—those of the Jesuit priest, the fur trader, and her father—but she does so only to create a context for and thus to highlight the voices of her mothers (be they foremothers, grandmothers, or her own mother).
39. The use of macrons in written Cree indicates the length of vowels. In the transition from *Bear Bones and Feathers* to *Blue Marrow*, Halfe has switched from *âtayohkân* to *âtayôhkan*. Unless I am quoting, I will use her spelling of the word as found in the revised edition of *Blue Marrow*.
40. Halfe, "Cree Glossary," 107.
41. Louise Bernice Halfe, *Bear Bones and Feathers* (Regina: Coteau Books, 1994), 128. This change in translation might be explained by the fact that there were different people involved in creating the Cree glossaries for Halfe's two collections of poetry. Whereas the Cree glossary in *Blue Marrow* was put together by Halfe herself and edited by Jean Okimâsis and Arok Wolvengrey, the one in *Bear Bones and Feathers* was established with the help of Judy Bear and Mary Jane Eley of Saskatchewan Indian Federated College, according to the book's copyright page.
42. Ibid., 10, 11.
43. LeClaire and Cardinal, *Alberta Elders' Cree Dictionary*, sv. "âtayohkan."

44. Marjorie Memnook-White, "Cree Words in Halfe's *Blue Marrow*," e-mail communication, 5 February 2007.
45. Joseph F. Dion, *My Tribe, the Crees*, ed. Hugh A. Dempsey (Calgary: Glenbow Museum, 1979), 56.
46. David G. Mandelbaum, *The Plains Cree: An Ethnographic, Historical, and Comparative Study* (Regina: Canadian Plains Research Center, University of Regina, 1979), 157.
47. Halfe, "Cree Glossary," 108.
48. LeClaire and Cardinal, *Alberta Elders' Cree Dictionary*, sv. "pawakan."
49. Mandelbaum, *Plains Cree*, 157.
50. Ibid., 160.
51. Dudek, "Begin with the Text," 101; emphasis added.
52. Dudek, ibid., reads the people and animals populating *Blue Marrow* as "the bones and marrow of the poems," but I believe Halfe's imagery to be more complex than that. Although the bones beneath *okâwîmâwaskiy* guide the narrator's fingers on the page, thus producing the narrative's grid, it is a particular component of the ancestors' bones, their marrow, that gives birth to the stories of *Blue Marrow*. It is indeed not ink but blood that the bones leave behind on the page as they guide the narrator's fingers ("See the blood" [3]): "My relatives wake. / Fingers and toes winged, / cord strung in our / infant moccasins. / We've gathered / splintered bones, / weave, mend / the blue marrow" (46). The narrator "weave[s] and mend[s]" that substance in bone cavities in which blood cells are produced. What makes the ancestors so precious to the narrator are these blood cells, the very stories that give life to and define the ancestors and, by extension, the narrator and her children.
53. Gerald McMaster, *Edward Poitras: Canada XLVI Biennale di Venezia* (Hull, QC: Canadian Museum of Civilization, 1995), 87.
54. See, for example, 15, 19, 23, 46, 51, 76, 77.
55. Dudek, "Begin with the Text," 102.
56. "women"; Halfe, "Cree Glossary," 104.
57. "your daughters"; ibid., 105.
58. Church of England, *The book of common prayer And administration of the sacraments, and other rites and ceremonies of the church, according to the use of Church of England; together with the Psalter or Psalms of David, pointed as they are to be sung or said in churches* (London, 1702; Eighteenth Century Collections Online, 3 September 2010), 44.
59. "1. the land/horizon of abundant beauty and life"; Halfe, "Cree Glossary," 108.
60. "1. earth, 2. soil, 3. dirt, 4. clay, 5. mud"; ibid., 103.
61. "1. sky, 2. the Heavens"; ibid., 105.
62. "love"; ibid., 108.
63. "kindness"; ibid., 105.
64. "Creator of All, Giver of Life"; ibid.
65. "the Thunders"; ibid., 108.
66. "the very Elderly Women; they are held in high esteem"; ibid., 107.
67. "the very Elderly Men; they are held in high esteem"; ibid., 105.
68. "deliberate, weighing thought"; ibid., 106.
69. "the Sweatlodge; the lodge where All Relations bear witness of tears and healing"; ibid., 105.

70. Mandelbaum, *Plains Cree*, 143.
71. This journey is linked to becoming a storyteller. The bone/marrow imagery passage quoted above also reveals this connection through the reference to moccasins: "My relatives wake. / Fingers and toes winged, / cord strung in our / infant moccasins. / We've gathered / splintered bones, / weave, mend / the blue marrow" (46).
72. Mandelbaum, *Plains Cree*, 227.
73. Ibid., 178.
74. Dion, *My Tribe*, 57.
75. Ibid., 58.
76. The cover design of the revised edition of *Blue Marrow* includes a photograph of four Cree women (Halfe's own grandmothers, according to the copyright page) set against a picture of the northern lights (*kânîmihitocik*). Communicating Cree culture on Cree terms, the cover image connects *kânîmihitocik* and the fore- and grandmothers telling their stories to the narrator with the bone/marrow imagery in the title of the book. The book's title thus represents a complex metaphor that points to the interconnectedness of people and their storied heritage or, to use Dudek's words, "the embodied nature of the stories."
77. This observation is further strengthened by the fact that the narrator, as she eventually admits, does "not recognize who speaks" (18, 61).
78. "s/he puts her/his land elsewhere"; Halfe, "Cree Glossary," 104.
79. Halfe, *Blue Marrow*, 1st ed., 1.
80. Ibid., 5.
81. Cook, "Bone Memory," 104. Cook's use of "membering" refers to what Warren Cariou (Métis) calls "a communitarian kind of memory, one that connects recollection with the idea of *membership* in a larger whole"; it is "a performance of social bonding"; Warren Cariou, "'We Use Dah Membering': Oral Memory in Métis Short Stories," in *Tropes and Territories: Short Fiction, Postcolonial Readings, Canadian Writings in Context*, ed. Marta Dvořák and W.H. New (Montreal: McGill-Queen's University Press, 2007), 195.
82. This chant is also included in the poem "Ditch Bitch" in Halfe's first collection of poetry; Halfe, *Bear Bones*, 50–51. Halfe describes it there as a song "sung by many Plains Cree people" (128).
83. *Ahâw* translates into "alright, okay, that's it"; Halfe, "Cree Glossary," 103. While the Cree glossary in *Bear Bones and Feathers* also gives "amen" as a translation of *ahâw* (Halfe, *Bear Bones*, 129), the Cree glossary in *Blue Marrow* does not.
84. Dennis Tedlock, *The Spoken Word and the Work of Interpretation* (Philadelphia: University of Pennsylvania Press, 1983), 161.
85. Thomas King, introduction to *All My Relations: An Anthology of Contemporary Canadian Native Fiction*, ed. Thomas King (Toronto: McClelland and Stewart, 1990), ix.
86. Except for "Ram Woman," an N N compound, all these chunks of language are phrasal.
87. Halfe, *Blue Marrow*, 1st ed., 90.
88. See also Chapter 2 (pp. 73, 93, 99–100), Chapter 3 (p. 134), and Chapter 4 (pp. 168–70) in this volume.
89. Cook, "Bone Memory," 97.

90. See Martha B. Kendall, who has argued that Northern Yuman personal names "must be considered abbreviated texts or allusions to narratives, whose significance is social as well as cultural"; Martha B. Kendall, "Exegesis and Translation: Northern Yuman Names as Texts," *Journal of Anthropological Research* 36.3 (1980): 261.
91. The first edition does not give the names of the female voices passed on by the narrator and thus lacks the rhetorical effect produced by these paraholophrases.
92. The first edition of *Blue Marrow* omits these evocations and so does not establish these important links to the opening. As a result, it lacks the textualization of orality that is achieved in the second edition.
93. The first edition of *Blue Marrow* contains only the bilingual recitation of this prayer; Halfe, *Blue Marrow*, 1st ed., 16.
94. See, for example, "All Women. Grandmothers and / the Eternal Grandmothers beseech / êy êy êy nôsisim ["my grandchild"] / here this needle / thread its eye / oh these âcimowinisa—" (63) and "All Women. Grandmothers / and Eternal Grandmothers endure / *mâto, nitânis* / Cry, my daughter. / The leaves have not collected our dust, / the veins crumpled into soil" (72). Other examples are on pages 30 and 85.
95. See, for example, "We will guide your feather, / dipped in ink" (27); "When the Voices roar, / I write. / Sometimes they sing, / are silent" (53); "They sing me to *kîwêtinohk*. / North. They bundle me home" (60); and "Thunderbirds woke me. / Wings flapping against their dance, / slamming doors, crashing windows. / I tucked my head. / Sliced fingers on these musty papers / where I singed their feathers" (79). Other examples are on pages 32, 33, 60, and 63.
96. Cook, "Bone Memory," 95.
97. LeClaire and Cardinal, *Alberta Elders' Cree Dictionary*, sv. "kiskeyitam."
98. Translating into "Bone-Pile-Up" or "Where the Bones are Piled"; Halfe, "Cree Glossary," 107.
99. That is, "Fast Flowing River, Strong Current River"; ibid., 108.
100. Stigter, "Dialectics," 52.
101. Cook, "Bone Memory," 94.
102. Gingell, "When X Equals Zero," 453.
103. Stigter, "Dialectics," 57.
104. Thomas King in Jennifer Andrews, "Border Trickery and Dog Bones: A Conversation with Thomas King," *Studies in Canadian Literature/Études en littérature canadienne* 24.2 (1999): 181.
105. Stigter, "Dialectics," 50.
106. *Cihcipistikwân* "Rolling Head" (Halfe, "Cree Glossary," 104) is a central figure in the Cree creation story (see Ahenakew, "Cree Trickster Tales," 309–13) and features prominently in Halfe's third collection of poetry, *The Crooked Good*.
107. For example, "kayâs-âcimowin nôtokwêsiw wîhtam" ("ancient story / old woman / she tells it" [25]); "*ohkomipan* continuous the confession" (21); "*câpân*, Grandmother, continues" (32).
108. For example, "ohkomipan, *I am she who speaks*" (20); "I am câpân, the grandmother who shamed her family when sound choked me" (31).
109. See the beginning of Glecia Bear's children's story in the appendix for an example of the frequent use of evidentials in traditional Cree storytelling.

110. Gérard Genette, *Figures of Literary Discourse*, trans. Alan Sheridan (New York: Columbia University Press, 1982), 54.
111. See Mandelbaum, *Plains Cree*, 229–32.

CONCLUSION

1. Arnold Krupat, *The Turn to the Native: Studies in Criticism and Culture* (Lincoln: University of Nebraska Press, 1996), 38.
2. Milman Parry, "Studies in the Epic Technique of Oral Verse-Making: I. Homer and Homeric Style," *Harvard Studies in Classical Philology* 41 (1930): 80.
3. Robin Ridington, "Dogs, Snares, and Cartridge Belts: The Poetics of a Northern Athapaskan Narrative Technology," in *The Social Dynamics of Technology: Practice, Politics, and World Views*, ed. Marcia-Anne Dobres and Christopher R. Hoffman (Washington: Smithsonian Institution Press, 1999), 179–80.
4. Richard Bauman, *Verbal Art as Performance*, with essays by Barbara A. Babcock et al. (Prospect Heights, IL: Waveland Press, 1984), 15–16.
5. Opening and closing frames in Indigenous literature, then, have to be distinguished from narrative frames found in Western novels, such as Emily Brontë's *Wuthering Heights* (London, 1847) or Joseph Conrad's *Heart of Darkness* (1902). Like the narrative frames in Western novels, opening and closing frames can involve fictive oral storytelling, but the purpose of opening and closing frames clearly goes beyond "the *imitation*, or *representation*, of a teller, his story, and an implied audience"; Robert Scholes and Robert Kellogg, "The Oral Heritage of Written Narrative," in *The Nature of Narrative*, by Robert Scholes and Robert Kellogg (1966; reprint, New York: Oxford University Press, 1971), 53.
6. Kenneth Burke, *A Rhetoric of Motives* (1950; reprint, Berkeley: University of California Press, 1969), 58.
7. Bauman, *Verbal Art*, 16.
8. Of course, Indigenous readers not familiar with the respective language and cultural traditions might still have some access to these contexts, depending on their backgrounds.
9. Scott Richard Lyons, "Rhetorical Sovereignty: What Do American Indians Want from Writing?" *College Composition and Communication* 51.3 (2000): 449–50.
10. Marianne Mithun, *The Languages of Native North America* (Cambridge, UK: Cambridge University Press, 1999), 38.
11. See Aristotle, *Rhetoric*, in *The Complete Works of Aristotle: The Revised Oxford Translation*, ed. Julian Barnes, 2 vols. (Princeton, NJ: Princeton University Press, 1983), Vol. 2, 1356a2–1356a21.
12. I owe this term to discussions with Ted Dyck.

APPENDIX

1. H. Christoph Wolfart, "Introduction to the Texts," in *kôhkominawak otâcimowiniwâwa/Our Grandmothers' Lives, as Told in Their Own Words*, by Glecia Bear et al., ed. and trans. Freda Ahenakew and H. Christoph Wolfart (Saskatoon: Fifth House Publishers, 1992), 31.
2. Glecia Bear, "Lost and Found," in *kôhkominawak otâcimowiniwâwa/Our Grandmothers' Lives, as Told in Their Own Words*, by Glecia Bear et al., ed. and trans. Freda Ahenakew and H. Christoph Wolfart (Saskatoon: Fifth House Publishers, 1992), 123–44.
3. H. Christoph Wolfart, "Notes," in *kôhkominawak otâcimowiniwâwa/Our Grandmothers' Lives, as Told in Their Own Words*, by Glecia Bear et al., ed. and trans. Freda Ahenakew and H. Christoph Wolfart (Saskatoon: Fifth House Publishers, 1992), 374.
4. Wolfart, "Introduction," 33.
5. Glecia Bear, *wanisinwak iskwêsisak: awâsisasinahikanis/Two Little Girls Lost in the Bush: A Cree Story for Children*, ed. and trans. Freda Ahenakew and H. Christoph Wolfart (Saskatoon: Fifth House Publishers, 1991), 2.
6. I would like to thank Dorothy Thunder (Cree; Faculty of Native Studies, University of Alberta) for proofreading my interlinear translation of Bear's story. All remaining errors, of course, are entirely my responsibility.

GLOSSARY

1. See Thomas King, *Green Grass, Running Water* (1993; reprint, Toronto: HarperPerennialCanada, 1999).
2. Monica Heller, introduction to *Codeswitching: Anthropological and Sociolinguistic Perspectives*, ed. Monica Heller (Berlin: Mouton de Gruyter, 1988), 1.
3. See Peter Koch and Wulf Oesterreicher, "Sprache der Nähe—Sprache der Distanz: Mündlichkeit und Schriftlichkeit im Spannungsfeld von Sprachtheorie und Sprachgeschichte," *Romanistisches Jahrbuch* 36 (1985): 15–43.
4. Eugene Nida and Charles A. Taber, *The Theory and Practice of Translation* (Leiden: E.J. Brill, 1969).
5. Neal McLeod, *Songs to Kill a Wîhtikow* (Regina: Hagios Press, 2005), 42.
6. *The Oxford English Dictionary*, 2nd ed., s.v. "Holophrasis."
7. Bernard Comrie, *Language Universals and Linguistic Typology: Syntax and Morphology*, 2nd ed. (Oxford: Basil Blackwell, 1989), 45.
8. Koch and Oesterreicher, "Sprache der Nähe," 21.
9. Martin Nystrand, "The Role of Context in Written Communication," *Comprehending Oral and Written Language*, ed. Rosalind Horowitz and S. Jay Samuels (San Diego: Academic, 1987), 206.
10. Ibid.
11. Ferdinand de Saussure, *Course in General Linguistics*, trans. Wade Baskin, ed. Charles Bally and Albert Sechehaye (London: Peter Owen, 1960).

12. See ibid.
13. Comrie, *Language Universals*, 45.
14. Ingo Plag, *Morphological Productivity: Structural Constraints in English Derivation* (Berlin: Mouton de Gruyter, 1999), 6.
15. Pavel Trost, "Tzv. Citátová komposita v němčině," *Cizí jazyky ve škole* 26.1 (1982–83): 18.
16. Richard Van Camp, *The Lesser Blessed* (1996; reprint, Vancouver: Douglas and McIntyre, 2004), 37.
17. Andrew Spencer, *Morphological Theory: An Introduction to Word Structure in Generative Grammar* (Oxford: Basil Blackwell, 1991), 319.
18. Ibid.

Works Cited

Abel, Kerry. *Drum Songs: Glimpses of Dene History*. Montreal: McGill-Queen's University Press, 1993.

Afable, Patricia O., and Madison S. Beeler. "Place-Names." In Goddard, *Languages*, 185–99.

Ahenakew, Edward. "Cree Trickster Tales." *Journal of American Folklore* 42 (1929): 309–53.

Alexie, Robert Arthur. *Porcupines and China Dolls*. Toronto: Stoddart Publishing, 2002.

Alia, Valerie. "Ipellie's Interior Visions." *Up Here* 5.5 (1989): 59.

Allen, Paula Gunn. *Grandmothers of the Light: A Medicine Woman's Sourcebook*. Boston: Beacon Press, 1991.

Alunik, Ishmael. *Call Me Ishmael: Memories of Ishmael Alunik, Inuvialuk Elder*. Inuvik, NWT: Kolausok Ublaaq Enterprises, 1998.

Alunik, Ishmael, Eddie D. Kolausok, and David Morrison. *Across Time and Tundra: The Inuvialuit of the Western Arctic*. Vancouver: Raincoast Books; Seattle: University of Washington Press; Gatineau, QC: Canadian Museum of Civilization, 2003.

Andrews, Jennifer. "Border Trickery and Dog Bones: A Conversation with Thomas King." *Studies in Canadian Literature/Études en littérature canadienne* 24.2 (1999): 161–85.

———. "Reading Thomas King's *Green Grass, Running Water*: Border-Crossing Humour." *ESC: English Studies in Canada* 28.1 (2002): 91–116.

Andrews, Thomas D., and John B. Zoe. "The Dogrib Birchbark Canoe Project." *Arctic* 51.1 (1998): 75–84.

Angilirq, Paul Apak. *Atanarjuat, the Fast Runner: Inspired by a Traditional Inuit Legend of Igloolik*. Toronto: Coach House Books and Isuma Publishing, 2002.

Aristotle. *The Complete Works of Aristotle: The Revised Oxford Translation*. Edited by Julian Barnes. 2 vols. Princeton, NJ: Princeton University Press, 1983.

Armstrong, Jeannette C. "Land Speaking." In Ortiz, *Speaking for the Generations*, 174–94.

Attla, Catherine. *K'etetaalkkaanee, the One Who Paddles among the People and Animals: The Story of an Ancient Traveller*. Translated by Eliza Jones. Nenana, AK: Yukon Koyukuk School District; Fairbanks: Yukon Koyukuk School District, Alaska Native Language Center, 1990.

Aupilaarjuk, Mariano, et al. *Cosmology and Shamanism*. Edited by Bernard Saladin d'Anglure. Vol. 4 of *Interviewing Inuit Elders*. Iqaluit: Language and Culture Program, Nunavut Arctic College, 2001.

Austin, Mary. *The American Rhythm: Studies and Reexpressions of Amerindian Songs*. Enlarged ed. 1930. Reprint, New York: Cooper Square Publishers, 1970.

Babcock, Barbara. "'A Tolerated Margin of Mess': The Trickster and His Tales Reconsidered." In *Critical Essays on Native American Literature*, edited by Andrew Wiget, 153–85. Boston: G.K. Hall, 1985.

Baker, Mark C. *The Atoms of Language*. New York: Basic Books, 2001.

Bal, Mieke. *Narratology: Introduction to the Theory of Narrative*. 3rd ed. Toronto: University of Toronto Press, 2009.

Balzer, Geraldine. "'Bring[ing] Them Back from the Inside Out': Coming Home through Story in Richard Wagamese's *Keeper 'n Me*." In Gingell, *Textualizing Orature and Orality*, 222–39.

Barber, Karin. *The Anthropology of Texts, Persons, and Publics*. Cambridge, UK: Cambridge University Press, 2007.

Bartelt, Guillermo. "American Indian English in Momaday's *House Made of Dawn*." *Language and Literature* 19 (1994): 37–53.

———. *Socio- and Stylolinguistic Perspectives on American Indian English Texts*. Lewiston, NY: Edwin Mellen Press, 2001.

Barthes, Roland. *Elements of Semiology*. Translated by Annette Lavers and Colin Smith. London: Cape, 1967.

———. "An Introduction to the Structural Analysis of Narrative." *New Literary History* 6.2 (1975): 237–72.

———. *Mythologies*. Selected and translated by Annette Lavers. New York: Hill and Wang, 1972.

Baugh, Albert C., and Thomas Cable. *A History of the English Language*. 5th ed. London: Routledge, 2002.

Bauman, Richard. *Verbal Art as Performance*. With essays by Barbara A. Babcock et al. Prospect Heights, IL: Waveland Press, 1984.

Bear, Glecia. "Lost and Found." In Bear et al., *kôhkominawak otâcimowiniwâwa*, 123–44.

———. *wanisinwak iskwêsisak: awâsisasinahikanis/Two Little Girls Lost in the Bush: A Cree Story for Children*. Translated and edited by Freda Ahenakew and H. Christoph Wolfart. Saskatoon: Fifth House Publishers, 1991.

Bear, Glecia, et al. *kôhkominawak otâcimowiniwâwa/Our Grandmothers' Lives, as Told in Their Own Words*. Translated and edited by Freda Ahenakew and H. Christoph Wolfart. Saskatoon: Fifth House Publishers, 1992.

Bennett, John, and Susan Rowley, comps. and eds. *Uqalurait: An Oral History of Nunavut*. Montreal: McGill-Queen's University Press, 2004.

Bennett, Simon. "Simon Bennett Stories." *Inuvialuit* (summer 1981): 13–17.

Bevis, William. "Native American Novels: Homing In." In Swann and Krupat, *Recovering the Word*, 580–620.

Biber, Douglas. *Dimensions of Register Variation: A Cross-Linguistic Comparison*. Cambridge, UK: Cambridge University Press, 1995.

Birk, Hanne. "Kulturspezifische Inszenierungen kollektiver Gedächtnismedien in autochthonen Literaturen Kanadas: Alootook Ipellies *Arctic Dreams and Nightmares* und Ruby Slipperjacks *Weesquachak and the Lost Ones*." In *Medien des kollektiven Gedächtnisses: Konstruktivität, Historizität, Kulturspezifität*, edited by Astrid Erll and Ansgar Nünning, 217–34. Berlin: Walter de Gruyter, 2004.

Blaeser, Kimberly M. *Gerald Vizenor: Writing in the Oral Tradition*. Norman: University of Oklahoma Press, 1996.

———. "Trickster: A Compendium." In *Buried Roots and Indestructible Seeds: The Survival of American Indian Life in Story, History, and Spirit*, edited by Mark A. Lindquist and Martin Zanger, 47–66. Madison: University of Wisconsin Press, 1994.

———. "Writing Voices Speaking: Native Authors and an Oral Aesthetic." In *Talking on the Page: Editing Aboriginal Oral Texts*, edited by Laura J. Murray and Keren Rice, 53–68. Toronto: University of Toronto Press, 1999.

Blondin, George. *Trail of the Spirit: The Mysteries of Medicine Power Revealed*. Edmonton: NeWest Press, 2006.

———. *When the World Was New: Stories of the Sahtú Dene*. Yellowknife, NWT: Outcrop, the Northern Publisher, 1990.

———. *Yamoria, the Lawmaker: Stories of the Dene*. Edmonton: NeWest Press, 1997.

Bloomfield, Leonard. *Sacred Stories of the Sweet Grass Cree*. Ottawa: National Museum of Canada, 1930.

"Blue Marrow." Coteau Books. www.coteaubooks.com/index.php?p=Books &listing id=27.

Bright, William. *A Coyote Reader*. Berkeley: University of California Press, 1993.

Brill de Ramírez, Susan Berry. *Contemporary American Indian Literatures and the Oral Tradition.* Tucson: University of Arizona Press, 1999.

Brontë, Emily. *Wuthering Heights.* London: T. C. Newby, 1847.

Brotherston, Gordon. *Book of the Fourth World: Reading the Native Americas through Their Literature.* Cambridge, UK: Cambridge University Press, 1992.

Burke, Kenneth. *A Rhetoric of Motives.* 1950. Reprint, Berkeley: University of California Press, 1969.

Burns, John. Rev. of *The Lesser Blessed*, by Richard Van Camp. *Georgia Straight*, 28 November 1996.

Campbell, Maria, trans. *Stories of the Road Allowance People.* Penticton, BC: Theytus Books, 1995.

Canton, Jeffrey. "Coyote Lives: Thomas King." In *The Power to Bend Spoons: Interviews with Canadian Novelists*, edited by Beverley Daurio, 90–97. Toronto: Mercury Press, 1998.

Cariou, Warren. "'We Use Dah Membering': Oral Memory in Métis Short Stories." In *Tropes and Territories: Short Fiction, Postcolonial Readings, Canadian Writings in Context*, edited by Marta Dvořák and W.H. New, 193–201. Montreal: McGill-Queen's University Press, 2007.

Carpenter, Edmund. "Image Making in Arctic Art." In *Sign, Image, Symbol*, edited by Gyorgy Kepes, 206–25. New York: G. Braziller, 1966.

Chafe, Wallace L. "The Deployment of Consciousness in the Production of a Narrative." In *The Pear Stories: Cognitive, Cultural, and Linguistic Aspects of Narrative Production*, edited by Wallace L. Chafe, 9–50. Norwood, NJ: Ablex Publishing, 1980.

———. *Discourse, Consciousness, and Time: The Flow and Displacement of Conscious Experience in Speaking and Writing.* Chicago: University of Chicago Press, 1994.

———. "Discourse Effects on Polysynthesis." In *Discourse across Languages and Cultures*, edited by Carol Lynn Moder and Aida Martinovic-Zic, 37–52. Amsterdam: John Benjamins Publishing, 2004.

———. "Integration and Involvement in Speaking, Writing, and Oral Literature." In Tannen, *Spoken and Written Language*, 35–53.

———. "Integration and Involvement in Spoken and Written Language." In *Semiotics Unfolding*, vol. 2 of *Proceedings of the Second Congress of the International Association for Semiotic Studies, Vienna, July 1979*, edited by Tasso Borbé, 1095–1102. Berlin: Mouton Publishers, 1979.

———. "Writing in the Perspective of Speaking." In *Studying Writing: Linguistic Approaches*, edited by Charles R. Cooper and Sidney Greenbaum, 12–39. Beverly Hills: Sage Publications, 1986.

Chafe, Wallace L., and Jane Danielewicz. "Properties of Spoken and Written Language." In Horowitz and Samuels, *Comprehending Oral and Written Language*, 83–113.

Chafe, Wallace L., and Johanna Nichols. Introduction to *Evidentiality: The Linguistic Coding of Epistemology*, edited by Wallace L. Chafe and Johanna Nichols, vii–xi. Norwood, NJ: Ablex Publishing, 1986.

Chafe, Wallace L., and Deborah Tannen. "The Relation between Written and Spoken Language." *Annual Review of Anthropology* 16 (1987): 383–407.

Chamberlin, J. Edward. "From Hand to Mouth: The Postcolonial Politics of Oral and Written Traditions." In *Reclaiming Indigenous Voice and Vision*, edited by Marie Battiste, 124–41. Vancouver: UBC Press, 2000.

Chandonnet, Ann. Preface to Oman, *The Epic of Quyaq*, vii–xii.

Chester, Blanca. "*Green Grass, Running Water*: Theorizing the World of the Novel." *Canadian Literature* 161–62 (1999): 44–61.

Church of England. *The book of common prayer And administration of the sacraments, and other rites and ceremonies of the church, according to the use of Church of England; together with the Psalter or Psalms of David, pointed as they are to be sung or said in churches*. London, 1702. Eighteenth Century Collections Online.

Comrie, Bernard. *Language Universals and Linguistic Typology: Syntax and Morphology*. 2nd ed. Oxford: Basil Blackwell, 1989.

Conrad, Joseph. "Heart of Darkness." In Conrad, *Youth: A Narrative and Two Other Stories*, 49–182. Edinburgh and London: William Blackwood and Sons, 1902.

Cook, Méira. "Bone Memory: Transcribing Voice in Louise Bernice Halfe's *Blue Marrow*." *Canadian Literature* 166 (2000): 85–110.

Cooley, Dennis. *The Vernacular Muse: The Eye and Ear in Contemporary Literature*. Winnipeg: Turnstone Press, 1987.

Daly, Richard. "Writing on the Landscape: Protoliteracy and Psychic Travel in Oral Cultures." In *They Write Their Dream on the Rock Forever: Rock Writings of the Stein River Valley of British Columbia*, by Annie York, Richard Daly, and Chris Arnett, 223–60. Vancouver: Talonbooks, 1993.

Davidson, Arnold E., Priscilla L. Walton, and Jennifer Andrews. *Border Crossings: Thomas King's Cultural Inversions*. Toronto: University of Toronto Press, 2003.

Dene Wodih Society, comp. *Wolverine Myths and Visions: Dene Traditions from Northern Alberta*. Edited by Patrick Moore and Angela Wheelock. Edmonton: University of Alberta Press, 1990.

Derrida, Jacques. *Of Grammatology*. Translated by Gayatri Chakravorty Spivak. Baltimore, MD: Johns Hopkins University Press, 1976.

Dion, Joseph F. *My Tribe, the Crees*. Edited by Hugh A. Dempsey. Calgary: Glenbow Museum, 1979.

Donaldson, Laura E. "Noah Meets Old Coyote; Or Singing in the Rain: Intertextuality in Thomas King's *Green Grass, Running Water*." *Studies in American Indian Literatures*, 2nd ser., 7.2 (1995): 27–43.

Doueihi, Anne. "Inhabiting the Space between Discourse and Story in Trickster Narratives." In Hynes and Doty, *Mythical Trickster Figures*, 193–201. Originally published as "Trickster: On Inhabiting the Space between Discourse and Story." *Soundings* 67.3 (1984): 283–311.

Dudek, Debra. "Begin with the Text: Aboriginal Literatures and Postcolonial Theories." In *Creating Community: A Roundtable on Canadian Aboriginal Literatures*, edited by Renate Eigenbrod and Jo-Ann Episkenew, 89–108. Penticton, BC: Theytus Books, 2002.

Dunn, Maggie, and Ann Morris. *The Composite Novel: The Short Story Cycle in Transition*. New York: Twayne Publishers; Toronto: Maxwell Macmillan Canada; New York: Maxwell Macmillan International, 1995.

Éjchenbaum, Boris M. "The Illusion of *Skaz*." Translated by Martin P. Rice. *Russian Literature Triquarterly* 12 (1975): 233–36.

Eliade, Mircea. *Shamanism: Archaic Techniques of Ecstasy*. Translated by Willard R. Trask. London: Routledge and Kegan Paul, 1970.

Erzgräber, Willi. *James Joyce: Oral and Written Discourse as Mirrored in Experimental Narrative Art*. Frankfurt am Main: Peter Lang, 2002.

Erzgräber, Willi, and Paul Goetsch, eds. *Mündliches Erzählen im Alltag, fingiertes mündliches Erzählen in der Literatur*. Tübingen: Gunter Narr Verlag, 1987.

Evans, Nicholas, and Hans-Jürgen Sasse. "Introduction: Problems of Polysynthesis." In *Problems of Polysynthesis*, edited by Nicholas Evans and Hans-Jürgen Sasse, 1–13. Berlin: Akademie Verlag, 2002.

Fagan, Kristina. "What's the Trouble with the Trickster? An Introduction." In *Troubling Tricksters: Revisioning Critical Conversations*, edited by Deanna Reder and Linda M. Morra, 3–20. Waterloo, ON: Wilfrid Laurier University Press, 2010.

Fee, Margery. "Writing Orality: Interpreting Literature in English by Aboriginal Writers in North America, Australia, and New Zealand." *Journal of Intercultural Studies* 18.1 (1997): 23–39.

Feeling, Durbin, comp. *Cherokee-English Dictionary*. Edited by William Pulte. Tahlequah: Cherokee Nation of Oklahoma, 1975.

Feldman, Carol Fleisher. "Oral Metalanguage." In *Literacy and Orality*, edited by David R. Olson and Nancy Torrance, 47–65. Cambridge, UK: Cambridge University Press, 1991.

Finnegan, Ruth. "What Is Orality—If Anything?" *Byzantine and Modern Greek Studies* 14 (1990): 130–49.

Flick, Jane. "Reading Notes for Thomas King's *Green Grass, Running Water*." *Canadian Literature* 161-62 (1999): 140–72.

French, David H., and Kathrine S. French. "Personal Names." In Goddard, *Languages*, 200–21.

Friedman, Susan Stanford. "Craving Stories: Narrative and Lyric in Contemporary Theory and Women's Long Poems." In *Feminist Measures: Soundings in Poetry and Theory*, edited by Lynn Keller and Cristanne Miller, 15–42. Ann Arbor: University of Michigan Press, 1994.

Gautreau, Evalyn. *Tale Spinners in a Spruce Tipi*. Ottawa: Borealis Press, 1981.

Genette, Gérard. *Figures of Literary Discourse*. Translated by Alan Sheridan. New York: Columbia University Press, 1982.

Gessell, Paul. "Dreaming in the Arctic." *Ottawa Citizen*, 6 February 1994, D5.

Gibert, Teresa. "Narrative Strategies in Thomas King's Short Stories." In *Telling Stories: Postcolonial Short Fiction in English*, edited by Jacqueline Bardolph, 67–76. Amsterdam: Rodopi, 2001.

Gill, Sam D. *Mother Earth: An American Story*. Chicago: University of Chicago Press, 1987.

Gill, Sam D., and Irene F. Sullivan, comps. *Dictionary of Native American Mythology*. Santa Barbara, CA: ABC-CLIO, 1992.

Gingell, Susan. Introduction in Gingell, *Textualizing Orature and Orality*, 1–18.

———. "Lips' Inking: Cree Writings of the Oral in Canada and What They Might Tell Educators." Paper presented at Celebrating the Local, Negotiating the School: Symposium on English Language and Literacy in Aboriginal Communities, Aboriginal Education Research Centre, University of Saskatchewan, Saskatoon, 7–8 November 2008. http://aerc.usask.ca/downloads/Gingell-DRAFTpager.pdf.

———. "'One Small Medicine': An Interview with Maria Campbell." In Gingell, *Textualizing Orature and Orality*, 188–205.

———. "Teaching the Talk that Walks on Paper: Oral Traditions and Textualized Orature in the Canadian Literature Classroom." In *Home-Work: Postcolonialism, Pedagogy, and Canadian Literature*, edited by Cynthia Sugars, 285–300. Ottawa: University of Ottawa Press, 2004.

———. "When X Equals Zero: The Politics of Voice in First Peoples Poetry by Women." *ESC: English Studies in Canada* 24.4 (1998): 447–66.

———, ed. *Textualizing Orature and Orality*. Special issue of *Essays on Canadian Writing* 83 (2004).

Goddard, Ives. "Synonymy." In *Arctic*, edited by David Damas, 5–7. Vol. 5 of *Handbook of North American Indians*, gen. ed. William C. Sturtevant. Washington, DC: Smithsonian Institution Press, 1984.

———, ed. *Languages*. Vol. 17 of *Handbook of North American Indians*, gen. ed. William C. Sturtevant. Washington, DC: Smithsonian Institution Press, 1996.

Goetsch, Paul. "Fingierte Mündlichkeit in der Erzählkunst entwickelter Schriftkulturen." *Poetica* 17.3–4 (1985): 202–18.

———. *Hardys Wessex-Romane: Mündlichkeit, Schriftlichkeit, kultureller Wandel*. Tübingen: Gunter Narr Verlag, 1994.

———. *The Oral and the Written in Nineteenth-Century British Fiction*. Frankfurt am Main: Peter Lang, 2003.

———, ed. *Dialekte und Fremdsprachen in der Literatur*. Tübingen: Gunter Narr Verlag, 1987.

———, ed. *Mündliches Wissen in neuzeitlicher Literatur*. Tübingen: Gunter Narr Verlag, 1990.

Goldman, Marlene. "Mapping and Dreaming: Native Resistance in *Green Grass, Running Water*." *Canadian Literature* 161–62 (1999): 18–41.

Gómez-Vega, Ibis. "Subverting the 'Mainstream' Paradigm through Magical Realism in Thomas King's *Green Grass, Running Water*." *Journal of the Midwest Modern Language Association* 33.1 (2000): 1–19.

Grant, Agnes. Introduction to *Our Bit of Truth: An Anthology of Native Canadian Literature*, edited by Agnes Grant, vi–x. Winnipeg: Pemmican Publications, 1990.

Griem, Julika. *Brüchiges Seemannsgarn: Mündlichkeit und Schriftlichkeit im Werk Joseph Conrads*. PhD diss., Universität Freiburg i. Br., 1995. Tübingen: Gunter Narr Verlag, 1995.

Gunn, Stacey Curry. "King Novel Popular in Canadian Literature Courses." *@ Guelph* 46.4 (27 February 2002). University of Guelph. www.uoguelph.ca/atguelph/02-02-27/articles/king.html.

Gzowski, Peter. "Peter Gzowski Interviews Thomas King on *Green Grass, Running Water*." *Canadian Literature* 161–62 (1999): 65–76.

Habermalz, Sabine. "'Signs on a White Field': A Look at Orality in Literacy and James Joyce's *Ulysses*." *Oral Tradition* 13.2 (1998): 285–305.

Halfe, Louise Bernice. *Bear Bones and Feathers*. Regina: Coteau Books, 1994.

———. *Blue Marrow*. Toronto: McClelland and Stewart, 1998.

———. *Blue Marrow*. Regina: Coteau Books, 2004.

———. "Cree Glossary." In Halfe, *Blue Marrow* (2004), 103–09.

———. *The Crooked Good*. Regina: Coteau Books, 2007.

Hamer, Penelope. "Beyond the Nineteenth Century: Thomas King's Decolonization of the Literary Image of the Native." MA thesis, Concordia University, 1995.

Hedge Coke, Allison Adelle. "Seeds." In Ortiz, *Speaking for the Generations*, 92–116.

Heller, Monica. Introduction to *Codeswitching: Anthropological and Sociolinguistic Perspectives*, edited by Monica Heller, 1–24. Berlin: Mouton de Gruyter, 1988.

Helm, June. "Dogrib." In *Subarctic*, edited by June Helm, 291–309. Vol. 6 of *Handbook of North American Indians*, gen. ed. William C. Sturtevant. Washington, DC: Smithsonian Institution Press, 1981.

———. "Tlicho (Dogrib)." In *The Canadian Encyclopedia*, revised by Thomas D. Andrews. www.thecanadianencyclopedia.com/index.cfm?PgNm=TCE&Params=A1ARTA0002332.

———. *Prophecy and Power among the Dogrib Indians*. Lincoln: University of Nebraska Press, 1994.

Helm, June, and Vital Thomas. "Tales from the Dogribs [Part I]." *The Beaver* 47.3 (1966): 16–20.

Hill, Archibald A. "The Typology of Writing Systems." In *Papers in Linguistics in Honor of Léon Dostert*, edited by William M. Austin, 92–99. The Hague: Mouton, 1967.

Hinnells, John R., ed. *The Penguin Dictionary of Religions*. Harmondsworth, UK: Penguin Books, 1984.

Hirschfelder, Arlene, and Paulette Molin, comps. *Encyclopedia of Native American Religions: An Introduction*. Updated ed. New York: Checkmark Books, 2001.

Hobson, Geary. Rev. of *The Lesser Blessed*, by Richard Van Camp. *Studies in American Indian Literatures*, 2nd ser., 10.4 (1998): 77–79.

Holm, Tom, J. Diane Pearson, and Ben Chavis. "Peoplehood: A Model for the Extension of Sovereignty in American Indian Studies." *Wicazo Sa Review* 18.1 (2003): 7–24.

Horne, Dee. *Contemporary American Indian Writing: Unsettling Literature*. New York: Peter Lang, 1999.

Horowitz, Rosalind, and S. Jay Samuels, eds. *Comprehending Oral and Written Language*. San Diego: Academic Press, 1987.

Hultkrantz, Åke. "A Definition of Shamanism." *Temenos* 9 (1973): 25–37.

——. "Die Religion der amerikanischen Arktis." In *Die Religionen Nordeurasiens und der amerikanischen Arktis*, by Ivar Paulson, Åke Hultkrantz, and Karl Jettmar, 357–415. Stuttgart: W. Kohlhammer, 1962.

Hutcheon, Linda. *A Theory of Parody: The Teachings of Twentieth-Century Art Forms*. New York: Methuen, 1985.

Hymes, Dell. "Discovering Oral Performance and Measured Verse in American Indian Narrative." *New Literary History* 8.3 (1977): 431–57.

Hynes, William J. "Mapping the Characteristics of Mythic Tricksters: A Heuristic Guide." In Hynes and Doty, *Mythical Trickster Figures*, 33–45.

Hynes, William J., and William G. Doty, eds. *Mythical Trickster Figures: Contours, Contexts, and Criticisms*. Tuscaloosa: University of Alabama Press, 1993.

Ipellie, Alootook. *Arctic Dreams and Nightmares*. Penticton, BC: Theytus Books, c. 1993.

Irniq, Peter T. "Speaking Notes: Inuit Spirituality." Address, 31st Annual Saskatchewan Prayer Breakfast, Regina, 4 April 2001.

Iser, Wolfgang. *Der Akt des Lesens: Theorie ästhetischer Wirkung*. Munich: Wilhelm Fink Verlag, 1976. Translated as *The Act of Reading: A Theory of Aesthetic Response*. Baltimore, MD: Johns Hopkins University Press, 1978.

Ives, Sumner. "A Theory of Literary Dialect." *Tulane Studies in English* 2 (1950): 137–82.

Jacobs, Melville. *The Content and Style of an Oral Literature: Clackamas Chinook Myths and Tales*. 1959. Reprint, Chicago: University of Chicago Press, 1971.

Jahandarie, Khosrow. *Spoken and Written Discourse: A Multi-Disciplinary Perspective*. Stamford, CT: Ablex Publishing, 1999.

Jaine, Linda, and Louise Halfe. "Traditional Cree Philosophy: Death, Bereavement, and Healing." *Saskatchewan Indian* (March 1989): 11. www.sicc.sk.ca/saskindian/a89mar11.htm.

James, Deborah, Sandra Clarke, and Marguerite MacKenzie. "The Encoding of Information Source in Algonquian: Evidentials in Cree/Montagnais/Naskapi." *International Journal of American Linguistics* 67.3 (2001): 229–63.

Justice, Daniel Heath. *Our Fire Survives the Storm: A Cherokee Literary History*. Minneapolis: University of Minnesota Press, 2006.

Kellogg, Robert. "Oral Narrative, Written Books." *Genre* 10 (1977): 655–65.

Kendall, Martha B. "Exegesis and Translation: Northern Yuman Names as Texts." *Journal of Anthropological Research* 36.3 (1980): 261–73.

Kennedy, Michael P. J. "Alootook Ipellie: The Voice of an Inuk Artist." *Studies in Canadian Literature/Études en littérature canadienne* 21.2 (1996): 155–64.

Keeshig-Tobias, Lenore. "Stop Stealing Native Stories." *Globe and Mail*, 26 January 1990, A7.

Kilpatrick, Alan. *The Night Has a Naked Soul: Witchcraft and Sorcery among the Western Cherokee*. Syracuse, NY: Syracuse University Press, 1997.

King, Thomas. "Godzilla vs. Post-Colonial." *World Literature Written in English* 30.2 (1990): 10–16.

———. *Green Grass, Running Water*. 1993. Reprint, Toronto: HarperPerennialCanada, 1999.

———. Introduction to *All My Relations: An Anthology of Contemporary Canadian Native Fiction*, edited by Thomas King, ix–xvi. Toronto: McClelland and Stewart, 1990.

———. *Inventing the Indian: White Images, Native Oral Literature, and Contemporary Native Writers*. Ann Arbor, MI: University Microfilms International, 1986.

———. *Medicine River*. 1990. Reprint, Toronto: Penguin Books, 1995.

———. *One Good Story, That One: Stories*. Toronto: HarperPerennial, 1993.

———. *A Short History of Indians in Canada*. Toronto: HarperCollins, 2005.

———. *Truth and Bright Water*. New York: Grove Press, 1999.

———. *The Truth about Stories: A Native Narrative*. Toronto: House of Anansi Press, 2003.

Kinkade, M. Dale, and Anthony Mattina. "Discourse." In Goddard, *Languages*, 244–74.

Kleist, Makka. "Pre-Christian Inuit Sexuality." In *Me Sexy: An Exploration of Native Sex and Sexuality*, edited by Drew Hayden Taylor, 15–19. Vancouver: Douglas and McIntyre, 2008.

Kleivan, Inge, and Birgitte Sonne. *Eskimos: Greenland and Canada*. Leiden: E.J. Brill, 1985.

Koch, Peter, and Wulf Oesterreicher. "Sprache der Nähe—Sprache der Distanz: Mündlichkeit und Schriftlichkeit im Spannungsfeld von Sprachtheorie und Sprachgeschichte." *Romanistisches Jahrbuch* 36 (1985): 15–43.

Krupat, Arnold. "Post-Structuralism and Oral Literature." In Swann and Krupat, *Recovering the Word*, 113–28.

———. *The Turn to the Native: Studies in Criticism and Culture*. Lincoln: University of Nebraska Press, 1996.

Lakoff, Robin Tolmach. "Some of My Favorite Writers are Literate: The Mingling of Oral and Literate Strategies in Written Communication." In Tannen, *Spoken and Written Language*, 239–60.

Laugrand, Frédéric, Jarich Oosten, and François Trudel. *Representing Tuurngait*. Translated and edited by Alexina Kublu. Iqaluit: Nunavut Arctic College, 2000.

Leach, Maria, ed. *Funk and Wagnalls Standard Dictionary of Folklore, Mythology, and Legend*. 2 vols. New York: Funk and Wagnalls, 1949–50.

Leap, William L. *American Indian English*. Salt Lake City: University of Utah Press, 1993.

LeClaire, Nancy, and George Cardinal, comps. *Alberta Elders' Cree Dictionary/alperta ohci kehtehayak nehiyaw otwestamâkewasinahikan*. Edited by Earle Waugh. Edmonton: University of Alberta Press, 1998.

L'Hirondelle, Lorna, et al., eds. *Plains Cree Grammar Guide and Glossary*. Edmonton: School of Native Studies, University of Alberta, 2001.

Lieber, Francis. "On the Study of Foreign Languages." *Southern Literary Messenger* 3 (1837): 162–72.

Linton, Patricia. "'And Here's How It Happened': Trickster Discourse in Thomas King's *Green Grass, Running Water*." *Modern Fiction Studies* 45.1 (1999): 212–34.

"Louise Halfe." Coteau Books. www.coteaubooks.com/index.php?p=Author&authorid=25.

Lowe, Ronald. Introduction to Lowe, *Siglit Inuvialuit Uqausiita Kipuktirutait*, xvii–xxviii.

———. *Siglit Inuvialuit Uqausiita Kipuktirutait/Basic Siglit Inuvialuit Eskimo Dictionary*. Inuvik, NWT: Committee for Original Peoples Entitlement, 1984.

Lutz, Hartmut. "First Nations Literature in Canada and the Voice of Survival." *London Journal of Canadian Studies* 11 (1995): 60–76.

———. "Thomas King." In *Contemporary Challenges: Conversations with Canadian Native Authors*, 107–16. Saskatoon: Fifth House Publishers, 1991.

Lyons, Scott Richard. "Rhetorical Sovereignty: What Do American Indians Want from Writing?" *College Composition and Communication* 51.3 (2000): 447–68.

Mace, Renate. *Funktionen des Dialekts im regionalen Roman von Gaskell bis Lawrence*. PhD diss., Universität Freiburg i. Br., 1986. Tübingen: Gunter Narr Verlag, 1987.

Mackenzie, Alexander. *The Journals and Letters of Sir Alexander Mackenzie*. Edited by W. Kaye Lamb. Toronto: Macmillan of Canada, 1970.

Mailhot, José. "L'étymologie de 'esquimau' revue et corrigée." *Études Inuit/Inuit Studies* 2.2 (1978): 59–69.

Malinowski, Bronisław. *The Language of Magic and Gardening*. Vol. 2 of *Coral Gardens and Their Magic: A Study of the Methods of Tilling the Soil and of Agricultural Rites in the Trobriand Islands*. London: Allen and Unwin, 1935.

Mandelbaum, David G. *The Plains Cree: An Ethnographic, Historical, and Comparative Study*. Regina: Canadian Plains Research Center, University of Regina, 1979.

Markoosie. *Harpoon of the Hunter*. Montreal: McGill-Queen's University Press, 1970.

Mattina, Anthony. "North American Indian Mythography: Editing Texts for the Printed Page." In Swann and Krupat, *Recovering the Word*, 129–48.

McGrath, Robin. *Canadian Inuit Literature: The Development of a Tradition*. Ottawa: National Museums of Canada, 1984.

McLeod, Neal. *Cree Narrative Memory: From Treaties to Contemporary Times*. Saskatoon: Purich Publishing, 2007.

———. *Songs to Kill a Wîhtikow*. Regina: Hagios Press, 2005.

McMaster, Gerald. *Edward Poitras: Canada XLVI Biennale di Venezia*. Hull, QC: Canadian Museum of Civilization, 1995.

Melville, Herman. *Moby-Dick; Or, The Whale*. New York: Harper, 1851.

Merkur, Daniel. *Becoming Half Hidden: Shamanism and Initiation among the Inuit*. New York: Garland Publishing, 1992.

———. "Eagle, the Hunter's Helper: The Cultic Significance of Inuit Mythological Tales." *History of Religions* 27.2 (1987): 171–88.

Mignolo, Walter D. *The Darker Side of the Renaissance: Literacy, Territoriality, and Colonization*. Ann Arbor: University of Michigan Press, 1995.

Mithun, Marianne. *The Languages of Native North America*. Cambridge, UK: Cambridge University Press, 1999.

Momaday, N. Scott. *The Man Made of Words: Essays, Stories, Passages*. New York: St. Martin's Press, 1997.

Moses, Daniel David, and Terry Goldie, eds. *An Anthology of Canadian Native Literature in English*. 3rd ed. Toronto: Oxford University Press, 2005.

———. "Traditional Orature: Southern First Nations." In Moses and Goldie, *An Anthology of Canadian Native Literature in English*, 1–5.

———. "Two Voices." Preface to the 1st ed. of *An Anthology of Canadian Native Literature in English*, reprinted in Moses and Goldie, xiii–xxii.

Muro, Junko. "Living in a Time for Celebration: An Interview with Richard Van Camp." In *Across Cultures/Across Borders: Canadian Aboriginal and Native American Literatures*, edited by Paul DePasquale, Renate Eigenbrod, and Emma LaRocque, 297–311. Peterborough: Broadview Press, 2010.

Nelson, Edward William. *The Eskimo about Bering Strait*. 1899. Reprint, New York: Johnson Reprint, 1971.

Neuhaus, Mareike. "The Marriage of Mother and Father: Michif Influences as Expressions of Métis Intellectual Sovereignty in *Stories of the Road Allowance People*." *Studies in American Indian Literatures*, 2nd ser., 22.1 (2010): 20–48.

Nicosia, Nicole. "May I Suggest." Rev. of *The Lesser Blessed*, by Richard Van Camp. *Indian Country Today*, 22 December 2004, www.indiancountrytoday.com/archive/28172764.html.

Nida, Eugene A. *Toward a Science of Translating: With Special Reference to Principles and Procedures Involved in Bible Translating*. Leiden: E.J. Brill, 1964.

Nida, Eugene A., and Charles A. Taber. *The Theory and Practice of Translation*. Leiden: E.J. Brill, 1969.

"Northern Games." Inuvialuit Regional Corporation. www.irc.inuvialuit.com/culture/northerngames.html.

Nowak, Elke. "Is Inuktitut a Morphological Argument Language?" TS, 1999. http://ling.kgw.tu-berlin.de/staff/Nowak/HALLE-AU.doc.

Nuligak (Bob Cockney). *I, Nuligak*. Translated and edited by Maurice Metayer. 1966. Reprint, Richmond Hill, ON: Pocket Books, 1971.

Nungak, Zebedee, and Eugene Arima. "A Review of Central Eskimo Mythology." In Nungak and Arima, *Unikkaatuat sanaugarngnik atyingualiit Puvirngniturngmit*, 111–37.

———, eds. *Unikkaatuat sanaugarngnik atyingualiit Puvirngniturngmit/Eskimo Stories from Povungnituk, Quebec, Illustrated in Soapstone Carvings*. Ottawa: National Museum of Canada, 1969.

Nystrand, Martin. "The Role of Context in Written Communication." In Horowitz and Samuels, *Comprehending Oral and Written Language*, 197–214.

Ochs, Elinor. "Planned and Unplanned Discourse." In *Discourse and Syntax*, edited by Talmy Givón, 51–80. New York: Academic Press, 1979.

O'Donovan, Leo J. "Mutual Teachers." *America: The National Catholic Weekly*, 29 August 2005, www.americamagazine.org/gettext.cfm?articleTypeID=1&textID=4325&issueID=540.

Oman, Lela Kiana. *The Epic of Qayaq: The Longest Story Ever Told by My People*. Edited by Priscilla Tyler and Maree Brooks. Ottawa: Carleton University Press; Seattle: University of Washington Press, 1995.

Oosten, Jarich, and Frédéric Laugrand. "The Bringer of Light: The Raven in Inuit Tradition." *Polar Record* 42.3 (2006): 187–204.

Ortiz, Simon J., ed. *Speaking for the Generations: Native Writers on Writing*. Tucson: University of Arizona Press, 1998.

Page, Norman. *Speech in the English Novel*. London: Longman, 1973.

Parry, Milman. "Studies in the Epic Technique of Oral Verse-Making: I. Homer and Homeric Style." *Harvard Studies in Classical Philology* 41 (1930): 73–147.

Perreault, Jeanne, and Sylvia Vance, comps. and eds. *Writing the Circle: Native Women of Western Canada: An Anthology*. Edmonton: NeWest Press, 1990.

Petitot, Émile. *Autour du Grand Lac des Esclaves*. Paris: A. Savine, 1891. Early Canadiana Online. www.canadiana.org/ECO/ItemRecord/11181?id=c916b31f945a8bf2.

———. *The Book of Dene: Containing the Traditions and Beliefs of Chipewyan, Dogrib, Slavey, and Loucheux Peoples*. Yellowknife: Department of Education, Government of the Northwest Territories, 1976.

———. *Traditions indiennes du Canada Nord-Ouest*. Paris: Maisonneuve et C. Leclerc, 1886. Early Canadiana Online. www.canadiana.org/ECO/ItemRecord/15869?id=c916b31f945a8bf2.

Pitseolak, Peter. *People from Our Side: A Life Story with Photographs*. Oral biography by Dorothy Harley Eber. 1975. Reprint, Montreal: McGill-Queen's University Press, 1993.

———. *Pictures out of My Life*. Edited from tape-recorded interviews by Dorothy Eber. Montreal: Design Collaborative Books, in association with Oxford University Press, Toronto, 1971.

Plag, Ingo. *Morphological Productivity: Structural Constraints in English Derivation*. Berlin: Mouton de Gruyter, 1999.

Polanyi, Livia. "Literary Complexity in Everyday Storytelling." In Tannen, *Spoken and Written Language*, 155–70.

Powell, Peter J. *Sweet Medicine: The Continuing Role of the Sacred Arrows, the Sun Dance, and the Sacred Buffalo Hat in Northern Cheyenne History*. 2 vols. Norman: University of Oklahoma Press, 1969.

Pullum, Geoffrey K. "The Great Eskimo Vocabulary Hoax." In *The Great Eskimo Vocabulary Hoax and Other Irreverent Essays on the Study of Language*, 159–71. Chicago: University of Chicago Press, 1991.

Rainwater, Catherine. *Dreams of Fiery Stars: The Transformations of Native American Fiction*. Philadelphia: University of Pennsylvania Press, 1999.

Rasmussen, Knud. *Across Arctic America: Narrative of the Fifth Thule Expedition*. 1927. Reprint, Fairbanks: University of Alaska Press, 1999.

———. *Fra Grønland til Stillehavet: Rejser og Mennesker fra 5. Thule-Ekspedition 1921–24*. 2 vols. Kobenhavn: Gyldendalske boghandel, 1925–26.

———. *The Mackenzie Eskimos: After Knud Rasmussen's Posthumous Notes*. Edited by H. Ostermann. Copenhagen: Gyldendal, 1942.

Redeker, Gisela. "On Differences between Spoken and Written Language." *Discourse Processes* 7.1 (1984): 43–55.

Ricketts, Mac Linscott. "The Shaman and the Trickster." In Hynes and Doty, *Mythical Trickster Figures*, 87–105.

Ridington, Robin. "Dogs, Snares, and Cartridge Belts: The Poetics of a Northern Athapaskan Narrative Technology." In *The Social Dynamics of Technology: Practice, Politics, and World Views*, edited by Marcia-Anne Dobres and Christopher R. Hoffman, 167–85. Washington, DC: Smithsonian Institution Press, 1999.

———. "Theorizing Coyote's Canon: Sharing Stories with Thomas King." In *Theorizing the Americanist Tradition*, edited by Lisa Philips Valentine and Regna Darnell, 19–37. Toronto: University of Toronto Press, 1999.

Robinson, Eden. *Blood Sports*. Toronto: McClelland and Stewart, 2006.

Robinson, Harry. *Write It on Your Heart: The Epic World of an Okanagan Storyteller.* Compiled and edited by Wendy Wickwire. Vancouver: Talonbooks, 1989.

Rodgers, Wendy. "Circumscribing Silence: Inuit Writing Orature." *Northern Review* 17 (1996): 48–59.

Rood, David S. "North American Languages." In *International Encyclopedia of Linguistics*, edited by William J. Frawley, 167–72. 2nd ed. Vol. 3. Oxford: Oxford University Press, 2003.

Rooke, Constance. "Interview with Tom King." *World Literature Written in English* 30.2 (1990): 62–76.

Saladin d'Anglure, Bernard. "An Ethnographic Commentary: The Legend of Atanarjuat, Inuit, and Shamanism." In Angilirq, *Atanarjuat*, 196–227.

———. "From Foetus to Shaman: The Construction of an Inuit Third Sex." In *Amerindian Rebirth: Reincarnation Belief among North American Indians and Inuit*, edited by Antonia Mills and Richard Slobodin, 82–106. Toronto: University of Toronto Press, 1994.

———. "Nanook, Super-Male: The Polar Bear in the Imaginary Space and Social Time of the Inuit of the Canadian Arctic." In *Signifying Animals: Human Meaning in the Natural World*, edited by Roy Willis, 178–95. London: Unwin Hyman, 1990.

———. "The 'Third Gender' of the Inuit." *Diogenes* 52.4 (2005): 134–44.

Saltman, Judi. "Richard Van Camp Interview." 29 September 2003. www.hanksville.org/storytellers/VanCamp/JSaltman.html.

Saussure, Ferdinand de. *Course in General Linguistics.* Translated by Wade Baskin. Edited by Charles Bally and Albert Sechehaye. London: Peter Owen, 1960.

Schafer, Edward H. "The Sky River." *Journal of the American Oriental Society* 94.4 (1974): 401–07.

Scholes, Robert, and Robert Kellogg. "The Oral Heritage of Written Narrative." In *The Nature of Narrative*, 17–56. 1966. Reprint, New York: Oxford University Press, 1971.

Schorcht, Blanca. *Storied Voices in Native American Texts: Harry Robinson, Thomas King, James Welch, and Leslie Marmon Silko.* New York: Routledge, 2003.

Schwarz, Herbert T. *Elik, and Other Stories of the MacKenzie Eskimos.* Toronto: McClelland and Stewart, 1970.

Scobie, Stephen. "Double Voicing: A View of Canadian Poetry." In *O Canada: Essays on Canadian Literature and Culture*, edited by Jørn Carlsen, 38–49. Aarhus, Denmark: Aarhus University Press, 1995.

Seidelman, Harold, and James Turner. *The Inuit Imagination: Arctic Myth and Sculpture*. Vancouver: Douglas and McIntyre, 1993.

Silko, Leslie Marmon. "Language and Literature from a Pueblo Indian Perspective." In *English Literature: Opening up the Canon*, edited by Leslie A. Fiedler and Houston A. Baker, Jr., 54–72. Baltimore: Johns Hopkins University Press, 1981.

Spalding, Alex, comp. *Inuktitut: A Multi-Dialectal Outline Dictionary (with an Aivilingmiutaq Base)*. Iqaluit: Nunavut Arctic College, 1998.

Spencer, Andrew. *Morphological Theory: An Introduction to Word Structure in Generative Grammar*. Oxford: Basil Blackwell, 1991.

Spencer, Robert F. *The North Alaskan Eskimo: A Study in Ecology and Society*. Washington, DC: Smithsonian Institution Press, 1959.

Standiford, Lester A. "Worlds Made of Dawn: Characteristic Image and Incident in Native American Imaginative Literature." In *Three American Literatures: Essays in Chicano, Native American, and Asian-American Literature for Teachers of American Literature*, edited by Houston A. Baker, Jr., 168–96. New York: Modern Language Association of America, 1982.

Stigter, Shelley. "The Dialectics and Dialogics of Code-Switching in the Poetry of Gregory Scofield and Louise Halfe." *American Indian Quarterly* 30.1–2 (2006): 49–60.

Sutherland, Xavier. "cahkâpêš nêsta mâka mistâpêskwêwak/Chahkabesh and the Giant Women." In *âtolôhkâna nêsta tipâcimôwina/Cree Legends and Narratives from the West Coast of James Bay*, translated and edited by C. Douglas Ellis, 104–09. Winnipeg: University of Manitoba Press, 1995.

Swann, Brian, and Arnold Krupat, eds. *Recovering the Word: Essays on Native American Literature*. Berkeley: University of California Press, 1987.

Swift, Jonathan. *Gulliver's Travels*. Vol. 3 of *Works*. Dublin: George Faulkner, 1735.

Swink, Helen. "William Faulkner: The Novelist as Oral Narrator." *Georgia Review* 26.2 (1972): 183–209.

Tannen, Deborah, ed. *Spoken and Written Language: Exploring Orality and Literacy*. Norwood, NJ: Ablex Publishing, 1982.

———. *Talking Voices: Repetition, Dialogue, and Imagery in Conversational Discourse*. 2nd ed. Cambridge, UK: Cambridge University Press, 2007.

Tedlock, Dennis. *The Spoken Word and the Work of Interpretation*. Philadelphia: University of Pennsylvania Press, 1983.

Thalbitzer, William. "Die kultischen Gottheiten der Eskimos." *Archiv für Religionswissenschaft* 26.3–4 (1928): 364–430.

Ticasuk (Emily Ivanoff Brown). *The Longest Story Ever Told: Qayaq, the Magical Man*. 2nd ed. Fairbanks: University of Alaska Press, 2008.

Tierney, Frank M., and Angela Robbeson. Preface to *Bolder Flights: Essays on the Canadian Long Poem*, edited by Frank M. Tierney and Angela Robbeson, 1–5. Ottawa: University of Ottawa Press, 1998.

Trost, Pavel. "Tzv. Citátová komposita v němčině." *Cizí jazyky ve škole* 26.1 (1982–83): 18.

Tyler, Priscilla, and Maree Brooks. Introduction to Oman, *The Epic of Qayaq*, xiii–xx.

Tyron, Thomas. *The Other*. New York: Alfred A. Knopf, 1971.

Uluksuk. "A Brief History." Introduction to Alunik, *Call Me Ishmael*, 4–23.

Van Camp, Richard. *The Lesser Blessed*. 1996. Reprint, Vancouver: Douglas and McIntyre, 2004.

Vecsey, Christopher. Rev. of *Native American Religious Action: A Performance Approach to Religion and Mother Earth: An American Story*, by Sam D. Gill. *American Indian Quarterly* 12.3 (1988): 254–56.

Vizenor, Gerald R. *Manifest Manners: Postindian Warriors of Survivance*. Hanover, NH: University Press of New England, 1994.

Voegelin, Erminie W. "Coyote." In Leach, *Funk and Wagnalls Standard Dictionary*, 1: 257–58.

———. "Creation." In Leach, *Funk and Wagnalls Standard Dictionary*, 1: 259–60.

Wagamese, Richard. *Keeper 'n Me*. Toronto: Doubleday Canada, 1994.

Warkentin, Germaine. "In Search of 'The Word of the Other': Aboriginal Sign Systems and the History of the Book in Canada." *Book History* 2.1 (1999): 1–27.

Watt, Ian. "Oral Dickens." *Dickens Studies Annual* 3 (1974): 165–81.

Weaver, Jace. "Notes from a Miner's Canary." Introduction to *Defending Mother Earth: Native American Perspectives on Environmental Justice*, edited by Jace Weaver, 1–28. Maryknoll, NY: Orbis Books, 1996.

———. *That the People Might Live: Native American Literatures and Native American Community*. New York: Oxford University Press, 1997.

White, Frederick H. "Language Reflection and Lamentation in Native American Literature." *Studies in American Indian Literatures*, 2nd ser., 18.1 (2006): 83–98.

Wiebe, Armin. *Tatsea*. Winnipeg: Turnstone Press, 2003.

Wiesenthal, Christine. *The Half-Lives of Pat Lowther*. Toronto: University of Toronto Press, 2005.

Willett, Thomas. "A Cross-Linguistic Survey of the Grammaticization of Evidentiality." *Studies in Language* 12.1 (1988): 51–97.

Williams, David. *Imagined Nations: Reflections on Media in Canadian Fiction*. Montreal: McGill-Queen's University Press, 2003.

Williamson, Robert G. "Eskimo Underground: Socio-Cultural Change in the Canadian Central Arctic." Uppsala: Almqvist & Wiksell, 1974.

Willinsky, John. "The Paradox of Text in the Culture of Literacy." *After Literacy: Essays*. New York: Peter Lang, 2001. 59–82.

Wissler, Clark, and D.C. Duvall, eds. *Mythology of the Blackfoot Indians*. 1908. Reprint, Lincoln: University of Nebraska Press, 1995.

Wolfart, H. Christoph. "Introduction to the Texts." In Bear et al., *kôhkominawak otâcimowiniwâwa*, 17–37.

———. "Notes." In Bear et al., *kôhkominawak otâcimowiniwâwa*, 351–406.

Wolfart, H. Christoph, and Janet F. Carroll. *Meet Cree: A Guide to the Cree Language*. Rev. ed. Edmonton: University of Alberta Press, 1981.

Wolfe, Alexander. Introduction to *Earth Elder Stories: The Pinayzitt Path*, xi–xxii. Saskatoon: Fifth House Publishers, 1989.

Womack, Craig S. "A Single Decade: Book-Length Native Literary Criticism between 1986 and 1997." In Womack, Justice, and Teuton, *Reasoning Together*, 3–104.

———. "Theorizing American Indian Experience." In Womack, Justice, and Teuton, *Reasoning Together*, 353–410.

Womack, Craig S., Daniel Heath Justice, and Christopher B. Teuton, eds. *Reasoning Together: The Native Critics Collective*. Norman: University of Oklahoma Press, 2008.

Index

This index includes most personal names (with the exception of the names of fictional characters) and publications referred to in this book. In the case of multiple authors, the book or article in question is listed under the name of the first author or editor; in the case of multiple editors, only the first editor is listed; frequently titles are shortened.

A

Abel, Kerry, 112; *Drum Songs*, 255-56

Afable, Patricia O.: "Place-Names," 257

Ahenakew, Edward: "Cree Trickster Tales," 266

Ahenakew, Freda, 225; *kôhkominawak otâcimowiniwâwa/Our Grandmothers' Lives, as Told in Their Own Words*, 272; *wanisinwak iskwêsisak/Two Little Girls Lost in the Bush*, 272

Alexie, Robert Arthur, 20; *Porcupines and China Dolls*, 111, 240

Alia, Valerie: "Ipellie's Interior Visions," 249, 254-55

allegory, 13, 118-19, 123, 127, 139-40, 196, 199

Allen, Paul Gunn: *Grandmothers of the Light*, 261

allusion, 52, 127, 176-77

Alunik, Ishmael, 105, 140, 219, 222; *Across Time and Tundra*, 35-36, 242, 253; *Call Me Ishmael*, 2, 16, 31, 34-38, 94, 101, 123, 139, 178, 239, 242; content and structure of, 79-80, 103, 106; holophrastic analysis of, 39-44, 46, 49-50, 52-55, 59, 61-67; holophrastic traces in, 107, 220-21; paraholophrases in, 84, 98, 115-16

Andrews, Jennifer, 164, 174, 207; "Border Trickery and Dog Bones," 258, 263-64, 270; "Reading Thomas King's *Green Grass, Running Water*," 264

Andrews, Thomas D., 132; "The Dogrib Birchbark Canoe Project," 257

Angilirq, Paul Apak: *Atanarjuat, the Fast Runner*, 246, 251-52

Arctic Dreams and Nightmares. See Ipellie, Alootook

Arima, Eugene, 76, 78

Aristotle: *Categories*, 242; *Rhetoric*, 223, 271

Armstrong, Jeannette C., 2, 24, 222; "Land Speaking," 1, 233, 240

art, fine, 103, 105; pictorial, 65; verbal, 64-65, 84, 103-5; written, 66

Attla, Catherine: *K'etetaalkkaanee, the One Who Paddles among the People and Animals*, 247

Aupilaarjuk, Mariano, 72; *Cosmology and Shamanism*, 245-47, 249-52

Austin, Mary, 11

Austin, William M.: *Papers in Linguistics in Honor of Leon Dostert*, 237

B

Babcock, Barbara: "A Tolerated Margin of Mess," 259

Baker, Houston A.: *Three American Literatures*, 238

Baker, Mark C.: *The Atoms of Language*, 233-34, 239-40

Bal, Mieke: *Narratology*, 262

Balzer, Geraldine: "Bring Them Back from Inside Out," 235

Barber, Karin: *The Anthropology of Texts, Persons, and Publics*, 241

Bardolph, Jacqueline: *Telling Stories*, 235

Barnes, Julian: *The Complete Works of Aristotle*, 242, 271

Bartelt, Guillermo, 7, 18; "American Indian English in Momaday's *House Made of Dawn*", 234; *Socio- and Stylolinguistic Perspectives on American Indian English Texts*, 234, 240

Barthes, Roland, 4-5, 25, 28; *Elements of Semiology*, 241; "An Introduction to the Structural Analysis of Narrative," 234; *Mythologies*, 241

Bateson, Gregory, 218

Battiste, Marie: *Reclaiming Indigenous Voice and Vision*, 237

Baugh, Albert C.: *A History of the English Language*, 238

Bauman, Richard, 218; *Verbal Art as Performance*, 245, 271

Bear, Glecia: "Lost and Found," 272; et al., *kôhkominawak otâcimowiniwâwa/Our Grandmothers' Lives, as Told in Their Own Words*, 272; *wanisinwak iskwêsisak/Two Little Girls Lost in the Bush*, 272

Bennett, John: *Uqalurait*, 247, 250, 254

Bennett (Bennettin), Simon, 36; "Simon Bennett Stories," 242

Bentley, David, 182

Bevis, William, 110; "Native American Novels," 255

Biber, Douglas: *Dimensions of Register Variation*, 236, 241

Birk, Hanne, 106; "Inszenierungen," 255; "Kulturspezifische Inszenierungen kollektiver Gedächtnismedien in autochthonen Literaturen Kanadas," 252

Blaeser, Kimberly M., 11, 13; "Trickster," 260; "Writing Voices Speaking," 238

Blondin, George, 114; *Trail of the Spirit*, 256; *When the World Was New*, 256-57; *Yamoria, the Lawmaker*, 256

Bloomfield, Leonard: *Sacred Stories of the Sweet Grass Cree*, 266

Blue Marrow. See Halfe, Louise Bernice

Boas, Frank, 78

Booth, Wayne C., 10

Borbe, Tasso: *Semiotics Unfolding*, 236

Bright, William: *A Coyote Reader*, 260

Brill de Ramírez, Susan Berry, 10, 12-13; *Contemporary American Indian Literatures and the Oral Tradition*, 236, 238

Brooks, Maree, 53

Brotherston, Gordon: *Book of the Fourth World*, 237

Burke, Kenneth: *A Rhetoric of Motives*, 218, 271

C

Call Me Ishmael. See Alunik, Ishmael

Campbell, Maria, 24, 182; *Stories of the Road Allowance People*, 18, 20, 240

Canton, Jeffrey: "Coyote Lives," 258, 260

Cariou, Warren: "We Use Dah Membering," 269

Carlsen, Jørn: *O Canada*, 266

Carpenter, Edmund, 103; "Image Making in Arctic Art," 254

Cary, Thomas, 182

catalyses, 4-5

Chafe, Wallace L., 3-4, 16; "The Deployment of Consciousness in the Production of a Narrative," 233; *Discourse, Consciousness, and Time*, 234; "Discourse Effects on Polysynthesis," 233, 239, 254; *Evidentiality*, 239; "Integration and Involvement in Spoken and Written Language," 236; *The Pear Stories*, 233; "Properties of Spoken and Written Language," 233, 254, 258, 264; "The Relation between Written and Spoken Language," 241; "Writing in the Perspective of Speaking," 234

Chamberlin, J. Edward, 11; "From Hand to Mouth," 237

Chester, Blanco: *"Green Grass, Running Water:* Theorizing the World of the Novel," 259

circumlocutions, 73, 80

Cockney, Bob, 74; *I, Nuligak,* 81, 250, 252

code switching, 9, 14, 28, 31, 207, 216, 219, 229; in *Arctic Dreams,* 73, 100, 104-5, 221; in *Blue Marrow,* 180, 183, 205, 214; in *Call Me Ishmael,* 58-59, 66; in *Green Grass,* 165, 168; in *The Lesser Blessed,* 116, 129, 140

colloquialisms. *See* language, colloquial

compounding, 31, 67, 178, 205, 207, 220-21, 223

compounds, 15, 67, 97, 101, 105, 140, 202, 210, 221, 239; A N, 169, 175, 207, 229; A N N, 207-8; complex, 15, 59-60, 67, 105, 208; deverbal, 16, 59-60, 67, 101, 105, 133, 169, 175, 207-9, 214; N, 214; N N, 16, 59-60, 67, 100-101, 105, 131, 133-34, 170, 207-9, 214, 230, 269; quotation, 16, 130-31, 133, 140-41, 169-70, 175, 207, 209, 214, 221, 231; root, 15, 231, 239; synthetic, 15-16, 60, 67, 101, 105, 169, 208-9, 221, 231, 239; V N, 16, 231

Comrie, Bernard: *Language Universals and Linguistic Typology,* 233, 272-73

concatenations of signs, 20-24, 27-28, 217

conversive criticism, 12

Cook, Méira, 180; "Bone Memory," 235, 265-66, 269-70

Cooley, Dennis: *The Vernacular Muse,* 237

Cooper, Charles R.: *Studying Writing,* 234

copula, 99

Creenglish, 9

D

Daly, Richard: "Writing on the Landscape," 237

Damas, David: *Handbook of North American Indians,* 246

Daurio, Beverley: *The Power to Bend Spoons,* 258

Davidson, Arnold E., 164; *Border Crossings,* 258, 263

de Saussure, Ferdinand: *Course in General Linguistics,* 272

deictics, 175

Dene Wodih Society, 114

DePasquale, Paul: *Across Cultures/Across Borders,* 255

Derrida, Jacques: *Of Grammatology,* 236

dialogue, 4, 12-13, 29

Dion, Joseph F.: *My Tribe, the Crees,* 268-69

discourse, 4, 18, 27, 152, 172, 174-75; devices of, 33, 216; types of, 29, 31, 129, 165, 177, 210, 218, 225. *See also* Indigenous discourse

Dobres, Marcia-Anne: *The Social Dynamics of Technology,* 263, 271

Donaldson, Laura E.: "Noah Meets Old Coyote," 261, 263

double voicing, 183, 215

Doueihi, Anne, 145; "Inhabiting the Space between Discourse and Story in Trickster Narratives," 260, 262

Dudek, Debra, 186; "Begin with the Text," 266, 268

Dunn, Maggie, 70; *The Composite Novel,* 249

Dvorák, Marta: *Tropes and Territories,* 269

E

Eber, Dorothy Harley: *People from Our Side*, 246, 253

Eigenbrod, Renate: *Creating Community*, 266

Éjchenbaum, Boris M., 10; "The Illusion of *Skaz*," 236

Eliade, Mircea, 79; *Shamanism*, 251

ellipses, 172, 175, 212

Ellis, C. Douglas, 17; *Cree Legends and Narratives from the West Coast of James Bay*, 239

engagement of reader. *See* participation

English language: analytic morphology of, 131, 141; colloquial uses of, 61; as Indigenous language, 6-7, 130; and loan translation, 177, 209, 214, 221; as oralized, 8, 130. *See also* languages

Erll, Astrid: *Medien des kollektiven Gedächtnisses*, 252

Erzgräber, Willi: *James Joyce*, 237; *Mündliches Erzählen im Alltag fingiertes mündliches Erzählen in der Literatur*, 237-38

ethnopoetics, 214

Evans, Nicholas: "Introduction," 233; *Problems of Polysynthesis*, 233

evidentiality, 16-18, 62-64, 67, 138, 174, 177-78, 220-21, 229

evidentials. *See* evidentiality

F

Fagan, Kristina: "What's the Trouble with the Trickster?" 146, 260

Fee, Margery, 9, 11; "Writing Orality: Interpreting Literature in English by Aboriginal Writers," 235, 238

Feeling, Durbin: *Cherokee-English Dictionary*, 167

Feldman, Carol Fleisher, 11; "Oral Metalanguage," 237

Fiedler, Leslie A.: *English Literature*, 248

figures of speech, 24, 45, 51, 217; in *Arctic Dreams*, 83, 88, 92, 97, 100, 105, 220; in *Blue Marrow*, 193, 199, 202, 213, 220; in *Call Me Ishmael*, 50, 54, 220; in *Green Grass*, 158, 161-62, 164-65, 178; in *The Lesser Blessed*, 119, 123, 136, 139, 220. *See also* speech, figurative

Finnegan, Ruth, 30; "What is Orality—If Anything?" 242

Flick, Jane, 163, 168; "Reading Notes for Thomas King's *Green Grass, Running Water*," 261-65

formulaic clusters, 43, 158-60, 165, 170, 176, 203, 217

fragmentation, 32, 67, 105, 141, 175, 177, 213, 219-20

frames. *See* narrative frames

Frawley, William J.: *International Encyclopedia of Linguistics*, 233

French, David H., 99; "Personal Names," 254

French, Kathrine, 99

Friedman, Susan Stanford, 182; "Craving Stories," 266

G

Gautreau, Evalyn: *Tale Spinners in a Spruce Tipi*, 114, 256-57

Genette, Gérard, 24, 213; *Figures of Literary Discourse*, 240, 245, 271

genre, 214, 220, 222

Gibbs, George, 143

Gibert, Teresa: "Narrative Strategies in Thomas King's Short Stories," 235

Gill, Sam D.: *Dictionary of Native American Mythology*, 244, 247, 259-61; *Mother Earth*, 267

Gingell, Susan, 29, 180, 182; "Lips' Inking: Cree Writings of the Oral in Canada and What They Might Tell Educators,"

235; "One Small Medicine," 240; "Teaching the Talk that Walks on Paper," 241; *Textualizing Orature and Orality*, 235, 237, 240-41, 265; "When X Equals Zero," 235, 245, 265-66, 270

Givon, Talmy: *Discourse and Syntax*, 236

Goddard, Ives: *Languages*, 240, 254, 257; "Synonymy," 246

Goetsch, Paul, 10; *Dialekte und Fremdsprachen in der Literatur*, 238; "Fingierte Mündlichkeit in der Erzählkunst entwickelter Schriftkulturen," 236; *Hardys Wessex-Romane*, 237; *Mündliches Wissen in neuzeitlicher Literatur*, 238; *The Oral and the Written in Nineteenth-Century British Fiction*, 238

Goldie, Terry: "Two Voices," 235

Goldman, Marlene, 155; "Mapping and Dreaming," 261-64

Gómez-Vega, Ibis: "Subverting the 'Mainstream' Paradigm through Magical Realism in Thomas King's *Green Grass, Running Water*," 264

Goody, Jack, 11

grammars, 3-4, 30, 133, 136, 169, 210, 212

Grant, Agnes: *Our Bit of Truth*, 242

Green Grass, Running Water. See King, Thomas

Griem, Julika: *Brüchiges Seemannsgarn*, 237

Gunn, Stacey Curry: "King Novel Popular in Canadian Literature Courses," 259

Gzowski, Peter, 8; "Peter Gzowski Interviews Thomas King on *Green Grass, Running Water*," 235, 258-59, 263

H

Habermalz, Sabine: "Signs on a White Field," 241

Halfe, Louise Bernice, 14, 183, 190, 219, 222; *Bear Bones and Feathers*, 179-80, 185, 206, 267, 269; *Blue Marrow*, 2, 31-32, 178-82, 220-21, 265, 269-70; holophrastic analysis of, 184-86, 189, 192-93, 197-202, 205-10, 212-15, 218; "Cree Glossary," 265, 267-70; *The Crooked Good*, 179-80

Hamer, Penelope: "Beyond the Nineteenth Century," 263

Harper, Elijah, 168

Havelock, Eric, 11

head (part of a compound), 229

Hedge Coke, Allison Adelle, 7; "Seeds," 235

Heller, Monica: *Codeswitching*, 238, 272

Helm, June, 112-13; "Dogrib," 255-56; *Prophecy and Power among the Dogrib Indians*, 114, 256; *Subarctic*, 255; "Tales from the Dogribs," 256; "Tlicho (Dogrib)," 256

Highway, Tomson, 14

Hill, Archibald A.: "The Typology of Writing Systems," 237

Hill, Roberta J., 206

Hinnells, John R.: *The Penguin Dictionary of Religions*, 261

Hirschfelder, Arlene: *Encyclopedia of Native American Religions*, 259

Hobson, Geary, 109, 140

Holm, Tom: "Peoplehood," 257

holophrases, 5, 11, 13, 15, 17, 20-21, 27, 30-32, 169, 222, 229, 234, 239; in *Arctic Dreams*, 72, 84, 88, 92, 97-99, 102, 104, 107; in *Blue Marrow*, 193, 199, 202-3, 209, 215-16, 221; in *Call Me Ishmael*, 45, 51, 56-61, 66-68; definition of, 1-3, 6, 20; in *Green Grass*, 153, 155, 162, 168, 171, 176-77; in Indigenous discourse, 3-5, 8-9, 14, 16, 25, 63, 66, 225; in *The Lesser Blessed*, 119, 123-24, 128, 133-34, 140; significance of, 20, 25, 225; structure of, 22, 24, 31, 60, 101-2, 130, 141, 175, 177, 210; translation of, 19, 25, 30; visual images in, 66, 103-5, 221, 234

holophrasis, 6, 13, 61, 101, 229

holophrastic traces, 15, 28, 30-31, 57, 64, 66, 216, 220-21, 223, 230; in *Arctic Dreams*, 100, 102, 104-5, 107; in *Blue Marrow*, 205,

INDEX

214; in *Call Me Ishmael*, 67; as culturally specific strategies, 25, 32, 133; direct, 15, 19, 59-60, 67, 101, 131, 139-40, 169-70, 176-77, 202, 207, 221; in *Green Grass*, 168, 178; indirect, 15-16, 18-19, 59, 61-63, 67, 101, 134-36, 174, 176-77, 213-14, 220; in *The Lesser Blessed*, 132-34, 138, 141

holoscheme, 223

Horne, Dee, 153; *Contemporary American Indian Writing*, 261

Horowitz, Rosalind: *Comprehending Oral and Written Language*, 233, 241, 254, 258, 264, 272

Howe, LeAnne, 14

Hultkrantz, Åke, 75-76, 79; "A Definition of Shamanism," 251; "Die Religion der amerikanischen Arkis," 244, 249-51

humour, 13

Hutcheon, Linda, 20; *A Theory of Parody*, 240

Hymes, Dell, 182, 214; "Discovering Oral Performance and Measured Verse in American Indian Narrative," 266

Hynes, William J.: "Mapping the Characteristics of Mythic Tricksters," 263; *Mythical Trickster Figures*, 245, 260, 263

I

imagery, 186

Indigenous autobiography, 37

Indigenous discourse, 5, 19, 61, 63-64, 66, 137

Indigenous English, 7-8, 19

Indigenous knowledge, 37. *See also* knowledge, traditional

Indigenous languages, 8, 16, 27, 59, 63, 132, 142, 212, 235, 238; holophrases in, 13, 51, 56-57, 60-61, 84, 88, 92, 97, 99, 134, 199, 202-3, 215, 221; as discourse feature, 67, 101, 104; and paraholophrases, 119, 123-24, 128, 153, 155, 162, 216; polysynthesis in, 98, 214; structure of, 9, 62, 133, 171, 177, 180, 182, 209, 222; and translations, 6, 20

Indigenous literatures, 1, 10, 12, 19, 24, 34, 64, 111, 176, 222-23

Indigenous oratures, 8, 13, 29, 43, 104, 107, 113, 143, 158, 174, 215-21; narrative frames in, 51, 66, 94, 124, 139; openings and closings in, 43, 45, 83, 116, 119

Indigenous poetry, 36

Indigenous story-writing, 1, 67

intertextual references. *See* intertextuality

intertextuality, 31, 217, 218; in *Arctic Dreams and Nightmares*, 77, 82-84, 87-88, 92, 97; in *Blue Marrow*, 197; in *Call Me Ishmael*, 43-45, 52-56, 66; in *Green Grass*, 158, 164-165, 169, 171, 176-177; in *The Lesser Blessed*, 112, 119, 123, 127, 141

intratextual references. *See* intratextuality

intratextuality, 31, 217; in *Arctic Dreams and Nightmares*, 88, 92, 95, 97; in *Blue Marrow*, 195-197, 199-200, 202, 205, 215; in *Call Me Ishmael*, 45-47, 50-51, 54, 56, 66; in *Green Grass*, 153, 162; in *The Lesser Blessed*, 121, 123, 127-128, 140

involvement of author, 13, 23, 32, 218-20; in *Arctic Dreams*, 84, 95, 100, 102, 104-5; in *Blue Marrow*, 200, 203, 205, 210, 212, 214-15; in *Call Me Ishmael*, 62, 66-67; in *Green Grass*, 165, 168, 173-74, 177; in *The Lesser Blessed*, 119, 128, 131, 133, 135, 139-41

involvement of speaker, 4, 7, 45, 137, 202

Ipellie, Alootook, 92, 140-41, 219, 222; *Arctic Dreams and Nightmares*, 2, 16, 31-32, 65, 68-74, 76-78, 134, 139, 168, 178, 218, 220-21, 239; holophrastic analysis of, 79-82, 84-88, 90-91, 93-107; narrative strands in, 123; paraholophrases in, 115-16

Irniq, Peter, 48, 75; "Speaking Notes," 246

irony, 50, 55-56, 119, 199

Iser, Wolfgang, 10, 135; *Der Akt des Lesens*, 258

Ives, Sumner: "A Theory of Literary Dialect," 238

J

Jacobs, Melville, 43; *The Content and Style of an Oral Literature*, 245

Jahandarie, Khosrow: *Spoken and Written Discourse*, 241

Jaine, Linda: "Traditional Cree Philosophy," 267

James, Deborah: "The Encoding of Information Source in Algonquian," 239

Justice, Daniel Heath, 142; *Our Fire Survives the Storm*, 235, 258

K

Keeshig-Tobias, Lenore: "Stop Stealing Native Stories," 242

Keller, Lynn: *Feminist Measures*, 266

Kellogg, Robert, 10; "Oral Narrative, Written Books," 236

Kendall, Martha B.: "Exegesis and Translation," 270

Kennedy, Michael P.J., 69; "Alootook Ipellie," 249

Kepes, Gyorgy: *Sign, Image, Symbol*, 254

Kilpatrick, Alan: *The Night Has a Naked Soul*, 167, 264

King, Thomas, 8, 12, 22, 198, 207, 222, 235; *All My Relations*, 269; "Godzilla vs. Post-Colonial," 238, 259; *Green Grass, Running Water*, 2, 16, 20, 23, 31-32, 141, 178, 218, 220-21, 239-40, 248, 272; holophrastic analysis of, 107, 155-58, 160-71, 173, 175-76; structure of, 143, 145, 147-48, 150-51; *Inventing the Indian*, 143, 259; *Medicine River*, 143, 164, 169; *The Truth about Stories*, 138, 144, 245, 258; *Truth and Bright Water*, 142-43, 164, 263

Kinkade, M. Dale, 17; "Discourse," 240, 254

Kleist, Makka: "Pre-Christian Inuit Sexuality," 252, 255

Kleivan, Inge, 75; *Eskimos*, 246-47, 250-51

knowledge, traditional, 46, 58, 64. *See also* Indigenous knowledge

Koch, Peter, 29; "Sprache der Nähe—Sprache der Distanz," 241-42, 272

Kolausok, Eddie D., 35-36, 39

Kongitok, Hellen, 106

Kroetsch, Robert, 182

Krupat, Arnold, 8-9; "Post-Structuralism and Oral Literature," 10; *The Turn to the Native*, 235, 271

L

Lakoff, Robin Tolmach: "Some of My Favorite Writers Are Literate," 236

Lamb, W. Kaye: *The Journals and Letters of Sir Alexander Mackenzie*, 256

language, 170, 206, 223; colloquial, 7, 10, 129, 136, 212; figurative, 16, 24, 136, 141, 178, 182, 203, 213-15, 217, 220-21; grammar of, 5, 25; poetic, 135, 178. *See also* grammars

language production, 29, 32, 66, 105, 141, 177, 214, 219-21, 230

language use, 29, 31-32, 230; context of, 51, 66, 105, 140, 177, 219, 221; as involvement, 51, 66, 140, 194, 219; as participation, 51, 66, 140, 194, 219. *See also* involvement; participation

languages: analytic, 21; ancestral, 8-9, 19, 105, 108, 128, 140-41, 165, 222-23; non-polysynthetic, 16; polysynthetic, 15, 103, 177, 209, 233; figurative use of, 133, 136, 217; holophrases in, 4-5, 21, 27; role of verbs in, 3, 16, 28, 62, 173; structure of, 59-60, 132, 135, 205; synthetic, 21, 209, 238

languages, Indigenous. *See* Indigenous languages

langue, 6, 22, 24, 230

Laugrand, Frédéric, 49; *Representing Tuurngait*, 246-47, 249, 251-52

Leach, Maria: *Funk and Wagnalls Standard Dictionary of Folklore, Mythology, and Legend*, 259-60

Leap, William L., 7; *American Indian English,* 234-35

LeClaire, Nancy: *Alberta Elders' Cree Dictionary,* 256, 267-68, 270

L'Hirondelle, Lorna: *Plains Cree Grammar Guide and Glossary,* 254

Lieber, Francis, 9; "On the Study of Foreign Languages," 235

Lindquist, Mark A.: *Buried Roots and Indestructible Seeds,* 260

Linton, Patricia: "And Here's How It Happened," 260

literary criticism, 19, 25, 27

Lowe, Ronald: *Basic Siglit Inuvialuit Eskimo Dictionary,* 48, 58, 234, 246, 248

Lutz, Hartmut, 143; *Contemporary Challenges,* 258; "First Nations Literature in Canada and the Voice of Survival," 258; "Thomas King," 258

Lyon, George Francis, 76, 82

Lyons, Scott Richard, 222; "Rhetorical Sovereignty," 271

M

Mace, Renate: *Funktionen des Dialeks im regionalen roman von Gaskell bis Lawrence,* 238

Mackenzie, Alexander: *Journals and Letters,* 113

Mailhot, José: "L'étymologie de 'esquimau' revue et corrigée," 246

Malinowski, Bronisław, 23; *The Language of Magic and Gardening,* 240

Mandelbaum, David G., 185, 189; *The Plains Cree,* 268-69, 271

markers, structural, 205

markers, textual. *See* textual markers

Mattina, Anthony, 17; "North American Indian Mythography," 234

McGrath, Robin, 37, 64-65, 97; *Canadian Inuit Literature,* 242-43, 247-49, 252-53

McLeod, Neal, 14, 28, 146; *Cree Narrative Memory,* 260, 266; *Songs to Kill a Wihtikow,* 241, 272

McLuhan, Marshall, 11

McMaster, Gerald: *Edward Poitras,* 268

Melville, Herman: *Moby-Dick,* 39-40

Merkur, Daniel, 75, 78-79; *Becoming Half Hidden,* 250-52; "Eagle, the Hunter's Helper," 252

metacommunication, 218

metafictionality, 56, 64, 203-5, 215

metalanguage, 27

metaphor, 13; in *Arctic Dreams,* 73, 79, 83, 88, 92, 97; in *Blue Marrow,* 192, 195, 197, 199, 203-4; in *Call Me Ishmael,* 43, 45, 50; in *Green Grass,* 162, 166; in *The Lesser Blessed,* 117, 119, 123-24, 126, 130-32

metonym, 83, 192

Mignolo, Walter D.: *The Darker Side of the Renaissance,* 237

Mills, Antonia: *Amerindian Rebirth,* 250

minimalism of text, 4, 13, 62, 104, 135-36

Mithun, Marianne: *The Languages of Native North America,* 233, 271

Moder, Carol Lynn: *Discourse across Languages and Cultures,* 233, 254

Momaday, N. Scott: *The Man Made of Words,* 236

Moore, Patrick: *Wolverine Myths and Visions,* 114, 256

morphemes, 2-3, 5, 15, 59, 101, 132

morphology, polysynthetic, 206

Morris, Ann, 70

Morrison, David, 35-36; *Across Time and Tundra,* 243; "Time and Tundra," 242

Moses, Daniel David: *An Anthology of Canadian Native Literature in English,* 235; "Traditional Orature: Southern First Nations," 235

Muro, Junko: "Living in a Time for Celebration," 255

Murray, Laura J.: *Talking on the Page,* 238

myth, 28, 64, 106

N

narration, 10, 31, 46, 50, 66, 94, 104
narrative, 97, 103, 137, 152, 158, 175-76, 186; structure of, 140, 145, 152, 163-65, 176, 215
narrative frames, 31, 51; in *Arctic Dreams*, 80, 85, 88, 93-94, 98; in *Blue Marrow*, 183, 194, 202, 217-18, 221; in *Call Me Ishmael*, 39, 43, 45, 50, 54; cyclical structure of, 104, 139, 198; in *Green Grass*, 147-48, 152, 173-74, 176-77; in *The Lesser Blessed*, 118, 120, 123; opening and closing of, 63, 66
narrative functions, 5; significant, 23-24, 160, 171, 203, 215; and figures of speech, 51, 54, 136; in oral discourse, 225; and paraholophrases, 205, 218, 223
narrative grid, 66, 84, 176-77, 223
narrative strand, 110, 138, 147; mythological, in *Green Grass*, 147-48, 150-55, 157-58, 163-64, 170-71, 174-75, 178; mythological, in *The Lesser Blessed*, 111, 113, 115, 118, 121-24, 127-28, 137; psychological, in *The Lesser Blessed*, 111, 115, 117, 123-24, 126-27, 136; realistic, in *Green Grass*, 147-48, 150-53, 155, 157-58, 163, 168, 171-72, 174-76, 178, 221
narrative technology, 147, 163, 165, 176, 217
narrative units, significant, 4-6, 23, 27; in *Arctic Dreams*, 84, 88, 92, 97, 104; in *Blue Marrow*, 217; in *Call Me Ishmael*, 45, 56; in *Green Grass*, 153, 155, 157, 162, 165; in *The Lesser Blessed*, 119
Nelson, Edward William, 41, 87; *The Eskimo about Bering Strait*, 243-44, 252
Neuhaus, Mareike: "The Marriage of Mother and Father," 240
Nichols, Johanna, 17
Nicosia, Nicole: "May I Suggest," 255
Nida, Eugene A., 19; *The Theory and Practice of Translation*, 14, 238, 272; *Toward a Science of Translating*, 238
noun-epithet formulas, 170-71, 175, 177-78
novel, 70, 107, 140, 143, 222
Nowak, Eike: "Is Inuktitut a Morphological Argument Language?" 254
Nungak, Zebedee, 76, 78; *Eskimo Stories from Povungnituk, Quebec*, 243, 251; "A Review of Central Eskimo Mythology," 243, 251
Nutaraaluk, Lucassie, 47
Nystrand, Martin: "The Role of Context in Written Communication," 241, 272

O

Ochs, Elinor: "Planned and Unplanned Discourse," 236
O'Donovan, Leo J.: "Mutual Teachers," 240
Oesterreicher, Wulf, 29
Okimasis, Jean, 180
Olson, David R., 11; *Literacy and Orality*, 237
Oman, Lela Kiana: *The Epic of Qayaq*, 53, 247-48
Ong, Walter, 11
Oosten, Jarich: "The Bringer of Light," 243-44
oral strategies, 1, 31-32, 138, 175, 177, 194, 220, 222, 230
oral traditions, 36, 38, 42, 52-53, 55, 65, 77, 87-88, 112, 141, 145, 217; in Indigenous cultures, 11, 37, 40, 163, 171, 218; textualizations of, 113-14; writing of, 34, 39, 43, 58, 64, 67, 107, 111, 139
orality, conceptual, 29-30, 32, 105, 124, 194, 214, 219, 221
Ortiz, Simon J.: *Speaking for the Generations*, 1, 233, 235
oxymoron, 92, 118, 120

P

Page, Norman: *Speech in the English Novel*, 237
paraholophrases, 2, 20, 22-23, 25, 27, 30-32, 66, 153, 217-19, 221-23, 230, 240, 252, 270; in *Arctic Dreams*, 79-80, 84, 88, 92, 94-95,

97-98, 100, 104-5, 107; in *Blue Marrow*, 180-81, 183, 193-94, 199-200, 202-5, 213-15; in *Call Me Ishmael*, 39, 43, 45-46, 51, 54-55, 57-58, 61, 66; as culturally specific strategies, 25, 28, 33, 216; definition of, 6, 21; as discourse devices, 21, 24, 31, 33, 107; in *Green Grass*, 143, 152-53, 155, 157-58, 161, 164-65, 171, 176-77; in *The Lesser Blessed*, 115-16, 119, 121, 124-25, 128, 136, 139-40; in narrative frames, 56, 85; significance of, 140-41

parody, 20, 184, 186, 189, 198, 215, 218

parole, 6, 22, 24, 230

Parry, Milman, 217; "Studies in the Epic Technique of Oral Verse-Making," 271

participation of listener, 4, 7, 32, 136

participation of reader, 13, 23, 218-20; in *Arctic Dreams*, 84, 94-95, 100, 102, 104-5; in *Blue Marrow*, 180, 200, 202-3, 205, 207, 210, 212, 214-15; in *Call Me Ishmael*, 45, 50, 52, 56, 59, 61-62, 66-67; in *Green Grass*, 165, 168-71, 173, 176; in *The Lesser Blessed*, 119, 124, 128, 131-36, 139-41

Patsauq, Markoosie: *Harpoon of the Hunter*, 103, 249

Paulson, Ivar: *Die Religionen Nordeurasiens und der amerikanischen Arktis*, 244, 249

Perreault, Jeanne: *Writing the Circle*, 179

Petitot, Émile: *Autour du Grand Lac des Esclaves*, 113, 256; *The Book of Dene*, 114, 256-57; *Traditions indiennes du Canada nord-ouest*, 256-57

pictographs, 65, 234, 237

Pitseolak, Peter, 97; *People from Our Side*, 37, 96, 103, 246, 253; *Pictures out of My Life*, 103

Plag, Ingo: *Morphological Productivity*, 234, 273

poems, 193, 222; free verse, 110, 121, 135-36, 180, 213; prose, 135-36

poetry, traditional, 54, 182

Polanyi, Livia: "Literary Complexity in Everyday Storytelling," 236

polysynthesis, 2-3, 15, 18, 220, 230; and discourse, 6, 16, 59, 176, 212; and evidentiality, 63, 137, 174; in Indigenous languages, 136, 171, 214

Powell, Peter J.: *Sweet Medicine*, 262-63

productivity (of language), 21-22, 231, 234

prolepsis, 119

pronoun copying, 19, 61, 67, 102, 141, 172-73, 176, 210, 212-14, 220-21, 223; as holophrastic traces, 16, 18, 101, 105, 134-35, 171, 177-78, 205

prose, 37, 178, 213; poetic, 110, 121, 135-36, 180

prosody, 32, 66-67, 105, 141, 177, 210, 213, 219-20

Pullum, Geoffrey K.: "The Great Eskimo Vocabulary Hoax," 257; *The Great Eskimo Vocabulary Hoax and Other Irreverent Essays on the Study of Language*, 257

Pulte, William: *Cherokee-English Dictionary*, 264

pun, 170

R

Rainwater, Catherine, 164; *Dreams of Fiery Stars*, 263

Rasmussen, Knud, 75-76, 78; *Across Arctic America*, 244, 250-51; *Fra Grønland til Stillehavet*, 250; *The Mackenzie Eskimos*, 244

reader-response criticism, 12-13

Red English, 7

Redeker, Gisela: "On Differences between Spoken and Written Language," 258, 264

Reder, Deanna: *Troubling Tricksters*, 260

redundancy, 32, 66, 105, 141, 177, 213, 219-20

repetitions, 62-63, 67, 220-21

rhetorical object, significant, 20, 25

Ricketts, Mac Linscott: "The Shaman and the Trickster," 245

INDEX

Ridington, Robin, 163-64, 176, 217; "Dogs, Snares, and Cartridge Belts," 263, 271; "Theorizing Coyote's Canon," 263

Robbeson, Angela, 182-83

Robinson, Eden: *Blood Sports*, 108

Robinson, Harry, 8, 12; *Write It on Your Heart*, 17, 240

Rodgers, Wendy, 64; "Circumscribing Silence," 243, 248

Rood, David S.: "North American Languages," 233

Rooke, Constance: "Interview with Tom King," 258

S

Saladin d'Anglure, Bernard, 48, 74; "An Ethnographic Commentary," 246, 252-53; "From Foetus to Shaman," 250; *Interviewing Inuit Elders*, 249; "Nanook, Super-Male," 251-52; "The Third Gender of the Inuit," 250

Saltman, Judi: "Richard Van Camp Interview," 255

satire, 13, 97

Schafer, Edward H.: "The Sky River," 253

Scholes, Robert: *The Nature of Narrative*, 271; "The Oral Heritage of Written Narrative," 271

Schorcht, Blanca, 12-13; *Storied Voices in Native American Texts*, 238

Schwarz, Herbert T.: *Elik, and Other Stories of the MacKenzie Eskimos*, 244, 248

Scobie, Stephen: "Double Voicing," 266

Scofield, Gregory, 14

Seidelman, Harold, 49, 72, 77; *The Inuit Imagination*, 246-47, 249-51, 254

semiotic theory, 105, 217

Silko, Leslie Marmon, 12, 56; "Language and Literature from a Pueblo Indian Perspective," 248

simile, 20, 88, 92, 120, 123

slang, 136

Sonne, Birgitte, 75

source citing, 64, 68, 106-7, 138-39, 141, 213

Spalding, Alex: *Inuktitut*, 247, 249, 251-53

speech, direct, 66, 152, 172, 174; figurative, 162. See also figures of speech; free indirect, 172, 175; oral, 61-62, 67, 101-2, 129, 131, 135, 137, 139, 172-73, 212

Spencer, Andrew: *Morphological Theory*, 239, 273

Spencer, Robert F.: *The North Alaskan Eskimo*, 244, 248, 255

Standiford, Lester A., 11, 13; "Worlds Made of Dawn," 238

Stigter, Shelley, 180; "The Dialectics and Dialogics of Code-Switching in the Poetry of Gregory Scofield and Louise Halfe," 235, 265, 270

story cycle, 52, 70, 73, 77, 80, 84, 92, 94, 98-107, 153, 157, 165, 222

story, oral, 39, 44, 163; structure of, 155, 157

story-within-a-story, 52, 137

story-writing, 67

storyknifing, 65

storytelling, 6, 21, 64, 103, 138, 147-48, 166, 182, 197, 213; and audience, 42-43; as oral performance, 8, 12, 39, 56, 65, 68, 129, 137, 152, 173, 176, 237

Sturtevant, William C.: *Handbook of North American Indians*, 240, 254-55, 257

subject dropping, 67, 102, 141, 172-73, 177; as holophrastic traces, 16, 62, 101, 105, 134, 171, 205, 210-14, 220-21, 223; in narrative strands, 176, 178

suffixes, enclitic, 6

Sugars, Cynthia: *Home-Work*, 241

Sutherland, Xavier, 17-18; "Chahkabesh and the Giant Women," 239

Swann, Brian: *Recovering the Word*, 234, 236, 255

Swift, Jonathan: *Gulliver's Travels*, 252

Swink, Helen: "William Faulkner," 237
symbol, 83, 88, 92, 97, 119, 123, 199
synecdoche, 73, 93, 99-100, 104, 168-69, 185, 201, 206, 219, 221, 223, 263

T

tags, 17-18, 174
Tannen, Deborah: *Spoken and Written Language*, 236; *Talking Voices*, 236
Taylor, Drew Hayden: *Me Sexy*, 252
Tedlock, Dennis, 43, 182; *The Spoken Word and the Work of Interpretation*, 245, 269
text, heteroglossic, 181
text minimalization. *See* minimalism of text
textual markers, 66, 100, 141, 169, 174, 178, 209, 214, 219, 221
textual silences, 4, 16, 214, 220
textualization of orality, 2, 7-8, 10, 25, 28, 30, 61, 65, 67, 133, 178, 231, 237, 241; as culturally specific strategy, 9, 11, 13, 63, 84, 223; in *Arctic Dreams*, 100-102, 104-5; in *Blue Marrow*, 200, 210, 212-13; in *Green Grass*, 158, 165, 169-71, 173, 175-77; in *The Lesser Blessed*, 119, 128, 131, 134-36, 138, 140-41; and holophrases, 14, 168, 174-75, 214, 216; in Indigenous literatures, 1, 6, 11, 13, 28-30, 32, 34; and paraholophrases, 56, 66, 98, 141, 180, 183, 194, 203-4, 219, 221-22; strategies for, 25, 45, 50; as strategy, 6, 9, 14, 38-39, 51, 59, 61-62, 64, 94, 100
textualization of orature, 29, 35, 67, 197, 214, 231, 237
Thalbitzer, William: "Die kultischen Gottheiten der Eskimos," 244
The Lesser Blessed. *See* Van Camp, Richard
Thomas, Vital, 113
Ticasuk, Emily Ivanoff Brown: *The Longest Story Ever Told*, 248
Tierney, Frank M., 182-83; *Bolder Flights*, 266
toponym, 132-33, 206
translation, English loan, 177, 209, 214, 221
translations, 6, 14, 47, 58, 99-100, 180, 185, 205-6
Trost, Pavel: "Tzv. Citátová komposita v nemcine," 273
Tungilik, Victor, 48
Turner, James, 72; 77
Tyler, Priscilla, 53

U

Ute English, 7

V

Valentine, Lisa Philips: *Theorizing the Americanist Tradition*, 263
Van Camp, Richard, 8, 33, 108, 114, 132, 222; *The Lesser Blessed*, 2, 16, 31-32, 107, 109-13, 115, 140-41, 168, 239, 242, 251, 255, 257, 273; figures of speech in, 178, 213; holophrastic analysis of, 116, 119, 122-24, 128-31, 134-39; holophrastic traces in, 220-21
Vance, Sylvia, 179
verbs, affixation of, 207-8; conjugation of, 102, 118-19; holistic, 13, 18-19, 173, 233; polysynthetic, 5, 16, 62, 101, 135, 213
Vizenor, Gerald R., 13; *Manifest Manners*, 258
Voegelin, Erminie W.: "Coyote," 260; "Creation," 259
voicing, double. *See* double voicing

W

Wagamese, Richard, 14; *Keeper 'n Me*, 110, 138, 235, 258
Walton, Priscilla L., 164

Warkentin, Germaine: "In Search of 'The Word of the Other,'" 237

Watt, Ian, 11; "Oral Dickens," 237

Waugh, Earle: *Alberta Elders' Cree Dictionary*, 185, 206, 256, 267

Weaver, Jace: *Defending Mother Earth*, 267; "Notes from a Miner's Canary," 267; *That the People Might Live*, 258

Welch, James, 12

White, Frederick H.: "Language Reflection and Lamentation in Native American Literature," 235; *Studies in American Indian Literatures*, 235

Wiebe, Armin: *Tatsea*, 114, 256-57

Wiesenthal, Christine: *The Half-Lives of Pat Lowther*, 254

Wiget, Andrew: *Critical Essays on Native American Literature*, 260

Willett, Thomas: "A Cross-Linguistic Survey of the Grammaticization of Evidentiality," 239

Williams, David: *Imagined Nations*, 237

Williamson, Robert G.: "Eskimo Underground," 252

Willinsky, John, 10; *After Literacy*, 236; "The Paradox of Text in the Culture of Literacy," 236

Willis, Roy: *Signifying Animals*, 251

Wissler, Clark: *Mythology of the Blackfoot Indians*, 261

Wolfart, H. Christoph: "Introduction to the Texts," 272; *Meet Cree*, 239, 266; "Notes," 272

Wolfe, Alexander, 36; *Earth Elder Stories*, 242

Wolvengrey, Arok, 180

Womack, Craig S., 6, 146; "A Single Decade," 260; *Reasoning Together*, 234, 260

word bundle, 25

words, loan, 66

words, monolexical, 104

words, onomatopoeic-like, 133, 175

Y

York, Annie: *They Write Their Dream on the Rock Forever*, 237

Z

Zoe, John B., 132

ABOUT THE AUTHOR

Mareike Neuhaus completed her PhD in English at Philipps-Universität Marburg, Germany, in 2008. She was an Andrew W. Mellon postdoctoral fellow at the Jackman Humanities Institute, University of Toronto, from 2008 to 2010 and now holds a Government of Canada postdoctoral research fellowship in the Department of English at the University of Toronto. Her research interests include North American Indigenous literatures and languages as well as Canadian literature. Mareike is also currently writing a multilingual children's book.

ABOUT THE TYPE

The text in this book is set in *Adobe Arno Pro*. Named after the river that runs through Florence, the center of the Italian Renaissance, *Arno* draws on the warmth and readability of early humanist types of the 15th and 16th centuries. While inspired by the past, *Arno* is distinctly contemporary in both appearance and function. Designed by Robert Slimbach, Adobe principal designer, *Arno* is a meticulously crafted face in the tradition of early Venetian and Aldine book types. Embodying themes that Slimbach has explored in typefaces such as *Minion*® and *Brioso*™, *Arno* represents a distillation of his design ideals and a refinement of his craft.